FIRST
MIGRANTS

For my father, Edwin Arthur Bellwood (1905–1959), and also for the Pink family, in memory of Jerome (1985–2012).

FIRST MIGRANTS

Ancient Migration in Global Perspective

MIGRANTS

Peter Bellwood

WILEY Blackwell

Blackwell Publishing was acquired by John Wiley & Sons in February 2007. Blackwell's publishing program has been merged with Wiley's global Scientific, Technical, and Medical business to form Wiley-Blackwell.

Registered Office
John Wiley & Sons Ltd, The Atrium, Southern Gate, Chichester, West Sussex, PO19 8SQ, UK

Editorial Offices
350 Main Street, Malden, MA 02148-5020, USA
9600 Garsington Road, Oxford, OX4 2DQ, UK
The Atrium, Southern Gate, Chichester, West Sussex, PO19 8SQ, UK

For details of our global editorial offices, for customer services, and for information about how to apply for permission to reuse the copyright material in this book please see our website at www.wiley.com/wiley-blackwell.

Library of Congress Cataloging-in-Publication Data applied for

Bellwood, Peter S.
First migrants: ancient migration in global perspective/Peter Bellwood.
   p.   cm.
Includes index.
ISBN 978-1-4051-8909-5 (hardback) – ISBN 978-1-4051-8908-8 (paper)   1. Human beings–Migrations.   2. Prehistoric peoples.   3. Migrations of nations.   4. Archaeology and history.   I. Title.
GN370.B45 2013
930.1–dc23

2013016299

A catalogue record for this book is available from the British Library.

Cover image: Hokule'a, replica of traditional Polynesian voyaging canoe, Kaneohe Bay, Oahu, Hawaii © Stock Connection / SuperStock.
Cover design by Nicki Averill Design & Illustration.

Set in 10.5/13pt Dante by SPi Publisher Services, Pondicherry, India
Printed in Malaysia by Ho Printing (M) Sdn Bhd

Contents

List of Figures

Preface

All of us alive today owe our very existences to the many layers of migration undertaken by our remote ancestors, going back far into time, even beyond the rise of humanity itself to the prehuman beginnings of life on earth. Working hand in hand with the processes of evolution, migration has spread the evolutionary products of biological mutation and cultural innovation to all regions where humans exist. Our genes, our languages, our systems of food production and technology, all exist *in part* because of migration. I emphasize *in part*, because migration cannot be seen in its own right as a biological or cultural cause of mutation or innovation. But as a mechanism of spread, it often meant that internally generated mutations and cultural innovations in the broadest senses could find new and fertile ground and proliferate to a degree unthinkable if the carriers all stayed at home. If all our ancestors had remained immobile, we simply would not exist as the environmentally demanding and dominating species that we have become today.

This book is about migration in all periods of human prehistory, from the initial spread of hominins out of Africa about two million years ago, down to the continental migrations of agricultural populations within the past 10,000 years. In general, I draw the line when history starts, so the Huns, Goths, Mongols, Conquistadores, and Victorians do not feature. We know something about them from history, even if the history is sometimes rather thin. On the other hand, some nonliterate peoples migrated over huge distances very recently in time, even contemporary with the European Middle Ages, but they did so in their own fully prehistoric circumstances. The Bantu-speaking peoples in Africa, the Eastern Polynesians, and the Inuit of the North American Arctic were all migrating as Gothic cathedrals arose in Europe, therefore they people the following pages.

As I was writing this book, an invitation from Immanuel Ness in New York gave me the opportunity to edit Volume 1 (Prehistory) of the *Encyclopedia of Global Human*

Migration (Ness and Bellwood 2013), an opportunity that allowed me to select and invite as authors some of the world's foremost scholars in the prehistoric sciences of archaeology, human biology and comparative linguistics. One of the developments that surprised me during the editing of this volume was the increased importance given in so many disciplines to processes of migration in human affairs, both ancient and modern. When I was a student of archaeology in the 1960s, migration was becoming an uncomfortable concept for many archaeologists, and home-grown independence or *multiregionalism* was becoming the favored perspective on the past in both human evolution and archaeology. The very different modern view of the 2010s reflects the huge advances in the biological sciences in recent years, especially in genetics, since DNA research now makes it very obvious that migration has always been of great significance. Before the 1970s, archaeologists and comparative linguists could not easily demonstrate the reality of migration without direct historical evidence, and neither indeed could geneticists at that time. Spreading cultures and languages in themselves are not automatic evidence for actual population migration, as opposed to cultural diffusion, although they can be argued to have been so in specific circumstances.

As with modern migration, prehistoric migration always needed a reason. One very common reason in many situations was growth in the size of the human population. A group of prehistoric humans living in complete demographic and environmental equilibrium would never have needed to move, unless the environment changed in an adverse way or the average couple switched to having more than two children. As we all know, human life has never existed in such idyllic circumstances, neither in the past nor in the present. Populations can grow in numbers, new land can be required, resources can diminish for many environmental and human-impact reasons, enemies can attack and force people to flee and not return, utopias can beckon. Circumstances can induce a group of humans to spread or migrate, whether consciously or unconsciously, by choice and group agreement, or simply through a less conscious transgenerational success in procreation.

In some ways, this book is a sequel to my earlier *First Farmers*, published by Blackwell in 2005, except that here I cover hunter-gatherers as well as farmers and go back much further in time to the beginnings of the genus *Homo* over two million years ago. The chapters are arranged partly in chronological order and partly in geographical order, but the main separation is into hunter-gatherer migrations (Chapters 3–5) and agriculturalist migrations (Chapters 6–9). I commence with two comparative chapters (1 and 2) on migration as a process of human movement and on how the multidisciplinary evidence for it might be perceived and interpreted by prehistorians, these being scientists from many disciplines (not just archaeology) who strive to understand the human past prior to the beginnings of written records.

The writing of this book has been a challenge for me because of the great breadth of information that I have had to collect. I have realized, over many years of research, that simply trying to interpret prehistory from a viewpoint of archaeology, or comparative linguistics, or genetics, or any other discipline alone is really rather a pointless exercise and one that can lead to a remarkable narrowness of perspective, not to mention time-wasting errors that can penetrate the literature and then echo down through the years. Overall, I have found the collection of multidisciplinary data to be an immensely energetic and stimulating exercise, given the phenomenal rates of publication in newly developing scientific disciplines, and genetics in particular. I stopped reading in February 2013, and any revolutionary observation published since then will not have made these pages.

A Note on Dating Terminology

Chronological statements in this book are always based on solar years, expressed as 'years ago' for periods before 10,000 years ago, and thereafter as years BC (before Christ) or AD (Latin *anno domini*, in the year of the Lord, or after Christ). In a broad scale review such as this, there is no need to refer to individual uncalibrated laboratory radiocarbon determinations.

The terms *Pleistocene* and *Holocene* refer to geological epochs. The former spanned the period from 2.58 million to 12,000 years ago (Gibbard et al. 2009). The latter has spanned the past 12,000 years (or 10,000 uncalibrated radiocarbon years), and is still unfolding. It commenced during the final glacial retreat at the end of the Younger Dryas miniglaciation (circa 13,000–11,600 years ago), and corresponds with the establishment of current interglacial climatic conditions across the world. The Pleistocene was preceded by the Pliocene, within which the earliest recorded stages of human evolution occurred in Africa. None of the events discussed in this book occurred as long ago as the Pliocene.

The Pleistocene is divided into three periods of unequal length (Figure 3.2): Lower (or Early) Pleistocene from 2.58 million years ago to the Brunhes-Matuyama paleomagnetic reversal at 780,000 years ago; the Middle Pleistocene from 780,000 to 120,000 years ago; and the Upper (or Late) Pleistocene from 120,000 years ago to the beginning of the Holocene, at 12,000 years ago. The Upper Pleistocene contained the penultimate interglacial and final glacial periods, a time of massive change in global environments in which anatomically and behaviorally modern humans were propelled into prominence and all other hominin species finally succumbed to extinction. The Holocene has witnessed the rise of agriculture, civilization, and our current state of overpopulated misery or technological glory, depending upon one's point of view.

Acknowledgements

In writing this book, I have on occasion had to ask colleagues for help, advice, and information, especially in disciplines or parts of the world with which I am not very familiar. They include Debbie Argue, Robert Attenborough, Vaclav Blažek, Murray Cox, Max Friesen, Colin Groves, Norman Hammond, Jane Hill, Bill Jungers, Ian Keen, Pat McConvell, Campbell Macknight, Marty Magne, R.G. Matson, Mehmet Özdoğan, Nicolas Peterson, Sasha Vovin, and three anonymous reviewers kindly supplied by the publisher. None are responsible for any errors. I would like to thank the Australian National University (ANU) for the research infrastructure that allowed this book to be written, and Multimedia Services in The College of Asia and the Pacific at ANU (especially Kay Dancey, Jenny Sheehan, and Karina Pelling) for some of the base maps, to which I have added my own interpretations using Adobe Illustrator CS5. Peter Johnson of Wollongong also helped me with some tricky aspects of Adobe Illustrator. Finally, my wife Claudia has given me continuous and invaluable support, plus some very valuable help with editing. I could not have written this book without her.

Chapter 1
The Relevance and Reality
of Ancient Migration

This chapter examines the great importance of migration in human history and in creating human patterns of diversity, both biological and cultural. It also examines some examples of migration as recorded in early historical sources and in the ethnographic records of indigenous peoples made during the early colonial era. An ability and a propensity to migrate over large distances have always been defining features of our human species, Homo sapiens, *right across the globe. The focus of this book, however, is on prehistoric and indigenous populations and their migrations, prior to the massive global movements of the past few centuries.*

We only need to look at our neighbors, at large crowds, or television, to realize that the world of humanity is very diverse. Human populations have different kinds of behavior, speak different languages, and look different from each other in biological terms. How has all this diversity come about? Has it evolved in place through the 60 or more millennia since the ancestors of *H. sapiens* first spread across the Old World, purely as a result of differing adaptations to varied natural and cultural environments? To a degree, the answer must be "yes," given that we can see so much environmentally related biological variation if we compare, for instance, Europeans, southern Africans, and eastern Asians. But does it also reflect the results of successive episodes of population migration, in many different times and places, erasing or mixing the old patterns and creating strikingly new ones? The answer is emphatically also "yes."

Recent history tells us a great deal about major population migrations, about how Europeans and Africans migrated to the Americas, Britons to Australia, Russians to Siberia, Dutch to South Africa, and Chinese to Taiwan. Recent history leaves no doubt that migration has been absolutely fundamental in the creation of our modern world, even if some of those migratory episodes occurred with little attention to the basic human rights that concern so many of us today. Going back in time, we read how Arabs migrated from Arabia into Iraq and Egypt, Turks from central Asia into Anatolia (now Turkey), Vikings from Scandinavia to Greenland, and Anglo-Saxons from across the North Sea to England. Before this we have the Roman Empire, Han Dynasty migration from central into southern China, and Greek and Phoenician colonies in the Mediterranean. And before the Greeks? History before 3000 years ago rather lets us down, certainly if we go back beyond the Old Testament and the ancient Indian

First Migrants: Ancient Migration in Global Perspective, First Edition. Peter Bellwood.

Rig-Veda. But the research tools of archaeology, comparative linguistics, and human biology are at hand.

What can these three disciplines reveal to us? Old rubbish has a tale to tell. If it did not, there would be no archaeologists, although any archaeologist will rightfully insist that the archaeological record consists of far more than just rubbish. Artifacts, offerings to the dead, art and architecture, ways of acquiring and processing food, technology in stone and metal, and human–environment relations, all play major roles in interpreting the past. When taken together, they allow us to read how ancient lifestyles, as expressed in material culture, migrated hand in hand with human populations across continents and oceans.

Comparative linguistics tells us how related languages have evolved within families, have spread, mixed, and sometimes died. Language families are an absolutely fundamental source of data on ancient migrations. In the historical record, the main mechanism behind their large-scale and long-distance spreads and their establishments as the long-term vernaculars of whole populations, not just elites, has always been migration of their speakers. Large-scale linguistic switching (or 'language shift' in linguistic terms) on a permanent basis without migration of any kind has generally been of limited geographical significance.

Skeletons and genes tell us how biological populations of humanity have evolved and migrated. Living populations such as sub-Saharan Africans, Western Eurasians (including North Africans), eastern Asians (including Native Americans and many Pacific peoples), and Australasians (Indigenous Australians and Melanesians), all form major geographical and biological foci of variation that are of great significance in the human migration story. But all human populations also have blurred biological boundaries and reveal histories of admixture, some no doubt on many occasions if we go back far enough in time.

What is *migration*? More to the point, what might the concept have meant during deep prehistory, before written records began? Historians and sociologists discuss many variations in the modern world.[1] But the many complex categories within the modern concept of migration cannot be identified easily in the records of the prehistoric past. For the purposes of the prehistoric and early historical record of human affairs described in this book, migration was simply *the permanent movement of all or part of a population to inhabit a new territory, separate from that in which it was previously based*. Permanent translocation is an essential part of this definition.[2]

I suggest this simple baseline definition because, as we go further back in time, it becomes more difficult to identify migratory activity in any exact and practical way, for instance, separating warfare or disaster refugees from economic migrants searching for food or land. It also becomes more difficult to determine if the migrants spread gradually and continuously from a source, or if they undertook one or more long-distance jumps (*leap-frogging*) across large areas of intervening terrain. For instance, we know for certain that early humans had achieved the colonization of the habitable regions of the world before the end of the Pleistocene geological epoch, except for Antarctica and some remote oceanic islands. But exactly where the very first Paleolithic colonists in each region placed their footprints in the earth, how many people took part in each component migration, and what languages they spoke will never be known to us with any exactitude.

The concept of migration has another complicating factor. The first migrations were necessarily into regions that had no prior inhabitants. But after our hominin ancestors, both archaic and modern, had established their first colonies across the globe, so new migrants had to enter regions that already had populations in residence, unless they could settle in remote islands or environments too hostile for previous occupation. For this kind of activity we can use the term *immigration*, as used for late prehistoric archaeological contexts by some archaeologists,[3] retaining the term *colonization* for migration into territories previously devoid of human inhabitants.

Migration is more than mere mobility. Hunters, pastoralists, and many species of mammals (including marine ones) and birds move regularly along well-defined routes through territories that are often of enormous size. Ethologists and anthropologists often use the term *migration* in this mode, and it might have allowed certain groups of humans to learn the distant landscape features that could assist them to undertake a permanent migration, as just defined. But, if involving return to a home territory, this kind of movement is not considered to be migration in the sense used in this book.

Similarly, the migrations of single individuals or very small groups in prehistory cannot easily be recognized within the archaeological, linguistic, or genetic records, except in very rare cases. For instance, strontium isotope ratio analysis of ancient human bone from cemeteries can allow analysts to establish the geochemical location of a person's place of birth and childhood (Montgomery 2010). This analytical technique has developed greatly in recent years, but it is necessarily restricted to ancient *individuals* (sometimes more than one in any given archaeological site), who in many cases are hard to relate to the global sources of the populations to which they belonged. Individuals will always have been migrating locally as they found partners, fell out with relatives, or searched for new resources, exactly as they do now. But such migration is only of direct interest for this book if it can be related to an actual episode of population migration beyond the individual level. The focus is on the large-scale *permanent* translocations of population that changed prehistory, in all cases covering many generations in time, many hundreds or thousands of kilometers in space, and with repercussions on humanity that still live with us today.

How can we recognize the existence of migration in the prehistoric record? Most records are proxy, in the sense that they are not direct representations of ancient biological populations moving in time and space. Only ancient human bones and the ancient DNA contained in them can be witnesses in this way, and then only if the data obtained are interpreted correctly, especially bearing in mind the very small sample sizes that are generally available for study using these techniques. On a broader level, it is by comparing the patterns implied by the independent sets of data derived from biology, archaeology, linguistics and the paleoenvironmental sciences (to name the most significant data sources), rather than human biology and genetics alone, that the science of reconstructing human population prehistory makes real progress. None of these disciplines alone shows us real populations actually on the move in the deep past. Historical judgment will always matter – we cannot expect significant prehistoric human migrations to become revealed in entirety by one technique, no matter how new or clever.

Migration has always been important for humankind. According to Anthony Marsella and Erin Ring (2003:3), it is "inherent in human nature – an instinctual and inborn disposition and inclination to wonder and to wander in search of new opportunities and new horizons." They add rightly that migration has led to the separation of the human species into "its myriad ethnic, cultural, linguistic, and racial groups." Russell King (2007:16) drives this home by stating "In a sense, humans are born migrants: our evolution is fundamentally linked to the act of migration, to moving from one place to another and adapting to that environment."

For every migration, there will always be a hierarchy of underlying environmental and cultural causes, and these causes need to be identified and understood by prehistorians. The real value of migration is that it imposes new patterns in culture, language, and biology, both through time and in space, that were not present before. As such, it rearranges the component parts of preexisting circumstances and presents new patterns of variation upon which the processes of both biological and cultural evolution can act anew.

Migration in Prehistoric Times

A vast number of migrations occurred within the course of human prehistory, just as they did in historical times. Some were doubtless very minor in extent and importance, but others were immensely significant in laying down very resistant and lasting foundation layers beneath the worldwide patterning of human variation. Language families, religions, domesticated animals and major food crops all exist where they do, at least in part, because groups of humans migrated with them at some time in the past. Of course, biological features can spread through gene flow, religions can spread through conversion, and domesticated animals can be traded or exchanged, but these processes operating alone are not enough to explain the full story.

Although migration has been an eternal factor throughout human prehistory, there are three highly researched phases of migration in overall human evolution that are currently the foci of a great deal of research:

1. migrations of extinct members of the genus *Homo*, such as *Homo erectus* and later the Neanderthals, after 2.5 million years ago, within and out of Africa and through Eurasia;
2. migrations of ancestral modern humans (*H. sapiens*) through most of the world, including Australia and the Americas, between 120,000 and 10,000 years ago;
3. migrations of farmers, herders, and boat builders in many separate groups, across most oceans and in all continents except Antarctica, during the past 10,000 years.

There is, of course, a fourth historical and far more recent migration phase, that of the rather staggering diaspora of approximately 150 million people in three massive flows peaking between the 1840s and the 1950s. One went from western Europe to the Americas and Australasia. Another went from India and China to the Indian Ocean rim, Southeast Asia, and the South Pacific. A third migration spread from Russia and China into central and northeastern Asia (McKeown 2004: 156). These three recent streams indicate that, while migration has always been a continuous activity on a small scale, it has also been subject to major pulses separated by periods of relative quiescence. Perhaps I do not need to add that migration, both forced and free, is still a vital element of our modern society. The refugee crisis that currently perplexes the governments of many countries, including Australia, my adopted home country, is continuing evidence of this.

Some prehistoric migrations seem quite extraordinary to us today. The human ability to migrate through vast landscapes and waterscapes to reach and settle new territories is one of the most striking aspects of our shared species history. Easter Island (Isla de Pascua, or Rapa Nui) is isolated across 2000 km of open ocean from its nearest inhabited Polynesian neighbors, Pitcairn and Henderson Islands (Figure 8.4). It was reached soon after AD 1000 by its first Polynesian colonists. They sailed there in one or more outrigger or double canoes with plank sides lashed on to dugout keels, crafted using polished stone tools and propelled by paddles and pandanus matting sails. Between 1000 and 800 years ago, Polynesians achieved this crossing, and many more, to equally isolated islands such as New Zealand, the Marquesas Islands, and Hawaii. Those who might see this as something of a record will be surprised to learn that people related to Polynesians probably made an equally astounding crossing about 2500 years earlier (1500 BC), over 2300 km of open sea from the Philippines to the Mariana Islands in western Micronesia.[4]

Humans, indeed, are the only mammal species to have colonized all regions of the world capable of supporting life *through their own energy and culture*. Our domestic animals and plants traveled with us, as did our commensals such as rats, weeds, and viruses, but it was the humans who made these diasporas possible.

Was there a likely common driving factor behind all successful prehistoric migrations? Accidents and disasters (e.g., a storm at sea, a volcanic eruption, or tidal wave) can trigger minor situations of unplanned migration, but only on a small scale. The eruption of Vesuvius in AD 79 did not drive all surviving southern Italians to the other side of the Roman Empire, or indeed cause any measurable hiccup in the development of Roman civilization. It is becoming fashionable nowadays to look for the causes of ancient migrations in climate change, particularly with respect to severe rainfall and temperature variations. I do not doubt the importance of such natural causes, especially for people living in fragile 'edge of the range' environments, where unexpected drought or a shrinkage in the average length of the growing season by a few days could have a disastrous impact on food production. But, in my view, the real energy behind the world's major colonizing migrations was human and demographic, in the sense that increasing human populations required new resources, especially territory, and more so if other groups or declining environmental conditions impinged on a long-term basis on the territories they already held. Shrinking populations would never have made successful colonists if they just continued to shrink, unless by migrating to richer habitats they reversed their demographic trajectory.

The question for prehistorians to answer, therefore, is why such demographic engines of expansion evolved in the first place, sufficient to drive peoples, languages, and societies across whole continents? Without migration there would be no human species, at least not outside a small region of Africa.

Hypothesizing About Prehistoric Migrations

This book deals with major migration episodes in human prehistory that can be reconstructed using multiple and independent sources of information. Whatever the information source, understanding of the prehistoric human past requires that hypotheses be considered against available information. I have presented one such hypothesis earlier, namely that demographic growth can drive migration. It can also be suggested that specific developments in technology, clothing, shelter and subsistence allowed many episodes of population growth and migration to occur, for instance by hunter-gatherers into Arctic latitudes or by early farming populations looking for fertile new lands in which to plant their domesticated crops or graze their animals. The sources of such hypotheses can either lie within recovered data (which are sometimes extremely few, especially if we rely on the archaeological record alone), or they can be drawn from broad comparative considerations of human behavior in the historical, ethnographic, and modern worlds. In reality, they are drawn from both approaches.

For instance, a major hypothesis, used in the later chapters of this book, is that many major language families and their early human speakers migrated together, on many separate occasions in different parts of the world, following the adoption of systematic food production during the Holocene.[5] This early farming dispersal hypothesis is based on worldwide comparisons of archaeological, linguistic, genetic, and other scientific data. It is also based on detailed region-specific archaeological and biological evidence. My general approach in developing and assessing such hypotheses follows Fogelin's (2007) strategy of "inference to the best explanation," by eliminating explanations that are less well supported by the evidence. I hope that my chosen explanations, especially for migrations during the past 10,000 years, will also accord with Fogelin's call for explanations that are empirically broad, general, modest, conservative, simple, testable, and that address many perspectives.

There are two further points that I wish to make here in order to set the concept of prehistoric migration in a fuller context. Firstly, historical accounts inform us that many relatively recent situations that we tend to think of as 'migrations' had, in reality, little long-term impact on the subsequent genetic, linguistic and cultural patterns in the areas to which they penetrated. This was because the migrants/conquerors and their descendants existed in relatively small numbers and were absorbed into the larger indigenous communities around them. The populations of many ancient conquest hegemonies and empires met this fate, including those of the Hellenistic kingdoms in Asia and Egypt following the conquests of Alexander the Great, many of the Germanic and Turkic-speaking populations who migrated across continental Europe during post-Roman times, the

Vikings in continental Europe, the Normans in England, the Crusaders in the Levant, the Mongols across their vast Eurasian empire, and many European colonial states in tropical Africa and Asia.

Conquest, imposition of government, and taking of tribute can have dramatic short-term effects, but over the long term many such events left few permanent traces, especially in terms of language replacement. Despite the magnificent conquests of Alexander the Great, and a few centuries of Greek influence in central Asia, hardly anyone living outside Greece and Cyprus today, except for modern migrants to countries like Australia and the United States, speaks Greek as a first language. Examples such as these can tell archaeologists that while material culture and imposed forms of government can often spread far and sometimes have significant cultural impact, they do not necessarily have to be associated with significant levels of permanent migration.

My second point is more philosophical, and it concerns the concept of *origin*. Let us consider two populations who have achieved fame in the world record of ethnography – the Khoe-San populations of southern Africa and the Maori of New Zealand. The Khoe-San, according to current archaeological and especially genetic data, have an ancestry in southern Africa that extends back for at least 100,000 years, perhaps as much as 300,000 years if one accepts a set of new molecular clock genetic calculations for the antiquity of the modern human genome.[6] The ancestors of the Maori arrived in New Zealand in the twelfth or thirteenth century AD, at a time when many famous monuments of Medieval Asia and Europe were under construction. We might rightfully think of the Khoe-San peoples as 'old' in ancestry and therefore origin, and the Maori as 'young'. Yet both groups are equally as modern, in human biological terms, as the rest of us. Both have prehistories of equal length, going back into the foundation layers of human origin in Africa. The only real difference is that the Khoe-San developed as distinctive populations within a completely African environment, whereas the Maori developed via many episodes of migration and ancestral residence, through at least 50,000 years, in many parts of tropical Asia and Oceania. Khoe-San ancestors tended to stay at home, Maori ancestors tended to migrate and sail away over the horizon in canoes.

In this sense, the 400 years or so of Maori residence in New Zealand, prior to the European discovery of these islands by Abel Tasman in 1642, are little more than a veneer. The Maori arrived in New Zealand as Polynesian fisher-farmers around AD 1250, just as complex in cultural terms as they were on the eve of the first serious European arrival, in 1769 by the British explorer James Cook (Tasman did not land). It is for this reason that my perspective in this book is focused on human populations and the routes they have traveled through time and space, and not simply on the archaeological records of modern nations. There is far more to Maori population prehistory over the long term than the prehistory of New Zealand, even if we cannot recognize entities in the lands of ancestral occupation, in Africa, southern China, Southeast Asia, or Oceania, that can specifically be termed *Maori*, as opposed to less specific categories such as modern human, Neolithic, Austronesian, or Polynesian (see Chapter 8).

Migrations in History and Ethnography

A most important body of comparative data on premodern migrations comes through history and ethnography, from situations in which writers consciously described what they perceived to be the histories and reasons for actual episodes of migration. Classical authors such as Herodotus and Julius Caesar led the way more than 2000 years ago, but the most remarkable records of kinship-based cultures in migration mode were made by European explorers, missionaries, administrators, and eventually anthropologists in the century between 1850 and 1950. I focus on a sample of these recorded migrations here because the societies described are likely to have resembled prehistoric societies in their sociopolitical and demographic structures, at least more so than would migrants from the Industrial Revolution in nineteenth-century Europe or modern refugees fleeing ethnic and political oppression.

The Helvetii

Let us start at one extreme of the migration spectrum, that of a large group migration that seems to have occurred as a single event, the first of its kind to be recorded in detail in world history. In 58 BC, according to Julius Caesar, Gaul (modern France) had three parts. The Belgae lived in the north, the Celts in the center, and the Aquitani in the south, with the Germans to the east across the Rhine. One group of Celts, the Helvetii, who lived around Lake Geneva in what is now Switzerland, were short of land, pressured by German tribes from the north, and wished to break out into more productive farming areas. Alas for the Helvetii, the route chosen for entry into Gaul would have taken them into the relatively new Roman province in southern Gaul (Provence, as it is still called today), a move which Caesar opposed. So they switched to a more northerly route across the upper Rhone valley into central Gaul, where they faced the pro-Roman Aedui. The Helvetii lost in their conflict with the Romans and their allies, but Caesar's description of their behavior is most illuminating:

> ...they determined to prepare for emigration by buying up all the draught cattle and wagons they could, sowing as much land as possible in order to secure an adequate supply for the journey, and establishing peaceful and friendly relations with their neighbors. They thought two years would suffice for completing these preparations [during which time their leader Orgetorix died, but the Helvetii did not give up]...As soon as they considered themselves ready, they burnt all their twelve towns and four hundred villages...and also the whole of their grain, except what they intended to take with them; for they thought that, if there was no possibility of returning home, they would be more willing to face all the perils that awaited them (Handford 1951: 29–30).

Caesar's legions, at least according to Caesar himself, brought them to a halt within Aedui territory, west of the Rhone, and the Helvetii were ordered back to their homeland after a military defeat. According to their own records, described by Caesar as written in their own language using a Greek script, the migration into Gaul involved a total of 368,000 people, of whom 92,000 were fit for military service. The migration traveled about 150 km before its eventual defeat.

The Helvetian migration had four interesting elements: a clearly stated intention, a large participating population, land shortage, and pressure from neighbors. It occurred into already-inhabited territory, but it was not successful. Many Classicists have suggested, perhaps not surprisingly, that Caesar may have magnified much of his account to impress the Senate and People of Rome. Perhaps he did, but the point here is that the Helvetii offer us a Roman mind model of what migration in western Europe might have involved 2000 years ago, even if some of the truth might have been distorted.

The migration of the Helvetii into Gaul is the first *detailed* record we have of a specific large group migration attempt within history. Herodotus (circa 440 BC) earlier mentioned the ancestral migrations of other populations, such as the Scythians who crossed the Araxes River, on the border between Iran and Armenia, to settle the Western Eurasian steppes adjacent to the Caspian and Black Seas.[7] But he gave less on-the-ground detail and, unlike Caesar, was not a direct eyewitness.

Ancient China

Overlapping in time with Caesar's account, Chinese historical records refer to the government-sponsored migration of a staggering seven to eight million people out of central China between 250 BC and AD 400, one of history's earliest accounts of migration on a scale approximating that of the recent colonial era. The migrants traveled from the alluvial plains of the Yellow, Yangzi and Wei rivers southwards into lands previously conquered by Qin and Han Dynasty armies, extending as far as northern Vietnam. Another two million non-Chinese people apparently moved into China from the steppes to the north at about the same time, further triggering the southward Chinese migrations.[8] Admittedly, this situation involved an ancient state rather than a small tribe, but it is interesting in terms of its size and because more than half of the populations of some Chinese homeland counties joined the migration. Recently, genetic research has supported the concept of north to south male-dominated movement within China from the evidence of both the male-inherited Y chromosome and female-inherited mitochondrial DNA. The archaeology of this period records the same process via a spread of Han Dynasty material culture, such as well-fired geometrically stamped pottery, ceramic tomb furniture, elite burials in brick or stone chamber tombs, and occasional artifacts with short inscriptions in Chinese script, through large regions of southern China and northern Vietnam.[9]

In cultural terms, the Chinese were migrating into regions already long settled by non-Sinitic populations, especially the Bai Yue, close cultural cousins and possible ancestors for many of the modern Tai-speaking peoples of southern China and Southeast Asia. The Chinese accounts do not give anthropological details, but the situations of linguistic and genetic admixture that accompanied these migrations produced eventually much of the Sinicized cultural landscape that we today term 'China'. The assimilation was not always one way, however, only in favor of the Chinese. The southern Chinese provinces of Guizhou, Guangxi and Yunnan still contain millions of indigenous Tai speakers today. The Vietnamese maintain a non-Sinitic linguistic and cultural identity, even though the northern half of the country was ruled by China during most of the first millennium AD. Modern Vietnamese is an Austroasiatic language with a significant amount of borrowed Sinitic vocabulary, but it is certainly not a Sinitic language in a genealogical sense. In the long term, both the Vietnamese and the indigenous Tai-speaking populations of northern Vietnam maintained their strong identities under the first millennium AD Sinitic domination, as did many peoples on the fringes of other powerful ancient empires – the Celtic Britons during the period of Roman Conquest (AD 43–410), for instance, or the Nubians on the southern frontier of Ancient Egypt.

Medieval Iceland

Another interesting example of early historical colonization, this time into virtually uninhabited territory, was that of the Norwegian Vikings who settled Iceland in the late ninth century AD.[10] Iceland was seemingly empty of permanent settlers before the migration, although a few Irish Christian monks and hermits might have visited it on a temporary basis before the first permanent settler population, of 404 men and 13 women, arrived from Norway in 874. Subsequent settlers came from both Norway (the Norse themselves, mostly men) and northern Britain, the latter being the source of the Gaelic wives (eventually 60% of Icelandic settler women) who accompanied many of the Norsemen.

It is estimated that about 10,000 people migrated to Iceland during the settlement period, between 874 and 930, and all available farmland was allotted to settler families within this time. Like their migrant Eastern Polynesian contemporaries in the Pacific, the earliest settlers lived more on fish than on farming or livestock owing to the initial wealth of previously unexploited maritime resources and the need for their herds to increase in size. Notwithstanding, some Icelanders by 980 were ready to move on to colonize southwestern Greenland – perhaps Iceland itself was already starting to feel a little crowded. Apparently, the population doubled every 200 years under Free State conditions, prior to Norwegian rule from the late thirteenth century onwards. By 1300, it had reached a total of about 40,000 people and there were close to 6000 farms across the island.

The Icelandic example points again to demographic success, as in ancient China, but this time in relative isolation. However, both examples were presumably well supported by backup migration from source regions and, unlike that of the Helvetii, did not happen just once. However, we must remember that the Helvetii were certainly not alone amongst their fellow Celts in having migratory inclinations. Many others, such as the Galatians of central Anatolia, the Boii of central Europe, and the Gallic invaders of the Po valley (circa 400 BC) in northern Italy have also come down to us in history as long-distance migrants.[11]

The Nuer of Sudan

In ethnographic times, especially during the nineteenth and early twentieth centuries, colonial records tell us of the expansions of many specific populations with traditional lifestyles and technologies. The Nuer (Nilo-Saharan language speakers – see Chapters 5 and 9) of East Africa offer a remarkable example of nineteenth-century migratory expansion, between 1818 and 1890, over more than 75,000 km², along a 600 km west to east trajectory across the tributaries of the Upper Nile in Sudan. According to Raymond Kelly (1985:1): "Nuer displacement of the Dinka (and Anuak) represents one of the most prominent instances of tribal imperialism contained in the ethnographic record."

Both the Nuer and the Dinka were related linguistically. Both had similar traditional lifestyles involving cultivation of millets and other grains, fishing, and herding of cattle in a landscape of wet season flooding and dry season pasture, the latter subject to increasing shortage as the dry season intensified. But the Nuer were able to raise huge forces of armed men combined from many tribal groups and were thereby able to expand through vast areas settled by Dinka populations, who were organizationally less able to defend themselves. As the expansion occurred, so the inflow of captive Dinka women, children and cattle fuelled further population growth amongst the Nuer, leading to a snowball that was only controlled early in the twentieth century by the advance of rinderpest, a virulent infectious cattle disease, and colonial era pacification.

How can we explain the level of Nuer success? This is the essence of Kelly's remarkably detailed book. The Nuer, by virtue of their widespread extra-tribal systems of patrilineal alliance, were able to call together huge forces of up to 1500 men, often organized to advance on an enemy in several columns. The Dinka, with a more matrilineal emphasis in their social organization, were normally unable to combine in defense beyond the level of the local group, making up just a few hundred men at most. In terms of total population size, relatively few people (mostly males) were killed in the Nuer attacks, but Kelly models the likely demographic advantage for the Nuer vis-à-vis the Dinka of the incorporation of young Dinka females and children. Dinka females were also valuable because of their ability to attract bride-price payments in cattle into Nuer communities, and it is the Nuer bride-price system that Kelly places at the center of his causal chain of explanation.

Nuer marriages at the end of the nineteenth century required that 40–60 head of cattle passed from the groom's to the bride's family, whereas Dinka bride-price requirements were much smaller and offset by return flows from the bride's relations. All in all, the Nuer needed twice as many cattle as the Dinka to support their marriage alliances and to fulfill commitments to the patrilineal kin of the bride, hence twice as much scarce dry season pasture. Thus, they needed access to land, and were prepared to fight for it. The result of all this conquest was that the Nuer population, with its large incorporation of ethnic Dinka, grew from an estimated 127,000 people in 1818 to 200,000 in 1890 (Kelly 1985: 228) and advanced over 600 km to the east of its former homeland. This offers us a classic example of conquest-driven assimilation, with Nuer and Dinka mixing genetically on a huge scale. However, it appears that the Nuer and Dinka identities and languages did not merge as a result of all this genetic admixture, but remained distinct, as they still do today. As Michael Hunley and colleagues (2008) have noted for similar population interactions in western Melanesia, genes cross population boundaries more easily than do languages, such that genetic interchange with language retention and bilingualism in each of the interacting populations is, in overall terms, more likely than total language replacement.

What started the Nuer expansion? Why did the Nuer demand so many cattle for their bride wealth payments? Those are good questions that are not easy to answer. Kelly places the origins of the system several centuries back in time, far beyond the reach of the ethnographic record and unfortunately far beyond the archaeological record in this troubled part of the world. In another related arena, however, James Barrett 2010 has recently suggested that young men who needed to search for bride-price resources provided one stimulus behind the Viking diaspora in Europe and Russia, in this case involving both plunder and colonization.

The Iban of Sarawak

Another most interesting example of ethnographic population expansion concerns the Austronesian-speaking Iban of Sarawak (western Borneo), rice farmers with long fallow land requirements who successively occupied river basins across a territory of equatorial rainforest stretching over 850 km from northwestern Kalimantan, through Sarawak, to Brunei Bay. Like those of the Nuer, these migrations were encouraged by high population growth and assimilation of captives, and continued for possibly a century until being eventually controlled after the imposition of British rule in 1841.

To an extent, Iban migration, like that of the Nuer, was self-reinforcing because of the constant assimilation of captured groups. The Iban were an ethnic group well defined by language and identity who engaged in fairly aggressive territorial expansion through success in warfare, headhunting, agricultural production, and the ability to establish new longhouse settlements in areas that previously supported only small populations, often of foragers. Indeed, achievement of the male status position of *raja berani* depended very much on one's possession of the aforementioned skills. Success bred more success, in the sense that a constant inflow of war captives, who were eventually enfranchised into Iban society, fuelled the population growth further, a situation similar to the Nuer incorporation of Dinka populations described earlier.

Derek Freeman 1970: 76 has described the incentives and methods that fuelled the Iban migration process as follows:

> The main incentive behind the remarkable migrations of the Iban has been a desire to exploit new tracts of primeval forest, and the tendency has been for communities to abandon their land as soon as a few lucrative harvests have been reaped, and move on to fresh precincts. In this way, the frontier of advance was pushed forward, first by one community, and then by another moving up from the rear. All these communities, it should be noted, were sections of the same tribe, and their members were all inter-related, in varying degrees, by cognatic ties.

The process was thus assisted by Iban cognatic social organization, in which family groups lived relatively independent lives in dwelling units constructed alongside each other within their raised-floor longhouses. Each family was free to leave its longhouse and join another whenever it desired, meaning that each new community would form around a newly constructed longhouse into which families from different origin longhouses could immigrate. This allowed a kind of social freedom which we might see as particularly useful for people wishing to expand into new territory in the manner chosen by the Iban. New longhouses could rapidly attract the labor and the warriors needed for successful establishment in a new territory, especially when other potentially hostile populations were present in the vicinity.

In a classic sense, the Iban expansion, like that of the modern Yanomami of the upper Orinoco River of Venezuela, represents a clear case of expansion of food producers into terrain inhabited either by foragers or by other less aggressive food producers. For the Yanomami, continuing migration occurred partly due to disagreements over wife-exchange in situations of male polygyny, as well as to the circumstances of remarkable population growth that required frequent foundation of new villages that could eventually reach 250 inhabitants. Until 1990, recorded average family sizes for Yanomami women who survived to age 50 were 8.2 births, despite high infant mortality rates as well as high adult male mortality in warfare. Even so, the Yanomami expanded their territory by an estimated 200–300% during the twentieth century.[12]

Relevance for Prehistoric Migration?

The examples just described are a mixed bunch, and we can hardly compare state-sponsored migration over many centuries in ancient China with the activities of individual tribal groups such as the Nuer or Iban. The latter were migrating under situations of developing colonial control and circumscription, rather than with the backing of an imperial army. Nevertheless, it is clear that such ethnographic migrations could sometimes be rapid, demographically powerful, and capable of covering quite large distances – many hundreds of kilometers in a century or less in the Nuer and Iban cases. It is quite possible that some of the vast and sometimes shadowy migrations that we will be considering in the following chapters involved similar bursts of migratory activity, at least from time to time. The existence of such episodes can become apparent when the data are rich and multidisciplinary. Excellent examples would be the very rapid Neolithic settlements of central Europe about 7500 years ago (Linearbandkeramik – Chapter 7) and the western Pacific about 3000 years ago (Lapita – Chapter 8).

The prehistoric migrations to be described in the following chapters generally took place over much greater extents and timescales than the recorded examples described earlier, often involving whole continents, and millennia rather than centuries. Therefore, they need to be considered as long-term processes rather than brief events. Most were undertaken by evolving populations with many genealogically related member societies, rather than single societies such as the Nuer or Iban. This was especially true of the food producer migrations that took place during the Holocene, which often involved the expansions of related populations in many different directions, through many thousands of years. So perhaps did the most significant migrations of Pleistocene hunter-gatherer populations, although we face an increasing elusiveness of data as we go back in time.

However, the ethnographic examples, even if small in scale on a global canvas, can certainly tell us something useful about motives for migration in kinship-based circumstances. In terms of fundamental economic causes, the Nuer expansion was fuelled by demands for cattle-grazing land, and those of the Iban and Yanomami by demands for crop lands (the Yanomami grow bananas and manioc). Additional behavioral and social persuasions that assisted these migrations operated through bride-price payments in the case of the Nuer, polygyny in the case of the Yanomami, and headhunting prowess and the instilling of fear in subjugated groups in the case of the Iban. But such social persuasions were generally icing on the cake, and desire for land to increase food production seems to have been the major factor behind successful migration, especially in tribal circumstances. European colonial powers might have conquered in the first instance for God and gold, not to mention trade in general and the wealth that accrued from it, but these were certainly not essential motives behind the migrations of ancient tribal societies. Even European colonial powers rapidly despatched settlers whenever they found territories where indigenous resistance was light and where climates suited European agricultural traditions.

Another factor that was especially important in stimulating migration, also widely reported in historical and ethnographic circumstances, was an ideological focus on giving high status and considerable political power to the founders of new settlements, especially in societies that recognized genealogical ranking by birth order. This was a cultural predilection found widely amongst expansive groups such as the Polynesians and Micronesians of the Pacific. It was often characteristic of ranked societies in which younger siblings inherited less productive land than older ones, and so had to consider out-migration to found a new settlement. For instance, amongst many populations in Oceania, the founding of new communities became a high-status activity and a major source for the embellishment of epics and mythology. In tribal agricultural societies with institutionalized forms of land ownership, where status and rights to land were to some degree determined by ancestry, gender, and birth order, there would always have been situations in which younger sons, able to found only lineages of junior rank at home, would have sought to establish a new senior line by migration to new territory. If such desires are institutionalized and given formal social approval, then a very powerful motivating force for active migration will be unleashed.[13]

Such systems of 'founder rank enhancement' underpinned the statuses of descendant individuals, families and lineages in many diverse societies around the world. Specific examples in the literature include the rice-growing Kelabit of Sarawak, the early Norse Icelanders, and the Shang Dynasty Chinese during the sixteenth to eleventh centuries BC. For the latter, Chang Kwang-chih (1983:16) wrote:

> At some point in the royal lineage's life there would arise reasons for sending one of its male members away from the royal domain to establish a new polity. He would be a brother, an uncle, or a cousin of the ruler, and he might be accompanied by a sizeable group of people in order to relieve population pressure, to open up new arable land, or to shore up defense...Thus, a new line of lineage segments would be initiated...

If the new lineage remained within the power structure of the foundation royal lineage, it could never rise to highest status. But if the young man concerned was able to claim independence for himself and his followers, then he would automatically rise to the highest status level in the local aristocracy. What better motive to migrate somewhere and find a place to call one's own?[14]

Recent colonial migrants of course had the same idea, albeit without the prominent underpinning of rank and status that occurred in Polynesia or ancient China. The American historian Ray Allen Billington (1967) describes in great detail how European migrants moving westwards through North America in the nineteenth century achieved land, wealth, and eventual community leadership, all by virtue of a process of founder rank or wealth enhancement. The same story for Australia has been told by Geoffrey Blainey (1966), and put into a novel about early nineteenth-century ex-convict and Aboriginal Sydney by Kate Grenville (2005).

The aforementioned examples all stress the significance of demographic success in migration, measured by increasing population size, except for the unfortunate Helvetii who met Caesar's army before they could settle down and procreate. Sometimes, people were lucky enough to break through and colonize landscapes, like Iceland, that had hardly or never seen humans before. Such was the good luck, on a much vaster scale, of the human populations who first reached Australia, New Guinea, and the Americas during the Late Pleistocene, and much later the Pacific Islands and Madagascar. But even in these cases, the first migrants would have depended on population growth for successful establishment.

Population growth amongst the first generations of colonists or successful immigrants is a phenomenon that is particularly well recorded in recent history. In my *First Farmers*, I discussed a number of examples from Chinese Taiwan, Pitcairn Island, colonial Australia, and late prehistoric New Zealand and Hawaii. A new analysis of Quebec birthrate records indicates that seventeenth- and eighteenth-century French pioneers on the mobile rural frontier in northeastern Quebec reproduced at a rather staggering average rate of 9.1 births per women, compared to a still fairly impressive 7.9 births for women who remained in the settled towns to the rear of the migration front. European women in 1840s Australia lagged only slightly behind at an average of 6.8 births per woman. These examples are all from situations where the settler population found itself in a temperate landscape that was either uninhabited, or only lightly settled by indigenous peoples, where food was plentiful, and where threats of disease were small. Pioneers in new lands that were not already densely settled were potentially very highly advantaged, especially in terms of passing on their genes and cultural habits to the following generations. The indigenous populations were not so lucky, as we can see from the devastation wreaked on contact-era populations in parts of Australia and the Americas.[15]

Not so lucky either were the great conquering armies of the Medieval era, such as those of the Yeniseian or Turkic-speaking Huns under Attila or the Mongols under Genghis Khan. These were not able to convert themselves into successful and permanent migrants, no matter how far their conquests took them. There were simply too many competitors already in place, even if Genghis Khan himself was highly

---

successful in leaving descendants.[16] Alexander the Great's followers faced exactly the same problem. Successful migrants needed advantages, demographic as well as cultural, if they wished to have a leading role in human biological and cultural evolution, rather than an ephemeral presence at the rear of the stage.

Notes

1. See the *Encyclopedia of Global Human Migration* (Ness and Bellwood 2013).
2. See also Cabana and Clark 2011 for the use of a similar definition.
3. For instance, by archaeologists Rouse 1986 and Batty 2007: 17.
4. Hung et al. 2011. This claim has generated some debate (Hung et al. 2012; Winter et al. 2012; Carson et al. 2013), but the archaeological record is in strong support.
5. Bellwood 2001, 2005a; Bellwood and Renfrew 2002.
6. Scally and Durbin 2012.
7. Both Griffith 1996: 377, footnote 11, and Cunliffe 2008: 264 assert that the Araxes of Herodotus was the Volga River, in accordance with the Pontic steppes view of Indo-European linguistic origins which I discuss in Chapter 7. However, the original Greek text of Herodotus refers unambiguously to the Araxes (Elizabeth Minchin, ANU, pers. comm.).
8. See the discussion of the Xiongnu and the Yeniseian languages in Chapter 7.
9. LaPolla 2001: 227–30 (linguistics and history); Wen et al. 2004 (genetics); Allard 2006 (archaeology).
10. Smith 1995; Sigurdsson 2009a, 2009b.
11. Collis 2003; Sims-Williams 2008.
12. The Iban are well described by Sutlive 1978 as well as Freeman 1970. For Yanomami, see Chagnon 1992; Merriwether et al. 2000.
13. Bellwood 1996a; Anthony 1997; Bellwood and Hiscock 2009: 294–5.
14. For the Kelabit see Barker et al. 2008: 128 and Smith 1995 for Iceland. The operation of founder rank enhancement is also suggested for Neolithic contexts (circa 5400 BC) in central Europe, where different household groups in the Neolithic settlement of Vaihingen in Germany had access to different territories with varying potentials for food production (Bogaard et al. 2011).
15. Bellwood 2005a: 14–9; Moreau et al. 2011 (Quebec); Vamplew 1987: 55 (Australia); O'Fallon and Fehren-Schmitz 2011 (colonial era depopulation in North America).
16. Zerjal et al. 2003.

Chapter 2
Making Inferences About Prehistoric Migration

In this chapter we examine some assumptions necessary for recognizing the existence of prehistoric migrations, using data from various disciplines and comparing their perspectives. Genes, languages and material cultures all contribute to our understanding of the human past, yet the data they yield can often be incomplete and ambiguous. On the one hand, the migration of a human population into an uninhabited landscape can provide a historical situation in which genes, languages and cultures moved in relative cohesion. Immigration into a previously settled landscape, on the other hand, can be expected to have led to situations of more complex interaction and admixture between populations of different origin.

Significant migrations that lead to permanent settlement into new territory will always leave a signature. Our problem is to recognize that signature. We can expect that with any significant level of migration there will be visible changes in language, material culture and biology, even if there is a considerable amount of admixture between indigenous and immigrating populations.

Are any signatures of ancient migration likely to be clear and unambiguous? Archaeologists, comparative linguists, geneticists, biological anthropologists and ethnologists are all able to consider this question. They must also be willing to consider it in a cross-disciplinary collaborative framework, *triangulating* across the borders of their specializations. This is a concept used to great effect by archaeologists Patrick Kirch and Roger Green (2001:42) in their detailed reconstruction of ancient Polynesian society:

> We seek to develop a *triangulation method* in which the subdisciplines of historical linguistics, archaeology, comparative ethnology, and biological anthropology independently contribute their data and assessments to the common objective of historical reconstruction.

Kirch and Green also point out that prehistorians work with 'polygons of error' rather than the precise intersection points of real surveyors, but the triangulation metaphor is still very apt.

First Migrants: Ancient Migration in Global Perspective, First Edition. Peter Bellwood.
© Peter Bellwood. Published 2013 by John Wiley & Sons, Ltd.

The existence of polygons of error rather than precise intersections is the main reason why biology, language and culture do not always covary in unison. People procreate and contribute 50% of their genes to each offspring, but a male and female from different ethnolinguistic communities do not create a new language from 50% of the linguistic resources of each of them drawn at random, or build a house split down the middle to reflect their separate architectural traditions. This is partly why, if we travel in Africa, Southeast Asia and the western Pacific, even Europe and India, we find millions of people who speak closely related languages, but who are as different in biological appearance as western Europeans and northern Indians (Indo-European speakers), Melanesians and Filipinos (Austronesian speakers), or Iraqis and Ethiopians (Afroasiatic speakers). There is nothing terribly mysterious about all of this.

Changes in Time and Space – Genes, Languages, Cultures

Any prehistoric migration is obviously going to be most visible if an endogamous group of people with their language and material culture moved across a landscape in a tight isomorphic combination. To investigate this further, we need to consider three questions in terms of comparative likelihood. Under what circumstances might the spread of an archaeological culture have been equivalent to the spread of a language, or a group of closely related dialects? Secondly, could the spread of a language have been equivalent to the spread of a relatively endogamous breeding population? Thirdly, could the spread of a relatively endogamous breeding population have been equivalent to the spread of an archaeological culture? And, of course, vice versa in each case.

The answers to these questions will always be "sometimes, but not always," and will differ according to whether the migration landscape was pristine and without prior human inhabitants, or already inhabited by other populations. In the case of a pristine landscape, genes, languages and material culture would have evolved initially within the founder community via parent to child transmission and peer interaction. Before the existence of modern transportation and mass communication, the initial migrants would always have arrived in a new landscape with only a subset of the biological and cultural variation present in the much larger homeland population, via a winnowing process termed *founder effect*. In the new land, the components of this cultural and biological founder configuration would have become duly magnified as the population grew in size and became increasingly differentiated from the source configuration.

If a landscape was already occupied, however, then genes, languages and material items would have been transmitted and exchanged between at least two different populations right from the start.[1] Gene flow, contact-induced change in languages, and cultural borrowing are all examples of such interaction or network-based processes, sometimes referred to as *reticulation*.[2] Even a new population in a pristine landscape would rapidly have experienced at least some interaction between its own dispersing and differentiating components as numbers grew. Indeed, in any real situation it can be almost impossible to separate the results of inheritance and interaction conclusively, except in totally isolated and very small populations (very rare in actuality), and at the level of the human individual, who can only inherit directly at birth from two parents and not receive genes from peers (modern gene transplants of course excluded!). The values of vertical descent and horizontal interaction, as concepts, lie in broad implications for reconstructing human prehistory at the population level, rather than in precise identification and separation in every situation.

If genealogical differentiation of entities in biology or culture is to develop at all, there must be separation between ancestral forms that formerly shared a common origin in a restricted territory. Such separation will always require expansion or migration, whether the entities happen to be genetic, linguistic, or cultural.[3] Differentiation cannot occur effectively if the foundation entity never spreads because any incipient diversity will tend to be swamped back into the main pool, especially as that pool grows in numbers. The result will be the transmission of a single society or population through time rather than many differentiating variants. Had human prehistory been without subsequent migration after the initial dispersals of *Homo sapiens* (Chapter 3), then we would expect human variation today to be differentiated only along natural and environmental boundaries. The world is not structured in this way, and never has been.

Human Biology, Genetics, and Migration

Biological ancestry at the individual level is highly complex if we wish to work back for thousands of years, especially in terms of the recombining parts of the nuclear genome, comprising the alleles (alternative forms of genes) that coil together as equal maternal and paternal contributions in the chromosomes of new offspring. However, some aspects of human ancestry can become clearer if we focus on genes transmitted through only one parent in every generation, either the mother, who transmits mitochondrial DNA (mtDNA) to all her children, or the father, who transmits the nonrecombining part of the Y chromosome (NRY) to his sons (males do not transmit mtDNA to their children). These *haploid* (as opposed to diploid) genetic systems change only through mutation, by a process known as nucleotide substitution, and not by chromosome recombination at meiosis. Thus, they form transgenerational lineages. Specific mtDNA and NRY lineages have proven very useful in tracing population ancestries, especially when they are widespread and occur in many populations.

Until recently, much genetics literature on ancient human migration was driven by mtDNA research. An early study in 1987 led to the exciting announcement that all living humans descend from a so-called African Eve who lived about 200,000 years ago. The ancestry is only partial, since African Eve only founded our mitochondrial lineages, not all our nuclear DNA. Even so, it is striking that all living humans share a limited number of mtDNA lineages (or haplogroups in genetic terminology) that are of ultimate African origin, and that the deepest ones in terms of time depth and phylogenetic differentiation occur amongst populations who today inhabit southern Africa. Current research on the NRY draws the same conclusion for males, albeit on a younger time scale. These observations help to explain why an origin for *H. sapiens* (modern humans) in Africa is so widely accepted by geneticists and paleoanthropologists today.[4]

In recent years, many genetic scenarios for human prehistory have been based on analyses of the haploid mtDNA and NRY genetic systems, using molecular clocks to determine dates and places of haplogroup origin. These clocks have generally depended on inferred rates of nucleotide substitution, calibrated against an estimated age derived from the fossil record for human-chimp separation (circa six million years ago, but opinions differ). The dates derived from these clocks are always associated with large degrees of error. There are also disagreements over which clock, based on which part of the genome, gives the most reliable results. Autosomal DNA located within the nuclear and recombining portion of the genome is today giving results that are often greatly different from those derived from the haploid sectors of the genome. For instance, the most recent autosomal molecular clock, based on mutation rates determined from family pedigrees rather than a human-chimp separation time, gives much older dates for the emergence of *H. sapiens* than those obtained from mtDNA.[5]

There are other issues in the interpretation of haploid genetic prehistory that also need to be considered. A number of recent genetics papers have raised the possibility that mtDNA haplogroup distributions are subject to natural selection (e.g., Balloux et al. 2009), given that mtDNA generates energy from glucose in cells. There is as yet no consensus on this rather difficult issue. It is also obvious that the survival chances of specific mtDNA haplogroups are subject to processes of genetic drift due to differential demographic success from one generation to the next. Some haplogroups can become very common, others can disappear with the passage of time, especially in small isolated populations where differential fertility can have a major impact on the composition of subsequent generations.

Also, knowing where and when a specific mtDNA or NRY lineage mutated into existence does not mean we know from exactly where a population that carries that mutation commenced its most significant episode of migration (Goldstein and Chikhi 2002). For instance, a percentage of the British who settled in Australia and the United States during the nineteenth century, arrived with mtDNA lineages in their cells that had mutated tens of millennia earlier in Paleolithic Europe, yet the migration itself originated far more recently in Britain. A lot of confusion in genetic understanding of human prehistory has arisen in recent years owing to the unfortunate tendency to equate the molecular clock age of a given mtDNA haplogroup mutation with a significant migration of the human carrier population, often in the face of very strong contradictory evidence from other disciplines.

I return to current genetic perspectives on human population histories in the following chapters, but it is quite remarkable that much that was written even five years ago on mtDNA and the NRY from a molecular clock perspective can now be seen as very dated due to advances in the interpretation of autosomal genetic data, and also to advances in the analysis of ancient DNA from bone. Whole genome scanning is now being achieved both for living individuals and for ancient DNA, and it is becoming standard for reconstructing historical relationships between modern populations. In fact, as I write this chapter, my feeling about the science of population genetics is that it is about to enter a new and very exciting era, driven by autosomal whole-genome comparative databases and by ancient DNA from skeletal remains, rather than by the mitochondrial and NRY phylogeographic methods based only on living populations that have dominated during the previous 25 years.

Demic Diffusion

When intermarriage occurs between adjacent populations, genetic characteristics can spread by local processes that need not involve any long-distance migration, for instance through local migration and spouse movement within an already settled landscape. This process is called gene flow. Over time, as a result of cross-boundary mating, it is likely that genes will spread. But they will not spread far unless people physically carry them, or unless they have a very high selective value. Marriages generally occurred close to home in most traditional societies, so the prolific gene flow in our modern global situation is not a good parallel for interpreting the tribal past. For instance, Jonathan Friedlaender (2007:4) reports that 80% of unions during the 1960s amongst inland gardening communities on Bougainville Island in western Melanesia occurred between partners who lived less than 1 km apart. The distances moved would have tended to be greater in more mobile hunter-gatherer societies (Hill et al. 2011), but a total randomness of mating across a large area would clearly have been impossible in such situations.

The situation changes if there is demographic growth that necessitates expansion in search of new land or resources into terrain already inhabited by other groups. Such expansion will tend to occur in the directions that offer the best resources and the least resistance, leading us to the concept of *demic diffusion*. As long as there is some kind of centrifugal spread or directionality in the process, then demic diffusion can be regarded as one aspect of the broader migration category of human behavior. It fits the Nuer and Iban expansions discussed in Chapter 1 very well, since these groups migrated into terrain that was already inhabited. But, of course, demic diffusion was not relevant for the Paleolithic colonizations of Australia or the Americas since there were no people there beforehand.

Demic diffusion is normally propelled by a wave of advance, which generally translates into radial or linear movement with an obvious migration component fuelled by population growth along a frontier. The wave of advance concept was adopted by Albert Ammerman and Luca Cavalli-Sforza (1984:67) to describe the actual population spread behind the expansion of Neolithic cultures through Mesolithic Europe between 6500 and 4000 BC:

> In the wave of advance model, population growth and local migratory activity are seen as producing a diffusion process that takes the form of a population wave expanding outward at a steady radial rate.

Demic diffusion *and* population growth take place simultaneously under this model, the latter mainly within the wave of advance itself rather than in the more densely populated hinterland. However, the genetic consequences become more and more watered down with respect to the source configuration as the wave of advance spreads through other unrelated populations and mixes with them, moving further and further away from the source region. Colin Renfrew (2002) has referred to this process as a "staged population interaction wave of advance," and the implications are very important. As Cavalli-Sforza (2002:153) points out, an immigrant population attracting gene flow from indigenous populations, at a rate of 5% per generation, will see 87% of its genes replaced over a period of only 1000 years. Naturally, a great deal of backup migration will tend to obviate such watering down, as during the nineteenth-century colonial migrations of Europeans in fleets of ships. But if there was no backup migration, then demic diffusion through a populated territory could lead to very considerable biological change from a fully immigrant population at the start to a completely different one (albeit not, of course, a fully indigenous one) at the end. Such movement, however, could carry cultures and languages over large distances with only limited modifications, depending on the demographic, technological, and social statuses of the immigrants *vis-à-vis* the indigenes.

Alan Fix (2011) has recently proposed a variant of the general model of demic diffusion to deal with situations where immigrant populations were very small, for instance in agriculturally marginal environments such as the equatorial rain forested interior of West Malaysia, where some hunter-gatherer populations have survived to the present day. He terms this "trickle effect colonization," and models a movement of 50 farmers into a new territory, where they mix at a rate of 10% every generation with the indigenous hunter-gatherers, and also receive a 10% addition each generation by continuing immigration from the farmer source region. The modeling presented by Fix produces a population of 4000 farmers from the initial 50 migrants in 30 generations, or about 750 years, a healthy increase over an archaeological timescale. It is clear that some migrant groups in prehistoric circumstances would have been very large, others very small, dependent no doubt upon the environmental suitability of the new region for food production and the nature of hunter-gatherer population density and resistance.

Although many archaeologists have since questioned some of the ideas behind the wave of advance model, especially that of a steady or unidirectional rate of expansion, the concept is sound and fits many examples of ancient immigration into inhabited territory. The golden rule is that real migration studies in prehistory must take account of both large group migrations in integrated episodes backed up by positive decision making, sometimes with geographical leap-frogging over intervening occupied terrain, as well as slow and halting demic diffusion or trickle effect colonization via fingers of demographic advance.[6] Perhaps fingers are better metaphors than waves in inhabited terrain in this regard, given that the idea of a migration *wave* has generated some resistance amongst archaeologists and historians in the recent past.

Language Families and the Study of Migration in Prehistory

The extents of language spread required to explain the distributions of the world's most extensive language families, of foragers and food producers alike, would have required significant migration of native speaker communities and not just language shift alone, although any situation of admixture between linguistically different populations will automatically have involved the latter process to some degree. As stated by linguist Nicholas Ostler in his survey of major language histories across the world during the past 4500 years:

> The most eminent judgment to emerge from our global survey is that migrations of peoples, the first force in history to spread languages, dominates to this day. (Ostler 2005: 534)

This statement gives considerable food for thought, not just for individual historical languages, but for whole language families as well.[7]

Genealogical (or genetic) relationship between different languages revolves around comembership in language families. The approximate distributions of the major language families of the world in AD 1500 are shown in Figure 2.1 and Figure 2.2. Languages are placed in such families because they share sets of common *retentions* that have descended from initial *proto-languages*, such as Proto-Indo-European or Proto-Austronesian. Within such families, sets of two or more languages form subgroups defined by uniquely shared *innovations* (inherited as *cognates*) that came into existence during episodes of common residence in a geographical homeland. Subgroups of languages in turn descend from proto-languages at different temporal and geographical levels. Such intermediate proto-languages record the history of the language family like a shrub or tree, from outer branches to root system. However, in reality, some root systems can often be located on the outer geographical fringes of the language families to which they gave birth; for instance, Taiwan for Austronesian, Mesoamerica for Uto-Aztecan, or West Africa for the Niger-Congo and Bantu languages (Chapters 8 and 9).

Comparative linguistic reconstruction is not always easy, for many reasons. Cognates can be difficult to recognize due to undocumented phonological change through time, especially in language families that are not well recorded. They can also be replaced through time by innovation or borrowing. Expansions of certain subgroups or individual languages can also erase former traces of other languages and subgroups within the same family. This has happened with the large-scale spreads of literary state languages such as the major Sinitic languages within China, Russian and other Slavic languages within eastern Europe, and the Romance languages derived from Latin in Mediterranean Europe.[8] These languages of state identity not only replaced many unrelated languages, but also assimilated many of their close linguistic cousins through language shift. Unfortunately, the extinction of an unwritten language is forever, and attempts by linguists to determine language family homelands purely on the basis of modern language distributions can give results that are at odds with archaeological and genetic data.[9]

Because languages change and differentiate continuously (just compare Anglo-Saxon of AD 950 with modern English), there is a time limit to how long relationships will be retained between related languages and subgroups before all traces of common ancestry have disappeared. There is no sharp boundary here because some linguistic

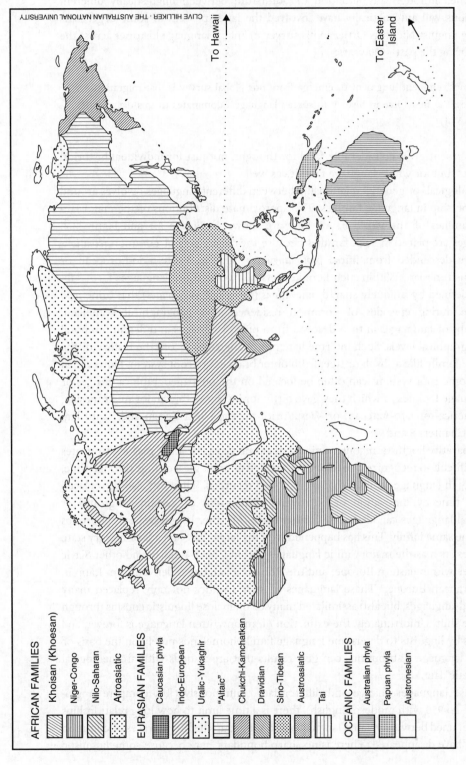

Figure 2.1 Major language family distributions across the Old World at AD 1500. Some small families and isolates are omitted, for instance, Hmong-Mien and Basque. The 'Altaic' family contains Japonic, Korean, Aimu, Mongolic, Turkic, and Tungusic (see Figure 7.6). Original drawn by Clive Hilliker as Bellwood 2005a, Figure 1.1, using data from Ruhlen 1987.

AFRICAN FAMILIES

Khoisan (Khoesan)

Niger-Congo

Nilo-Saharan

Afroasiatic

EURASIAN FAMILIES

Caucasian phyla

Indo-European

Uralic-Yukaghir

"Altaic"

Chukchi-Kamchatkan

Dravidian

Sino-Tibetan

Austroasiatic

Tai

OCEANIC FAMILIES

Australian phyla

Papuan phyla

Austronesian

To Hawaii

To Easter Island

CLIVE HILLIKER · THE AUSTRALIAN NATIONAL UNIVERSITY

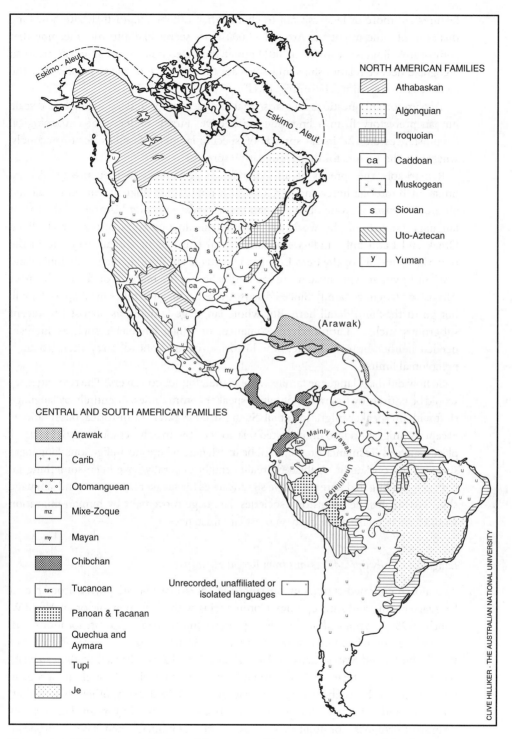

Figure 2.2 Major language families of the New World at AD 1500. Many small families and isolates are omitted, and the large areas marked as "unrecorded, unaffiliated" reflect in part the widespread native language loss since European settlement began. Original drawn by Clive Hilliker as Bellwood 2005a, Figure 1.2, using data from Ruhlen 1987.

features are more or less resistant to change than others. Linguists debate how long this span of time might be. Around 12,000 years seems likely to me, meaning that comparative linguists can tell us little about the Paleolithic. Some linguists claim to recognize deeper relationships and advocate the existence of *macro-families*, but the evidence can sometimes be ambiguous.[10]

Two important questions now arise that are relevant for understanding broad-scale human prehistory from a linguistic perspective. Firstly, under what chronological circumstances did the initial spreads of specific language families occur? Secondly, what were the vectors for those foundation spreads?

Remarkably, the spreads of all major language families to their precolonial era limits, of hunter-gatherer and agriculturalist populations alike, occurred in full and absolute *prehistory*. None of the initiations, spreads, and early histories of the major language families of the world are recorded in documentary history at all. Even Greek and Latin only underwent fairly trivial episodes of spread very late in the remarkable history of the Indo-European language family. Akkadian/Babylonian and Ancient Egyptian were little more than branches on the margins of the much vaster Afroasiatic language family. Since I discuss these language families in Chapter 7, I will not go further into detail here. But whole language families, as opposed to recent subgroups such as Latin-derived Romance, or single languages such as English, needed neither historical states nor historical conquerors to carry them to their precolonial limits.

So how did these language families spread their foundation layers? The two extremes would be entirely by migration of native speaker communities, or entirely by language shift with no speaker migration at all. Such extremes rarely fit historical observations, except for migration into uninhabited territory or the massive colonial settlements of places such as Tasmania or the Caribbean Islands, where no indigenous languages survived the onslaught. Prehistoric reality might generally have been something in-between, leading to different relative significances for speaker movement and language shift. For small-scale prehistoric societies, language movement by human migration would have been far more likely in most circumstances.

Language Family Spread: Lessons from Recent History

The aforementioned statement on language spread can be supported from recent language history and anthropology. Commencing with the former, historian Alfred W. Crosby (1986) has pointed out how European colonization in temperate locations with few indigenous inhabitants, such as Argentina, Chile, Uruguay, much of southern Brazil, the United States, Canada, New Zealand, and Australia, led to the establishment of what he termed 'Neo-Europes'. In these countries, 50 million European immigrants in the century between 1850 and 1950 (and many others before that) founded predominantly European populations speaking European languages – Spanish, Portuguese or English in most of the aforementioned cases. European-introduced epidemic diseases with their 'devastating scythe-like effects', domesticated Eurasian crops and animals, tough weeds, and high levels of European population fecundity in newly found fertile lands led to a tragedy for the indigenous populations of absolutely unparalleled proportions.

For instance, William Denevan has estimated indigenous population declines of between 74 and 99% (the latter in Hispaniola) across the moving frontier of European conquest after 1492 in the Americas, an estimate given fairly substantial backing from modern genetic research. Even in the early nineteenth century, traveler and artist George Catlin was able to suggest that North America had an indigenous population of 16 million before Europeans arrived, and that 12 million had since died – 6 million as "victims to the small-pox" and another 6 million "to the sword, the bayonet, and whiskey."[11] As another example, New Zealand in 1870 supported 250,000 Europeans and nine million sheep, but less than 40,000 Maoris, who continued to dwindle in numbers from their 1769 precontact high of perhaps 100,000 or more, until the population rebounded in the twentieth century (Miller 1958: 104; Crosby 1986: 265). By the mid-nineteenth century, relatively few Maori and Australian Aboriginal women were able to conceive owing to the devastating impacts of introduced diseases (especially smallpox and venereal diseases), land taking, and many unfortunate cases of settler brutality, especially towards indigenous women. On the other hand, European women in colonial territories during the seventeenth to nineteenth centuries were giving birth to rather phenomenal numbers of children, as we saw in Chapter 1. Indigenous languages survived wherever indigenous population networks remained numerous enough to maintain them, but the overall impact of Spanish, French, and British colonization in these regions was and still is absolutely obvious, especially in the language situation today.

Crosby went on to compare the Neo-Europes with locations that clearly were *not* Neo-Europes, mostly Old World tropical to equatorial locations with their own diseases to which Europeans had no resistance, and all with dense populations living at high levels of social and political integration. The Middle East with North Africa, many regions of tropical Africa, and southern and eastern tropical to temperate Asia (including China) offer many examples. The tropical Americas do not to such a high degree because the linguistic outcome was so heavily driven in favor of European languages by the massive impact of introduced diseases and the lack of any major reverse impact on the Europeans. All of this means that European nations were unable to colonize very successfully in the Old World tropics, and their languages faded from memory once their empires had decayed. Try speaking Dutch today in Indonesia, French in Vietnam, or even English in many remote corners of India. As Crosby (1986:63) commented, rather amusingly, on the attempts of the Crusaders to conquer the Holy Land: "the conquerors, taken collectively, were like a lump of sugar presiding in a hot cup of tea."

It is true that some nations with immense linguistic diversity have decided to adopt a European language as a national language since World War II (e.g., Nigeria with English), but even in cases such as Papua New Guinea, with English and Motu as parliamentary languages and Tok Pisin as the main lingua franca, we must ask if the total population will one day speak *only* English or Tok Pisin, having abandoned all their native vernaculars.[12] Modern conditions of literacy, schooling, mass communication and centralized government might one day enforce this, but I am doubtful that such circumstances could ever have existed in prehistory.

The conclusion that can be drawn from the recent colonial past is that a single language, when introduced into a new territory, will normally only take hold on a permanent basis, as a whole-population vernacular, if it is imported in the mouths of substantial numbers of native speakers, or if a modern state hastens its adoption through literacy and schools. Going back a little further into history we find much the same situation. As linguist Nicholas Ostler (2005:273) states, after examining the history of the written languages of the world, from Egyptian and Akkadian of 2500 BC onwards to recent times:

> The cases where serious language change failed to follow on from conquests expose the hollowness of much military glory – the conquests in western Europe by Franks, Vandals and Visigoths, even the conquests in Britain by Romans and Normans.

His conclusions are that the languages of imperial administrations and trader lingua francas did not survive for very long after the systems that nourished them went into decline, *unless* there were implantations of very large numbers of their native speakers or only low densities of aboriginal population.

Language Family Spread: Lessons from Anthropology

One reason why language spread only occurred in rough proportion to the degree of permanent population immigration is related to the issue of language loyalty. This clearly matters to healthy and non-oppressed indigenous populations, for whom language loss can be a serious and stressful process (Mithun 1999: 2). Indeed, large numbers of indigenous language speakers, even if conquered and induced to learn imposed national languages, can give some immunity against total language swamping from outside. Stephen Schooling (1990:123–4) has demonstrated this very clearly for New Caledonia, where native Austronesian languages are successfully resisting the domination of French:

> Relationships are the glue that binds people together. If all the members of a community are individually bound to each other by a specific relationship, they form a solid block which will tend to stick together and conform to the same norms. This is DENSITY. If people are bound together by many different relationships, the link between them is like a many-stranded rope – very difficult to break. This is MULTIPLEXITY. People bound into a closely compacted social network have plenty of opportunity to be exposed to the standards and norms of that network. As long as there is a motive for remaining part of a network there is every reason to conform to its norms – to speak the language and do those things that are normal for that group. Even should there be a conscious desire to break free from such a network, it may be quite difficult to do so. Sanctions that can be applied to maintain conformity are often considerable.

Perhaps one can understand from the preceding that language very often serves as a badge of identity – people do not give up native vernaculars lightly. Even in cases of preferred intermarriage between members of different language families, as in parts of northwestern Amazonia, people still do not mix languages or undergo continuous language shift. Instead, they maintain a situation of multilingualism, using their languages as relatively stable bases of ethnolinguistic identity (Aikhenvald 2002: 23). Multilingualism, indeed, was probably as common in prehistoric societies as it is in many societies today, and is an extremely important mechanism for allowing different groups to maintain ethnic independence and continuity, without the need for a resulting 'win' of one language over another.

Dating the Spreads of Language Families

It is difficult to date language families using internal linguistic data alone. Language family geography sometimes offers a relative chronological order for language family spreads, especially when certain language families have become layered on top of others through time. In Mainland Southeast Asia, for instance, the extensive but spotty distribution of Austroasiatic languages from eastern India to the Malay Peninsula records overlay by the more recent and compact spreads of Indic (Indo-European), Tibeto-Burman, Thai, and Malay languages (Figure 8.2). All linguists agree that the Austroasiatic language family has a greater antiquity in this region than do the other families, although some of the pattern also reflects the internal expansions of Khmer and Vietnamese in historical times, both of these also being Austroasiatic in origin.

Yet, care is very much needed here. There can be no universal rule for interpreting the geography of language spread. The Hmong and Mien languages of southern China and northern Mainland Southeast Asia also have a scattered distribution, rather like that of many Austroasiatic languages. But in this case, they are known to have spread southwards very recently from China. The Hmong-Mien scattered distribution is quite different from the extensive and continuous distributions of state languages such as Thai and Burmese, which spread hand in hand with Indicized kingdoms over very large areas, involving conquest, state establishment, literacy, and firm management of territorial borders. On the contrary, the Hmong and Mien were nonliterate populations of upland farmers, seeking small pockets of land across a vast region that was already claimed for rice growing at lower altitudes by the inhabitants of the major states. They lacked the military and unified demographic strength to take over such large territories.

As far as absolute (rather than relative) dates for language families are concerned, a linguistic technique termed glottochronology dates language splits from percentages of cognates between related pairs of languages, according to an assumed regular rate of lexical change through time (rather like a molecular clock in genetics). As with molecular clocks, such a regular rate has often been shown to be wrong (e.g., Blust 2000b for Austronesian), but there have recently been some interesting developments in precision and methodology (Holman et al. 2011). Statistical techniques derived from evolutionary biology have also allowed some recent and fairly convincing estimates of proto-language age to be calculated for the Indo-European and Austronesian families, as discussed in Chapters 7 and 8.

I will finish this brief section on linguistic chronology by suggesting that the most significant point of change in recent world linguistic prehistory, at least within the agricultural (temperate and tropical) latitudes, was the transition from hunting and gathering into food production, as also suggested by Colin Renfrew (1991, 1996). The various agricultural transitions that occurred between roughly 8500 BC and AD 1, depending on which part of the world is under focus, could well turn out in combination to have marked the most significant fault line for language spread and replacement in human prehistory, only matched again by the colossal population and language upheavals that occurred during the colonial era, since AD 1500.

Cultures in Archaeology – Do They Equate with Linguistic and Biological Populations?

Modern archaeology has evolved hand in hand with the concept of the archaeological *culture* – a relatively homogeneous assemblage of items which occur together in sites across a given region within a given span of time. However, archaeological theorists such as David Clarke (1968) have been pointing out for many years that archaeological cultures were not always homogeneous within and sharply bounded without. Clarke borrowed the term *polythetic* to describe them, as opposed to a *monothetic* concept of total homogeneity. Clarke also pointed out that the geographical distributions of culture-defining artifact types in the archaeological record will not always have been coterminous. Different kinds of artifacts can have different distributions, depending both on their functions and on their associations with cultural identity.

Despite all these qualifications, the concept of the archaeological culture, as it was defined by the archaeologist Gordon Childe, still carries a very significant meaning and level of usefulness in archaeology:

> In each functional class archaeologists can distinguish a variety of types current over a restricted area at a given period in archaeological time. The totality of recognized types current simultaneously in a given area is termed a "culture." (Childe 1948: 25–6)

Childe went on to state that an archaeological culture must correspond to a social group which sanctified the distinctive conventions enshrined within that culture, but he did not demand that culture and language were necessarily always locked together.

The reality is that some archaeological cultures are well bounded, others not; some are internally homogeneous, others not. Some offer clear traces of widespread interaction, others do not. Thus, the concept of the archaeological culture is not a meaningless universal. Just as some language groupings stand up well as coherent genetic structures and others tend to collapse into bundles of isolates, so do archaeological cultures. In some periods we witness very broad extents of material culture (defined as technocomplexes or culture groups by David Clarke), covering almost continental areas, internally homogeneous, tightly dated to specific chronological horizons and telling us that something, somehow, has spread. At other times we find situations where, try as we may, there are simply no coherently defined cultures at all. At such times everything can indeed be fluid, dynamic, and reticulate.

There can be little doubt that stylistic variation in material culture does equate to some degree with the concept of a social group or endogamous population, at least according to observations made within the ethnographic record. A number of African examples, chosen from many, can be used to illustrate this. For instance, Gosselain (2008) reports how stylistic and technological factors can mark ethnic identity in Nigeria, especially through variations in pottery decoration and shape. He also notes that such defining features are not normally borrowed between different potting communities. Wallaert (2008) reports how pottery traditions are closely tied to individual villages in one region of Cameroon, such that women who copy from other village traditions cannot sell their pots within their own village, but only to outsiders. Another example comes from northern Cameroon, where pottery decoration represents cosmological and religious concepts, leading to the statement that "The interrelatedness of pottery decoration and symbolic structures justifies widespread use of decoration as the prime index of ethnicity preserved in the archaeological record" (David et al. 1988: 365). Such examples are not just restricted to Africa.

However, it is one thing to be able to point to ethnographic situations where identity and style appear to be closely related, but another to turn such observations into strong statements of what is likely to have occurred in fully prehistoric situations. Only historical records, and not archaeological material culture, would ever reveal the existences of prehistoric Kurds, Jews, and Minangkabau as distinctive ethnic groups in an unrecorded prehistoric context. To deal with this problem, the stance I take in this book is that material culture combinations are likely to reflect human populations who shared languages and relatively endogamous breeding networks *if* they were complex and internally coherent, geographically widespread, rapid in appearance, and can be inferred to have undergone histories of descent-based (phylogenetic) differentiation.

Demonstration of descent-based differentiation for archaeological categories through space and time is becoming a major focus of research in modern archaeology, just as it has been for a long time in human biology and linguistics (Steele et al. 2010). An excellent example, amongst many, is focused on the spread of Neolithic plant economies of western Asian origin into Europe between 6500 and 5000 BC (Coward et al. 2008). This phylogenetic analysis of 250 early Neolithic crop assemblages from archaeological sites demonstrates the existence of two separate culturally-defined crop combinations moving along two routes, one via the Mediterranean and the other through central Europe north of the Alps. The crops concerned (Chapter 7) were manifestly not present in either of these regions before the Neolithic. The overall pattern fits the well-established picture, derived from other aspects of archaeology, linguistics and genetics, of a two-pronged Neolithic migration from the Near East into Europe starting around 6500 BC.

Of course, demonstration of lineage-based relationships between these sets of crops does not automatically imply that their transportation was by human migration, as opposed to exchange or trade. The crops could have moved by themselves if indigenous hunter-gatherers all adopted agriculture from each other by some kind of chain reaction. But I doubt the reality of such a scenario for the European Neolithic.

Archaeology and the Study of Migration in Prehistory

It is because of the lack of any *total* congruence between patterns in language, culture, and biology that we find the identification of ancient migrations to be a difficult and often controversial matter, especially for the archaeologist. As I have indicated, material culture in itself is not always a reliable marker of population identity. But as material culture becomes more complex, and distributed across more functional and stylistic categories, then the reliability of inferring an attachment to community and a replacement by immigration can increase. If there is a totally dramatic replacement of material culture in all categories in a broad region across a very short period of time, we are surely entitled to think of immigration as a possible explanation.

Nevertheless, the dangers of using *only* the archaeological record to argue for migration will be brought home very quickly by looking at some historical examples. What appear to us now to have been great cultural replacement events in early history were accompanied sometimes by substantial immigration, and sometimes not.

One End of the Spectrum – Intensive Culture Change without Significant Migration

As a striking example of culture change in a nonmigration situation, we have the shift through imperial conquest from Iron Age to Roman Britain, from the Claudian conquest year of AD 43 into the later first century AD. Admittedly, the British population had already been softened up by a century of intermittent contact with the Roman world since the initial and brief conquest by Julius Caesar in 55 BC. But AD 43 still marked a very dramatic transition in British affairs. The Romans introduced roads, forts, cities, villas, brick and stone monuments, Latin inscriptions, and fine wheel-made pottery from Gaul. Within a few decades, within the regions under Roman control (excluding northern Scotland and Ireland), these icons of Mediterranean civilization began to replace indigenous Iron Age earthwork fortifications, timber and thatch villages of round huts, storage pits, 'Celtic' metallurgical art, mostly handmade pottery (except in southeastern England), and the general situation of illiteracy. The marching legions quickly met indigenous resistance with the insurrection of Boudicca and her Iceni warriors in East Anglia, but the Romans won. If we had no history, we might think of this as reflecting an immigration of new Roman colonists from Italy or Gaul in large numbers into a former tribal landscape, like the British settlement of Australia.

But, of course, we do have history, and it tells us quite clearly that the conquest of Britain did not involve very much free settler immigration. The Roman Empire did not encourage such a concept in its outer provinces, except by the foundation of special cities called *coloniae* for giving conquered land to veteran soldiers and officials, most of whom were probably outnumbered by natives. Only four *coloniae* were apparently founded in Britain, at Colchester, Gloucester, Lincoln, and York. "Colonization was not at the leading edge of Roman imperialism" (Brennan 1990: 498), and free farmer-colonists did not sail in from Italy, Spain, or any other part of the empire in large numbers to dispossess the Britons.

This, however, is not to state that migration was never important in the Roman world as a whole. Scheidel (2005) calculates that some two million adults were relocated within Italy during the last two centuries BC, and possibly two to four million slaves were imported into Italy over the same period. Many colonies with Italian settlers were founded in late Republican and early Imperial times in Spain, Gaul, Dalmatia, and Africa. But Britain was more remote from Rome and indigenous population continuity there was evidently much stronger, especially given the lack of evidence for widespread indigenous adoption there of a Romance language derived from spoken Latin.

A roughly contemporary and equally impressive example of great change without migration, in this case based on religious rather than military conquest, would be the spread of Indic religions, philosophies, and architectural concepts between AD 500 and 1300 across many regions of Southeast Asia.[13] The legacy of this today consists of huge stone and brick temples such as the Angkor complex in Cambodia, Borobodur and Prambanan in Java, the My Son complex in central Vietnam, and the Pagan complex in Burma. In this case, there was no lasting military conquest from South Asia, and there were very few ethnic Indian as opposed to indigenous rulers. But there was enormous influence on indigenous elites, via the Hindu and Buddhist religions, that led eventually to the formation of Indic-style kingdoms. As one suspects happened in Roman Britain, the common people with their languages and genes changed little, apart from a few Indian genes that entered regions intensively visited by Indian traders, such as Bali, where about 12% of men today still carry Indian NRY chromosome lineages.[14] Islam spread in similar ways beyond the Arab world into South and Southeast Asia, mostly without spoken vernacular Arabic, as distinct from the seventh-century Arabic used to recite the Koran. Of population replacement, there was apparently rather little.

Material culture, especially that connected with the elite, can be quite misleading in such circumstances if we are looking for evidence of migration. In Roman Britain and Indic Southeast Asia, the archaeological record shows sharp changes in material culture and associated beliefs in situations where no significant immigration over an existing native population can be inferred. In Southeast Asia, the magnitude of the change is exacerbated by the fact that archaeologists gravitate towards large Indic-style monuments, where cultural aggrandizement is rather heavily indicated. Were they to concentrate more on contemporary life in villages they would probably see no change in identity at all. The people who inhabit Southeast Asia now, in the villages around Angkor and Borobudur, descend fairly directly in genetic and linguistic terms from the people who lived there 3000 years ago, long before Shiva and Buddha entered local consciousness.

The Other End of the Spectrum – Intensive Cultural Change
with *Significant Migration*

At the other end of the spectrum, there certainly have been historical situations where real change in the archaeological record can be correlated with unambiguous evidence for the arrival of a new population. During the fifth and sixth centuries AD, there was a historically and linguistically significant immigration of Anglo-Saxons and allied Germanic language speakers across the North Sea to eastern and central England. This immigration is recorded unambiguously in the contemporary account of Gildas and in later sources such as the Anglo-Saxon Chronicle and the Ecclesiastical History written by The Venerable Bede. It is also recorded clearly in NRY (male) genetics and in the forging of English as a unified language out of the Anglo-Saxon dialects, a process brought to completion by the English kings Alfred the Great and Athelstan in the ninth and tenth centuries. Where Anglo-Saxons met Celts in eastern England, there were clearly enough of them to drive home their language advantage. There are even suggestions that they maintained this advantage by rules of genetic endogamy with respect to the native British.[15] John Hines (1996) points out how small was the Celtic linguistic substrate incorporated into the Anglo-Saxon language, whose descendant today we term English.

Archaeology and place-names reinforce this picture of large numbers of Anglo-Saxons arriving as settlers in eastern and central England, where they founded hundreds of villages with Germanic place-names, especially those ending in derivatives of – ingas, -inga, -ham, -leeh (-ley), -dun (-don) and – burh (-burgh, -borough).[16] They deposited cremation burials in decorated pottery urns, laid down inhumation burials with distinctive cupreous brooches and iron weapons, and constructed Germanic-styled sunken-floored huts (grubenhäuser) or framed wooden buildings,[17] all instantly recognizable as markers of a cultural phase very different from that of the terminal years of Roman Britain.

The Anglo-Saxons, however, did not settle everywhere. As during the Roman Empire in Britain a few centuries earlier, local Celtic languages continued to survive in the more mountainous and remote regions of Wales, the southwest of England, Ireland and Scotland, by now (fifth century AD) in combination with Christianity. Many aspects of these Celtic Christian cultures have survived to the present, to underpin modern Welsh, Irish, Cornish and Scottish identities. In East Anglia and the Midlands, however, Roman cities and their Celtic or Latin vernaculars faded from the scene, even though many former Roman cities kept the Latin suffix -chester or -cester ('military camp') in their names.

So, in Anglo-Saxon eastern and southern England, we could perhaps expect no better evidence for migration. It is almost as good as the archaeological evidence from Australia that documents what no one could possibly doubt. British colonization, from 1788 onwards, wrought a tremendous change in the colonized coastal regions (by no means the whole continent, of course), such that language, material culture, genetics, and written history are all in agreement and leave no doubt about the reality of the situation. In this colonial situation, as in many parts of British North America, genes, languages, and culture all arrived in unison in the first instance from Europe.

Yet, there are some grounds for concern. In three situations of really quite powerful change in archaeological culture, we find that two (Roman Britain and Indic Southeast Asia) were not associated with any substantial settler immigration or language replacement at all. But how can we differentiate such situations when they are restricted to prehistoric data, with no documentary history? The answer is that we probably cannot if we rely solely on the archaeological record, which is prone to ambiguity when considered in isolation from other disciplines. Hence, it is not surprising that some archaeologists in recent years have attempted to modify the Anglo-Saxon arrival into a process of cultural and linguistic diffusion, with no immigration from Germanic Europe at all. It is quite possible to do this, but doing it convincingly is another matter altogether.[18] Only a fully multidisciplinary investigation will suffice.

Notes

1. An exception here would be if successive migrant populations came from the same homeland.
2. Bellwood 1996b, 2001; Stark et al. 2008.
3. Kirch and Green 1987; Mace and Pagel 1994; Bellwood 1996b; Mace and Holden 2005; VanPool et al. 2008: 77.
4. See Cann et al. 1987 for the original paper on African Eve. Shi et al. 2010 discuss the NRY.
5. Scally and Durbin 2012 suggest up to 300,000 years as opposed to the more widely assumed 100,000 to 200,000 years for the origins of *H. sapiens* in Africa. They also doubt the validity of molecular clocks based on mtDNA alone.
6. Van Andel and Runnels 1995 describe leap-frog immigration for Neolithic Greece; Sheppard 2011 for Lapita in western Oceania.
7. See Diamond and Bellwood 2003; Bellwood 2008.
8. As Currie and Mace 2009 point out, the areas covered by individual languages have increased in size as their speakers have increased in social and political complexity.
9. See, for instance, the unlikely homelands calculated by Wichmann et al. 2010 for Indo-European and Afroasiatic. They state clearly that their calculations take no account of subgroup extinctions.
10. The suggestion by migration historian Patrick Manning 2005 that all major language families, except for Bantu and Austronesian, represent Pleistocene radiations linked to the spread of modern humans approaching 50,000 years ago is not based on linguistic analysis, and is not convincing.
11. Denevan 1992; Catlin 2004: 3–4; O'Fallon and Fehren-Schmitz 2011 (modern genetics). I am unsure about the accuracy of Catlin's estimates, but at least he was there to witness the devastation at first hand.
12. Tok Pisin, developed originally in German New Guinea, has an 80% English vocabulary and a Melanesian grammar and word order. It is neither Indo-European, nor Austronesian, nor Papuan, but a linguistic creation in its own right spoken by several million people in modern Papua New Guinea.
13. Higham 2001; O'Reilly 2007.
14. Ardika and Bellwood 1991 (Bali archaeology); Karafet et al. 2005 (Bali genetics).
15. On Anglo-Saxon genetics see Weale et al. 2002; Thomas et al. 2006.
16. Wainwright 1962; Cox 1975.
17. Dark 2002; Hills 2003.
18. For example, Matthews 1995. Oppenheimer 2007, interestingly, pushes back the date of some Germanic migration into Britain into pre-Roman times, using mtDNA molecular clock calculations.

Chapter 3
Migrating Hominins and the Rise of Our Own Species

This chapter first considers the early migrations of members of the genus Homo, both within Africa and into Eurasia, the latter movement commencing around two million years ago. Our own species, Homo sapiens, appears also to have migrated out of Africa into Eurasia much later in time, between 120,000 and 70,000 years ago, a process leading to complex patterns of both admixture and replacement with respect to archaic hominins. These human migratory achievements, both archaic and modern, were undoubtedly aided by culture and language, both evolving from simple to more complex forms through time. By 45,000 years ago, modern human hunter-gatherers had reached the habitable limits of the Old World.

The biological family that contains great apes and humans is termed the Hominidae. Within it, there is a taxonomic tribe of upright bipedal striding creatures called the Hominini, henceforth *hominins*. Nowadays, the hominins consist only of us (*Homo sapiens*), and all other hominin species have become extinct. Modern apes – gorillas, chimpanzees, orangutans, and gibbons – are not fully bipedal and are not classified as hominins.

All living humans share hominin ancestors extending back beyond two million years ago, this being the time in Africa when our genus *Homo* is widely agreed to have speciated from an ancestor within the genus *Australopithecus*. Also classified as hominins, and also African, are the more ancient and truly extinct genera *Kenyanthropus*, *Ardipithecus*, *Australopithecus*, and *Paranthropus*. Other putatively extinct hominins include former species within the genus *Homo*, such as *Homo erectus* in East Asia and *Homo neanderthalensis* (the Neanderthals) in western Eurasia.

Where did hominins emerge, and how did they spread? Between 2.5 and 1.8 million years ago, early in the Pleistocene, early hominins in East and South Africa were acquiring a number of rather fundamental characteristics that help us to define the genus *Homo*. These include an anatomically human postcranial skeleton, specifically carrying an upright bipedal posture that allowed striding and upright running, a precision grip between fingers and thumbs that allowed the handling and purposeful flaking of stone tools, and a parabolic and distinctively human 32-tooth omnivore dentition, well adapted for consumption of both plant foods and meat. The ancestor concerned is best termed "early *Homo*." We do not need here to immerse ourselves in the finer details of hominin taxonomy, but a current and widely accepted family tree for hominins is offered in Figure 3.1.[1]

First Migrants: Ancient Migration in Global Perspective, First Edition. Peter Bellwood.
© Peter Bellwood. Published 2013 by John Wiley & Sons, Ltd.

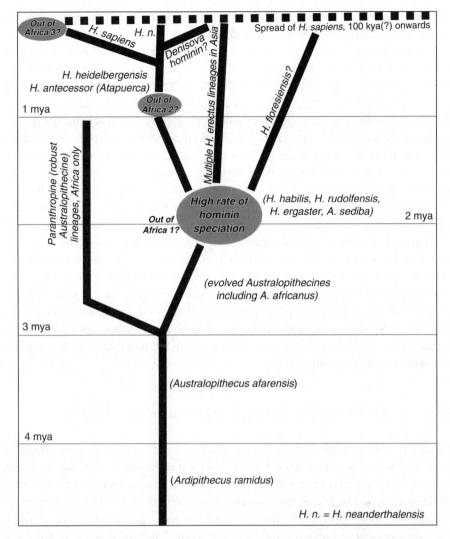

Figure 3.1   A current family tree for hominins, from Australopithecine ancestors to *Homo sapiens*, the only hominin species to have survived until the present. Drawn by the author.

Part of the problem in understanding fossil hominins relates to the rather confusing concept of 'the species' in the paleoanthropological record. Unlike most modern animal species that form closed breeding networks in the wild, the remains of fossil hominins can only be classified in terms of their surviving measurements and visible features, and more rarely through their ancient DNA (Groves 2013). Such classifications must deal with variations in chronology, since all species evolve through time, and also the biases of small sample size and fragmentary preservation, plus the huge time and space gaps in the fossil record. Thus, we should not necessarily think of fossil hominin species as being as different from each other as modern humans and chimpanzees. Some, despite being classified as separate species, have recently been revealed by modern research into ancient DNA to have interbred to a small degree.

This implies that, when one ancient hominin species met another as a result of migration, the result could have been far more complex than simple replacement of a loser by a winner, with no genetic interchange. Indeed, the concept of *extinction by assimilation* (Smith et al. 2012) holds that a dominant species will gradually incorporate the genes of a less dominant one if it is biologically able to do so, such that the genetic profile of the latter will decline in proportion continuously through time.[2] It is perhaps best to think of the ancient genus *Homo* at any one time as comprising a series of regional populations which marginally interbred, although not forming such a unified species as modern humanity due to the greater degrees of geographical isolation.

The immediate Pliocene ancestor for *Homo*, prior to 2.6 million years ago, would have been a member of the genus *Australopithecus*, a genus on present evidence confined entirely to Africa. By two million years ago, incipient *Homo* species were well established in southern and eastern Africa as an array variously termed *Homo habilis*, *Homo rudolfensis*, and *Homo ergaster*. Whether there really were three separate species of early *Homo* in existence in East Africa at the same time is a topic of current intense debate.[3] But it is clear that an early *Homo* population had migrated into western Asia by at least 1.8 million years ago, where, according to some authorities, it became distinguished as the species *H. erectus*, best known from the Pleistocene fossil sequences of Georgia, Java, and China.

Behavioral Characteristics and Origins of Early Hominins in Africa

Did our remote ancestors behave like us? When it comes to migration we cannot be sure. We know they moved, from Africa to Asia and eventually to Java, but we do not know if the moves were intentional, if they traveled in large or small groups, or if they could swim across large expanses of water. Most likely there would have been range expansions similar to those of other mammal species, dependent on environmental circumstances and probably without conscious intent. The precise details of any given range expansion will be forever lost to us, as they surely are for other ancestral species deep in time. But we can plot some of the approximate time and space coordinates of hominin expansions from the fossil record, and more controversially from genetic molecular clocks. We can also relate them to enabling environmental factors such as the existence of enticing warm climates, familiar food resources, fairly open country (neither intense desert nor dense rainforest), and the availability of land bridges between land masses that were at other times separated by sea.

Did early *Homo* at two million years ago already have the gendered pair bonding, cooperative sharing, and base-camp territorial systems that characterized ethnographic human hunter-gatherer populations?[4] This could be considered an insoluble question, perhaps an irrelevant one for migration studies. But an answer could help in the modeling of migration scenarios, if only because a species organized into large cooperating groups of both sexes, with permeable rather than rigid territorial group boundaries, and perhaps communicating with rudimentary spoken language, would have had a far better chance of successfully colonizing a new and unknown landscape than one without such advantages. They would have had an even better chance if, as suggested by Richard Wrangham (2009), they already knew the use of fire for cooking food by as early as two million years ago. Cooked food allows easier and more rapid digestion than raw food, thus making energy available to be utilized in brain development. Cooking is also an activity that can strengthen the bonds within a family unit, leading to increased male–female cooperation. Whether cooking really was known to hominins two million years ago remains debated, but chimpanzees and bonobos do not use fire and are strongly territorial, which may be partly why they have not had a very successful history of species radiation beyond the equatorial rainforests of Africa.

Getting down to more visible characteristics, the earliest members of the genus *Homo* in Africa were habitually bipedal, as demonstrated by the almost complete skeleton of the 1.6 million year old 'Turkana Boy' (*H. ergaster* or *H. erectus*) from Kenya. Bipedalism is important because it allows us to stride, run, and travel over very large distances, and doubtless allowed our ancestors to migrate much further than would the knuckle-walking posture of a chimpanzee or gorilla. This ability applied equally to both sexes, added to which the sexual dimorphism in body size that characterizes most other higher primates was under gradual reduction at this time, making males and females more equal in size. Overall body sizes for both sexes were also increasing, but brain sizes were still small two million years ago, varying between 500 and 900 ccs, depending on the species concerned. In contrast, Neanderthal and modern human brains of the past 50,000 years averaged over 1200 ccs in brain size.

As far as we know from extant finds, early hominins favored fairly dry tropical and temperate woodlands and parklands south of the fluctuating southern edge of the Sahara Desert, generally quite open, of varying tree and shrub density. In fact, given the presence of their fossilized (mineralized) bones in several caves in South Africa, as well as in East Africa, it is likely that early *Homo* populations occupied nearly the whole continent by two million years ago, except possibly for the most arid Sahara and Kalahari regions. This means that temperature-wise they would have been adapted to life in both tropical and temperate climates, from the Equator to almost 40° of latitude north and south. According to Ruxton and Wilkinson (2011), the loss of thick body hair in our own direct *H. sapiens* ancestry reflects selection to allow sweating in hot and open tropical environments, but there is no guarantee that all early hominins were hairless. Thick body hair might have been extremely useful to hominins living through a chilly winter in South Africa or Algeria.

In terms of the archaeological record, the earliest African *Homo* populations struck pebbles and stone nodules with stone hammers to make simple tools, utilizing both cores and flakes. Stone tool making has become one of the essential elements in the definition of *Homo*, given that no other hominins, apart perhaps from the latest Australopithecines, can yet be proven to have made them. Currently, sites with definite stone tools in Africa go back about 2.6 million years (Hovers and Braun 2009) and strongly suggest a partly meat-eating diet, even if archaeologists cannot easily decide whether the game was hunted by the hominins themselves or scavenged from abandoned carnivore kills. What is more, some of the stone raw materials were carried several kilometers across the landscape. Apes can be taught how to make stone tools by human mentors, and indeed sometimes use them as hammers or anvils in the wild. Some chimpanzees in West Africa leave discarded modified stones around their living places (Mercader et al. 2007), but chimps in the wild do not flake stone tools with focused intent.

How do we know the genus *Homo* evolved in Africa, and not elsewhere? Human evolution occurs constantly, and humans have certainly evolved as regional populations in Eurasia as well as in Africa. Some populations even moved back into North Africa from Asia during the Holocene, particularly via the Levant and Arabia (Chapter 7). Some have suggested that fossil species of *Homo*, especially *H. erectus*, might have evolved in Asia and done the same in the remoter Pleistocene past.[5] Once *Homo* populations were widespread in ancestral form across the Old World, then formation of a new species could have happened, in theory, anywhere within the range, allowing sufficient time and isolation (Stewart and Stringer 2012).

However, in terms of human evolution as a whole, from Miocene and Pliocene primate forebears to early *Homo*, Africa was undoubtedly our ultimate source. Our closest genetic relatives, chimps and gorillas, have never been found in fossil form elsewhere. All pre-*Homo* hominin fossils have been found in Africa, as well as the oldest dated stone tools. What is more, as far as modern humans are concerned, the greatest degree of genetic diversity in humans occurs in sub-Saharan Africa. All of the haploid DNA lineages of living people (*H. sapiens*) across the world first appeared there in their foundation forms, although genetics at present cannot demonstrate this for extinct species of hominin.

Where in Africa did the genus *Homo* originally speciate? Two regions have produced the bulk of the relevant hominin fossils: the Great Rift Valley of East Africa, and a series of ancient limestone caves in South Africa. In both cases, the landscapes assist paleontologists greatly, since alluvial/lacustrine and cave sediments trap and bury bones which can eventually fossilize, later to be exposed to view by uplift, erosion, or speleological good luck. Many of the geological deposits in the Rift Valley are also derived from volcanoes that feed on the crustal instability, and tuffs and lavas are very useful for radiometric and other forms of absolute dating. Hence, we know a lot about hominin evolution from these two regions.

However, in terms of the totality of Africa, these landscapes are rather localized. The Great Rift Valley is 6000 km long and runs beyond East Africa, via the Red Sea, into the Jordan Valley in the Levant. But much vaster and more stable areas of western and northern Africa do not reveal fossils so easily. Australopithecines dating from 3.5 million years ago have been found as far west as northern Chad in the Sahara, but they lived during a moist Pliocene climatic period long before the evolution of *Homo*, when the Sahara was apparently more habitable than now. So, was the source of the genus *Homo* actually in the woodlands and parklands of eastern and southern Africa, where so many fossils have been found? Or could it have been elsewhere?

Because of the hominin adaptation, via bipedalism, for extended bouts of walking and running (e.g., after ground-dwelling prey, or away from ground-dwelling predators), an origin in the eastern and generally drier side of sub-Saharan Africa does seem most likely. Hominins are not renowned for their tree-climbing capabilities, and many recent hunters and gatherers have found wet tropical rainforest to be rather difficult for food collection and hunting. In 1994, Yves Coppens proposed an "East Side Story" for the origin of humankind, in which humans became separated from the ancestors of chimps and gorillas as the Rift Valley formed and divided sub-Saharan Africa into a wetter west and a drier east. King and Bailey (2006) have put the spotlight on the Rift Valley itself, pointing out that hominins would have been hard-pressed to avoid predators in completely open flat country, whereas the Rift would have offered excellent opportunities for early humans to have foraged, hunted, and protected themselves in relatively rough terrain. They point to varied geomorphological features that exist owing to the tectonic instability, giving varied and abundant plants and animals, ample water in the form of lakes and rivers, security (cliffs, trees, rough places in general), and perhaps even opportunities for running down animal prey. They also note how the Rift Valley would have led people onwards into Asia when the Saharan and Arabian deserts allowed such movement to occur.

In the last few years, a number of scholars have also suggested a southern rather than eastern African origin for *Homo* (e.g., Pickering et al. 2011). If true, this would be rather interesting in terms of climatic adaptation, since the caves near Johannesburg that have produced so many fossils from the period between 3.5 and two million years ago lie at a latitude of about 30°S. As noted earlier, this would probably have meant cold winters and occasional frosts, especially since these caves are quite far inland. Given that the oldest hominins in Eurasia have also been found far from the Equator, at 41°N in Georgia, it is becoming apparent that archaic hominins as a whole, regardless of specific *H. sapiens* ancestry, were not entirely tropical creatures, but able to survive in much cooler temperate climates as well.

Yet, even here there may be a catch. Christine Hertler and colleagues (2013) suggest that early Australopithecines spread from tropical East Africa to temperate South Africa during a warm climatic phase about 3.5 million years ago. Then they spread back again, as the species *Australopithecus africanus*, during colder climatic conditions between three and two million years ago, eventually to give rise in East Africa to an early *Homo* species (*H. habilis?*) before two million years ago. This suggests an interesting level of climate-related migratory behavior for such an early time period, with *Homo* ancestors dodging the cold through forward and backward migration. But such scenarios can be little more than working hypotheses at present.

First Hominin Migration(s) — Out of Africa 1

As will be seen in the pages that follow, successful movements of hominins out of Africa into Eurasia probably occurred on at least three occasions, and quite possibly many more. To understand how and why these migrations occurred, we begin with the enormous cycles of climatic change that characterized the whole of the Pleistocene epoch, and thus the whole of the evolutionary time span for *Homo*.

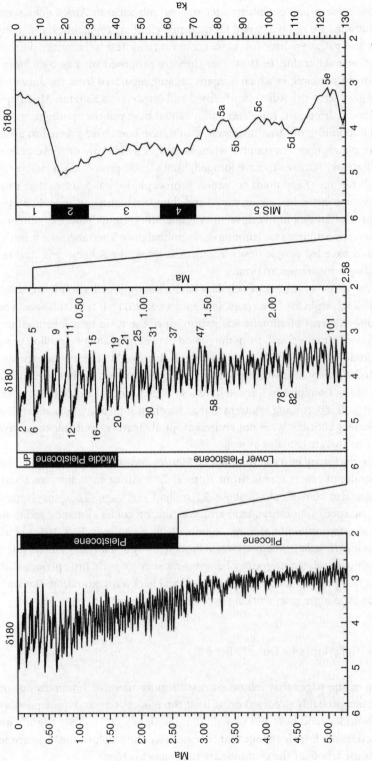

Figure 3.2 Oxygen isotope records reflecting global temperatures at increasing resolutions for the last 5.3 million years (left), the Pleistocene and Holocene (from 2.58 million years ago; center), and the Upper Pleistocene and Holocene (from 130,000 years ago; right). Higher temperatures are to the right, lower to the left. Interglacials are identified by uneven numbered marine isotope stages (MIS – the Holocene is 1), glacials by even numbers. This figure is from Hertler et al. 2013, and contains original data from Lisiecki and Raymo 2005. Reproduced courtesy of the authors.

Paleoclimatic studies have revealed the successive cycles of glaciation and deglaciation that influenced the world during the Pleistocene epoch, between 2.58 million and 12,000 years ago, especially in the northern hemisphere. Climates oscillated in many successive cycles, between extreme cold and dry glacial conditions on the one hand, and warm and wet interglacial conditions like those of today on the other (Figure 3.2). Furthermore, some of the swings were very abrupt indeed, jumping in just centuries or less between sharply different states. Such swings seem to have been especially strong around 2 to 1.8 million years ago, when early *Homo* was undergoing increased natural selection, dietary expansion, and engaging in its first attempts to move out of Africa.[6] The potential for migration offered by the rapid opening and closing of environmental transit zones is apparent, depending of course on the adaptability of the hominins concerned to new and often stressful conditions.

Glaciations undoubtedly offered very severe conditions for early hominins at high and middle latitudes. Snowlines dropped by up to 1 km in altitude and huge ice sheets extended southwards across Europe and North America to reach central England and the Great Lakes, although much of northern Asia east of the Taymyr Peninsula was too dry to support them. Prior to 0.9 million years ago, these glacial to interglacial cycles each lasted about 40,000 years, reflecting the cyclical changes in the orientation of the earth's orbit around the sun. After 0.9 million years ago, during the Middle and Late Pleistocene, the cycles lengthened to about 120,000 years, and have kept that extended range until now. Within these major cycles, much smaller oscillations with a periodicity of a millennium or so have constantly spiced up the suddenness of change.[7]

It is quite obvious that these glacial to interglacial swings would have had powerful effects on world climate, not just in truly glaciated regions but also in the tropical and warm temperate regions of the world that appear to have been favored by early hominins. The tropics became much drier in glacial periods than in interglacials, and deserts expanded. In the temperate zone, many landscapes switched from being habitable during interglacials to being marginal or completely uninhabitable (under ice) during glaciations. Such changes would have pulled populations into new territories during interglacials and expelled them back or driven them to local extinction during glacials (Dennell et al. 2011), although much would depend on how hardy and resourceful were the populations concerned.

Our best example of an interglacial is the current Holocene epoch, in which we are now living. This reached its peak of temperature and moisture between 9000 and 4000 years ago, as did its predecessor (the last interglacial) between 128,000 and 118,000 years ago, when average global temperatures were 2 °C higher than now and sea levels up to 9 meters above the present.[8] As we will see below, it was probably during the last interglacial that our own ancestors (*H. sapiens*) first left Africa and moved into Israel and Arabia. In central and northern Africa, the northward expansion of tropical monsoon rainfall during such interglacials led to periodic dampening of the Sahara and Arabia, and the formation of lakes and river channels where today there is only dry sand. During the early Holocene, parklands and grasslands spread right into the interior Saharan massifs and supported human populations who hunted cattle and harvested wild millets, at least until increasing desertification around 6000 years ago

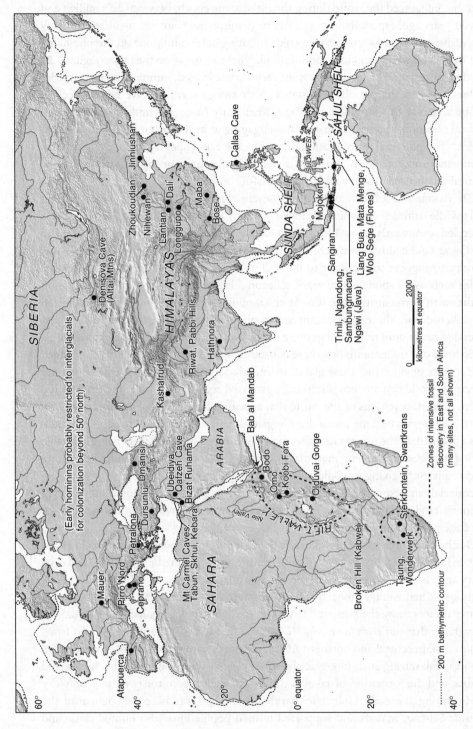

Figure 3.3 Early hominin (pre-Neanderthal and pre-*sapiens*) fossil find places and archaeological sites in the Old World. Background map by Multimedia Services, ANU, details added by the author.

gradually expelled them (Chapter 5). The main point here is that the Saharan and Arabian deserts quite regularly became habitable and traversable for hunter-gatherers during the Pleistocene. These intervals might have lasted only for a few millennia and have been tens of millennia apart, but given the two million or more years of existence of the genus *Homo*, chances to move from Africa into Eurasia could and perhaps did occur relatively often.

Indeed, Leroy et al. (2011) estimate that no less than 42 interglacial warm and wet phases occurred worldwide during the Early Pleistocene alone, between 2.58 and 0.78 million years ago. Adding to these the nine longer amplitude cycles during the Middle and Late Pleistocene, we face a rather staggering 50 or more *potential* chances for archaic humans to have left Africa and entered Eurasia. Of course, it is very likely that some of the low and high points of these cycles were more extreme than others. But the existence of so many possibilities should at least make us stop and think, particularly given the rather fragmentary fossil and archaeological records available to us. The prospects are daunting, especially for the colder Eurasian latitudes, where each such spread might have been followed by a glacial phase population retraction or extinction, leading to a very complex situation for understanding the course of human biological evolution outside the tropics.[9] Similar population retractions might have occurred after each time hominins penetrated the Sahara from the south during interglacials.

Homo populations appeared first in Africa, but by what routes might they have spread from Africa into Asia? Robin Derricourt (2005) has suggested that the Nile Valley was the most likely conduit towards Sinai and the Levant. During the last 6000 years, the Egyptian Nile Valley has been an amazingly fertile band of country – after all, Egyptian civilization flourished here on the narrow strip of alluvium between the river and the desert. During moist Pleistocene interglacials, river channels and humid corridors existed not only along the Nile but also across other regions of the Sahara, giving potential access for Lower Paleolithic populations to the North African coast.[10]

An alternative to the Nile is the narrow Bab al Mandab Strait that separates Djibouti and Yemen at the southern end of the Red Sea, only a few kilometers wide during periods of glacial low sea level, albeit never quite dry land altogether.[11] Could early hominins swim? Could they make rafts? Unfortunately for would-be migrants, the lowest glacial sea levels, hence the narrowest crossing of the Bab al Mandab, corresponded with weak monsoons and increased aridity in the Sahara and Arabia. The greater monsoon-induced moisture that perhaps opened up those deserts for human passage correlated with higher interglacial sea levels, hence wider and perhaps more stressful sea crossings. Early modern humans might have crossed by this route, as we will see, but for archaic ones there is less certainty.

The big question behind early hominin migration, both within and out of Africa, remains *why*. By at least 1.5 million years ago, hominins had attained a territorial distribution in tropical to temperate latitudes from southern Africa to China and Java (Figure 3.3). In this regard, they were unique in the contemporary mammal world. Leopards, lions, cattle, pigs, and wolves were also very widespread in the wild, the first three in parts of both Africa and Eurasia. Wolves, like mammoths and reindeer (caribou), extended from Asia into the Americas. But most large terrestrial mammal species were far less widespread, including our great ape cousins the gorillas and chimpanzees. In the case of hominins, one is tempted to invoke increasing brain size, intelligence, dietary omnivorousness, and the evolution of human curiosity about the unknown to be relevant factors behind early migration. Whether or not we can include language at 1.5 million years ago remains unknown. However, the idea that the grass is always greener on the other side might be more ancient than we think.

Other factors related to mutation and diet might also have been involved in allowing range expansion for hominins. Giuseppe Rotilio and Eliana Marchese (2010) suggest an interesting hypothesis whereby genetic mutations that gave some individuals a lesser survival ability in a situation of environmental change might have induced them to migrate to another location, in which by chance their altered abilities suddenly acquired a much greater survival value. As an example, they suggest that a genetic mutation that lessened jaw robusticity in early hominins led them to vacate a chimpanzee-like arboreal diet in forest in favor of a ground-based and partially carnivorous diet, meat being easier to masticate than hard nuts. In turn, this would have increased the amount of metabolic energy available via digestion of fat to promote the evolution of the early hominin brain, as well as an increased ability through a broadening of diet to withstand marked fluctuations in food supply. Both developments would have given great encouragement to any tendencies towards migration into new habitats, especially given the wide-ranging habits of many of the large herbivore species that the hominins presumably followed and consumed. As noted, debate exists over whether early hominins hunted themselves, or scavenged carnivore-kill meat, but meat eating in itself is evidenced by cut marks on some of the oldest African animal bone assemblages.[12]

Unfolding Species in Time and Space

The oldest hominin finds outside Africa come from Dmanisi in Georgia, where four crania and other mandible fragments dated to about 1.8 million years ago are generally attributed today to the species most successful in migrating out of Africa – *H. erectus*.[13] They had quite small brains at 650-800 ccs and were found with an 'Oldowan' stone tool industry consisting of small flakes and cores, named after Olduvai Gorge in Tanzania (Figure 3.3 and Figure 3.4).

Moving further east, it is not absolutely clear when hominins reached China. A calotte (skull top) from Lantian in central China overlaps with the Dmanisi skulls in cranial capacity (780 cc) and is morphologically more archaic than the *H. erectus* skulls from the Zhoukoudian limestone caves, near Beijing, which have recently been dated to 780,000 years ago. Lacustrine and alluvial deposits exposed by uplift and erosion at Sangiran in central Java have also yielded remains of *H. erectus* dating rather shakily from perhaps 1.8 or 1.6 million years ago, but most are younger than one million years. However, some early sites in China that were once claimed to have hominin fossils and stone tools at almost two million years ago, such as the cave of Longgupo in Sichuan province, are now subject to uncertainties involving the potential presence of an unidentified hominin-like 'mystery ape'. Apes at that time were far more widespread and species-rich in eastern Asia than they are today.[14]

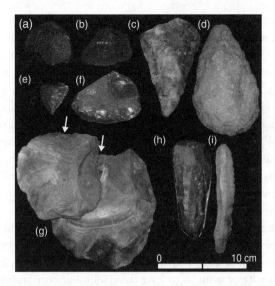

Figure 3.4 Major Paleolithic stone tool forms considered by archaeologists to be diagnostic in discussions about human evolution. (a, b) Oldowan basalt pebble core and large flake (ventral view) from Koobi Fora, Lake Turkana, Tanzania; (c) Acheulian flint bifacial hand axe from Britain; (d) a quartzite example (shown with opposite orientation) from West Bengal, India; (e, f) Mousterian retouched flake scraper and point, Combe Grenal cave (Dordogne), France; (g) Levalloisian 'tortoise' (prepared) flint core with a detached flake (modern copy – white arrows show direction of strike); (h, i) prismatic blade core and long blade of flint (Upper Paleolithic, France). All from the collections of the School of Archaeology and Anthropology at ANU, photos by the author.

Many other sites without fossils in Asia are also associated with Oldowan stone tool industries. Those well dated by radiometric techniques include Goudi in the Nihewan Basin in Hebei Province, northern China, with paleomagnetic dates between 1.66 and 1.36 million years, and Wolo Sege and Mata Menge in central Flores island in eastern Indonesia, dated to 1.02 million years ago. Bizat Ruhama in Israel has Oldowan lithics in sediments dated paleomagnetically to between 1.96 and 0.78 million years ago, Pirro Nord in Italy to between 1.6 and 1.3 million years ago, and Dursunlu near Konya in Turkey to between 0.99 and 0.78 million years ago.[15]

Moving west, in southern Europe, the breccia-filled cave of Sima del Elefante at Atapuerca in northern Spain has yielded Europe's oldest hominin mandible, dated to 1.2 or 1.1 million years ago by measuring radioactive decay in rare chemical elements contained in buried stone tools. Interestingly, slightly younger hominin remains from the neighboring Gran Dolina at Atapuerca, dated to around 800,000 years ago, reveal the world's oldest evidence for bone damage resulting from nutritional cannibalism, a habit also practiced by their Neanderthal successors.[16]

Despite the difficulties with dating, it is apparent that populations of early *Homo*, still relatively small bodied and small brained, were able to migrate across Asia to as far as China and Indonesia soon after two million years ago. Perhaps the major window for expansion was between 1.8 and 1.6 million years ago, when environmental changes were particularly rapid and when bovids are also known to have undergone a great deal of speciation and expansion (de Menocal 2011). Such a time span would have been quite early in the Quaternary history of Himalayan tectonic uplift (mostly between 2 and 0.5 million years ago), when passage through interior Asia during interglacial warm phases should have been easier than now. As for the ability to survive in cool climates, some hominins had already adapted to temperate latitudes, as noted earlier, prior to the exodus from Africa. Dmanisi in Georgia lies at 41°N, a similar latitude to Zhoukoudian and Nihewan, both near Beijing, a very cold place in winter even during present interglacial conditions. As discussed earlier, it is possible that such temperate latitude excursions were assisted by a use of fire, an invention of obvious utility that remains very elusive in the archaeological record, but which does appear to have been available to *H. erectus* and the Neanderthals.[17]

Early humans leaving Africa had the abilities needed to migrate through the tropical and warmer temperate latitudes of Eurasia, through parklands, woodlands, grasslands, and possibly even semi-deserts, allowing that drinking water supplies would always have been necessary. They would only have faced fully equatorial rainforests far away in Malaysia and Indonesia, although they must have passed through or around some of these in order to reach Java, which lies south of the Equator. All of these habitats would have offered them meat, nutritious nuts and tubers, aquatic and coastal resources, and a vast variety of edible insects, reptiles, worms and other delicacies. In terms of meat, open vegetation would have provided better hunting or scavenging possibilities than dense rainforest, in which many prey species live high in the tree canopy and probably out of reach for those who lacked bows, arrows and blowpipes, all believed to be relatively recent human inventions. But rainforests often have tubers and seasonal fruits, and my general impression is that while rainforests probably slowed human expansion down, the only environments capable of stopping early hominin expansion altogether, once it had started from Africa, would have been absolute deserts, wide seas, or very cold climates under ice, tundra, or coniferous *taiga* forest.

Java, Flores, and Crossing the Sea

The island of Java is very important in the history of human evolution, a status attained when Eugène Dubois recovered the first 'Java Man' or *Pithecanthropus* fossil at Trinil in 1891. It was the furthest point from Africa reached by early hominins until the presumably later settlement of Flores further to the east, and its periodic isolation by high sea levels and equatorial rainforest renders the story of its colonization potentially very interesting.[18] Java reveals a history of over one million years of evolution within the species *H. erectus*, with crania or parts thereof recovered from Lower and Middle Pleistocene sediments at Sangiran, Sambungmacan, Trinil and Mojokerto, onwards to the presumed Late Pleistocene and large-brained Solo River series of *H. erectus* from Ngandong and Ngawi. This long series of fossils spans a period of time from possibly 1.8 million to as recently as 50,000 years ago, depending upon which radiometric dates on geological materials one chooses to believe. During this long period, there was an evolution of the hominin brain from around 750 ccs to almost 1200 ccs in average size.

Java itself was joined by periodic land bridges across the Sunda continental shelf to the present Malay Peninsula of mainland Asia, especially during glacial periods of low sea level (Figure 3.3). This means that hominins could have reached it on more than one occasion, at least in theory. Given evidence for the fairly sudden appearances in Java at around 0.8 million years ago of new animal species such as water buffalo, cattle, pigs, Javan rhinoceros, tigers and macaque monkeys[19], it is possible that a new population of *H. erectus* also arrived in Java at that time from the Asian mainland. A poorly dated change in the *H. erectus* fossils from a highly robust form (*Meganthropus* of older authors) to a more gracile morphology provides possible support for this hypothesis, although agreement is elusive.[20] Whatever the final answer, only one hominin species appears to have existed in Java *after* about 0.8 million years ago (Kaifu et al. 2008).

Moving beyond Java, the Lesser Sunda islands east of Bali lie beyond the Sunda continental shelf and were always divided from each other and from mainland Asia by sea passages. They belong to a biogeographic province of intergradation between Eurasian placental and Australian marsupial mammalian faunas that has been termed *Wallacea*, after Alfred Russel Wallace, a contemporary of Darwin and codiscoverer of the evolutionary theory of natural selection. One of these Wallacean islands is Flores, another is Sulawesi, and yet another is Luzon in the Philippines. Any hominin that could reach any of these islands had to have some form of watercraft, something to float upon, or a phenomenal swimming ability.

That hominin was perhaps the ancestor of a tiny female skeleton discovered from a depth of 6 m in the cave of Liang Bua, on the island of Flores, firmly within non-land-bridged Wallacea. Dated originally[21] to only about 18,000 years ago, her skeleton was associated with simple stone tools of evolved Oldowan affinity and bones of young pygmy stegodons (proboscids, related to elephants) with butchering marks, yet with no sign of any bone or shell body ornaments or pigments, artifact categories that else-where are presumed to signify the presence of behaviorally modern humans (Westaway et al. 2009). The woman appears to have died and slumped into a pool of water, and there are also bone fragments of other very small individuals in the cave. All have been dated so far to between 95,000 and 15,000 years ago and express the same phenotypic characteristics – tiny body size at about 1 m tall, tiny brain (380–417 ccs), short legs, relatively long arms and feet, and a cranial shape that resembles much older hominins in Africa and Georgia (Aiello 2010). Some recent analyses[22] suggest that the ancestor perhaps departed from Africa before 1.6 million years ago, and was part of the migra-tion that also gave rise to the small hominins at Dmanisi. If so, it might have entered Indonesia as part of the earliest very small-brained *H. erectus* population also found at Sangiran. Others believe that some of the size reduction occurred in the small island of Flores itself during the past one million years from a larger *erectus* ancestor, given that mammal and human size reduction on small islands is a common biogeographical trend.[23]

Regardless of how this debate over *Homo floresiensis* is resolved, two important matters are now very widely agreed upon. This hominin was not a deformed modern human, as some have suggested.[24] Furthermore, it was not a prey animal at the hands of another hominin species since its bones show no cutting marks, unlike those of the contemporary juvenile pygmy stegodons found in the cave, which clearly served as food. *H. floresiensis* was probably testimony to a very early hominin migration across sea gaps between eastern Indonesian islands, presumably with stone tool use since Oldowan style lithics dating to about one million years ago have been found in other sites in Flores, such as Wolo Sege and Mata Menge. It is not clear how often hominins might have reached Flores, but if they did so only once, then the record speaks to us of utter isolation on a small island for one million years, a remarkable and unprecedented 'experiment' in human evolution.

How did the initial population get to Flores, across two sea gaps if traveling from Java? These gaps are 25 km nowadays between Bali and Lombok, and 9 km between Sumbawa and Flores. Had there once been a land bridge one would expect early Pleistocene Sundaland mammals such as deer and pigs to have migrated from Java as well, and either still exist on Flores today or be represented in fossil faunal assemblages. There are none, apart from stegodons. In fact, in glacial periods of low sea level these straits were narrower, and probably flushed by powerful currents flowing from north to south – a circumstance that has led some to suggest that both stegodons and the ancestors of *H. floresiensis* came with currents from Sulawesi rather than from Java.[25] So far, there is no clear evidence for this, but whatever the answer, an attachment to something afloat would have been necessary to make the journey.

Another very small hominin metatarsal (foot bone) dated to 67,000 years ago from Callao Cave on Luzon in the northern Philippines, also in a non-land-bridged part of Wallacea, opens the possibility that tiny hominins were not only located on Flores (Mijares et al. 2010). Luzon also once had stegodons, but none were found in Callao Cave, only pigs and deer. Unfortunately, the Callao Cave metatarsal was not associated with stone tools, but some of the deer bones found with it show cutting marks. The possibilities are still under analysis, and more human remains have been found in this cave since the initial discovery was made, but the metatarsal does overlap in size with some of the small Agta ('Negrito') populations who still live in northern Luzon today, as well as with *H. floresiensis*, so a definite attribution to the latter would at this stage be premature. Even so, the prospects for further discoveries in Wallacea are exciting.

Out of Africa 2?

The likelihood that archaic hominins left Africa on more than one occasion during the Lower and Middle Pleistocene has already been raised several times. But so far there is really only one situation in the combined archaeological and fossil records that suggests this. In eastern Africa, the distinctive bifacial hand axe industry that archaeologists term the Acheulian (Figure 3.4) had developed in nascent form from its Oldowan predecessor by 1.8 million years ago. There is a general assumption by archaeologists that the Acheulian represented something technologically and conceptually different from the Oldowan, even though some developed Oldowan tools were bifacially flaked. Outside Africa, Acheulian technology occurs at Ubeidiya in the Jordan valley in Israel by possibly 1.6 million years ago and perhaps earlier than one million years ago in southern India.[26] But its spread was fairly limited until about 800,000 years ago, after which bifacial hand axes are found in many regions of Africa and Eurasia, to as far north as Great Britain and eastwards to the Black Sea, Kazakhstan, the Altai Mountains, and Mongolia.[27]

These widespread Acheulian industries in the western and central Old World are believed to be associated with *Homo heidelbergensis*, a fairly brainy hominin (averaging about 1250 ccs in cranial capacity) represented by fossils from a number of African and Eurasian locations that include Broken Hill (Kabwe) in Zambia, Bodo in Ethiopia (dated to 600,000 years ago), Mauer (near Heidelberg) in Germany, Ceprano in Italy, Petralona in Greece, and Hathnora in the Narmada Valley in India. Because of the large number of fossil and hand axe discoveries, there is considerable support for a migration, around 800,000 years ago, of *H. heidelbergensis* from Africa into Western Eurasia, with part of the species remaining in tropical Africa and undergoing separate evolution there in the direction of modern *H. sapiens* (Figure 3.1).

H. heidelbergensis was thus the potential common ancestor for both evolving modern humans in Africa, *and* Neanderthals and allied species such as the Denisova hominin (see following text) in Eurasia. The genetic split between these two groups has been dated recently by nuclear DNA molecular clock calculations to something under 840,000 years ago, alas a little uncertain, but still within the range of an Out of Africa 2.[28] In Europe, incoming *heidelbergensis* presumably replaced or mixed with the earlier hominins represented in Sima del Elefante and Gran Dolina at Atapuerca in northern Spain, and then evolved into the Neanderthals of the Upper Pleistocene.

Some of the contemporary Paleolithic assemblages of China, Korea and Java also have bifacial hand axes, together with the more ubiquitous unifacial pebble and flake tools, for example, the finds from Bose in Guangxi, southern China.[29] Nevertheless, the hand axes do not seem to be sufficiently prominent for a separate layer of human migration to be invoked in these regions. However, the evidence for a possible arrival in Java of a new hominin species at about 800,000 years ago could be relevant here. The Javan fossils cannot be assimilated into *H. heidelbergensis* and are firmly *erectus* in taxonomic terms, but this possible secondary arrival could have been a repercussion of other population movements elsewhere on the Asian mainland. It is therefore possible that *heidelbergensis*, in the strict biological sense, did not migrate beyond India, but that cultural and perhaps even some biological repercussions extended as far as China and Indonesia.

H. heidelbergensis was also the first species to penetrate really cold latitudes, up to 53°N in southern England, Germany, and possibly the Altai Mountains of Russia. As discussed already, questions arise concerning hominin survival at such latitudes during glaciations, or through extremely cold winters in interglacial periods, remembering that actual glaciers and ice sheets were features only of northern Europe and North America. The drier parts of Siberia east of the Taymyr Peninsula would have been mostly in the grip of deep permafrost rather than ice sheets. Perhaps people either retreated south during glaciation periods, or simply died out. Clothing and fire would naturally have been useful during such northerly excursions. As discussed in Chapter 5, it is clear from ethnographic accounts that Australians could withstand very cold winter temperatures in regions such as Tasmania with only marsupial fur cloaks wrapped around their upper bodies, showing a fortitude that greatly impressed early European visitors (Mulvaney 2008). Perhaps earlier hominins were equally hardy.

As for penetration of such regions when conditions were good, Leroy et al. (2011) point out that movement into high Eurasian latitudes would have been easiest during the early phases of glacial retreat, rather than during interglacial high points. This is because the spread of dense temperate forest and the drowning of continental shelves by rising seas lagged several millennia behind the commencement of postglacial temperature rise, as explained by Broecker (2000). In other words, warmer temperatures developed whilst land bridges and open rather than densely forested landscapes still remained, for a few millennia at least. Faunal and pollen data from many archaeological sites indicate that early hominins in Eurasia, as in Africa, preferred open grassland or forest steppe conditions rather than dense forest. Some southerly *heidelbergensis* populations, such as those from Atapuerca in Spain, were able to occupy open woodlands virtually continuously, through hundreds of millennia, but such benign conditions would have diminished quite rapidly north of southern France.[30] Indeed, we know that a major expansion from southern refuges into northern Europe occurred as conditions improved after the last glaciation, between 19,500 and 14,000 years ago (see Chapter 5), so it is likely that hominins congregated for warmth in similar southern latitudes during earlier glaciations as well.

There are also suggestions of very prolonged periods of aridity in southwestern Asia that would have hampered both mammal and hominin migration from Africa. Van der Made (2011), for instance, suggests that such conditions existed between 1.8 and 0.9 million years ago, which agrees quite well with the suggested commencement date for *heidelbergensis* migration from Africa into Eurasia around 800,000 years ago. However, a contrasting suggestion is that early hominin migrations into Eurasia were not attached directly to those of other mammal species at all (O'Regan et al. 2011). If this is true, then hominins might have acted alone in their migratory quests, perhaps assisted by increasing investments in cultural paraphernalia. This raises a fundamental question; were early hominins rigidly bound by climatic parameters in their migratory movements, or could they ignore them as brain capacity evolved, to an increasing degree through time? We are still far from knowing the answer for hominin species prior to the appearance of *H. sapiens*, but I would expect the latter answer to be at least partly correct.

Out of Africa 3? The Origins of *H. sapiens*

In the mid-twentieth century, there was general agreement amongst paleoanthropologists that only one hominin species existed at any one time across the Old World and that its members evolved from Australopithecus to *H. sapiens*, assisted by extensive gene flow, through grades that many would then have termed habiline, erectine, neanderthal and sapient, succeeding one another through time. However, even when such multiregional scenarios for human evolution were the vogue, cracks were developing in the façade. As early as 1960, William Howells (1960:336–9) was disagreeing with what we regard today as the multiregional hypothesis, stating that *H. sapiens* must have evolved in a region separate from the Neanderthals, expanding from there to interbreed with them and eventually to replace them. Howells did not know where that area was and just referred to it as the 'main area', probably tropical, somewhere in Africa or Asia.

The arguments against multiregionalism were solidified by advances in genetics and fossil discoveries during the late 1980s and 1990s, especially the identification of African Eve in 1987 through mtDNA analysis. These advances gave rise to the specific 'out of Africa' hypothesis for anatomically and behaviorally modern humans that dominates much thinking today. This is focused on an expansion from Africa within the past 100,000 years (or thereabouts) that led to the extinction of all previous hominin species across the Old World. Multiregional evolution never really recovered from the shock provided by the mtDNA bombshell. The concept also suffered with the growing realization that some close hominin cousins of *Homo* undoubtedly became extinct, especially the robust Australopithecines who survived in Africa, alongside species of *Homo*, down to almost one million years ago (Figure 3.1).

However, was it all as coldhearted and final as it might seem for the archaic pre-*sapiens* species of *Homo*, species that must have become extinct across the whole of Eurasia very rapidly if one accepts a 100% out of Africa model for *sapiens* ancestry? These other hominin species included *H. erectus* in Java and China, the Neanderthals in western Eurasia, *H. floresiensis*, the Denisova hominin from the Altai Mountains, and possibly other late-surviving archaic hominins in parts of Africa. The modern genetic record is now suggesting that small levels of interbreeding between such extinct hominin species and our own ancestors may have happened on many occasions. Prominent amongst these are the recently announced low levels of interbreeding in Eurasia between early modern humans on the one hand, and Neanderthals and Denisovans on the other.[31]

Given this new information, we should perhaps not think of these Late Pleistocene species as always forming closed populations for breeding purposes, as advocated earlier in this chapter in connection with the species concept in hominins in general. We are such a closed species today because all other hominin species are either extinct or assimilated without obviously identifiable survivors. Interestingly, as members of *H. sapiens* we are all perfectly capable of successful interbreeding, regardless of geographical origin, even though our ancestral diversification in Africa is currently estimated from various molecular clock analyses and the fossil record to have commenced between 100,000 and 300,000 years ago.[32] The Neanderthal-*sapiens* evolutionary bifurcation out of *H. heidelbergensis* occurred perhaps 600,000 to 800,000 years ago. From such dates, we can begin to understand that complete genetic barriers to successful procreation might have required upwards of a million years to develop. Indeed, Garrigan and Kingan 2007 have noted that two species of baboon are still capable of producing fertile offspring after an estimated genetic separation time of five million years.

All of this makes possibilities for hybridization throughout the whole of the hominin fossil record rather large. Extinction by assimilation rather than total extermination becomes an attractive hypothesis for those archaic hominin species that came face to face with modern humans. Sharp confrontation between out of Africa and multiregional models for the emergence of *H. sapiens* are therefore no longer productive. It is time for a compromise, as long as the compromise recognizes the importance of migration out of Africa as a foundation factor in the rise of modern humans.

The Recognition of Modern Humans in Biology and Archaeology

The concept of *modern human* has three components – anatomical (skeletal), genetic, and behavioral. The anatomical modernity enshrined in the taxon *H. sapiens* is defined by Richard Klein (2009a: 623–4) as a mean brain size over 1350 ccs, prominent forehead and chin, a cranium generally globular in shape with its widest point above the ears (rather than close to the ears as in most earlier hominins), and a high degree of facial retraction and gracility. Cranial remains with these characteristics have been found in a number of sites in Africa, especially in the east and south, dating radiometrically between 100,000 and 200,000 years ago.

The most significant examples come from the Omo-Kibish and Herto localities in Ethiopia (Figure 3.5). These remains still carry archaic features no longer strongly marked in most modern humans, such as brow ridges and occipital crests at Herto, but they are agreed by most authorities to be directly within the anatomical ancestry of modern *H. sapiens*. The Omo remains were found with Acheulian tools. Their dates, approaching 200,000 years ago, obviously support an origin for anatomically modern humans in eastern Africa, being considerably older than any similar remains from southern Africa or Eurasia.[33] The Herto remains, from two adults and one child, are dated to 160,000 years ago and carry traces of defleshing, for unknown reasons, but not necessarily cannibalistic. Stratigraphically-related deposits in the Herto region contain a late Acheulian industry with a component of prepared cores (Levalloisian technology – see Figure 3.4), transitional to what, in Africa, is generally termed the Middle Stone Age. This was a period of great importance in early modern human affairs, associated in Africa with the appearance of a number of archaeological indicators of an increasingly sentient humanity.[34]

One aspect of *H. sapiens* biology that supports an origin in a tropical region, such as Ethiopia and East Africa generally, rather than in the more temperate far north or south of Africa, is that all modern humans are relatively free of body hair. This was probably lost to allow more efficient heat loss by sweating in open and hot tropical environments (Ruxton and Wilkinson 2011). Eventually, this allowed modern humans to acquire, through migration and adaptation to differing levels of ultraviolet radiation, the latitudinal variations in skin pigmentation that we regard today as so definitive a marker for the geographical divisions within our species. Our lack of body hair also renders us susceptible to the effects of extreme cold, and this is perhaps why, during the past 50,000 years, carefully prepared clothing of cut and shaped animal skins or woven textiles has been developed in northern latitudes.

The genetic record has been revealing the same picture of an African origin for *H. sapiens* at regular intervals since 1987, especially for mtDNA and NRY lineages, although the molecular clock dates for the evolution and dispersal of modern humans are currently undergoing a great deal of flux. Human genetic diversity declines with distance from Africa, reflecting passage through a number of small population bottlenecks and leading to loss of some haploid lineages as populations split and moved away from each other.[35] Interestingly, a similar observation has recently been applied to phonemic diversity in languages, which also diminishes with distance from Africa, a situation that Quentin Atkinson (2011) believes tracks the early dispersals of *H. sapiens* through language bottlenecks.[36] However, as populations became established in these new locations, so those genetic lineages that survived the bottlenecks would have aggrandized themselves very quickly as their carrier populations grew in numbers, thus giving opportunity for new mutations to occur and spread. MtDNA analysis suggests a rapid appearance of new haplogroups as early modern humans spread through southern Asia.[37]

We must now turn to the third factor listed earlier, behavioral modernity. Richard Klein (2009a: 742, 2009b), focusing mainly on the western Old World, has suggested that archaeological markers of a modern level of human behavior include the following:

1. a substantial increase in the numbers of recognizable artifact types, with new categories such as projectile points, grinding and pounding tools, spear throwers, nets, bone flutes, eyed needles, beads, and pendants;
2. an increase in the range of raw materials utilized, including bone, ivory, shell, clay (sometimes baked), and pigments such as ochre;
3. an appearance, particularly in the Upper Paleolithic of eastern Europe and Russia, of definite dwellings, in some cases incorporating mammoth bones as structural elements;
4. evidence for ritualized activities such as burial and art, the latter on portable objects as well as on cave walls and undoubtedly present by at least 40,000 years ago in Europe;
5. increasing attention to aquatic resources, from both riverine and marine sources;
6. increasing ability to transport raw materials over tens or even hundreds of kilometers;[38]
7. the ability, using multiple-layered fitted clothing (Gilligan 2010), and doubtless fire, to penetrate the Arctic Circle to as far as the northern coastline of Asia, and from there eventually to move east into the New World.

Some of these behaviors were present in earlier Eurasian cultural settings. Neanderthals, for instance, buried their dead quite frequently, but whether or not they intentionally placed offerings with those burials is more controversial. They also used bone awls in France, perhaps to make clothing, and used mammoth bones to construct windbreaks of some kind (not necessarily closed huts) in Ukraine (Demay et al. 2012). They knew also how to use fire. So, while most categories in the aforementioned list still seem to be restricted to an association with *H. sapiens*, many archaeologists nowadays argue against assuming an exclusive correlation.[39]

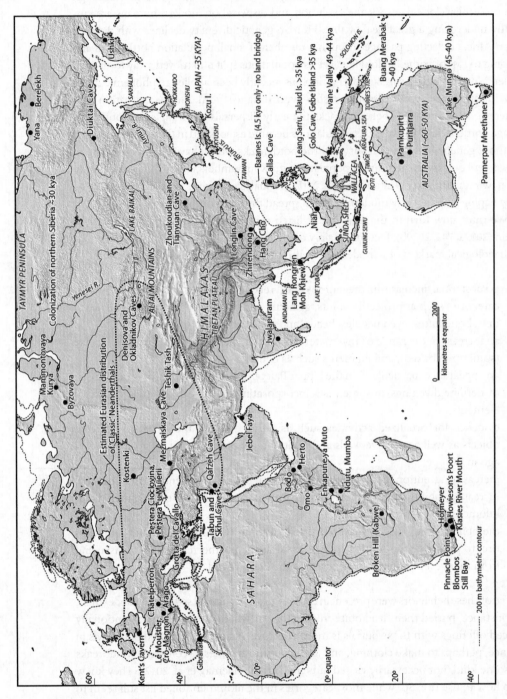

Figure 3.5 Old World localities associated with biological and cultural remains of Neanderthals and early *H. sapiens*. Kya = thousands

Ushki

Yana
Berelekh

Diuktai Cave

TAYMYR PENINSULA

Mamontovaya
Kurya

Byzovaya

Colonization of northern Siberia ~30 kya

Yenesei R.

SAKHALIN

AMUR R.

HOKKAIDO

HONSHU

JAPAN ~35 KYA?

Kozui I.

KYUSHU

RYUKYUS

TAIWAN

Batanes Is. (4.5 kya only – no land bridge)

Callao Cave

SOLOMON IS.

Buang Merabak
>40 kya

Ivane Valley 49–44 kya

Leang Sarru, Talaud Is. >35 kya
Golo Cave, Gebe Island >35 kya

TORRES STRAIT

ARAFURA SEA

Parnkupirti
Puritjarra

AUSTRALIA (~60–50 KYA)

Lake Mungo (45–40 kya)

Parmerpar Meethaner

LAKE BAIKAL

ALTAI MOUNTAINS

Estimated Eurasian distribution
of 'Classic' Neanderthals.

Denisova and
Oklandnikov Caves

Teshik Tash

Kostenki

Peştera Cioclovina,
Peştera Cu Măierii

Mezmaiskaya Cave

HIMALAYAS

TIBETAN PLATEAU

Zhoukoudian and
Tianyuan Cave

Longlin Cave

Zhirendong

Hang Cho?

Niah

SUNDA SHELF

WALLACEA

ROTI

TIMOR

GUNUNG SEWU

LAKE TOBA

Lang Rongrien
Moh Khiew

ANDAMAN IS.

Uwalapuram

Jebel Faya

Bodo

Omo
Herto

Enkapune ya Muto

Ndutu, Mumba

SAHARA

Broken Hill (Kabwe)

Pinnacle Point
Blombos
Still Bay

Hofmeyer
Howieson's Poort
Klasies River Mouth

Kent's Cavern

Le Moustier,
Cro-Magnon

Châtelperron

Arago

Grotta del Cavallo

Gibraltar

Tabun and
Skhul Caves

Qafzeh Cave

0° equator

20°

40°

60°

40°

20°

0° equator

20°

40°

0   2000

kilometres at equator

200 m bathymetric contour

Beyond the level of material culture represented in the earlier list, other questions arise concerning the origins of complex language and kinship systems. How did they evolve, and are they unique to modern humans? Both are intricately intertwined, two sides of the same coin, since kinship can hardly exist without language. At the beginning of this chapter, I questioned if early hominins really had kinship reckoning as we know it. We do not know the answer, but early *H. sapiens* certainly had kinship reckoning in some form. Existing hunter-gatherer societies differ from other primate ones in having cohabiting and interacting groupings of nuclear families, recognized affinal ties based on marriage ('in-laws'), and conscious recognition of kin relationships that tie separate communities across very large areas.[40] Hunter-gatherers (including our *sapiens* ancestors) are mobile, and draw marital partners from wide geographical regions. This means that very early *H. sapiens* societies could probably have extended as cooperating units across larger areas, in both geographical extent and population, than could non-*sapiens* hominin bands.

What of language, that most remarkable of our combined biological and cultural creations? Human language is an incredible creation within the biological world, and no other creatures even begin to approach us in linguistic complexity. If an ancient hominin group with language ability like ours met another hominin group without such ability, the result in terms of any significant competition is not hard to imagine. The main question is really one of evolutionary tempo. Was the acquisition of human language by our ancestors a punctuated event, or did it happen gradually over hundreds of thousands of years? There has been a great deal of debate on this issue, and genetics and physiology play important roles in our understanding. But the answer, in fact, is not known, even though some Neanderthals, and even *H. heidelbergensis* 500,000 years ago in the Sima de los Huesos at Atapuerca, might have had speech capabilities very close to ours, to judge from their possession of a hyoid (tongue supporting) bone very like that of modern humans. However, a new reading of the whole genome of a hominin finger bone from Denisova Cave in the Altai Mountains of Siberia, estimated to be 80,000 years old and thus contemporary with Neanderthals, suggests that this archaic human did not have the full expression of the FOXP2 gene that is believed to be associated with the speech capacity of modern humans (Meyer et al. 2012).

I suspect that questions about *when* human language and kinship appeared during our evolution will never be answered conclusively. However, I find myself in agreement with the widespread view that the *rates* of both biological and cultural evolution increased dramatically with the appearance of *H. sapiens*, both inside and outside Africa, thus allowing the out of Africa movement of modern humans to occur with such success. Richard Klein (2009a: 649) favors rapid neural reorganization of the human brain "that launched the fully modern ability to manipulate culture as an adaptive mechanism." He believes that this occurred amongst an African breeding population of about 10,000 adults, just prior to the modern human crossing (or crossings) into Eurasia. This is a view that at present cannot be easily dismissed, although the question of the *date* of modern human emergence out of Africa is currently highly contested.

The Expansion of Modern Humans Across the African and Eurasian Continents, 130,000–45,000 Years Ago

Africa

Africa served as the homeland for *H. sapiens*, and the fossil record favors East Africa, owing to its excellent fossil record and its location close to the Nile River and the Bab al Mandab as likely routes of passage. But new genetic evidence from modern hunter-gatherer populations in southern Africa is now pointing to that region as another likely source for *H. sapiens*, an observation supported by close resemblances between the Late Paleolithic Hofmeyr skull from South Africa and roughly contemporary Upper Paleolithic skulls from Eurasia.[41] Certainty is elusive, partly because genetic geography in Africa has changed on a massive scale due to subsequent migrations since early modern humans first left its shores (Chapters 5 and 9). But my preference for an origin region remains the eastern tropical part of Africa rather than the south. East Africa is much closer to Eurasia, and it still contains the most significant ancestral fossils for modern humans, from Omo and Herto.

To review the archaeology of early *H. sapiens*, however, we must begin with developments in Middle Stone Age southern Africa. Excavations in a large number of caves in South Africa and Namibia have produced a range of artifacts connected with the so-called Still Bay and Howieson's Poort lithic technologies, dated overall in several sites to between 77,000 and 59,000 years ago. These artifacts are technologically more advanced than contemporary assemblages associated with Neanderthals and *H. erectus* in Eurasia. Here, in far southern Africa, we seem to have some of the first clear traces of modern human behavior in the world, to the extent that it can be discerned from the intentionality enshrined in the design and manufacture of material culture. Claims for a similar antiquity of modern human behavior in North Africa, connected with the Middle Stone Age lithic industry known as the Aterian, are also appearing in the literature, but the South African material is currently receiving most attention, due in part to the very large number of excavations taking place there.[42]

In South Africa, seemingly innovative stone artifacts include Still Bay bifacial leaf-shaped projectile points (some manufactured by pressure flaking after heat treatment), Howieson's Poort backed geometrics and crescents that were perhaps hafted as barbs on projectile weapons, and narrow and sharp-edged blades struck with soft hammers of bone or horn rather than stone. A presence of the bow and arrow has been suggested, and the idea of hafting was apparently another important development at this time.[43] Bone points, incised pieces of ostrich shell, perforated gastropod shell beads, and pieces of red ochre (hematite) with engraved markings also made their appearances. Ochre has long been a source of pigment for body and cave painting, but appears not to have been used regularly by archaic hominins. Furthermore, the Klasies River Mouth cave has early *H. sapiens* human remains in association with these types of artifacts.

The genesis of this Middle Stone Age complex and its sapient human creators might have begun long before 77,000 years ago, given a report of worked pieces of red ochre and stone bladelets, some subjected to heat treatment to improve their flaking qualities, from another coastal site in South Africa called Pinnacle Point Cave 13B. This assemblage has been luminescence-dated to a surprising 162,000–90,000 years ago, and carefully prepared red ochre mixed with crushed bone and charcoal, stored in abalone shells, is also claimed to date from about 100,000 years ago in nearby Blombos Cave.[44] These are the oldest occurrences of such material to date in Africa, but one wonders how this reflects research intensity rather than an absolute origin for modern humans in South Africa. Unfortunately, few archaeological traces resembling the Still Bay and Howieson's Poort manifestations have been found in eastern Africa, although backed geometrics and ostrich eggshell beads occur in the rock shelters of Mumba in Tanzania and Enkapune Ya Muto in Kenya, claimed to date to before 46,000 years ago. Early blade industries dated to possibly 60,000 years ago are also reported from the Nile Valley in Egypt, and Aterian projectile point industries in North Africa are claimed to be even older.[45] But the dating in many of these contexts remains uncertain.

Given the archaeological and fossil records for early modern humans in Africa, could it be that they were quite widely distributed by about 120,000 years ago, especially in the northeast of the continent, ready to move into Asia? In my view, this is quite likely. Oddly enough, however, both the Still Bay and Howieson's Poort technologies disappeared mysteriously in southern Africa after 59,000 years ago, raising the unsolved issue of what happened to their makers. Industries of this type were certainly not carried by the first *H. sapiens* to move into Asia. Furthermore, there is genetic and fossil evidence for a survival of archaic hominins in central Africa until about 35,000 years ago, or even later (Hammer et al. 2011), making an instant domination of the whole continent by *H. sapiens* very unlikely. Indeed, it has recently been argued by Smith et al. (2012) that modern humanity can be traced specifically to an Omo and Herto ancestry, and that many cranial remains of younger age from both northern and southern Africa, for instance from the cave at Klasies River Mouth, represent gene flow between anatomically archaic and modern populations.

Another observation is very relevant. Ian Gilligan (2010) has suggested that the archaeologically-visible elements of modern human behavior were always more apparent in temperate and cool regions that demanded more complex tool kits for survival than did the tropics. This would have been true in Africa as well as in Eurasia. For instance, cooler regions would have required animal skin clothing and shelters in winter, especially during glacial climatic conditions. Blades, points, and scrapers like those found in the South African caves would have been very useful for working hides, and we return to this important issue below in connection with the settlement of the colder latitudes of Eurasia. Lithic complexity might have been related as much to environmental factors as to inherited factors of human cognition.

Regardless of where *H. sapiens* evolved initially in Africa, the most debatable issue at present seems to be the question of *when* the exodus into Eurasia occurred. If we accept all the archaeological, paleoanthropological and genetic dating estimates for Eurasia at face value, using both radiometric and molecular clock chronologies, we have an incredibly wide range of possibilities. Early modern humans *could* have migrated through tropical and temperate latitudes, from western Asia to southern Siberia, China, and Australia, at pretty much any time between 135,000 and 50,000 years ago. These are outer limits, but the range spans an awfully long period of time.[46]

Could the expansion of H. sapiens throughout Eurasia really have been as slow and drawn out as this? The answer might be *yes*, given that humans throughout recorded history have been incapable of launching such a major population replacement again throughout such a vast area of Europe and Asia. Colonial era migration since AD 1500 has had minimal biological impact in Asia south of Siberia, as in Africa, as discussed in Chapter 2, although the impact was certainly much greater in the Americas and Australia due to the diseases introduced into these locations by the Europeans. The answer might also be *no*, especially if some of the chronological calculations in the literature turn out to be wrong, leaving only one chronology (but which one?) as correct.

My preference is for the *yes* answer, since the evidence suggests to me that the settlement of Eurasia by early H. sapiens was actually quite a long and drawn-out process that might have been fed by more than one episode of population migration from Africa into Arabia and the Levant. In order to explain why, we need to look at some evidence.

The Levant and Southern Asia

If the widely held view of a single exit from Africa for early *sapiens* is correct, the implication must be that all non-Africans have a common source in one movement from Africa into the Levant or Arabia. Geneticists and paleoanthropologists are still divided on this issue. The single-exit view is derived mainly from haploid genetics (mtDNA and the NRY), but the multiple-exit view fits better with the paleoanthropological record.[47] My own view is that an intelligent hominin who could cross Sinai or the Bab al Mandab could most probably have done it more than once, particularly if tens of thousands of years of time were available. After all, within Eurasia itself there were evidently separate colonizing movements by early modern humans through tropical and temperate latitudes both south and north of the Himalayas, into Southeast Asia on the one hand and northern Eurasia (Europe across to China) on the other, with the former movement in the more inviting tropics perhaps occurring earlier than the more stressful movement to the north.[48]

The initial movement of early modern humans out of Africa presumably occurred via the Levant, given the general lack of evidence for a sea passage via Gibraltar (Van der Made 2011). In the Levant, the caves of Es Skhul and Qafzeh in Israel have both produced human burials that are very close to being anatomically modern and that date between outer limits of 135,000 and 90,000 years ago, hence within the warm and wet last interglacial. They are far older than any other well-dated anatomically modern human remains from Eurasia, all of which (apart from some uncertain claims from China) date to younger than 70,000 years. The Skhul and Qafzeh assemblages reveal a rather confusing cultural mixture of putatively modern human characteristics, such as intentional burial, ochre and shell beads, but a Mousterian/Middle Paleolithic (putatively Neanderthal) lithic technology. Given that Neanderthal skeletal remains actually appear in younger levels dated between 75,000 and 45,000 years ago in caves in the same region (Shea 2010b), a very widespread view has developed that this early *sapiens* population in Israel failed, either due to adverse climatic shifts or to competition from the Neanderthals. The latter seems to me very unlikely, given that Neanderthal replacement of modern humans never appears to have happened anywhere else. It also seems unlikely that climates in the Levant, after the time of Skhul and Qafzeh, became so inhospitable that this lineage of anatomically modern humans died out, whereas the Neanderthals survived. After all, the Es Skhul and Qafzeh caves were near the warm eastern coastline of the Mediterranean and the hominins concerned lived there during the last interglacial. Even during the last glacial maximum, the Levant served as an important refuge zone for modern human populations, especially in the Jordan Valley.

If the Skhul-Qafzeh population did become extinct, then it would leave open the door for a single successful modern human exit from Africa much later in time, possibly after 70,000 years ago, as some haploid molecular clocks and archaeological perspectives focused on Upper Paleolithic technology would appear to demand. For instance, the most recent calculation of the age of mtDNA haplogroup L3 in central and eastern Africa is only 60,000–70,000 years, much too young to apply to Skhul and Qafzeh. Given that L3 was the root haplogroup for the foundation Eurasian mtDNA haplogroups M and N, one might argue that any out-of-Africa movement into the Levant should have postdated its mutation. However, one can also argue around this problem by suggesting that the original mtDNA haplogroups of the Skhul-Qafzeh population were replaced as a result of significant levels of secondary migration from Africa. One can also argue that the molecular clock used is giving results that are, for various reasons, too young.[49]

At present, one can neither confirm nor deny any of these possibilities, especially without assistance from ancient DNA. However, if a complete replacement of more ancient Skhul-Qafzeh mtDNA haplogroups in the Levant is the answer, possibly in a still-restricted region of early modern human settlement, then we do at least have precedents. Some mtDNA haplogroups can disappear and others become greatly magnified in small populations as a result of assimilation and founder effects. I will examine some examples, for central Europe and Polynesia specifically, in Chapters 7 and 8. The important point here is that the descendants of the Skhul and Qafzeh populations might have been assimilated into later arrivals of *H. sapiens* from Africa, rather than pushed into extinction. Palaeoclimatic records from East African lakes and the Levant reveal a regional increase in rainfall about 75,000 years ago (Scholz et al. 2007), so perhaps this was a good time for a secondary migration out of Africa by modern humans carrying mtDNA haplogroups L3, M and N.

A number of paleoanthropologists have recently suggested that the descendants of the Skhul-Qafzeh population were actually the ones who moved through tropical Asia towards Australia, long prior to the development in colder Eurasian latitudes of the Upper Paleolithic blade industries normally associated by archaeologists with modern human spread (Figure 3.4).[50] The last interglacial is the obvious time for early movement to as far east as India, with a possible pause entering the wet rainforests of Southeast Asia, at least until a return of glacial conditions and tropical dry season corridors beyond Burma (see Chapter 5). The suggestion that early modern humans did indeed penetrate warm western regions of southern Asia beyond Israel as early as the last interglacial is currently receiving a boost from new work in the Arabian peninsula. Jebel Faya Cave in Sharjah (UAE) has a Middle Stone Age industry of hand axes, scrapers, and blades that the excavators (Armitage et al. 2011) date by optical luminescence to between 127,000 and 95,000 years ago, and trace to a northeast African origin during and after the last interglacial. They suggest an association with early modern humans, although the industry is rather different from that found at Skhul and Qafzeh. Rose (2010) extends the story further by claiming that there was a large refuge region, which he terms the Arabo-Persian Gulf Oasis, exposed as dry land by last glacial period low sea levels in what is now the Persian Gulf and adjacent shorelines of Arabia and the Red Sea. Here, in theory at least, early modern human populations were able to grow and expand during phases of extreme aridity further inland. The only drawback for this hypothesis at present is that the area concerned was drowned between 12,000 and 6,000 years ago by the rising postglacial sea level that formed the modern Persian Gulf, so a confirmatory archaeological record will be very hard to find.[51]

Early modern humans on the move through southern Asia as early as 75,000 years ago might also have experienced something rather frightening. About 74,000 years ago, the Toba volcano in northern Sumatra underwent one of the largest explosions in geological history, spewing out 2800 km^3 of tephra and presumably causing a volcanic winter of dark skies around the earth, although estimates of the exact size and impact of this eruption vary greatly. Williams et al. (2009) argue from geomorphological evidence that the eruption had a massive effect in the Indian Ocean region, causing cold arid climates for a millennium or more after the event. Some also claim that it wiped out large segments of the human population at that time (Oppenheimer 2003: 192–3).

More recent assessments (e.g., Timmreck et al. 2012), however, suggest that the Toba eruption did not impact humans on such a major scale. Indeed, recent excavations at a series of sites at Jwalapuram in southern India have revealed Middle Paleolithic artifacts and ochre both above and below a layer of volcanic ash associated with the Toba eruption, suggesting that the impact on the humans living in the area at the time was rather small. The excavators also raise the possibility that the pre- and posteruption populations were both anatomically and behaviorally modern, tracing them back via the Arabian Peninsula into the Levant and to a Skhul-Qafzeh related source.[52] If they are right, then modern humans might also have been in India during the last interglacial, although the evidence here is archaeological and not biological, so cannot be read as definitive on the issue. The Jwalapuram population appears to have maintained its Middle Paleolithic technology until about 35,000 years ago, when microlithic industries made an appearance in southern India and Sri Lanka. But these appear to be local developments unconnected with earlier backed geometric industries in Africa and may reflect local population growth and investment in a more complex hunting technology, as well as climatic cooling as the last glaciation approached. As we will see in Chapter 5, similar microlithic industries appear also to have developed independently in Australia and Sulawesi during the Holocene.

After 100,000 years ago, as the warm conditions of the last interglacial retreated, the temperate and arctic latitudes of Eurasia began a fluctuating slide downwards towards the cold climates of the last glacial maximum, which peaked about 20,000 years ago (Figure 3.2). By that time, Northern Europe and North America were covered by ice sheets, whereas northeastern Asia was too dry to support any major accumulation of ice, as opposed to permafrost. As noted, archaic human populations were evidently restricted to latitudes below about 55°N during interglacials, and presumably were forced to abandon large regions during full glacial maxima. *H. sapiens* populations were able to circumvent the cold to a degree, owing to their ability to build shelters, manufacture layers of fitted clothing and use fire. Even so, we see no signs of human occupation of the Arctic coastline of Asia until about 30,000 years ago. North America remained out of reach until about 16,000 years ago, when the postglacial climate had improved sufficiently to allow movement across Bering Strait into Alaska, and eventually into the rest of the continent via ice-free routes (Chapter 4).

Available genetic and skeletal evidence suggests that modern humans spread initially, from the northern Levant and the Caucasus, into northern Eurasia before the peak cold of the last glacial maximum, probably at the beginning of the Upper Paleolithic, circa 45,000 years ago.[53] This date is obviously very much later than that for the first modern humans in the Levant, as just discussed, and one must wonder why there was such a time lag. There are two fairly obvious reasons, related to cold climate and the presence of the Neanderthals. Early modern humans fresh from a tropical origin in Africa probably had less cold tolerance than Neanderthals, and if equipped with a Middle Paleolithic technology they would have had few other advantages over them. This brings up another factor – the Upper Paleolithic technology itself. I noted earlier that blade industries were present in northern Africa from about 60,000 years ago, so it may be that a transference of technology from Africa into the Levant occurred at about that time, or a little later. There is considerable uncertainty about this owing to the scarcity of data, but it seems quite possible to me.

By 130,000 years ago, the Eurasian Neanderthals had evolved their classic form, described in all textbooks of biological anthropology as being more rugged, heavily brow-ridged, chinless, and muscular than *H. sapiens*. As we have seen, modern DNA research suggests they might have hybridized with modern humans outside Africa on rare occasions. Their relatively low level of ancient mtDNA diversity appears to have been similar to that of modern Eurasians, and much less than observed in modern African populations. Perhaps, like modern Eurasians, they also underwent some degree of population expansion from a founder population bottleneck during and after the last interglacial. As noted, both Neanderthals and *sapiens* share a similarly-shaped lingual bone termed the hyoid, a shape deemed essential for speech, but Neanderthals were quite distinct from modern humans in Eurasia in body morphology and the specific lineages within their mtDNA.[54]

Importantly, Neanderthals were still universal in the habitable areas of Europe until at least 60,000 years ago. It has long been assumed that they survived in increasingly cold conditions in southerly parts of Europe (Iberia and Croatia) until perhaps 30,000 years ago, by which time they would surely have overlapped with modern humans. However, new dating analyses are raising the possibility that all Neanderthals had vanished from Iberia and the Caucasus by at least 37,000 or even 40,000 years ago, so the overlap may have been briefer.[55] Beyond Europe, Neanderthal bones have been found in caves in Israel, Iraqi Kurdistan, Uzbekistan, the Altai Mountains of Russia, and possibly even in China, where a Neanderthal-like partial cranium was found at Maba in Guangdong Province (Figure 3.5).

In the Gorny Altai region of Russia, well north of the Tibetan Plateau at 55°N, we actually find two archaic hominins – a Neanderthal child identified from its ancient DNA in Okladnikov Cave, and an unusual surprise thought to be about 80,000 years old from Denisova Cave. The Denisova hominin is known to us from two molar teeth and a finger bone, the latter with ancient mtDNA that indicates it belonged neither to a Neanderthal nor to a modern human. Instead, it belonged to a hitherto unknown hominin species that appears to have shared a common origin with Neanderthals and modern humans between 700,000 and 170,000 years ago, similar to the age range for Neanderthal–modern separation, and possibly another evolutionary product of out of Africa 2 expansion.[56]

I have already referred to Denisovans on several occasions in this chapter since they, like Neanderthals, interbred to a small extent with modern humans. Some of their genes have been traced in modern eastern Indonesians, Melanesians and Australians, but not in most modern East Asians or western Indonesians, the latter being more recent Holocene migrants from the Asian mainland (Reich et al. 2011; and see Chapter 8). However, it is not clear where this admixture took place since there has been so much subsequent Holocene population replacement in eastern Asia. Perhaps it occurred more than 50,000 years ago amongst colonizing *H. sapiens* populations in mainland Asia, before Australia and Melanesia were reached.

The early immigrant populations of *H. sapiens* clearly lived alongside these archaic Neanderthal and Denisovan hominins. But, apart from the much older Skhul/Qafzeh remains in Israel, anatomically modern human cranial remains with tight and convincing Pleistocene dates older than 40,000 years are relatively rare in the temperate to cold latitudes of western and northern Eurasia. In this regard, they correlate tightly with the spread of Upper Paleolithic technologies. The oldest modern human remains in Europe are a mandible from Peştera cu Oase Cave in Romania, directly dated by C14 to 42,000 years ago, a maxilla of similar date from Kent's Cavern in southern England, and molars also of similar date from Grotta del Cavallo in southern Italy.[57] Only bone fragments of modern humans are dated from this time period in the Levant, and the oldest anatomically modern temperate East Asian is the partial skeleton from Tianyuan Cave at Zhoukoudian near Beijing, directly radiocarbon dated to about 40,000 years ago.[58] A fragmentary modern human mandible from Zhirendong cave in Guangxi province is claimed to be 100,000 years old on the basis of uranium series dating of covering stalagmite deposits, but the report mentions no associated archaeology. Clearly, more support is needed if such an early date is to be accepted, although Zhirendong is on the fringe of the Southeast Asian tropics so an earlier *sapiens* presence might be expected.[59] As we will see in Chapter 4, a *sapiens* presence in tropical Southeast Asia is now documented back to perhaps 60,000 years ago, at Tam Pa Ling Cave in Laos.

The classic markers of Upper Paleolithic technology in Europe and the western and northern parts of Asia, but excluding southern China, Southeast Asia, and Australia, are long blades, many with blunting (or backing) down one side to facilitate holding or hafting, struck from prismatic cylindrical or conical cores that were different from the multidirectional cores more typical of the preceding Middle Paleolithic (Figure 3.4). As we have seen earlier, such blades with backing are reported from many regions of Africa, especially in the south, well prior to 50,000 years ago. In the Levant, they appeared (from the Nile Valley?) around 50,000 years ago, in the Balkans by 45,000 years ago, and in Spain and France by about 40,000 years ago. In Europe, they belong to what is most commonly termed the Aurignacian industry.[60]

It is worth noting that central France and northern Spain also harbor an Upper Paleolithic industry known as the Châtelperronian, contemporary with the Aurignacian and characterized by curved-backed blades, together with Aurignacian-like bone points and animal tooth pendants. Surprisingly, however, these items have been found in apparent association with Neanderthal cranial remains in at least two central French caves.[61] Opinions differ as to the significance of the Châtelperronian. Perhaps the Neanderthals independently invented some aspects of behavior normally attributed to modern humans, as suggested by Zilhão and Wong (2010). Perhaps they were acculturating to modern human behavioral norms, as suggested by Mellars (2011). Or perhaps the records have been affected by stratigraphic admixture or unclear recording, as suggested by Bar-Yosef and Bordes (2010). Recent radiocarbon dating of the Châtelperronian layers in Grotte du Renne makes disturbance a distinct possibility.[62] Opinion now seems to be swinging towards the view that Neanderthals and moderns might have been very different in their capacities for cultural expression.[63]

The Aurignacian proper is most commonly sourced to immediate origins in the Levant, rather than Africa itself, although this does not, of course, rule out an ultimate northern African origin. Industries of similar type occur along the North African littoral, but it is possible that these could reflect migratory back-movements into northern Africa at this time with the spread of Asian mtDNA haplogroups M1 and U6 (Olivieri et al. 2006). The most likely possibility seems to be that the blade-based immediate antecedents for the Aurignacian were developed in the Levant around 50,000 years ago, from an ultimate African origin, possibly by descendants of the Skhul and Qafzeh people. But there is no firm agreement on this.

In Eurasia, some of the oldest Upper Paleolithic industries appear to come from caves in the Altai region, where rich Upper Paleolithic assemblages commenced about 45,000 years ago. These industries are related to the Aurignacian, with blades, fully prismatic cores, bone points, and beads and pendants made of bone, shell, mammoth ivory, and egg shell. Russian archaeologists favor a continuous development of them from the preceding Mousterian,[64] but the typological situation is really no different from that in Europe, where replacement with some possible Châtelperronian-like admixture with Neanderthals, rather than exclusive continuity, is more widely accepted. Indeed, trying to trace a specific lithic industry such as the Aurignacian, no matter how recognizable, to a specific source will always be dogged by vagueness of chronology and by the simple observation that the visibility of origin will correlate directly with the speed of spread. The Aurignacian clearly spread quickly, wherever it might have originated, between Europe and the Altai within a few millennia. Such rapid movement cannot be easily plotted in terms of directionality through the dating methods that are available to us.

The Fate of the Neanderthals

How did modern humans actually replace the Neanderthals and their archaic contemporaries? One recent environmental explanation is that massive and roughly coeval volcanic eruptions in southern Italy (Campanian Ignimbrite eruption) and the Caucasus Mountains (Mt Elbrus) drove Neanderthals into virtual extinction before modern humans had a chance to appear on the scene in large numbers, similar to the earlier suggested impact of the Toba eruption 73,000 years ago (Golovanova et al. 2010). Such scenarios of volcanic cataclysm would be convincing if they were tied to massive regional episodes of animal extinction or species turnover, but in these cases it is my understanding that they are not.

Instead, most archaeologists nowadays regard Neanderthal extinction as a result of differential cultural and demographic behavior between this species and modern humans. Curtis Marean suggests that modern humans as dietary generalists would have had an edge over the more specialized and carnivorous (even cannibalistic) Neanderthals in any situations where territorial interests overlapped or clashed.[65] Another suggestion, already discussed earlier, focuses on the use of clothing. Basically, cold weather, especially with high levels of wind chill, would have required complex clothing and reliable shelter.[66] We have no direct evidence for Neanderthal clothing, which presumably consisted of layers of animal skins draped around the body. The clothing associated with early *H. sapiens*, however, was more complex, according to the quantities of bone or shell beads sewn on to now-vanished clothing in some Upper Paleolithic graves. Complex clothing involved multiple layering and attention to fit and shape, and could carry decoration. Its manufacture also required technological innovation, hence the finding of many tools such as skin scrapers, sharp cutting blades, bone points and eyed bone needles, the latter documented from about 35,000 years ago in the western Russian Upper Paleolithic sites of Kostenki and Mezmaiskaya Cave (Golovanova et al. 2010: 677). Neanderthals made some of these items, especially the stone ones, but not the whole package. Modern humans also evidently knew how to weave plant fibers (Soffer 2004). Woven garments, when necessary, would tolerate perspiration better than animal skins. Species of body lice that evolved in partnership with modern humans and their clothing support the view that *H. sapiens* and complex clothing traveled together, as Gilligan (2010) emphasizes. So too, perhaps, did certain forms of stomach bacteria and malaria parasites (Henn et al. 2012).

The impact of modern humans on archaic hominins must also have been of a demographic as well as a technological nature – our ancestors appear to have had more and healthier babies. A comparative analysis of archaeological (cave) site floor areas, artifact densities, and meat weights for the Mousterian, Châtelperronian and Aurignacian phases in the Dordogne region of southern France, spanning the crucial period from 45,000 to 35,000 years ago, reveals that the Aurignacians supported a population size nine times (or more) greater than that of the final Neanderthals.[67] Increasing birth rates, along with the better clothing and hunting technology to support them, are hard to deny. Did fecund and well-clothed modern humans gradually replace the sartorially less protected Neanderthals, forcing the latter into gradual extinction in the colder and less desirable regions of Europe and Asia? Modern humans would certainly have played a major role in Neanderthal demise if they stopped them from retreating south into warmer regions when the advance of high latitude glaciation after 45,000 years ago could have made it imperative. Did they impact on the Denisovans in central Asia in a similar way, pushing them eventually into chilly extinction? This is not certain, and much depends on the chronology for Neanderthal survival, which as noted earlier is at present under some dispute. But I suspect it is very likely.

Finally, another factor in the demise of Neanderthals might have been a use of dogs, or tame wolves, as aids in hunting by modern humans. This is an interesting possibility, and we return to similar but much younger situations of dog-aided hunter-gatherer expansion in Chapters 4 and 5. Bones of potentially domesticated canids have recently been reported in several Upper Paleolithic occupations in Europe and Siberia, but not in Mousterian ones. Dogs, it seems, have special abilities not only to smell game from afar, but also to communicate with us by observing the movements of our eyes. What better hypothesis to please a dog lover! As Pat Shipman (2012) states, perhaps our dogs domesticated us as we domesticated them.

Explanations?

The picture reconstructed so far is that early *H. sapiens* spread from Africa into the Levant during the last interglacial period, before 100,000 years ago, prior to the widespread development of blade and backed industries in Africa, carrying a Middle Paleolithic technology similar to that of many of its archaic contemporaries. By at least 75,000 years ago, perhaps well before, its descendants were on their way to India, possibly encouraged by a period of relatively high rainfall that made the Syrian, Arabian, Iranian and Thar deserts more passable. Movement into the Southeast Asian tropics beyond Burma did not, on present evidence, occur until after 70,000 years ago, although this date could very easily change with new discoveries. Movement into temperate Eurasia did not get underway until about 50,000 years ago, following the introduction of the necessary Upper Paleolithic technology from a likely (but still uncertain) northern African source. The final outcome of all of this was that modern humans spread over all habitable parts of Eurasia and into Australasia, and in the process assimilated (not exterminated!) all surviving populations of archaic hominins.

Of course, not all agree on this scenario, even allowing for some modest degree of assimilation of archaic hominins, or even successive migrations of modern ones. No interesting question in prehistory ever attracts full agreement. There are quite a large number of archaeologists and biological anthropologists who still favor direct phylogenetic continuity to modern humans in Eurasia from archaic hominins such as Neanderthals.[68] My own opinion does not favor such a high degree of multiregional continuity, partly because I cannot imagine any mechanism that could create a single species (*H. sapiens*) by convergence processes out of differentiated archaic hominin antecedents, including Neanderthals, Denisovans, erectines and even Floresians over the whole of the occupied Old World. I have already stressed this. However, my opinion does allow for some continuity through episodes of hybridization between archaic and modern humans, should such hybridization survive intensive genetic investigation in the near future.

The origins and dispersals of early *H. sapiens* remain among the most important and most debated issues in all the sciences devoted to human prehistory. One hundred percent continuity from archaic hominins in Eurasia versus one hundred percent out of Africa replacement would be simple answers, but neither is right. The search goes on relentlessly for more convincing answers. I hope that I have presented some here.

Notes

1. See Cameron and Groves 2004; Klein 2009a; Pickering et al. 2011; Leakey et al. 2012; Wood 2012; Hertler et al. 2013; Groves 2013 for discussion of some of the possibilities.
2. Unless, of course, something occurs to boost the birth rate amongst the descendants of the less dominant population. One can see such a process in operation amongst many indigenous Australian and American peoples today, as modern medical advances, social freedoms, and land rights replace colonial era repression, and reverse former population declines.
3. Anton 2012 recognizes five separate 'cranial morphs' in Africa at about 1.9–1.4 million years ago.
4. See Isaac 1978; Ryan and Jetha 2010 for strongly differing viewpoints. See also the differing viewpoints in Allen et al. 2008, and an analysis of modern Hadza hunter-gatherers (Tanzania) in Apicella et al. 2012. The significance of mutualistic collaboration in child-rearing and food-getting amongst hominins, as opposed to other primates, is discussed by Tomasello et al. 2012.
5. For example, Dennell and Roebroeks 2005; Ferring et al. 2011; Wood 2011.
6. Potts 2012; Magill et al. 2013.
7. Broecker 2000; Ruddiman 2005; Potts 2012.
8. Rohling et al. 2008; Dutton and Lambeck 2012.
9. See Dennell et al. 2011; Van der Made 2011; Stewart and Stringer 2012 for discussion of these issues.
10. Osborne et al. 2008; Castañeda et al. 2009.
11. Bailey et al. 2007; Chauhan 2009.
12. Balter 2010; Barham and Mitchell 2008:122–3.
13. On the Dmanisi hominins, see Rightmire and Lordkipanidze 2010; Agusti and Lordkipanidze 2011.
14. References for this paragraph: Ciochon 2009; Shen et al. 2009; Hyodo et al. 2011.
15. For these discoveries, see Dennell 2009; Güleç et al. 2009; Brumm et al. 2010; Hou and Zhao 2010; Zaidner et al. 2010; Arzarello et al. 2012; Groves 2013.

16. For Atapuerca see Carbonell et al. 2008, 2010a, 2010b; Bermudez de Castro et al. 2010.

17. Compare Roebrooks and Villa 2011, who favor a late appearance of fire usage by hominins, with Wrangham 2009, who favors a much earlier appearance with the evolution of *H. erectus* close to two million years ago. The oldest archaeological evidence for fire, dated to about one million years ago, is claimed by Berna et al. 2012 from Wonderwerk Cave in South Africa.

18. Sémah and Sémah 2013.

19. Van den Bergh et al. 2001; Van der Geer et al. 2010.

20. The possibility that such a new arrival occurred is discussed by Kaifu et al. 2005; Groves 2013.

21. At the time of writing, there are rumors (for want of a better word – nothing is published yet) that *H. floresiensis* could be older than the original dates suggested. If so, some of the problems raised in this section could dissolve.

22. Argue et al. 2006, 2009; Groves 2008; Morwood and Jungers 2009; Jungers and Baab 2009.

23. Lyras et al. 2008; Perry and Dominy 2009; Van Heteren and Sankhyan 2009; Kaifu et al. 2011.

24. Numerous perspectives on *H. floresiensis* are summarized in Indriati 2007.

25. Morwood and Aziz 2009; Van der Geer et al. 2010: 200.

26. On early hand axes, see Shea 2010a; Lepre et al. 2011; Pappu et al. 2011.

27. Langbroek 2004; Derevianko 2005.

28. Reich et al. 2010; Meyer et al. 2012.

29. Zhang et al. 2010; Brumm and Moore 2012.

30. Rodriguez et al. 2011; Garcia et al. 2011a.

31. Green et al. 2010; Reich et al. 2010; Abi-Rached et al. 2011; and see Hammer et al. 2011 for similar archaic admixture in Africa. Eriksson and Manica 2012 suggest that sharing of genetic material between archaic and modern humans reflects deeply shared ancestry in Africa rather than much later interbreeding in Eurasia.

32. Behar et al. 2008 suggest 150,000 years for mtDNA differentiation between southern Africans (especially Khoe-San) and the rest of humanity, whereas molecular clock calculations from the autosomal genome give a range between 100,000 and a possible 300,000 years (compare Schlebusch et al. 2012; Scally and Durbin 2012).

33. McDougall et al. 2005; Shea et al. 2007; Smith et al. 2012.

34. McBrearty and Brooks 2000; Clark et al. 2003.

35. Blum and Jakobsson 2011; Henn et al. 2011.

36. A number of comments on Atkinson 2011, published in *Science* on February 10 and March 2, 2012, indicate that the linguistic situation could be more complex than implied here. But phonemic simplification is attested in other contexts, for instance if one compares spoken Polynesian languages, located at the end of the Austronesian dispersal, with Taiwan or Philippine languages spoken near the commencement of that dispersal (Blust 1991). The question here is whether the reduction in phonemic diversity observed by Atkinson actually tracks back directly to the initial dispersal of modern humans, or if it reflects subsequent historical factors.

37. Oppenheimer 2003; Atkinson et al. 2008.

38. Ambrose 2001; Marwick 2005.

39. For instance, Shea 2011; Hiscock 2013a.

40. Hill et al. 2011; Tomasello et al. 2012.

41. Grine et al. 2007 (Hofmeyer); Henn et al. 2011 (genetics).

42. Garcea 2010; for South Africa see Henshilwood and Dubreuil 2011; for the Aterian see Balter 2011.

43. Ambrose 2010; Lombard and Phillipson 2010; Brown et al. 2012; McBrearty 2012.

44. On Pinnacle Point and Blombos see Marean et al. 2007; Marean 2010; Henshilwood et al. 2011.

45. Ambrose 1998 (Kenya); Vermeersch 2010; Pearson 2012.

46. The latest autosomal molecular clock based on pedigree (within-family) studies of mutation rates suggests that the major out of Africa migration of modern humans occurred between 130,000 and 90,000 years ago (Scally and Durbin 2012). See also Boivin et al. 2013.

47. Campbell and Tishkoff 2010; Wollstein et al. 2010; Reich et al. 2011 support a single exit from Africa of the common ancestors of modern humans on genetic grounds. Conversely, de Knijf 2010; Boivin et al. 2013; Gunz et al. 2009 and Schillaci 2008 all present multi-migration scenarios, the last two from paleoanthropology.

48. Rasmussen et al. 2011; Stoneking and Harvati 2013.

49. See the different perspectives on the mtDNA molecular clock with respect to this precise issue in Soares et al. 2012; Boivin et al. 2013.

50. Lahr and Foley 1998, Stringer 2007; Schillaci 2008; Boivin et al. 2013.

51. See also Walter et al. 2000 for a possible last interglacial occurrence of stone tools on the Red Sea coast of Eritrea.

52. On the Jwalapuram sites see Petraglia et al. 2007, 2009, 2010; Haslam et al. 2010; Clarkson et al. 2009, 2012; Petraglia and Korisettar 2012.

53. Oppenheimer 2003; Forster 2004; Macaulay et al. 2005; Roostalu et al. 2007.

54. Krause et al. 2007; Hublin 2007; Caramelli et al. 2008; Klein 2009a.

55. Zilhão et al. 2011; Pinhasi et al. 2011; Callaway 2012.

56. Krause et al. 2007, 2010; Reich et al. 2010; Gibbons 2011; Meyer et al. 2012.

57. On these discoveries see Trinkaus 2007; Higham et al. 2011b; Benazzi et al. 2011; Mellars 2011.

58. Shang et al. 2007; Keates 2010.

59. Liu et al. 2010; Kaifu and Fujita 2012.

60. Goebel 2007; Meignen 2011; Mellars 2011.

61. Zilhão and d'Errico 1999; Klein 2009a: 590–5.

62. Higham et al. 2010; disputed by Caron et al. 2011.

63. But see Zilhão 2010 for some strong opposition to this suggestion.

64. Derevianko and Shunkov 2005, 2011.

65. Marean 2007; Richards and Trinkaus 2009.

66. Gilligan 2007, 2010; Weaver 2009.

67. See also Bolus 2011 for the Swabian Alps in southern Germany and Mellars and French 2011.

68. For example, Derevianko 2005; Bednarik 2008; Shang et al. 2007; Liu et al. 2010; Wolpoff and Lee 2012.

Chapter 4

Beyond Eurasia: The Pioneers of Unpeopled Lands – Wallacea and Beyond, Australia, The Americas

In this chapter, we deal first with the colonization by Homo sapiens *of the islands of Wallacea (eastern Indonesia and the Philippines), Australia, and the inner islands of the western Pacific, an entirely tropical achievement requiring seacraft that occurred around 50,000 years ago. Then we move to the younger and far less tropical colonizations of Japan (circa 40,000 years ago) and the Americas (circa 16,000 years ago). The focus is on Paleolithic colonizations of previously uninhabited lands by processes that required crossing either a sea gap or a land bridge, or combinations of both. In the case of North America, some fairly rigid paleoenvironmental constraints determined the date of first settlement from an immediate Siberian homeland region located very close to the Arctic Circle.*

As discussed in Chapter 3, modern humans with a Middle Paleolithic technology spread from tropical Africa via the Levant and Arabia to tropical Sundaland by at least 70,000 years ago, without really needing to exit the warm latitudes below the tropic of Cancer (except in Iran and Pakistan). Life in the continuously warm tropics has certain obvious advantages. For a hunter and gatherer (or a farmer for that matter), it is not necessary to invest huge amounts of time in manufacturing warm clothing or substantial shelters. Ethnographic accounts of tropical Southeast Asian hunters and gatherers, like the Andaman Islanders described by Radcliffe-Brown (1922), indicate the use of quite flimsy pole and thatch shelters made of bamboo and palm products that were simply abandoned when the group moved. They had minimal clothing – fiber, leaf, or bark cloth waist bands (often nothing for children) – and carried little else apart from what appear to have been remarkably widespread traditions of body painting and scarification (tattooing was a Neolithic introduction into Southeast Asia).

Tropical Australian populations had similar forms of clothing and shelter at contact, although marsupial skin cloaks were required in the colder south of Australia and the island of Tasmania (Gilligan 2008). The series of photographs taken by Baldwin Spencer (1982) on his two Northern Territory expeditions in 1901–2 and 1911–2 reveal many remarkable details from the center and north of the continent – tree bough and bark shelters, neck and arm ornaments, waist strings of human hair or pandanus fiber,

First Migrants: Ancient Migration in Global Perspective, First Edition. Peter Bellwood.
© Peter Bellwood. Published 2013 by John Wiley & Sons, Ltd.

tasseled aprons for women and pubic coverings for men, and intricate body painting and cicatrization. Very often, no clothing was worn at all, and Spencer noted how remarkable it was that people, especially children, could go naked through the night in the middle of the fairly cold central Australian winter.[1]

Crossing the Sea Beyond Sundaland

Australia and New Guinea were reached by H. sapiens entirely through the tropical world, and across sea, by people carrying a Middle Paleolithic technology based on the removal of flakes from pebbles and other forms of stone core, the latter sometimes flaked in a unidirectional manner. This industry was certainly not classically Upper Paleolithic as defined in the previous chapter, because it lacked the blades, small blade-lets, backed tools, end scrapers, burins and bifacial points that made the western and central Eurasian Upper Paleolithic so distinctive. In fact, it was related more closely with the contemporary Mousterian and Levalloisian core and flake technologies found in the western Old World, associated especially with Neanderthals.

Indeed, the difficulty of distinguishing archaic versus modern human populations using Paleolithic artifacts is especially magnified in Southeast Asia, where a Middle Paleolithic unretouched flake tool technology, found unambiguously with skeletal remains of Homo sapiens, dominated many regions until the Holocene. Southeast Asia and Australia simply did not experience a sequence from Acheulian through a Middle Paleolithic into an Upper Paleolithic, even though Mainland Southeast Asia had an indisputably modern human population in residence by at least 50,000 years ago. Stone tools do not allow recognition of the activities of different hominin species in this part of the world. Modern humans could have arrived in tropical eastern Asia prior to 100,000 years ago in terms of the available rather conflicting data from genetic, archaeological, and fossil sources. Whether they actually did so is matter for future research to decide.

The oldest skeletal evidence for H. sapiens in Southeast Asia comes from Laos, where the Tam Pa Ling skull cap is dated to between 46,000 and 64,000 years ago, unfortunately with no associated archaeology. The skull from Niah West Mouth in Sarawak, Borneo, is dated to about 45,000 years ago, and other human remains that may be of a similar antiquity come from Tabon Cave on Palawan in the southwestern Philippines.[2] There is also the enigmatic metatarsal from Callao Cave in northern Luzon, dated to 67,000 years ago, but in this case it is hard to be certain if we are dealing with Homo sapiens or a small archaic hominin. In Australia, an ochre-covered inhumation burial at Lake Mungo from western New South Wales is dated to about 40,000 years ago by luminescence dating (Bowler et al. 2003), but the Australian archaeological record goes back further to beyond 50,000 years ago. This initial sapiens population undoubtedly overlapped in Mainland and Island Southeast Asia, but not in Australia, with late surviving populations of Homo erectus and H. floresiensis.[3]

Only modern humans appear to have traveled beyond Flores. Little floresiensis did not reach Australia as far as we know, or probably even Timor. The extreme degree of endemism expressed by this species suggests that ocean crossing was not a common event for archaic hominins, until modern humans crossed the Wallace Line to reach Australia and New Guinea about 50,000 years ago. It was perhaps about this time that someone invented a functional watercraft, presumably propelled by paddles.

With watercraft, we have a complex item of material culture that has excited the imagination of many an archaeologist. Did Paleolithic migrants to Australia use dugout canoes, bark canoes, rafts of bamboo, logs, or reed bundles, perhaps all of them? We will never know, but something was certainly required to carry humans from Indonesia to northern Australia, across at least 90 km of open although usually fairly quiet sea, especially during the southern hemisphere summer (December to February) when the winds and currents trend towards Australia from the northwest.[4] The sail was still unknown, given the absence of any evidence for its widespread indigenous use in the prehistoric Americas (Anderson 2010), settled by 16,000 years ago. Balsa sailing rafts plying the coasts of Peru and Ecuador before the Spanish conquest did have sails, but these could reflect late prehistoric contact with Polynesia.

Our best clues to the kinds of seacraft available in Pleistocene Southeast Asia come from Tasmania, isolated from southern Australia since about 13,000 years ago, when the rising postglacial sea level reached -50 m and began to drown the former Bass Strait land bridge.[5] Tasmanians did not use sails, but they did have very handy watercraft made of bundles of bark or reeds, described by George Robinson in 1831 as "perfectly safe", able to brave a rough sea (as occur very frequently around Tasmania), difficult to capsize, and in one case able to carry eight people (Plomley 1966: 119, 379). No argument involving European diffusion can explain these craft entirely. The methods they used were deeply indigenous and would have been valid for an attempted crossing to Australia 50,000 years ago, although tropical travelers would have had access to bamboo, a material unavailable in Tasmania.

Coastal groups in southeastern Australia also made canoes of single large sheets of bark, or several sheets sewn together, with sides kept apart by wooden stretchers (Roth 1908: 161). Dugout canoes are another possibility, given that edge-ground pebble axes occur in a few northern Australian Pleistocene sites (and in many sites in Japan – see page 82) from 35,000 years ago onwards, albeit not yet back to the period of initial settlement. Dugout canoes are very ancient in many parts of the world and their remains often survive in waterlogged sites, with examples dating before 8000 years ago in Africa, Japan, China, and Europe.[6] They can be made by burning and scraping out the interior of the log, even using shell scrapers, as well as by stone or shell adzing. However, the sewn plank and outrigger canoes made in recent times in northeastern Australia probably reflect contact with Austronesian-speaking populations to the north or west and are unlikely to be suitable models for Pleistocene watercraft. In addition to canoes, Joseph Birdsell (1977: 139) also believed that rafts comprising two layers of mangrove poles held together with driven hardwood pegs were a likely model for Pleistocene craft, based on records from northwestern Australia.

Many separate sea crossings between different islands would have been required in order to reach Australia or New Guinea from Sundaland, the exposed glacial-period continent formed around the present islands of Sumatra, Java, Borneo and Bali. Low glacial-period sea levels would have exposed dry land passages of varying width between New Guinea and Australia for most of the Pleistocene, across Torres Strait and the Arafura Sea, turning both land masses into a single emergent continent. But some quite wide sea gaps always had to be crossed, especially in the deep sea zones of eastern Indonesia. The largest of these, from Buru to Obi on the route from Sulawesi to New Guinea, or from Timor or Roti to the exposed continental shelf of northern Australia, would have been around 90 km when sea levels were low.[7] Those who commenced these voyages, intentionally or unintentionally, would not always have seen land ahead of them, although if they survived to half way across they would perhaps have seen land in both directions, as well as floating timber and the huge flocks of homing sea birds that predated human presence on all Oceanic islands.

All we really know is that viable populations reached low-lying Australia and more mountainous New Guinea by crossing sea gaps at least 50,000 years ago. Their genetic descendants are still there to register the fact. So too are their linguistic descendants, although the time depth is too great for any useful observations to be made from extant languages about the first human colonizations. We examine the archaeology behind all of this later, but it is first necessary to examine the potential demography of Pleistocene colonization.

How Many Settlers?

The future of the human species depends on its women. For any small community living in isolation and worried about its viability, having 10 women and only 1 man in the camp would be infinitely preferable to having 10 men and only 1 woman. So, let us imagine a small raft-load of people arriving on the beach of an uninhabited island in Wallacea, 50,000 BC. How many people would there need to be if the future community had any chance at all of coming into existence and remaining in existence as a viable breeding community?

First of all, we should remember that hunter-gatherers at 50,000 BC were probably far fitter *genetically* than we are today, given their unremitting exposure to natural selection and the lack of medical care. Anyone harboring a deleterious gene that produced chronic ill health or a highly visible physical defect would (in theory) have had a diminished chance of reproduction, and so the offending gene might have had a short life within the population. *Physical* good health outside genetic causation is, of course, another matter, and many no doubt would have had bodies that were rather heavily used, even battered and poorly repaired by our standards. But genetic procreation is the issue here, and a genetic profile well-honed by natural selection would presumably have lessened the chances of having offspring with life-threatening genetic disorders.

One of my former ANU colleagues, demographer Norma McArthur, attempted to address the *how many* question with some colleagues back in 1976. Computers were fairly basic then, and her simulation required that couples were always unadventurously monogamous. But the results were actually very interesting. McArthur calculated that just three monogamous couples of reproductive age landing together on one island would have had, on average, a 50% chance of assured genetic survival into the future – very good odds indeed if they found themselves in a healthy location with no serious predators or diseases. One simulated sextet went extinct because it ended up with all males, but another luckier one produced 250 descendants after about 225 years – all inside a computer, but still surely a success. McArthur also pointed out that an isolated community with 10 children could, by chance, have 9 boys and 1 girl – a potential disaster. But an isolated community with 100 children could not, statistically, hope to have more than 62 boys (or girls, as the case may be). Numbers mattered, and the more the better (McArthur et al. 1976).

The archaeological record, unfortunately, does not tell us how large were the colonizing populations of the Wallacean islands or Australasia. Geneticists can calculate rough likelihoods for founder population sizes from patterns of nucleotide diversity within mtDNA haplogroups, but these estimates have very large error ranges and it is not always clear if they relate to one migration or to several over a long period. However, the flow of migrants would have increased if people ('scouts' or explorers) were able to return home from a newly discovered island and tell the tale, as with Polynesian and European migration tens of millennia later. We cannot assume that Pleistocene voyagers had such abilities – those who headed off towards the Sahul Shelf might never have been seen or heard from again. But the return voyage possibility always has to be borne in mind.

Historical records give us some idea of just how quirky the trajectories of extremely small and completely isolated colonizing populations could be. Perhaps the most interesting case developed when Fletcher Christian and friends mutinied on the British ship *Bounty* in 1789, on its way to take breadfruit from Tahiti to the West Indies under the command of Captain William Bligh. A total of 28 people – 9 British mutineers (all male), 6 Tahitian men, 12 Tahitian women, and 1 infant girl – sailed from Tahiti and arrived on Pitcairn Island in southeastern Polynesia in September 1789.[8] There they hid until the colony was discovered in 1808, by now containing 35 people, or 7 more than the original number. Yet, by this time eight of the original nine British men were dead, either from murder or ill health. One male child born on the island evidently reached puberty around 1805 and procreated with one of the Tahitian women, who would have been about twice his age. Otherwise, in 1808, the population included, apart from the surviving adult males, 7 of the original Tahitian women close to the ends of their child-bearing careers, and 24 children – 13 boys and 11 girls. From 1810 onwards, these children procreated sufficiently to double the population every 20 years, at an astounding growth rate of 3.7% per year. By 1856, there were so many Pitcairners that the population had to be moved to Norfolk Island.

Demographically, the colonization of Pitcairn Island was a great success, but what might have happened had the women, and not the men, murdered each other, or if they ended up with 20 boys and only 4 girls? They would probably have died out, a fate that might have befallen the fully prehistoric Polynesians who occupied Pitcairn a century or two before the mutineers arrived, of whom nothing but archaeological traces remained in 1789.

Admittedly, the Pitcairners were farmers and not hunter-gatherers, but the facts of human procreation remain the same regardless, as long as there is sufficient food to support the population and a good role of the gender dice. The 24 children on the island in 1808 eventually produced a population of about 87 people by 1831, thus more than trebling in one short generation. There is no inherent reason why Pleistocene colonists in and beyond Wallacea could not have grown their numbers likewise, at least in the first few centuries of settlement (population growth always meets resource limits eventually). Joseph Birdsell stated much the same in 1957, suggesting that it could have required only 2200 years from first settlement by a small founder group for Australia to contain a population of 300,000 people.[9]

The First Australo-Melanesians

When I published my first book on Southeast Asian and Pacific prehistory in 1978, genetic data on population ancestries were very few and most interpretations were based on analyses of skulls and skeletons from caves and ancient cemeteries. The general opinion then was that the initial modern humans in Southeast Asia were the direct ancestors of the present indigenous populations of the western Pacific. These include the native peoples of Island Melanesia, New Guinea, Australia, and some of the so-called Negrito populations of the Andaman Islands, central Malaya (Semang), and parts of the Philippines (Agta, Aeta, Batak). Over the years, it has become convenient to refer to these populations as *Australo-Melanesians* (Figure 3.5).

Modern craniometric studies still reflect the same conclusion. The ancient and modern indigenous populations of the southwestern Pacific, especially in Melanesia and Australia, were and still are a coherent biological subdivision that can be differentiated (admitting lots of admixture) from the majority of Southeast Asian populations outside eastern Indonesia dating from the Neolithic to the present day.[10] Prior to the Neolithic, this Australo-Melanesian population appears to have been distributed across all of Southeast Asia and up into southern China.

Recent analyses of pre-Neolithic crania excavated from Southeast Asian caves confirm this perspective.[11] The relevant Mainland Southeast Asian remains, for instance, the burials from Moh Khiew Cave in southern Thailand (30,000 years old), Gunung Runtuh cave in Malaya (11,000 years old), and Hang Cho Cave in northern Vietnam (13,000 years old), are all described as Australo-Melanesian in cranial morphology. So too are many pre-Neolithic burials from caves in the Gunung Sewu region of central Java.[12] Even the oldest cranial remains from Island Southeast Asia, from Niah Cave and Tabon Cave, fit the same pattern, as of course do the Pleistocene remains from Australia, albeit with considerable variation along a range from gracile to robust. The general morphology still continues today with regional variations, overlain in Southeast Asia by about 4000 years of genetic admixture with immigrant Asian Neolithic populations.[13]

Modern and ancient genetic data also support the above reconstruction. Ancient mtDNA samples from skeletal remains found in Malay Peninsula caves, dating from 30,000 to about 10,000 years ago (including those from Moh Khiew, above), belong to haplotypes close to those of the modern Senoi (non-Malay) peoples of interior

Malaya. The Senoi, although now agriculturalists, are close linguistic and phenotypic relatives of the neighboring hunter-gatherer Semang Negritos (Oota et al. 2001). Both the Semang and the Andaman Islanders have very deeply rooted mtDNA haplotypes within haplogroup M that suggest to geneticists very long-term in-place evolution in relative isolation, probably from the period of initial modern human spread through tropical Asia.[14] Similar observations from the Y chromosome have been made for Philippine Negritos, who share several NRY haplotypes with Australians (Delfin et al. 2011).

Indeed, extremely long-differentiated mtDNA haplotypes within haplogroup M also occur in the New Guinea region and Australia. The most recent research suggests that both of these populations shared a common ancestry in Indonesia from one or more Paleolithic colonization events, perhaps migrating separately to New Guinea and Australia according to Y-chromosome data. These initial movements probably occurred around 50,000 years ago, and both regions have been fairly isolated genetically from each other since then.[15]

The picture has recently become slightly more complicated, as discussed in Chapter 3, by the observation that some living Australo-Melanesian populations share around 5% of their genetic material with the Late Pleistocene Denisova hominin from the Altai Mountains (Reich et al. 2011). This is similar to the degree of sharing between Neanderthals and Eurasians in general, but probably due to mixing events situated later in time. These Denisovan genes are not shared with nearby mainland Asians or western Indonesians, who are descended from populations who immigrated from more northerly Asian sources during Neolithic times, replacing or assimilating their Paleolithic forebears (Chapter 8). But they do indicate that the modern Australo-Melanesian populations are fairly direct in-place descendants of their early *sapiens* ancestors, who interbred with another hominin species that was already widespread in central and eastern Asia. Indeed, David Reich (2011) has suggested that the Denisovans might be represented by the Maba and Dali pre-*sapiens* skulls from China.

The Denisovan connection is interesting, especially given that recent uranium series dating of the late *H. erectus* skulls from Ngandong in Java suggest that this archaic hominin could have survived to as recently as 70,000–40,000 years ago (Yokoyama et al. 2008), possibly to overlap in time with *H. sapiens*. So too, of course, did *H. floresiensis*, and now we have the enigmatic and possibly non-*sapiens* discoveries from Guangxi in southern China referred to in footnote 2. There would have been plenty of scope in East and Southeast Asia generally for early migrating groups of modern humans to have acquired archaic gene sequences.

The Archaeology of Island Colonization – Wallacea, Melanesia, Australia

New Guinea and Australia remained joined as one landmass across Torres Strait until about 8000 years ago, and the exposed bed of the Arafura Sea was probably under open woodland at the time. The human presence in Sahul (the continent of Australia plus New Guinea, when joined by dry land) goes back to the limits of radiocarbon dating at about 50,000 years ago. A small number of dates based on optically stimulated luminescence, a method that dates by the intensity of trapped electrons in buried geological materials such as quartz sand grains, trickle back towards 60,000 years ago, but are not considered reliable by everyone (O'Connell and Allen 2012). A series of sites at 2000 m above sea level in the Ivane Valley in the eastern Highlands of Papua New Guinea, investigated by Glenn Summerhayes and colleagues (2010) and occupied probably with the intention of collecting starch-bearing pandanus nuts, have recently produced wood charcoal radiocarbon dates that indicate human occupation from 49,000 years ago. In radiocarbon terms, these are perhaps the oldest reliably dated sites in Sahul.

So far, no sites of quite such a high antiquity as those in the the Ivane Valley have been excavated in Wallacea outside Flores. But several caves in the northern Moluccas, Talaud Islands, Sulawesi and Timor have produced dates for human occupation that could go back as far as 40,000 years ago. The passage to the isolated Talaud Islands between Mindanao and Sulawesi at 35,000 years ago could have required crossing 100 km of open sea, perhaps the longest successful sea crossing in Wallacea by this time. On the eastern side of New Guinea, people also crossed Pleistocene sea passages to reach the Bismarck Archipelago, Solomon Islands and Admiralty Islands, the last across 200 km of open sea from New Guinea a little before 20,000 years ago.[16]

The passage to the Andaman Islands from Burma would also have been at least 50 km during low glacial sea levels, but here we have a mystery in that the archaeological record of these islands only extends back 2000 years (Cooper 1985), by which time the inhabitants had access to imported pottery and iron. Whether or not the ancestors of the Andamanese actually migrated to the Andaman Islands 50,000 years ago we do not know, but their endemic genetic lineages and isolated languages suggest that they have certainly been there a very long time. No trace of any population that could be a close biological or linguistic cousin for the Andamanese remains on the Asian mainland today, although there are deep-seated genetic sharings with the Semang Negritos of Peninsular Malaysia.

One island-hopping route that I suspect the early *sapiens* colonists did not follow was that from Taiwan to the Philippines via the Batanes Islands. There was no land bridge here because these seas are very deep and usually very rough. Our recent excavations in five Batanes caves have produced Neolithic deposits but no Paleolithic occupation whatsoever (Bellwood and Dizon 2008). The first permanent settlers arrived in Batanes by boat from Taiwan about 4000 years ago. Admittedly, Paleolithic settlers reached Luzon much earlier, perhaps by 67,000 years ago according to the dated metatarsal from Callao Cave discussed earlier, but from the south, via Sundaland (Borneo and Palawan). I cannot completely disprove that Pleistocene humans once passed through Batanes, but if they did so they were not persuaded to settle or even leave stone tools behind, perhaps because of the lack of resources on these small islands and the rough sea conditions.

As far as continuing maritime contacts between these island landmasses are concerned, there is evidence for very small scale movement of obsidian between islands in the Bismarck Archipelago. But the significance of this is disputed.[17] Perhaps it would be premature to think of interisland movement on the scale of that practiced by later seaborne Neolithic populations. It should also be noted that people cannot subsist entirely on protein from fish and shellfish, as clearly explained by Janet Davidson and Foss Leach (2001). Not only proteins, but also fats and carbohydrates are essential for human survival, requiring terrestrial hunting and gathering as well as shoreline foraging. Therefore, it is quite possible that many of the small islands of Wallacea and western Melanesia, which generally lacked terrestrial resources, especially wild mammals, were occupied only intermittently by early *sapiens* hunter-gatherer populations rather than on a permanent basis.

We might ask just what abilities these early modern humans in Southeast Asia and Australasia possessed that enabled them to colonize so many different environments, a question already asked about the modern human spread across Eurasia in general. These were people whose archaeological record, by at least 30,000 years ago, and in some sites long before, indicates a use of watercraft, grindstones, and occasional edge-ground pebble axes, involving transport of raw materials over distances up to 150 km.[18] They hunted in coastal rainforests (Niah Cave in Sarawak), subsisted from littoral resources (Timor, Talaud Islands, and Bismarck Archipelago), crossed narrow and fairly calm seas, and even climbed to a valley located 2000 m above sea level in the case of the Ivane Valley in New Guinea. The Ivane Valley is interesting in that it has no sign of human occupation during the last glacial maximum at 25,000–19,000 years ago, when local highland mean temperatures could have been as much as 9°C colder than now. There is, however, evidence for plentiful occupation of caves in southern Tasmania at this time, perhaps reflecting the helpful innovation of marsupial skin clothing at this far southern latitude (42°S).[19]

These populations also practiced both flexed and cremation burial at Lake Mungo. They used ochre pigment and necklaces of perforated shells. Convincingly dated cave art in Australia is still younger than 20,000 years (Davidson 2010), but even this antiquity makes likely an origin potentially contemporary with some of the celebrated cave art of Paleolithic France and Spain. These Sahul populations were arguably equal to any others in the Old World at the time in their abilities for creative subsistence and symbolism. Although currently a topic fraught with controversy, Rule et al. (2012) also suggest that the first Australians had a massive impact through fire and hunting on the naïve megafauna that inhabited the continent, leading to the extinction of many larger species.

The penetration of rainforests is a further interesting issue, since there has been a long debate in archaeology as to whether or not hunter-gatherers could occupy wet equatorial rainforest, particularly in inland environments far from the sea, as opposed to semi-deciduous and more open forests. During the 1980s, a number of anthropologists suggested that access to agricultural foods was essential for deep interior rainforest dwellers, given that wet rainforest resources are usually located high in the canopy, with relatively few animals or tubers available at ground level.[20] In opposition to this idea, however, archaeologists have pointed to definite cases of Late Pleistocene equatorial rainforest occupation at Niah Cave, also in a large series of caves occupied by pre-Neolithic hunter-gatherers in Peninsular Malaysia, and in the Bismarck Archipelago (the latter very close to the sea).[21] Hunters often managed very well in rainforests, especially if they had projectile weapons such as blowpipes or bows and arrows (neither documented, however, during the Southeast Asian Paleolithic).

But there are other circumstances that suggest that equatorial rainforests were not always so friendly for early humans, especially if they were extremely far inland. As Peter Brosius (1991) has pointed out, the ethnographic Penan (or Punan) hunter-gatherers of interior Borneo inhabit only very limited regions, mostly in the north and close to settled farming populations. Most of the interior rainforests of Borneo away from the major rivers supported no Penan or any other hunter-gatherer populations when ethnographic records began. Neither have surveys by archaeologists ever located any caves with convincing Paleolithic artifacts in central Borneo, as opposed to Neolithic pottery and burials (Fage and Chazine 2009). There is no reason as yet to assume that any Pleistocene hunter-gatherers penetrated far into interior Borneo beyond the thin coastal halo that held sites such as Niah Cave in Sarawak and several late Paleolithic sites in Sabah, all within 100 km of the sea, even during glacial periods of low sea level.

This conclusion is driven home by the archaeological record from the Malay Peninsula. Lots of interior caves were occupied by Hoabinhian hunter-gatherers, users of large and distinctive unifacial and bifacial pebble tools, especially between 12,000 and 4000 years ago, after which time agriculturalist populations arrived in the peninsula from Thailand. But human occupation is not attested during the last glacial maximum, even though it was present before it, about 40,000 years ago, at Lang Rongrien Cave in southern Thailand (Anderson 1990). During the early Holocene, the coastline lay within 100 km of most of these sites, but during last glacial maximum it lay 500 km to the west and almost 1000 km to the east. This suggests that Pleistocene humans were not willing to penetrate this far into interior wet rainforests in rugged and mountainous country, unless they could retain the option of walking easily to the coastline. Last glacial maximum radiocarbon dates are also rare in the sequence from the Niah Caves in Borneo (Higham et al. 2009), although in this case the site was closer to the sea and some limited occupation did occur.

Despite these difficulties with deep interior wet rainforest, the fact remains that early hominins and early modern humans who wished to migrate as far south as Java or Australia would have needed to pass through at least some, especially along the Equator in Indonesia. There are two possible answers to this problem. One is to walk around the coastline, not always easy and often an extremely long way around. The other is that the Southeast Asian rainforest during the last glacial period, following the wet conditions of the last interglacial, was cooler and drier than now, leading to the development of at least one 'dry-season corridor' running roughly from northwest to southeast down through the center of Sundaland.[22] But the actual extent of this corridor is debatable (Cannon et al. 2009), and it is not clear whether any archaeological sites were ever located within it. Whatever the answer to penetrating equatorial Sundaland, I still favor a model that recognizes considerable difficulties for deep interior wet rainforest occupation by hunter-gatherers, recognizing that Borneo is still today one of the least populated islands of Indonesia. As stated earlier, the earliest modern human settlement of Southeast Asia east of Burma might also have been delayed by an initial presence of dense rainforest, at least prior to about 70,000 years ago.

What of other seemingly challenging environments? Habgood and Franklin (2008) note that Australian dune field deserts and the northern Queensland coastal rainforest do not show signs of frequent occupation until the Holocene, although it is clear that central Australia was at least penetrated by humans before 40,000 years ago (Hiscock 2008: 47–8; see Puritjarra and Parnkupirti on Figure 3.5). So too were the southern semi-arid regions, for instance, the Willandra lakes with Lake Mungo in western New South Wales. Tasmania was reached by a land bridge that appears to have come into existence with lowered sea levels at about 43,000 years ago (Turney et al. 2008). Populations in the southwest of the island during the last glacial maximum were inhabiting caves (e.g., Parmerpar Meethaner, Figure 3.5) as protection against wind chill, hunting wallabies and wombats, manufacturing skin clothing using steep-edged stone thumbnail scrapers, and probably enjoying some of the coldest conditions ever faced by Pleistocene humans south of the Equator.[23]

All in all, the first Australians settled or penetrated virtually all regions of Australia fairly quickly, underlying their ability to adapt to environmental challenges. The question really becomes not one of total presence or absence of humans, but one of preference of habitat. Humans *could* penetrate wet rainforests and dry deserts, but this need not mean they occupied these areas intensively or even continuously. As O'Connell and Allen (2012) point out, the colonization of Wallacea and Australia by modern humans might have involved successive movements due to regional depletions of highly ranked prey species. Costs, benefits, and the reality of human dietary needs and efficient behavior meant that the most productive environments probably filled first.

Wallacean and southwest Pacific material culture at 50,000 years ago was different because it was not 'Upper Paleolithic' in the Western Eurasian sense. Beyond Flores, it was surely the handiwork of *H. sapiens*, given that there are no skeletal traces of earlier hominins, a point recently made by Iain Davidson (2010). We do not have this luxury for Eurasia in general, and archaeologists there still argue heatedly whether specific stone tool industries were made by archaic or modern humans, or both, when no fossils are present to clinch the matter. But Australia, in particular, gives us a clear-cut picture of what modern humans were capable of, by at least 50,000 years ago.

Heading North and Offshore Again – Japan

The Japanese islands consist of the isolated Ryukyus in the south, then the central islands of Kyushu, Shikoku and Honshu, with Hokkaido to the north (Figure 3.5). So far, Japan has no convincing evidence for human occupation before about 40,000 years ago. If people crossed from Asia at that time they would have been dealing with sea levels perhaps 70–80 m below present, when Sakhalin and Hokkaido would have been joined together and to the Asian mainland. They remained joined until about 12,000 years ago. Honshu, Shikoku and Kyushu formed a single large island under low sea level conditions, separated by permanent sea gaps from Hokkaido to the north and Korea to the west, although the emergence of several small islands in

Korea Strait might have made the Korea to Kyushu crossing little more than a hop between visible land masses.

How did the first human settlers enter Japan? An initial arrival across sea is actually most likely because the oldest sites occur in Kyushu and Honshu, rather than Hokkaido. But from where? Three islands in the Ryukyu chain to the south, Ishigaki, Miyako, and Okinawa, have produced some very mysterious human and extinct deer remains from caves, with almost no associated archaeology, some dating greater than 30,000 years ago (Kaifu and Fujita 2012). To reach these islands would have required several sea crossings, some perhaps over 100 km in length since they lie off the continental shelf. A migration route from Taiwan, which was joined to China at periods of low sea level, with the northwards-flowing Kuroshio Current is therefore possible, but very hard to assess. Ryukyu in the Paleolithic remains a great mystery.

The best choice for an initial population homeland for the major Japanese islands of Kyushu and Honshu seems to be Korea. However, the very distinctive early industries of these two Japanese islands, with their edge-ground axes and transverse-bladed ('trapezoidal') points, are so far not directly paralleled in Korea at this time depth (circa 40,000 years ago) and seem also to be very rare in Hokkaido.[24] This could reflect the great density of archaeological work in Kyushu and Honshu compared to the other regions, and both Korea and Japan certainly shared a rudimentary large blade technology at this time (Seong 2008). Possibly also, the first Japanese developed lithic industries suited specifically to the forested landscape of their main islands, given that the edge-ground axes would have been very useful for working wood (e.g., for boats). My understanding here is that this is the oldest edge-grinding technology in world prehistory. Edge-ground pebble axes also occur after 35,000 years ago in Late Pleistocene contexts in northern Australia, but in Korea, China and Southeast Asia they are not yet definitely reported from such early contexts as in Japan. Obsidian was also collected for tools by these initial Japanese settlers from a small volcanic island called Kozu, in the Izu Islands, that 35,000 years ago would have been about 40 km offshore from the mouth of Tokyo Bay (Ikawa-Smith 2009).

Rather mysteriously, the edge-ground axes disappeared from the archaeological record in Kyushu and Honshu at the time of a major volcanic eruption, with widespread ash falls (the Aira-Tanazawa tephra), that occurred about 28,000 years ago. Whether there was a cause and effect sequence here is not clear, but the Japanese archaeological record after the eruption underwent major changes, initially with a short-lived introduction to Kyushu of a tanged point industry from Korea.[25] Following this, there was a significant new immigration from eastern Siberia along the Sakhalin-Hokkaido-Kurile land bridge, but not into Honshu or Kyushu, where a different Jomon cultural tradition with early pottery developed after 20,000 years ago. The migration into Hokkaido took place a little before the last glacial maximum, prior to 24,000 years ago, and was associated with the introduction of bifacial points and microblades. Both of these now made their first appearances in Hokkaido as well as Korea (Aikens et al. 2009), with the microblades spreading onwards into the remainder of Japan (except Ryukyu), where bifaces already existed. Interestingly, this was also a period of major faunal immigration into Japan from several regions of mainland Asia, bringing in new species such as the wolf, brown bear, leopard, aurochs (wild cattle), and macaque monkeys (Van der Geer et al. 2010: 231).

Analysis of ancient DNA from skeletons excavated from several sites in Hokkaido reinforces the conclusion that these microblade-using immigrants were not the same population as the earlier makers of the edge-ground axes. Their descendants in Hokkaido continued the microblade tradition and shared a mtDNA ancestry with populations in the Amur valley in southeastern Siberia. A molecular clock traces this shared ancestry to about 22,000 years ago (Adachi et al. 2011), a date sufficiently close to the appearance of microblades in northern Japan (circa 24,000 years ago) to render these people too recent in time to have been the makers of the edge-ground axes. Instead, they were probably the main ancestors of the indigenous modern Ainu (non-Japonic-speaking) population of Hokkaido.[25] The earlier edge-ground axe users in Kyushu and Honshu were perhaps ancestral to later Jomon populations there, and to some of the indigenous (non-Yayoi) genetic components in the modern Japanese population (Chapter 8).

Were humans in Japan before 40,000 years ago? This country today has huge numbers of excavations and archaeologists. A rather staggering 14,000 Paleolithic sites are believed to exist there (Izuho 2011), including at least 1792 microblade-bearing sites (Sato and Tsutsumi 2007: 53). Were Japan really to contain convincing Lower Paleolithic sites and archaic hominin fossils, we would surely have evidence by now, as we do in China from a less intensive archaeological coverage. This suggests that Japan really was settled first by modern humans about 40,000 years ago, with an industry of large blades, transverse-bladed points and edge-ground axes, introduced by a probable sea crossing from Korea. These industries were eventually replaced by various combinations of microblades and bifacial tools, the former introduced prior to 24,000 years ago via Hokkaido. The prehistory of Japan after the last glacial maximum will be discussed later, but given its equable maritime climate it is likely that these islands offered a favored location for human occupation in the late Pleistocene, operating as a kind of refuge from the northeast Asian continental cold.

The Americas

In the fully tropical latitudes of Africa, Eurasia and Indonesia, within 23° of the Equator, the archaeological record of the earliest hominins before 0.5 million years ago is mostly limited to open air localities that contain eroding volcanic, alluvial and lacustrine sediments. The record becomes more and more dependent upon caves/rock shelters as we move into cooler latitudes in southern Africa and Eurasia, possibly because of a lesser rate of limestone solution in the cooler and drier conditions. Some of these caves contain remains of Early and Middle Pleistocene antiquity in their breccia fills, from Australopithecines in southern Africa through to *H. erectus* in China. In cool to cold climates, as Ian Gilligan (2007) has pointed out, caves can give some protection from wind chill if they open to face the sun, and we know that archaic hominins and modern humans in all pre-Neolithic periods lived in them quite intensively, in all parts of the world.

But can caves be expected to reveal the *first* presence of humans in landscapes subjected to initial settlement by early modern humans? In eastern Indonesia and Australia, some caves do indeed have records going back 50,000 years in some cases. Here, the answer would be a qualified *yes*, even though no one could ever guarantee that an excavated layer at the bottom of a deep cave was put there by absolute first generation colonists. However, we can perhaps assume that a large comfortable cave in a good location, facing the sun in cooler climates, along a route or coastline that might have been used for migration, will be likely to have been visited by the first humans to pass through. This kind of logic has already allowed me to state that Paleolithic humans most probably did not migrate from Taiwan to the Philippines through the open ocean route via the Batanes Islands.

When such logic is applied to the Americas, something becomes very obvious. The Americas, as a whole, have many limestone and eroded sandstone regions with caves/ rock shelters, and over the past century a very large number of these have been excavated, often very intensively. Yet *none* have any acceptable evidence for pre-last glacial maximum or even glacial maximum occupation. The records commence at the earliest only around 16,000 years ago. The human crossing of Beringia – the land either side of Bering Strait – occurred well after the last glacial maximum. This is powerfully reinforced by the paleoenvironmental observation that the ice-clad North American continent, beyond Alaska, was not accessible to humans attempting to migrate from Asia between 24,000 and 16,000 years ago. Impenetrable ice sheets extended then right into the sea along the west coast of Canada and along the Canadian Arctic coast to Greenland. The northern Canadian Arctic coastline was not occupied regularly until the middle Holocene (Chapter 5), and we have no indications that Paleolithic humans were able to exploit such ice-covered environments. A recent genetics-based suggestion that the Americas were first colonized from west to east, along the Arctic coast of North America, *prior* to the coldest part of the last glaciation (O'Rourke and Raff 2010), is undoubtedly interesting, but lacks any support from the archaeological record.

In fact, when we look at the Russian side of Bering Strait within the Arctic Circle, especially at the Chukotka Peninsula, we see the same absence of any convincing signs of a human presence during or before the last glacial maximum. In order to understand why, we need to examine the whole question of human penetration of high northern latitudes in Siberia.

Getting to Beringia

Late Pleistocene archaic hominins (Neanderthals and Denisovans) in northern Eurasia were evidently restricted to latitudes below about 55°N, a little north of the Altai Mountains, as discussed in Chapter 3. Modern humans with their presumably more advanced forms of clothing and shelter eventually penetrated much further north into the Arctic Circle. From here they were able to migrate into Alaska across the Bering Strait land bridge after the last glacial maximum.

However, hominins of uncertain taxonomic affinity also reached the northern coastline of Eurasia, close to the northern Ural Mountains, by soon after 40,000 years ago. Stone flakes and a worked proboscidean tusk have been directly radiocarbon dated to 36,000 years ago in a sequence of alluvial deposits at Mammontovaya Kurya, located at 66°N. A Middle Paleolithic industry of similar date exists nearby at Byzovaya. Another site much further east in Siberia, close to the delta of the Yana river at 71°N, has yielded a wild horse mandible, stone flakes, a woolly rhinoceros spear foreshaft, and carved artifacts of mammoth ivory, the foreshaft and other bones directly radiocarbon dated to about 28,000 years ago. The locations of these sites are shown in Figure 3.5.[27]

It is not entirely clear if these very northerly discoveries relate to a presence of archaic or modern humans, but none contained any blades or microblades. Yana, with its carved bone and ivory, seems likely to have been inhabited by *H. sapiens*. But could the two northern Ural sites have been the last hideouts of Neanderthals or Denisovans pushed north by invading *H. sapiens*, following the argument suggested at the end of Chapter 3? The excavators of Byzovaya actually claim Neanderthal affinities for their site, although no human bones were found. However, a 'last hideout of archaic hominins' scenario for the northern Urals is by no means impossible, albeit quite hotly debated.[28] We have a stalemate that only the discovery of human remains in these sites will resolve.

Despite these discoveries, the archaeological record for settlement before the last glacial maximum disappears east of Yana, in far northeastern Siberia. There may be a good glaciological reason for this. Northern North America and northwestern Eurasia, from Scandinavia around to the Taymyr Peninsula in Russia, are still uplifting due to a process termed isostasy, as the earth's crust beneath rebounds with the melting of the massive overburden of glacial ice. This means that ancient coastal landscapes in northern Europe and North America, with Paleolithic sites, are still above sea level, and rising. Northeastern Siberia and Beringia, on the other hand, were not glaciated extensively because their climates were too dry. There has been far less isostatic rebound here and the coastlines of 15,000 years ago are now drowned far offshore beneath the high postglacial sea, together with any coastal archaeological sites that might once have existed close in time to the last glacial maximum.

Despite this problem, it is possible to make some contextual reconstructions for getting to the Americas from knowledge of archaeological sites in inland regions of Siberia, which were never drowned by rising sea but which presumably had to be crossed. A broad summary of radiocarbon dated sites in Siberia (Brantingham et al. 2004) has concluded that humans with a large blade (but not microblade) and biface technology reached a latitude of about 60°N between 45,000 and 25,000 years ago, especially in the Altai Mountains and northwards. However, many other regions of Siberia appear to have been only minimally occupied, if occupied at all, at the peak of last glacial maximum, perhaps because of the severity of the conditions.[29]

After 25,000 years ago, at about the time of the last glacial maximum, the widespread microblade and wedge-shaped core technology made its first appearance, perhaps initially in the Altai and Baikal regions.[30] This technology appeared at the same time in Japan and the Yangzi basin in China, in the latter case with very early pottery.[31] Both Japan and the warmer regions of China could have served as refuges during the coldest climatic extremes of the Pleistocene, as did southern Europe. The general timing suggests that microblades might have been invented to cope with climatic extremes, possibly for specialized hunting equipment that utilized barbs set into slotted bone points. Their usage did continue into much warmer Holocene times in some areas of Asia and North America, but less so with the passage of time.

At this point, we must ask when and how humans migrated from central Siberia through the Chukotka Peninsula into Alaska, and what lithic technology they took with them. The Bering Strait land bridge, across which the first migrants to America are believed to have traveled, is located along the Arctic Circle at about 65–67°N (Figure 3.5 and Figure 4.1). At present, the Siberian side shows clear signs of human settlement starting only around 13,000 years ago, two millennia after the first colonists can be tracked within North America itself, and there are no sites directly adjacent to the formerly emergent parts of the land bridge itself.[32] However, the Ushki Lake sites on Kamchatka Peninsula have bifacial stemmed points at about 13,000 years ago (Ushki cultural layer 7), followed by a separate industry of microblades, wedge-shaped cores and burins by 12,600 years ago (Ushki cultural layer 6; Goebel et al. 2010). This is the same sequence that we see in central Siberia, with bifaces before microblades, but younger in time. Much further west at Berelekh, near the lower Indigirka Valley of northern Siberia, bifaces also occurred at a date similar to Ushki cultural layer 7.

The relative lateness of these dates suggests that some of the archaeological record may be under the postglacial rising sea, but the glacial maximum cold might also have kept people out of Beringia for long periods. Certainly, from a comparative perspective, it probably kept people out of the high altitude Tibetan Plateau during the last glacial maximum as well. Occupation here, above 3300 m altitude, apparently commenced around 20,000 years ago according to a mtDNA molecular clock, and around 15,000 years ago in archaeological terms.[33] The extreme cold of the last glacial maximum was a serious issue for human colonization of both regions.

Beringia today is divided by the 90 km wide and 50–60 m deep Bering Strait, between Chukotka and Alaska. Prior to 12,000 years ago, it was a vast emergent plain, up to 1000 km wide from north to south, covered with Arctic shrub vegetation and supporting bison, mammoths, horses, musk-oxen, saiga antelopes, caribou (reindeer in Eurasia), woolly rhinoceros, lions, and plentiful sea mammals (Brigham-Grette et al. 2004), all hunted by migrating humans. The coasts of the land bridge were fringed by sea ice until about 15,000 years ago, but thereafter became free of ice, allowing easier human passage (Goebel et al. 2008). This Beringian landscape extended eastwards into a partially unglaciated Alaska, beyond which stretched the enormous Laurentide ice sheet, up to 4 km thick and covering 13.4 million km² of Canada across to Greenland. South of Alaska, this ice sheet merged to its west with the Cordilleran ice sheet to form continuous ice cover right across North America to as far south as Pennsylvania. The Cordilleran ice sheet only began to melt sufficiently along its western edge to allow humans to pass south, along the coastline of British Columbia, at about 16,000 or 15,000 years ago. By 13,000 years ago, an ice-free corridor down the Great Plains to the east of the Rockies had also opened sufficiently between the two ice sheets to allow human passage southwards from Alaska and the Yukon (Figure 4.1).

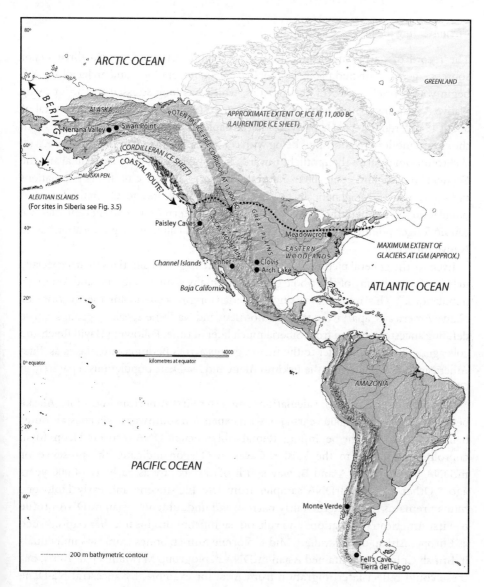

Figure 4.1 The colonization of the Americas. Extents of ice cover are only approximate, but the huge extent of the North American glaciers is evident. Background map by Multimedia Services, ANU, details added by the author.

A different possibility for settling in the Americas from Siberia would be island hopping along the Aleutian Island chain, from Kamchatka to the Alaska Peninsula. But current archaeological perspectives on these islands suggest that no settlement occurred before 7000 years ago, and not before 3500 years ago on the most westerly ones. The Aleutians were evidently settled from Alaska, not Kamchatka (Balter 2012a), during the Holocene. They cannot at present be considered a viable Pleistocene migration route from Asia.

The record of early American colonization (Figure 4.1) comes from three major sources – genetics (including ancient DNA), paleoanthropology, and archaeology. We begin with a brief review of the genetics, which has long stressed that most living Native Americans share five mtDNA haplogroups (A, B, C, D, and X), with a total of about 15 different internal haplotypes. These haplogroups are all of Asian origin, with the closest modern relationships being with central rather than far northeastern Asia.[34] Y chromosomes move the spotlight towards the Altai Mountains, Lake Baikal and the Yenisei River (Zegura et al. 2009). Naturally, however, there are no living populations in Asia who have been genetically fossilized since 15,000 years ago. Given the extent of population replacement that has occurred in northeastern Asia in recent centuries, we can no longer point to a precise spot on the map and call it an origin location for all Native Americans.

Even so, the general picture of Native American origins in Siberia is clear, especially in light of a new study of the whole genomes of many sampled Siberian and American populations.[35] This reinforces a single Siberian origin scenario for the majority of Native Americans, apart from the Eskimo-Aleut and Na-Dene-speaking groups whose defining ancestors arrived from Siberia much later in time. Following David Reich and colleagues (2012), I will refer to the first migrants across Beringia into Alaska as 'First Americans' and will discuss the Eskimo-Aleut and Na-Dene populations separately in Chapter 5.

Current molecular clock calculations suggest a First American entry into Alaska between 18,000 and 15,000 years ago, with expansion southwards via coastal routes being most likely in the beginning. Remarkably, ancient DNA recovered from fossil coprolites preserved in the Paisley Caves in Oregon indicates the presence of mtDNA haplogroups A and B, way south of the ice, by as early as 14,000 years ago.[36] Other ancient mtDNA samples from late Pleistocene and early Holocene human remains reinforce the fairly narrow and undoubtedly Asian mtDNA profile of First American populations and rule out significant origins in other regions such as Europe, Africa, or Australia.[37] Mid-Holocene human bones from two individuals in British Columbia contained Asian mtDNA haplogroup M (Malhi et al. 2007), but these could reflect later migration from Asia, for example, by ancestral Na-Dene speakers. Certainly, the First Americans appear to have brought in mtDNA haplogroups A, B, C, and D, which thereafter rose to almost complete dominance in varying combinations within the American population as a whole, from Alaska to Tierra del Fuego.

Some geneticists observe that the modern Native American mtDNA profile is sufficiently differentiated from related lineages in Siberia to suggest a population bottleneck with a strong founder effect, perhaps through a long period of relative isolation in a last glacial maximum refuge around the Sea of Okhotsk or the Sea of Japan.[38] This would allow the possibility of several subsidiary episodes of movement emanating from a large but genetically fairly homogeneous homeland region, similar to that suggested for modern humans leaving Africa in Chapter 3.[39] However, such subsidiary movements might again be hard to detect since it is quite possible that some early mtDNA or NRY lineages died out, as suggested for Skhul and Qafzeh, thus becoming detectable only through ancient DNA analysis. For instance, a burial dated to over 12,000 years ago from On Your Knees Cave in Alaska carried mtDNA subhaplogroup D4h3, which only exists today in a derived form in South America (Kemp et al. 2007). This suggests that not all First Americans transmitted their DNA directly to modern in-place descendants.

Although a single overall First American ancestral population is currently favored by geneticists, suggestions of more complex multiple migrations from Asia into America have come from the paleoanthropological record, as for out of Africa scenarios. Skeletal remains seem to be giving us a better, or at least different, reality in both of these crucial migratory situations than living genetic profiles. Hubbe and colleagues (2010) suggest two population entries between 17,000 and 15,000 years ago, based on measurable differences in ancient crania. The oldest 'Paleoindian' crania tend to be longer and to have more protruding faces than more recent ones, which in turn are more similar to contemporary eastern Asian populations.[40] A newly-reported female skeleton from Arch Lake in New Mexico, dated to 11,500 years ago, is stated to be a good representative of the early group, despite being rather short and broad across the skull. Unfortunately, her bones contained no ancient DNA, but her analysts (Owsley et al. 2010) describe her as "different from other ancient American skeletons in some respects, similar in others, and strongly differentiated from modern Native Americans."

These cranial differences raise an important question: why are the Asian resemblances greater with the younger remains? De Azevedo and colleagues (2011) perhaps resolve the controversy to a degree. They consider a similar database to Hubbe and colleagues, but draw the conclusion that there was only one significant but fairly heterogeneous First American migration from Beringia, followed by continuing gene flow with Asia concentrated in Arctic latitudes. As we will see in Chapter 5, Na-Dene and Eskimo-Aleut populations migrated from northeastern Siberia through Alaska into Canada during the Holocene, so they might well have been responsible for this later gene flow. However, their descendants generally remained in the north of the Americas and cannot be seen as the source of any significant secondary Asian influence in South America. Even so, this could explain why younger remains, at least in North America, are more Asian in morphology than earlier ones.

Perhaps we are close to a promising concordance of the linguistic, genetic, and archaeological evidence for the immediate origins of the First Americans that could eventually win the day, but exactly how this concordance will be structured remains to be seen. The situation has very obvious similarities with the debate over modern human migrations from Africa into Eurasia. At present, it is difficult to link the linguistic evidence for three successive First American, Na-Dene, and Eskimo-Aleut migrations with the geographically rather scattered results available from genetics and paleoanthropology.[41] But the main structural components that created American prehistory are becoming clearer as modern genetic research makes further progress into the realms of autosomal and ancient DNA.

The Rapid Unfolding of American Colonization

The story so far is that the first human colonists of the Americas crossed Beringia into Alaska about 16,000 years ago and began to move quickly down the ice-free western coast of North America towards California. By about 13,000 years ago, other groups were able to pass through an ice-free inland corridor from interior Alaska into the Great Plains and the eastern United States. Humans had reached the southern coastline of Chile by 14,000 years ago, and soon after as far as Tierra del Fuego. How could such a rapid movement have happened?

The answer might be demographic growth in extremely conducive conditions. A population of 100 founders growing at a fairly slow rate in healthy circumstances could easily reach 10 million people in 1000 years – sufficient to cover all of the Americas with an average human population density of 1 person/km². Such a high density is, of course, absolutely impossible for hunter-gatherer Pleistocene populations across both continents, but the point needs to be made. Like Australia and Maori New Zealand (Walter et al. 2010), early population growth and movement could have been very rapid indeed, especially if people targeted migrating herds of animals prior to their extinction, rather than settling down within restricted territories as specialist plant collectors.[42]

We know from the colonizations of Japan and Australia that people certainly had a knowledge of seacraft by the time the Americas were settled. The west coastal North American 'kelp corridor' that runs down to Baja California would have encouraged marine exploitation, with its rich shellfish, fish, marine mammal, seabird and seaweed resources. This is demonstrated by the finding of 13,000-year-old human occupation and skeletal remains on the Channel Islands of southern California, then perhaps 10 km offshore.[43]

What about the continental routes followed by the migrants after they arrived in the Americas? Having arrived in Alaska, how did they penetrate other regions to the south? Most of interior Canada was still inaccessible until as recently as 13,000 years ago, still under the Laurentide ice sheet, except for the western coastline and the ice-free corridor running down the eastern side of the Rockies. Both of these routes would have given access to the rest of the Americas, via the Isthmus of Panama, down to a still fairly frigid Tierra del Fuego. The northern coastline of Canada, Greenland, and the territories today occupied by Inuit peoples did not become available for human colonization until about 5000 years ago (Chapter 5).

In Alaska itself, the archaeological record starts at about 14,000 years ago with a most interesting duality. A number of sites belong to the Denali Complex and contain wedge-shaped cores and distinctive microblades, together with small bifaces. These are paralleled in some contemporary sites in Siberia, such as Ushki cultural layer 6 in Kamchatka and Diuktai on the Lena River, the latter located roughly 2000 km southwest of Bering Strait.[44] A second complex, the Nenana, lacks microblades and wedge-shaped cores and is characterized by large blades, scrapers, and small teardrop-shaped and triangular bifacial points. At Ushki, this Nenana-like biface industry is older (i.e., in cultural layer 7) than the Denali-like microblade industry.

In apparent agreement with this relative chronology, the Nenana biface complex preceded the Denali in some regions of central Alaska, as demonstrated by the succession of tools at the Dry Creek site in the Nenana Valley itself. Although the Denali occupation at Swan Point in the Tanana Valley is dated to about 14,000 years ago, hence apparently contemporary with Nenana, it appears that true microblades, as opposed to blade-like flakes, were not present in the basal layers of this site (Yesner and Pearson 2002). These observations suggest that the Nenana biface industry arrived in Alaska slightly before the Denali microblade industry. This is important for Na-Dene origins, as we will see in Chapter 5, given that the archaeology of Na-Dene-speaking regions was closely associated with microblades during the Holocene. While some archaeologists regard biface and microblade industries as reflecting different hunting activities in different seasons (Robinson 2008), this does not rule out separate origins and migrations of their users from Siberia.

In my view, the spread of the large blade and biface technology over most of the Americas, right down to Tierra del Fuego, suggests that this was the first to arrive and obtain a positive foothold. Microblade technology never expanded beyond northern and western North America, suggesting that it arrived with slightly later populations, who found the new continent already occupied. The oldest dated archaeological sites in the Americas, south of Alaska, are unequivocally associated with bifaces and large blades, not microblades. Meadowcroft rock shelter in Pennsylvania was occupied by users of small bifaces and prismatic blades (no micro-blades) about 15,000 years ago (Adovasio and Pedler 2004). Similar dates come from the partly waterlogged site of Monte Verde, located at 42°S in the southern coastal region of Chile, a rather staggering 16,000 km in a straight line from Alaska. The Monte Verde people lived next to a small creek about 30 km from the contemporary coastline and constructed wooden shelters that might have been covered with mastodon skins, traces of which were found in the site. They also imported medicinal plants from many kilometers away and manufactured wooden fire drills, spears, and a few small stone lanceolate bifaces.[45]

Although the 14,500 year ago date for Monte Verde has led to claims that humans must have reached Alaska before the last glacial maximum (LGM), in order to cover the 16,000 km distance between these two regions, I see absolutely no good reason why a mobile hunter-gatherer population equipped with good hunting technology and hunting dogs, a desire to follow migrating herds of animals, and reasonable boats should not have made its way down the long western edge of the Americas in just two short millennia between 16,000 and 14,000 years ago. Recently, I had the eye-opening experience of visiting my ANU colleague Chris Carter when he was conducting an archaeological project near Arica, in the Atacama desert of northern Chile. Occasional valleys extend towards the Pacific Ocean through this absolute desert, which is totally without plateau-level surface water. But these valleys carry vegetation and animals supported by significant underground water resources that can be tapped by farmers today, even though there are no permanent flowing rivers. Any humans migrating down this desert coastline 14,000 years ago, across 25° of latitude from northern Peru to central Chile, would perhaps have left small fishing settlements at the mouths of the more enticing valleys and sent on scouts quickly to find others. As well as the coastline, they could also have traveled along the better watered valleys at higher altitude further inland, beyond the desert proper. A few hundred pioneers doubling their population every 50 or 100 years or so would have had little difficulty in traversing such a distance very quickly, and keeping contact with other groups left behind. Indeed, Meltzer (2009: 213) estimates the rate for Clovis expansion in North America to have been 10–20 km per year, sufficient in theory to cover 20,000 km in only 1000 years. The Clovis people themselves did not migrate beyond central America, but others obviously did.

The Clovis Complex itself, dated between 13,200 and 12,800 years ago and one of the major markers of Paleoindian migration in the Americas, is distributed across the central and eastern United States with outliers southwards into Mexico and as far as Panama.[46] It lacks microblades, although it does have large blades and a few wedge-shaped cores. The classic Clovis artifact is an elongated and very finely made fluted bifacial point that presumably served as a projectile tip. For a time, it was believed that Clovis people were the very first migrants into North America, but the increasing archaeological record now raises doubts about this. Even so, Clovis was probably the first human manifestation in much of the United States east of the Rockies. Hamilton and Buchanan (2007) see it as representing a rapid population movement from the north, but Beck and Jones (2010) prefer an origin in the southern United States. The Debra L. Friedkin site in Texas offers a biface industry with end thinning that could represent a Clovis ancestor, perhaps dated back as far as 15,500 years ago (Waters et al. 2011a). Most archaeologists also relate Clovis back in terms of ultimate origin to the Nenana Complex in Alaska.[47] Both Clovis and Nenana have similar bone and ivory rods, but Nenana points do not have the characteristic Clovis fluting, which appears to have been an innovation south of the ice.

Wherever it began, Clovis clearly spread very quickly, until it funneled into other expressions in the narrow tropical isthmus of central America. Fluted points related to Clovis appeared in the far south of South America by 13,000 years ago, particularly at Fell's Cave in Patagonia. In North America, however, Clovis points did not spread into the western United States, where a different class of 'Western stemmed' projectile points occurred in the intermontane basins of the Rocky Mountains and in the Californian Channel Islands, the latter reachable only by boat. Similar stemmed points were contemporary with Clovis points in the Paisley Caves in Oregon, quite far west of the Clovis distribution, and also became widespread in South America.[48]

Some Clovis sites have remains of butchered and even unbutchered mammoths and bison, and no less than 13 butchered mammoths were excavated at the Lehner site in Arizona. Clovis people also transported raw materials on occasions over 500 km, attesting to their considerable mobility. In the face of such hunting prowess, one might ask if the First Americans really exterminated all those mastodon, mammoth, ground sloth, horse and camel populations, all presumably quite naïve in the face of a brand new situation of human predation, together eventually with their native predators like the saber tooth feline and the dire wolf? This issue has been a source of considerable controversy in recent years, as in Australia. It is very apparent to me that humans had a severe impact on such large mammals very early in the settlement sequence, possibly through both effective hunting and the use of fire. The First Americans brought Eurasian dogs, which rapidly became a major food source and hunting aid, as apparently in Upper Paleolithic Eurasia (Chapter 3).[49] Recent dating of the bones and fossilized dung of the extinct North American megafauna suggests that many became extinct suspiciously soon after the date of human arrival, with a lot of activity between 15,000 and 13,500 years ago.[50] Mastodon apparently survived to 11,500 years ago, according to direct AMS C14 dates on collagen and tooth enamel. A mastodon bone point embedded in a mastodon rib dated to 13,800 years ago from the Manis site in Washington reinforces human intention in its demise.[51]

Over 25 years ago, Joseph Greenberg suggested that all Native American language families, apart from Na-Dene and Eskimo-Aleut, belonged to a single macro-family that he termed *Amerind*.[52] This suggestion has perhaps been more disputed than any other in the recent history of linguistics, simply because Greenberg did not follow certain principles of linguistic comparison at the proto-language level. From the perspective of this chapter, however, what matters is whether Greenberg was correct in a historical sense. The indication that the Amerind languages (excluding Na-Dene and Eskimo-Aleut) could have developed from a single founder proto-language, introduced by the First American biological population into the Americas via Beringia around 16,000 years ago, is of great significance.

My own observation on this linguistic issue is that the Americas were obviously settled at a relatively recent date by Old World standards, sufficiently recently at circa 16,000 years ago to allow some extremely faint shadows of shared ancestry to survive between major language families that are now far separated in space. The Americas were also settled quickly, from Alaska to Tierra del Fuego, meaning that the language families recognized today form a rake-like arrangement of independent branches rather than a rooted tree. The foundation spread that led to initial linguistic differentiation was too fast to allow a gradual geographical unfolding of subgroup-defining innovations. Greenberg's Amerind might be essentially unverifiable, but that need not make it wrong.

Notes

1. See also Peterson 2003 for other remarkable photographs by Donald Thomson of traditional Aboriginal attire in northern Australia.
2. See Demeter et al. 2012 for Tam Pa Ling, Barker et al. 2007 and Higham et al. 2009 for the dating of Niah, and Détroit et al. 2004 for Tabon. Curnoe et al. 2012 report the discovery of a human cranium with an extremely wide face dated to 11,500 years ago from Longlin Cave in Guangxi Province, southern China, but it is unclear if it represents a late-surviving archaic species or a hitherto-unsuspected early *sapiens* dispersal separate from that which survives in living Asian populations.
3. Kaifu et al. 2008 demonstrate the reality of *erectus* extinction in Java, but not its date.
4. Irwin 1992: 26, 2010.
5. Sahultime 2007; Hiscock 2008: 130.
6. For instance, Habu 2004: 236; Ikawa-Smith 2009; McGrail 2010.

7. Birdsell 1977; Butlin 1993. The trip to Australia from Timor or Roti would be about 400 km today.
8. Terrell 1986: 188–94 gives an excellent account.
9. Birdsell 1957: 67. O'Connell and Allen 2012 qualify this estimate to reflect the impact of climatic changes. Henn et al. 2012 suggest that early modern human colonizing populations doubled in size every generation until regional population groupings of about 1000 people had been created, after which birth rates dropped.
10. Bulbeck et al. 2006; Pietrusewsky 2006; Bellwood 2007a.
11. Matsumura and Hudson 2005; Matsumura and Oxenham 2013.
12. Détroit 2006; Widianto 2006.
13. Storm 2001; Xu et al. 2012.
14. Macaulay et al. 2005; Thangaraj et al. 2005; Perry and Dominy 2009.
15. See Merriwether et al. 2005; Hudjashov et al. 2007; Mona et al. 2009; Pugach et al. 2012.
16. Spriggs 1997; Bellwood et al. 1998; Szabo et al. 2007; Ono et al. 2009; O'Connor et al. 2011a.
17. O'Connell et al. 2010; O'Connor 2010.
18. Habgood and Franklin 2008; Balme et al. 2009.
19. For Tasmania see Allen 1996; Gilligan 2008.
20. Bailey et al. 1989; Headland and Reid 1989; and see a series of papers in *Human Ecology* 1991.
21. For example Endicott and Bellwood 1991; Denham et al. 2009.
22. Bird et al. 2005; Bellwood 2007a: 33–6; Wurster et al. 2010.
23. Gilligan 2008; Hiscock 2008: 115.
24. Tsutsumi 2012; Yamaoka 2012.
25. Seong 2008; Morisaki 2011.
26. Hammer et al. 2006; Karafet et al. 2009 discuss the genetic ancestry of the modern Japanese.
27. For these sites see Pavlov et al. 2001; Pitulko et al. 2004; 2012; Slimak et al. 2011, 2012; Zwyns et al. 2012.
28. Zwyns et al. 2012 claim that the Byzovaya tools are Upper Paleolithic based partly on a presence of bifacial points. The issue is still under debate (Slimak et al. 2012).
29. Graf 2009, 2010 for the Yenisei valley.
30. Goebel 2002; Kuzmin et al. 2007: 2.
31. Shelach 2012; Wu et al. 2012.
32. Goebel 2002, 2004; Dillehay 2009; Meltzer 2009.
33. Zhao et al. 2009 for mtDNA; Brantingham et al. 2010 for archaeology.
34. Kidd et al. 2011; Long and Bortolini 2011; Southerton 2013.
35. Reich et al. 2012.
36. Gilbert et al. 2008; Jenkins et al. 2012.
37. Raff et al. 2011. Paleoindian origins from Europe, via the Upper Paleolithic Solutrean industry of France (circa 20,000 years ago), are sometimes argued, but have little support amongst specialists of this period (Balter 2012b).
38. Tamm et al. 2007; Volodko et al. 2008; Long and Bortolini 2011.
39. As implied by Perego et al. 2009; Ray et al. 2010.
40. Neves and Hubbe 2005; Klein 2009a; Pucciarelli et al. 2010.
41. In this regard, Reich et al. 2012 considered samples mainly from Central and South America, with very few from Canada and none at all from the United States.
42. Kelly and Todd 1988; Anderson and Gillam 2000.

43. Erlandson et al. 2007, 2011.

44. Hoeffecker et al. 1993 discuss Denali. Ackerman 2007; Kuzmin et al. 2007; Goebel et al. 2010 discuss the Siberian sites.

45. Dillehay 2009; Meltzer 2009; Pettitt 2013: 170–1.

46. Collins and Lohse 2004; Waters and Stafford 2007; Meltzer 2009, 2013; Beck and Jones 2010.

47. E.g. Hoeffecker et al. 1993; Dixon 2001; Goebel 2004; Matson 2007; Dillehay 2009.

48. Erlandson et al. 2011 (Channel Islands); Jenkins et al. 2012 (Paisley Cave).

49. Leonard et al. 2002; Tito et al. 2011.

50. E.g. Buck and Bard 2007; Gill et al. 2009; Tuniz et al. 2009. Mastodon extinction (below) is discussed by Woodman and Beavan 2009; Waters et al. 2011b.

51. However, a recent global analysis of Quaternary extinctions (Prescott et al. 2012) points to a combination of both climatic and human factors in these events.

52. Greenberg et al. 1986; Greenberg 1987.

Chapter 5
Hunter-Gatherer Migrations in a Warming Postglacial World

Chapter 4 followed the migrations of sapient hunter-gatherers into previously uninhabited regions, down to and including the colonization of the Americas, an event which occurred during the phase of climatic warming after the last glacial maximum. This chapter discusses other postglacial episodes of hunter-gatherer migration, continuing into recent millennia during the Holocene. It focuses on late Pleistocene population advances into formerly glaciated regions in Western Eurasia, on Na-Dene and Eskimo-Aleut migration into North America, on the colonization of the early Holocene 'green' Sahara, and on population adjustments (or absence thereof) in many regions as continental shelves were drowned by rising postglacial sea levels. It finishes with an examination of a possible episode of hunter-gatherer migration through much of Holocene Australia.

Postglacial warming presents us with one of the major questions of our modern world. What will happen to Holocene climates in coming millennia, even centuries or decades? Will world climate eventually revert to another ice age, or will it continue to get hotter with continuing carbon dioxide and methane production as a result of uncontrolled human exploitation of fossil fuels and other sources of greenhouse gas? Unfortunately, I cannot foretell the future. But I am sure that the postglacial warming that followed the last glacial maximum allowed our species to undergo unprecedented cultural and demographic expansion. This expansion still continues today, but now the environmental consequences are far more serious.

The colonization of the Americas was the greatest migration 'event' of the early postglacial world, assisted by a tame animal, the Eurasian dog. This colonization was a direct product of postglacial climatic amelioration, which allowed human migration through formerly impenetrable Arctic latitudes. As postglacial temperatures warmed, humans in Siberia were offered a few final millennia of existence of the Bering Strait land bridge combined with a relatively ice-free route into North America. As glacial-era land bridges gradually became submerged, people turned to an increasing use of boats.

As the Americas were being settled for the first time, other populations across the Atlantic moved from refuge regions in southern Europe back into the newly deglaciated northern latitudes. They also expanded from other refuges such as the Jordan Valley in the Levant and perhaps the Altai Mountains into regions of Asia that had

First Migrants: Ancient Migration in Global Perspective, First Edition. Peter Bellwood.
© Peter Bellwood. Published 2013 by John Wiley & Sons, Ltd.

previously been too cold for glacial maximum settlement. It is likely that some of these groups had dogs too.[1]

Seen in perspective, the colonization of the Americas was just the beginning of the massive investment in cultural expansion and migration by *Homo sapiens* during the postglacial millennia. There followed the several developments of food production and population expansion in all inhabited continents except Australia, followed later by the rises and falls of the ancient and medieval civilizations with their many attached episodes of population dislocation. World population grew from a possible five million at the end of the Paleolithic to seven billion today.[2]

Although agriculturalist migration has been a major phenomenon of the past 10,000 years, hunter-gatherer migration never really ceased. It can be tracked in some regions virtually into the colonial era, even though hunters have been allowed less and less land from which to make a living, or to escape into, as farmers expanded into their territories. Most hunters eventually became assimilated or squeezed into ever-smaller territories in the agricultural latitudes, such that very few traditional hunters and gatherers today can still subsist entirely from their indigenous resources. Nevertheless, the past 15,000 years have seen some quite extensive episodes of hunter-gatherer territorial expansion, especially in cold or dry regions beyond the focused interest of farmers. In some cases to be discussed in this chapter, such as the migrations of the Eskimo-Aleut and Apachean populations of North America, these hunter-gatherer expansions overlapped with the arrival of Europeans.

What has been rather rare in the recent recorded history of migration is any clear instance of a hunter-gatherer population replacing another one of similar density, technology, and economy, throughout a fully inhabited region (Krantz 1976). Most recorded hunter-gatherer migrations, such as those of the Eskimo-Aleut and Apacheans, were into territories either uninhabited or mostly abandoned by their previous inhabitants. This does not mean that such population replacements could never have occurred amongst *sapiens* hunter-gatherers in prehistoric times. But they would surely have required some form of demographic or technological advantage if they were to succeed.

Postglacial Recolonizations in Northern Eurasia

One very significant point stands out about the settlement of the ice-bound coasts of northern Alaska, Canada, and Greenland. No settlement occurred there until the peak phase of Holocene warmth, dating in these regions to around 5000 years ago. The Paleoeskimo colonization that occurred at this time eventually failed thereafter as the climate and landscape froze partially over again. The Thule Inuit had to wait until the next warm phase (the 'Medieval warming') before they could migrate into the same landscape, after AD 1200. First American populations 15,000 years ago did not have access to the full Arctic coastline of the Americas because of the permanent ice cover, and the ice-bound coasts of northern Europe and Asia were also unoccupied through the last glacial maximum. The permanent postglacial settlement of the northern Eurasian coastline by *H. sapiens* occurred, like that in North America, only during the Holocene.

In far northeastern Asia, too dry for major glacier formation, human occupation during the last glacial maximum appears to have been restricted to below 63°N, around the latitude of northern Kamchatka, quite some distance south of Bering Strait and the Arctic Circle. As discussed in Chapter 4, no one appears to have lived in Beringia at this time. Occupation was probably concentrated in coastal and/or relatively warm refuge localities such as Japan and the Altai. In the wetter climatic conditions of northern Europe and northwestern Asia, thick glacial maximum ice descended to reach central England (52°N), and extended as far east as the Taymyr Peninsula in northern Russia. These ice sheets began to melt about 20,000 years ago, encouraged by the warm Gulf Stream that enters the Norwegian Sea from the Caribbean. But the human population distribution in Europe was still affected by lingering glacial conditions until about 15,000 years ago, and it appears that most populations tended to huddle in warm southerly refuges close to the Mediterranean.

This is revealed to us by an analysis of many hundreds of C14 dates, plotted per millennium as proxies for latitudinal densities of human population between 25,000 and 11,500 years ago. It suggests five main phases of hunter-gatherer population distribution and northward migration in western Europe:

1. During the last glacial maximum, 25,000–19,500 years ago, populations were concentrated in caves and rock shelters in relatively warm refuge areas in Iberia and southwestern France;
2. Between 19,500 and 16,000 years ago, population expansion began from northern Iberia and southern France into continental Europe;
3. Between 16,000 and 14,000 years ago, northward expansion was at its most rapid. Settlement reached as far north as the British Isles and the north European Plain;
4. Between 14,000 and 12,900 years ago, recolonization was virtually complete, so this was a period of relative population stability;
5. Between 12,900 and 11,500 years ago, there was a sharp climatic decline with a return to glacial climatic conditions during the Younger Dryas. Populations apparently declined quite sharply in numbers.[3]

It might be asked if these late Pleistocene population movements, so clear in the archaeological record, can still be traced in the genetics of modern Europeans. The authors of the aforementioned study claimed a major genetic significance for this recolonization based on use of a molecular clock for mtDNA haplogroups. However, more recent mtDNA lineage time depths calculated using a slightly different molecular clock by Soares et al. (2010) place only 3 out of 16 major European mtDNA haplogroups within the 19,500–14,000-year time span for major human migration northwards. No less than six haplogroups date to between 13,000 and 6000 years ago, long after these migrations had ceased.

While the teams involved in this research argue against any importance for Neolithic migration in European population history, I will enter the debate from a very different perspective in Chapter 7. Current genetic data, especially from ancient DNA, do not make modern Europeans mainly the descendants of Mesolithic Europeans and there is no genetic evidence for population growth or significant migration during the European Mesolithic. Another genetics team (Garcia et al. 2011b) has attempted to find evidence for this postglacial recolonization in mtDNA profiles from northern Iberia, but without success. Postglacial population migration within Europe certainly happened, but not necessarily with significant long-term effect on the modern European population as a whole.[4]

What is striking from the aforementioned archaeological record from Europe is that the chronological pattern is almost identical to that for the First American migration into the Americas – a relentless push starting also around 16,000 years ago as the doors to new territory gradually opened. Similar movements led to the reoccupation of abandoned regions of western Asia, particularly during the Geometric Kebaran phase that started around 16,500 years ago in the Levant. South America and Australia did not have such strong glaciation as Eurasia and North America, but the glacial cold still had a major impact. Several regional plots of C14 dates for Australia and Tasmania indicate a substantial decrease in human activity through the duration of the last glacial maximum.[5] The southwest Tasmanian population peaked after it, as in Europe, perhaps reflecting a cool temperate adaptation to warming postglacial temperatures. Like the First Americans, Tasmanian populations would have benefitted directly from the time lag between deglaciation and its eventual environmental repercussions, in that a warming climate would have aided movement and hunting in what was essentially still a fairly open landscape with good hunting resources. However, population numbers and densities in mainland Australia only increased intensively within the past 5000 years, as I will discuss subsequently.

We might also ask if such postglacial population adjustments occurred in Arctic as opposed to temperate Europe. As in Arctic Canada and Greenland, the retreating ice sheets here would not have allowed easy human access beyond the Arctic Circle until at least the onset of the Holocene. Recent research in northern Finland and Norway reveals an initial postglacial occupation about 11,500 years ago, following the climatic warming after the end of the Younger Dryas mini-glaciation.[6] There is an important body of information concerning the history of the Uralic language family that is also potentially very relevant for this issue. This family includes Hungarian, Finnish, Estonian, and also the languages of some very widespread traditional hunters and gatherers, many converted recently to reindeer herding. These include the Saami and the Samoyedic-speaking Nenets and Nganasan, who occupy the Arctic coastline from northern Scandinavia eastwards to the Taymyr Peninsula.[7] The linguistic homeland of the Uralic language family appears to have been in the region between the Urals and the Yenisei River (Figure 5.1). The relative dating and traditional hunting and gathering lifestyles associated with its most northern speakers make it a good candidate to record a mid-Holocene colonization of the Arctic coastline, under conditions of maximum postglacial warmth.

A linguistic chronology for the migration of Uralic speakers is given by linguist Vaclav Blažek, who suggests that early Uralic and the ancestral Yukaghir languages of the Kolyma Basin in eastern Siberia separated about 6600 BC. Uralic languages then began to spread west of the Urals after 4000 BC, their speakers eventually spreading

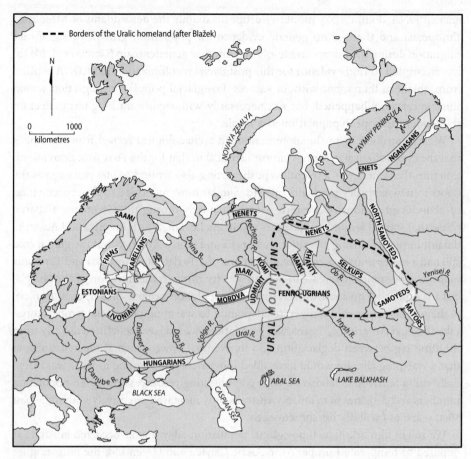

Figure 5.1 Suggested early migrations of the speakers of Uralic languages, after Blažek 2013b with minor modifications, reprinted courtesy of the author. Map production by Multimedia Services, ANU.

through the upper Volga basin to reach the Arctic and Baltic coasts, relatively recently perhaps in the case of the ancestral Saami.[8] Others, ancestral Samoyedic speakers, spread eastwards towards the Taymyr Peninsula. Some southerly groups close to the Urals eventually came into contact with Tocharian- and Indo-Iranian-speaking peoples (Chapter 7), and others in Europe became influenced by loans from Germanic and Baltic languages.

If this reconstruction is reasonable, then the northern Uralic speakers could have been the equivalents of the Paleoeskimos – early colonists of Arctic coastlines as they became available through summer ice melt during the Holocene. Sewn reindeer clothing (with the fur inside) probably assisted both movements, as did dogs. But the Uralic populations never developed such specialized maritime economies as the Paleoeskimos or the Inuit, and remained more terrestrial in orientation. Their early boating skills appear to have been quite impressive from linguistic reconstructions (Decsy 1990), and could have assisted rapid colonization along rivers.

After the First Americans: Further Migrations Across Bering Strait

We now move back to the Americas to examine Holocene migrations across Bering Strait, after the First American colonization discussed in Chapter 4. Two major North American language families, Na-Dene and Eskimo-Aleut, were carried from Siberia across Bering Strait into Alaska later in time than the First American (Amerind) migration. Both, unlike the Amerind language families, have living linguistic relatives in Siberia. Both also generated long-distance episodes of hunter-gatherer migration (Thule Eskimo and Apachean) during the past millennium.

Na-Dene and Yeniseian

American linguist Edward Sapir coined the term *Na-Dene* early last century to include a number of languages in the western part of North America. The main grouping, that occupies a very large interior region of Alaska and western Canada, is termed Athapaskan. This has offshoots on the coasts of Oregon and northern California and in the US Southwest, the latter including Navajo and Apache of Arizona, New Mexico, and adjacent regions (Figure 5.2). Related to the Athapaskan languages are Eyak and Tlingit of the coastlines of southern Alaska and northern British Columbia. The whole group makes up the Na-Dene family (Greenberg et al. 1986).

Most interestingly, recent research has led to linguistic suggestions that the Na-Dene languages are quite closely related to a group of languages termed Yeniseian in central Siberia, located on the middle Yenisei River (see location in Figure 7.6).[9] Today, only one Yeniseian language survives, called Ket, but at least five others died out during the nineteenth century. The Siberian Ket are now located more than 4000 km west of their Na-Dene relatives, the intervening terrain having been settled in recent millennia by Tungus and Turkic-speaking hunters and herders. Merritt Ruhlen (1998) was able to find several cognates shared between Ne-Dene and Yeniseian, although the two populations today no longer share any obvious DNA links, and the Na-Dene have similar mtDNA lineages to neighboring Native American populations.[10]

The explanation for this situation in terms of human migration is still debated. Linguistic borrowing alone as an explanation for the Yeniseian and Na-Dene sharings, owing to the great distance involved, is out of the question. An explanation involving shared ancestry and migration is more acceptable.

As discussed in Chapter 4, archaeologists recognize a distribution of microblade technology in northern North America, commencing after the initial spread of the large blade and biface technology that gave rise to Clovis. This microblade complex is first represented at the end of the Pleistocene (circa1 4,000–12,000 years ago) by the Denali industry in Alaska. Microblade technology then spread south during the early Holocene to the central coast of British Columbia, with outliers eventually appearing further south in coastal Oregon and northern California. Unlike Clovis and related bifacial point technologies, microblade technology remained restricted throughout its prehistory to these regions of northern and western North America. As discussed in

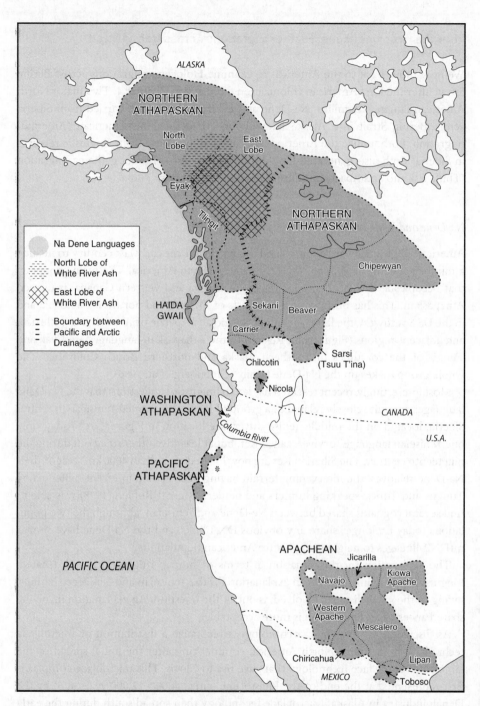

Figure 5.2 The distributions of Na-Dene languages and White River volcanic ash.
Reproduced with minor modifications from Matson and Magne 2013, courtesy of the authors.
Original map by S. Matson.

Chapter 4, the explosive spread of Clovis and related bifacial point complexes elsewhere in North America perhaps usurped any chances for further spread by microblade-using populations. It is also possible that microblade technology belonged to a specific barbed projectile technology for hunting, rather than plant collection, in cold northern latitudes where hunted meat was more important in the diet than collected plant foods.

Did microblades and ancestral Na-Dene languages spread together across Bering Strait from Siberia into Alaska? The North American microblade occurrences are very similar in their distribution to the Na-Dene languages, including Athapaskan, with the exception of the very recent Apachean migration into the US Southwest. A terminal Pleistocene or early Holocene origin for the Na-Dene languages is favored by archaeologists David Meltzer (2009: 193) and Ben Potter (2010). Linguistically, Na-Dene is unlikely to have a time depth over 8500 years, with Athapaskan proper having far less, but this time depth is still reasonable for early Holocene dispersal.[11] Indeed, James Kari (2010) makes a case for very slow linguistic change ('geolinguistic conservatism', reflecting a high intensity of interaction) to offer a possibly very early Holocene origin for the Na-Dene family as a whole, which would fit well with the microblade chronology. Genetic evidence does not throw direct light on these questions, although recent whole-genome analysis of single nucleotide polymorphisms suggests that the Na-Dene populations are distinct from Eskimo-Aleuts and 'First Americans', albeit more closely related to the latter, and could share a fairly high degree of common ancestry with Chinese populations.[12]

The Athapaskan languages proper underwent their main dispersal several millennia after the initial arrival of Na-Dene ancestors. R.G. Matson and Marty Magne trace the ancestry of the existing Athapaskan languages to a homeland located at about 2000 BC in the Yukon Territory of Canada and adjacent regions of Alaska and British Columbia (Figure 5.2). They note that archaeological sites associated with northern Athapaskan populations still have microblades into quite recent times, although they do not claim any specific continuity from much earlier complexes such as Denali.[13]

How can one explain the relationship between Na-Dene and Yeniseian? Often, an assumption is made that populations like the Yeniseians, who live in small pockets surrounded completely by unrelated groups, are stay-at-home survivors from a once more widespread distribution that has been submerged by subsequent migrations. A hypothesis based on this observation might thus place the Na-Dene homeland in central or eastern Asia. It is rather less likely that Yeneiseian somehow leap-frogged all the way to its current location from somewhere in northeastern Asia, although such leap-frogging is known in the histories of Turkic speakers in Siberia, Hmong and Mien in Southeast Asia, and many Amazonian populations. In these cases, very long distance migrations of mostly pastoralist or agriculturalist groups to circumscribed destinations occurred over quite short periods of time, often involving leap-frogging over intervening and unrelated groups. The Apacheans to be discussed later appear to have done likewise.

However, linguist Alexander Vovin 2000 has persuasively argued that the Yeniseian languages preserve traces of a former more widespread distribution in central Asia, preceding Turkic and Mongolian settlement in many areas and perhaps providing the linguistic source for the widespread term *khan* (leader). A Yeniseian language was perhaps also spoken by the Xiongnu warriors and pastoralists who afflicted the northern frontiers of the Chinese Empire during the Qin and Han dynasties, after 250 BC, persuading First Emperor Qin Shi Huang Di to construct his version of the Great Wall. Unfortunately, the Chinese sources on the Xiongnu are rather slim and ambiguous, and other linguists associate the Xiongnu language with Turkic or Mongolian. But we return to Yeniseian again later, in connection with the Neolithic prehistory of central Asia and the rather contentious search for Indo-European origins via migrations through that region.

Whatever the ultimate linguistic links, the arrival and dispersal of the ancestral Na-Dene speakers in North America offers a particularly interesting example of a postglacial hunter-gatherer migration, subsequent to that of the First Americans and far more constrained in its eventual distribution. Although reservations exist about the apparent concordance of the archaeological dates for microblades and the linguistic dates for Na-Dene origins, there is sufficient agreement to support a secondary population movement from Siberia into North America at some time between 12,000 and 9000 years ago.

The Apachean Migration

The Athapaskans also underwent a much more recent leap-frogging migration, covering 3000 km from Canada into the US Southwest. This was the Apachean migration, that led the ancestors of the modern Navajo, Apache, and related groups into Arizona, New Mexico, and western Texas. With the Thule Inuit migration (see following text), it offers us one of the longest-distance recorded migrations by hunters and gatherers in recent prehistory.

The details of this Apachean migration have also been carefully reconstructed by Matson and Magne (2007). One ultimate trigger for population movement, far to the north in Yukon Territory, might have been a massive eruption that produced the White River ash shower about AD 800. Perhaps this caused human movement to the south, with a kind of domino effect that eventually split the ancestral Apachean population from its Carrier and Chipewyan (Athapaskan) linguistic relatives in southwestern Canada. The Apachean migration then followed a route through the intermontane basins of the Rockies, eventually emerging through northern Wyoming into the western fringes of the Great Plains. As pedestrian (pre-horse) hunters of bison, elk, and deer, ancestral Apachean groups reached the US Southwest by about AD 1450 (Figure 5.2). Although horses existed in North America during the Pleistocene, they did not survive the Paleoindian period, and the ethnographic-period horses of the Americas were introduced in the sixteenth century by the Spanish.

As they entered the terrain of the former Pueblo cultures of New Mexico and southern Colorado, the ancestral Apacheans would have found large areas abandoned following the thirteenth-century retraction of maize farming peoples eastwards towards the Rio Grande (Chapter 9). Hence, they stayed in the region and the Navajo eventually adopted maize farming from surviving Uto-Aztecan or Tanoan-speaking neighbors, and also sheep pastoralism after Europeans arrived. Today, the Navajo form the largest Native American population north of Mexico. The Plains Apache retained a more mobile horse-riding and hunting lifestyle into the nineteenth century. Both of these groups offer us one of the best-documented hunter-gatherer migration histories from any period of the human past.

The Holocene Colonizations of Arctic Coastal North America

The Na-Dene migrations just described were mostly terrestrial phenomena, undertaken by land-based hunters and gatherers. Perhaps some ancestral Na-Dene once lived along the coastlines of Beringia and western Alaska, but nowadays almost all the coastal populations of these regions speak Eskimo-Aleut languages (Figure 5.3) and the only truly coastal Na-Dene live further south. The northern Athapaskans are completely terrestrial, and we have no good evidence that they ever seriously colonized the ice-bound coasts of northern Alaska, northern Canada, or Greenland. There is a suggestion that Na-Dene languages spread with the Arctic Small Tool tradition which records the first human colonization of the Arctic coastline of North America (Dumond 2010), but the vast majority of North American linguists and archaeologists associate this tradition with ancestral Eskimo-Aleuts, or Paleoeskimos.

Robert McGhee (2005) provides an excellent description of what must have been one of the most challenging environments to be occupied by prehistoric humans. The Arctic Circle offers a good living for people who can hunt off treeless tundra and sea-ice, with very high biomasses of large mammal species such as seals, whales, walrus, polar bears, musk oxen and caribou (reindeer). It is a land of spring and summer plenty, and the key to survival is to withstand the winter, via the use of efficient technology for clothing, hunting, food storage and shelter. The first human migrations into these North American high latitudes occurred around 5000 years ago, during the period of maximum mid-Holocene warming.

The Arctic Small Tool tradition, sometimes referred to as the Paleoeskimo Tradition, also made its first appearance about 5000 years ago, initially as the Denbigh archaeological complex on Seward Peninsula in Alaska (Figure 5.3).[14] Denbigh/Paleoeskimo descendants spread east along the northern coastline of Canada, to appear as the Pre-Dorset and Dorset cultures of Baffin Island, and the Saqqaq and Independence I cultures of Greenland, all evidently in place by 2500 BC (Ellis 2008). The Saqqaq people have recently hit headlines with the extraction of a 79% complete DNA profile from male hair preserved in the Greenland permafrost (Rasmussen et al. 2010). The owner, surprisingly, revealed little genetic similarity to existing Native American populations, including modern Eskimo-Aleuts. It matched most closely the modern Chukchi and Koryak populations of northeastern Siberia and the Uralic-speaking Nganasans of the Taymyr Peninsula far to the west. These are all indigenous Siberian hunters and gatherers and recent herders of reindeer.

The archaeological material culture and economy behind the Arctic Small Tool tradition and its many local descendants, from St Lawrence Island in the west to Greenland in the east, was particularly complex, befitting the colonization of a frozen landscape. It included microblades and small blade-like flakes, burins (engraving tools), ground stone adzes and knives, soapstone lamps, fiber-tempered and stamped pottery, portable skin tents weighted down by boulders, tailored skin clothing, bone and antler harpoons and arrowheads, skin-covered boats like ethnographic kayaks, and the spear hunting of fish, seals, caribou, and plentiful musk oxen.[15] Dogs were also present.

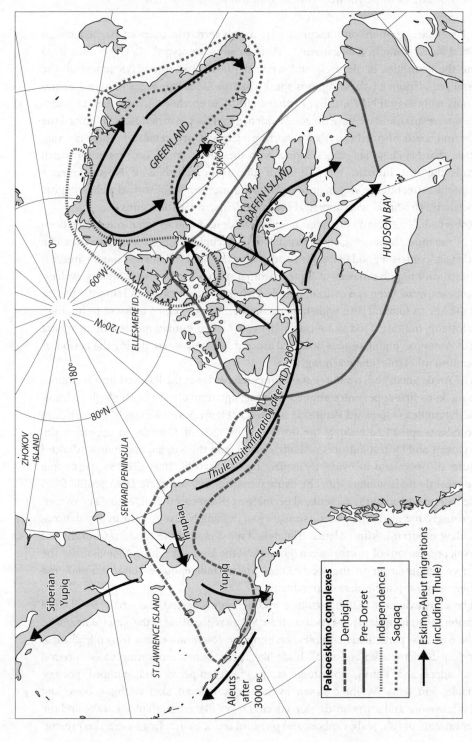

Figure 5.3 The distributions of Paleoeskimo archaeological complexes (circa 2000 BC), superimposed by the linguistic migrations of Eskimo-Aleut populations, especially the major Thule Inuit migration after AD 1200. Background map by Multimedia Services, ANU, with original data

The pottery is interesting, given its manufacture in much of the world by sedentary groups, mainly farmers. It was being made by 5000 BC in the Lena Basin of Siberia, but did not spread into Alaska or northern coastal Canada until much later .[16] In fact, the aforementioned items did not all appear together in the archaeological record, but most seem to have been present by the time of the Norton culture of Alaska, circa 500 BC.

One very interesting attempt to place the Arctic Small Tool tradition into a broader historical perspective is that by linguist Michael Fortescue (1998). He regards the major Uralic, Eskimo-Aleut and Yukaghir language families as being all related in a macro-family termed Uralo-Siberian. I noted the existence of Nganasan (Uralic) and Saqqaq (Eskimo-Aleut) genetic links earlier. Whole-genome analysis of single nucleotide polymorphisms also relates modern Uralic and Eskimo-Aleut speakers quite closely, at least when compared to other Native Americans and Eurasians (Reich et al. 2012). The origin of the Uralo-Siberian macro-family is postulated to have been in southern Siberia, in the Lake Baikal region between the Yenisei and Lena rivers, prior to the extensive migrations through here of Turkic and Tungusic-speaking hunters and pas-toralists. Fortescue believes that ancestral Eskimo-Aleuts split from their Uralo-Siberian linguistic relatives at about 4000 BC and ultimately reached Beringia, and then Alaska, carrying the Arctic Small Tool tradition. As discussed earlier (page 99), the ancestral Uralic languages presumably started to move west at about the same time.

Uralo-Siberian is completely separate from Dene-Yeniseian, and the two macro-families show very little sign of ancient contact or borrowing. The unrelated Na-Dene languages were probably present in Alaska at the time of Uralo-Siberian expansion, as were similarly unrelated Chukotko-Kamchatkan languages in Beringia and Kamchatka. These distributions suggest again some kind of leap-frogging movement, as well as continuous territorial expansion, by the early Eskimo-Aleuts.

Other groups of unknown ethnolinguistic identity penetrated the northeastern coastline of Siberia at around the same time as the Paleoeskimos settled in the Arctic coastline of Canada, reaching Zhokov Island at about 76°N in one of the most north-erly forays of hunter-gatherers in prehistory.[17] The Zhokov people constructed semi-subterranean houses, used stone microblades, mammoth ivory picks and ground stone adzes, and hunted reindeer and polar bear. The excavator reports radiocarbon dates of 9000–6000 BC on wood and animal bone, but also notes that the island contains much driftwood preserved by permafrost. These dates can perhaps be questioned since radiocarbon analysis dates the death of the tree, not the date of human usage of the wood, so one wonders if this movement could actually have been contemporary with that of the Paleoeskimo settlers of Alaska, closer perhaps to 3000 BC.

The Thule Migration and the Inuit

The Eskimo-Aleut language family as a whole developed in coastal Alaska, and has a relatively short time depth of 5000 years, or less.[18] From a purely linguistic perspective, one of its first recorded spreads (the Paleoeskimo languages are extinct, so we cannot know what languages they spoke) appears to have been that of ancestral Aleut speakers from the Alaska Peninsula into the Aleutian Islands.[19] Elsewhere on the coastlines around Bering Strait, the ancestors of the living Eskimo languages diverged ultimately into the four present-day members of the Yupik subgroup, from which the Inuit dialect chain separated during the thirteenth century AD to migrate eastwards in a remarkably rapid 5000 km movement that reached as far as Greenland (Figure 5.3).[20] The southern and western coastlines of this huge Arctic island were already settled at this time by Norse from western Europe, who arrived historically from Iceland in AD 985. This would have been one of the first meetings[21] between Native Americans and Europeans, brought about by remarkable migratory achievements from both directions. It is perhaps worth remembering, however, that only the Native Americans survived in Greenland to the present, the Norse having withdrawn during the fifteenth century.

The Thule migration appears to have retraced some of the routes taken by Paleoeskimo migrants over 3000 years before. By AD 1000, technology had advanced to include an increasing use of polished slate tools, larger boats perhaps similar to the ethnographic *umiak*, dog-drawn sleds, more advanced forms of bone or ivory harpoon heads, and the use of iron tools. The iron was obtained either from meteoric sources in northwestern Greenland, or from the Norse hunters and traders who came to Disko Bay in western Greenland. McGhee (2005) notes that iron was also in use in coastal Alaska from about 2000 years ago, perhaps obtained from Chinese or Korean sources.

The entire migration from Alaska to Greenland perhaps took only a few decades, reflecting the vast distances between exploitable resources in the landscape. What was the stimulus? Archaeologists variously suggest that the movement was encouraged by a desire for Greenland iron, hunting of caribou and musk oxen, and by the mobility required to hunt Arctic bowhead whales. As Michael Fortescue (2013: 340) notes, the migration was rapid enough to be traceable through linguistic studies alone:

> In fact, the Thule migrations from North Alaska as far as East Greenland about a thousand years ago represent a paradigm case for the rapid expansion of a language into virtually uninhabited regions, with ensuing gradation of innovations and losses away from its original homeland.

By the time of the Thule migration, few of the earlier Paleoeskimo populations, such as the genetically distinctive Saqqaq referred to earlier, appear to have survived in the eastern Arctic (hence Fortescue's reference to virtually uninhabited regions). One isolated non-Inuit group, the Sadlermiut, survived until 1902 in northern Hudson Bay.[22] The Inuit presumably incorporated most preceding populations linguistically and genetically into their own communities. There are few traces of language mixing or convergence between Inuit and other unrelated languages, and language shift rather than intensive multilingualism was the main route towards assimilation (Fortescue 1998).

Why were the Inuit such successful long-distance migrants? By the thirteenth century AD, the 'Great Warming', described rather lucidly by Brian Fagan (2008), was releasing coastal resources again from the ice. One question that arises, therefore, is whether the two successive Eskimo-Aleut migrations about 4000 years apart – the Paleoeskimo and the Thule Inuit – were the results of the successive episodes of warm mid-Holocene and Medieval climate, allowing easier access to what would otherwise have been largely ice-bound coastal resources?[23]

I suspect they were, and return again to the suggestion by Krantz (1976), introduced in Chapter 4, that hunters and gatherers rarely migrated within landscapes that were already occupied by human populations of similar technological and demographic capacity. They would have done only into relative or absolute population voids. The migrations discussed in this chapter, especially the Thule and Apachean migrations, fit this perspective very well. But while there is truth in Krantz's observation, I would also point to the apparent ability of hunters and gatherers to respond to situations of technological innovation. Thule material culture was more complex than that of the Paleoeskimos. The skin boats, harpoons, polished slate knives and dog sleds that apparently distinguished the Thule Inuit all come to mind in this regard. They surely gave their owners some advantages, even though there might have been few surviving Paleoeskimo populations still around to experience the impact.

The Early Holocene Colonization of a Green Sahara

I now move to an opposite climatic extreme, from a polar to a very hot desert, albeit once a much greener one than now. After the Younger Dryas mini-glaciation, the African summer monsoon moved north between 9000 and 4000 BC. What is now the southern half of the Sahara became a remarkable landscape of grassland under the relatively reliable summer monsoonal rainfall, then at least 200 mm per year as opposed to less than 100 mm now.[24] The northern edge of the Sahel grassland zone extended virtually to the middle of what is today the Sahara Desert, at least 850 km north of its present boundary. Herds of wild animals and stands of wild millet existed widely where now there is only sand, especially in the better-watered Tibesti, Air, and Hoggar uplands.[25]

Populations of hunter-gatherers took advantage of these improved conditions, colonizing a previously empty southern and central Sahara, decorating it with a great deal of remarkable rock art and carrying a material culture of pottery decorated with wavy line and impressed punctate patterns.[26] The earliest examples of this pottery date from about 9000 BC. It occurs in many sites distributed from the Western Desert of southern Egypt and Sudan, through the central Saharan massifs, to as far west as Ounjougou in the Niger Valley in Mali (Figure 5.4). So far, however, it has not been reported from the northern Sahara, perhaps because this northerly region would have remained as desert rather than grassland, as it is today. Initially, this pottery was rather homogeneous in decoration but later it developed regional styles, suggesting initial dispersal via a population radiation. It is believed to have been used for boiling small grass seeds, and perhaps for making beer.[27] These people were also capable boat builders and subsisted by freshwater fishing. Bone harpoons occur in many sites, and an 8.5 m long dugout canoe dated to 6500 BC has been found at Dufuna, on a greatly expanded early Holocene Lake Chad.[28]

Wild cattle were a major source of meat, and later (after their eventual domestication) of milk. The oldest dates for cattle bones occur in the east, especially in the

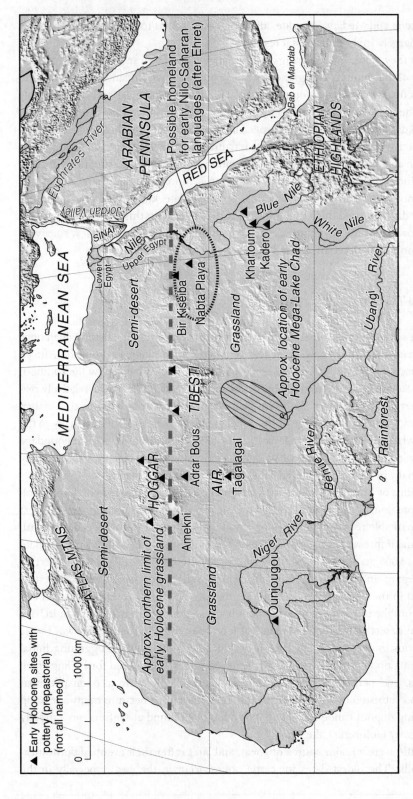

Figure 5.4 Pre-pastoral human occupation in the Green Sahara during the mid-Holocene. Background map by Multimedia Services, ANU, details added by the author.

Nabta Playa and Bir Kiseiba sites in the Western Desert of Egypt (circa 8000 BC). But it is very interesting that cattle only spread westwards very slowly, reaching the Niger River in Mali around 2000 BC.[29] There have been suggestions that cattle were being herded and managed in Nabta Playa by 8000 BC, but there is no actual evidence for domestication at this time. It is far more likely that these animals were hunted, at least until about 5000 BC, when evidence for consumption of cow's milk appears in southern Libya (discussed further on page 213). The slowness of the spread indicates that not all of the early Holocene Saharan hunters lived on beef. Barbary sheep seem also to have been important for their meat in some regions.

We might ask if any of these early Holocene colonizing hunter-gatherers have descendants today. It is clear that this Saharan occupation occurred before ancestral Afroasiatic-speaking populations began to arrive in northeastern Africa from the Levant, after 6000 BC, bringing in Fertile Crescent food production with sheep and goat herding (Chapter 7). Even though the descendants of these Afroasiatic-speaking immigrants eventually occupied much of northern Africa, they did not replace another very important ethnolinguistic population that still dominates many regions of Chad, southern Sudan and northern Kenya today. We met two of their member populations as the Nuer and Dinka in Chapter 1. They are the speakers of Nilo-Saharan languages (Figure 2.1 and Figure 9.3).

For many years, linguist Christopher Ehret has taken the view that the early inhabitants of the Holocene Sahara were ancestral speakers of Nilo-Saharan languages. It is difficult to see any other convincing possibility.[30] The linguistic homeland of the Nilo-Saharan language family appears to have been the middle Nile region of Sudan, south of the confluence of the White and Blue Niles and close to Khartoum (Figure 5.4). Ehret's protolanguage vocabulary reconstructions for various stages in the history of the family indicate that the initial migrating groups had no firm commitment to food production. Later groups did, of course, as cattle, sheep, and goat herding spread after 5000 BC. Had they not acquired this commitment, they would have been most unlikely to survive in the forbidding Saharan environment to the present day, in competition with adjacent populations of Cushitic and Omotic (Afroasiatic) herders and farmers.

Whether early Nilo-Saharan-speaking peoples spread through the whole of the Sahara, from coast to coast, we will never know, since so much of this part of the world is occupied today by Niger-Congo and Afroasiatic speakers (Chapter 9). But modern genetic evidence supports the existence of the Nilo-Saharan-speaking population as a major genetic node in the African pattern of diversity. Using data on the distributions of a large number of autosomal DNA polymorphisms distributed across sub-Saharan Africa, Evelyne Heyer and Jorge Rocha have identified 14 'associated ancestral components', each associated with a different major ethnolinguistic and geographical population.[31] Their Nilo-Saharan component occurs in its highest frequencies around the middle Nile in Sudan, suggested also as the region of Nilo-Saharan linguistic origin by Ehret. The distribution of the Nilo-Saharan component overlaps greatly with that of the Cushitic (Afroasiatic) component, suggesting a great deal of genetic interchange between these two populations in recent millennia.

Continental Shelves and Their Significance for Human Migration

Like desert greening, sea level change has undoubtedly been a major factor in allowing (or perhaps even forcing) humans to migrate. But how major? Were the Americas settled because the ice retreated, or because the falling sea level exposed the Beringian land bridge? Probably, both factors were important in Arctic circumstances. But sea level changes have been invoked in the past as major reasons for migration in warmer latitudes, especially during the Holocene drowning of the very extensive Sundaland continental shelf in Southeast Asia. During the last glacial maximum, Sundaland formed a 2.2 million km^2 exposed subcontinent. The sea level rise of 120 m between 15,000 and 7000 years ago reduced this land mass to its present large but separate islands (Borneo, Sumatra, and Java being the largest), and in the process roughly doubled the extent of coastline (Dunn and Dunn 1977).

Several authors have regarded this relatively rapid drowning of Sundaland as a fundamental driver in the Palaeolithic colonization of other nearby regions such as the Philippines and western Oceania.[32] Some have even related it to the human colonization of much of the world during the Holocene. For instance, Stephen Oppenheimer (1998) and Peter Watson (2012) hypothesize mass emigration due to rising sea levels out of Sundaland about 8000 years ago, giving rise to many significant populations, including even the early Sumerians of the Ubaid period in southern Iraq (5000–3000 BC). According to such cataclysmic scenarios, people literally became washed off the land and conveniently invented boat technology as a result. But could it really have been as dramatic as this (Bellwood 2000)?

In fact, there is no archaeological, linguistic, or genetic evidence at all for such a major dispersal out of Sundaland during the postglacial period of sea level rise.[33] It is quite true that the early Holocene rises in worldwide sea level were sometimes very rapid, particularly that of 60 m between 9650 and 5000 BC (Smith et al. 2011). But, by 4000 BC, sea levels had become virtually stable, simply fluctuating within a few meters of the present. These were the conducive conditions that stimulated Pacific ancestors to invent efficient boats in coastal waters off southern China and in Southeast Asia. During Pleistocene periods of rapid sea level change, coastal hunters and gatherers would have found it very difficult to exploit coastal resources successfully. Rising sea levels would have drowned such resources; falling sea levels would have exposed salt flats or coral cliffs. At times, the rates of change would have been so rapid that people would have been forced to move. But because the major oceans are linked worldwide their levels would have changed everywhere in relative unison, so coastlines everywhere would have been equally affected, allowing for localized factors such as isostasy and tectonic movement. There would be no reason in such circumstances to expect significant migration, except for moving further inland, nor indeed is there evidence for any.

Human groups on Sundaland presumably moved and adapted locally during such difficult times by emphasizing the exploitation of terrestrial resources, although it is rather difficult to demonstrate this archaeologically since sites close to the coastline that were occupied before 4000 BC are naturally now under the sea. This problem applies in all continental shelf situations that were not glaciated. In glaciated regions, isostatic uplift kept pace with sea level rise as the ice melted, as discussed for Arctic North America in Chapter 4. Coastal archaeological sites there have remained above sea level. But these very cold regions played little role in the great demographic increases in late Holocene agricultural latitudes.

Holocene Australia – Pama-Nyungan Migration?

Australian archaeologists rarely discuss post-colonization immigration from an outside source as a possibility for Australian prehistory, partly because the record of flaked lithic tools does not reflect deeply on such issues. Material categories that do appear to carry group-focused style, such as rock art, are highly localized to suitable rock surfaces, nonportable, and extremely difficult to date. However, Australian archaeology was not a static phenomenon over its 50,000 year hunter-gatherer time span. Many changes in population distribution and artifact form can be identified during its prehistory, especially since 4000 years ago.

The retraction of human occupation that occurred within mainland Australia during the last glacial maximum has already been noted. As Peter Hiscock (2008: 61) comments: "Abandonment of local areas, even entire regions, perhaps the extinction of human groups, demonstrates that Pleistocene foragers were subjected to severe stress in the extreme environmental conditions of the time." Populations seem to have remained small into the early Holocene, but after 4000 years ago there developed an increasing site density over much of mainland Australia, especially in productive eastern regions such as Cape York, central Queensland and coastal New South Wales. The reasons for this are debated. Population increase due to better resource densities is one suggestion.[34] Or perhaps younger sites preserve better and are more visible in the landscape than older ones.[35] I suspect, however, that a significant population change might also have been involved. In terms of lithics, as well as site numbers, there were major changes across much of mainland Australia (excluding Tasmania) between 4000 and 3000 years ago.

One of the classic mid-Holocene artifacts found across most of mainland Australia is the hafted and multipurpose 'backed blade', made on what archaeologists technically term a blade-like flake (Robertson et al. 2009). Another common form is a backed microlith of geometric shape, usually triangular, crescentic or trapezoidal (Figure 5.5). This backing technology developed initially in an uncertain but probably eastern region of Australia in the late Pleistocene or early Holocene, and there is no credible link to the Eurasian Upper Paleolithic. But the main period of popularity of such tools, as plotted by Peter Hiscock (2008: 157), lasted from roughly 3500 to 2500 years ago, whereupon they gradually disappeared from the record well prior to European contact. Even more interesting is the distribution of these items in space, since they do not occur in the Kimberley and Arnhem Land regions of tropical and monsoonal northern Australia.[36] Different kinds of tools were used here, especially bifacially flaked points and edge-ground axes. Neither do backed blades and microliths occur in prehistoric Tasmania, isolated from Australia

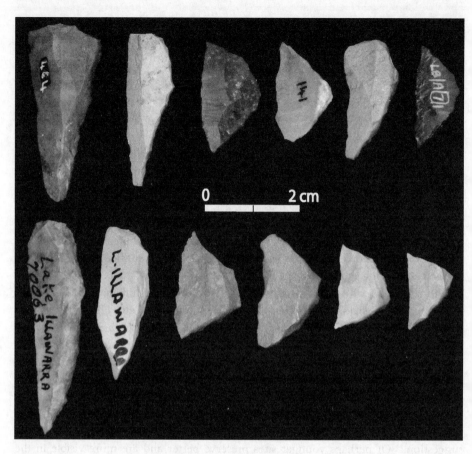

Figure 5.5 Backed artifacts and geometric microliths from Australia and the southwestern arm of Sulawesi. Top row: two backed blade-like tools and four microliths (geometric and crescentic in shape) of chert from Leang Burung shelter 1, South Sulawesi, excavated by Mulvaney and Soejono 1970. Bottom row: matching tools of chert and silcrete from southern Australia (including the two backed blade-like tools marked "Lake Illawarra"), from collections of the National Museum of Australia on loan to the School of Archaeology and Anthropology at ANU. Photos by the author.

by the postglacial sea level rise and apparently beyond the capacity of available watercraft to reach (Figure 5.6).

Another appearance in late Holocene Australia (but not Tasmania) was the dingo, a domesticated descendant of the Eurasian wolf, like all other ancient dogs. The dingo was presumably transmitted into Australia via an ancestral bottleneck population in Indonesia, given the high degree of mtDNA homogeneity that living dingoes still carry.[37] The date for this transfer is unlikely to have been much before 3500 years ago, based on the Southeast Asian archaeological record. Their movement can be associated with the arrival of Austronesian-speaking populations with domesticated dogs in Indonesia (Chapter 8). Bones of wolves and dogs, nonnative animals in Southeast Asia, are totally absent from the archaeological record in this region prior to this time,

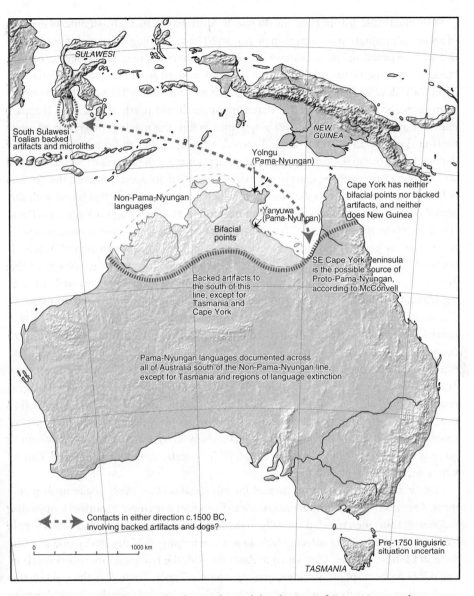

Figure 5.6 Australia, showing the almost identical distributions of Pama-Nyungan languages with backed artifacts, and Non-Pama-Nyungan languages with bifacial points. The northern Cape York Peninsula and New Guinea lack both artifact categories. Also shown is a possible sea route linking Sulawesi and Australia, utilizing historical parallels for Makassan *teripang* collectors. Background map by Multimedia Services, ANU, details added by the author.

although they do occur during the early Holocene in southern China. A recent molecular clock claim that dogs were introduced from Mainland Southeast Asia into Indonesia and Australia between 18,300 and 4600 years ago (Oskarsson et al. 2012) is without archaeological or biogeographical support – the dates are far too old to refer to their actual transference.

Do backed blade distributions and dingoes in Australia equate with a significant episode of secondary migration in Australian prehistory? The archaeological record cannot tell us this with certainty, and perhaps never will. But it is interesting to note that similar backed blades and geometric microliths occur in the southwestern arm of the island of Sulawesi, in central Indonesia. This industry, known to archaeologists as the Toalian, is best reported from caves and rock shelters in the Maros limestone district north of Makassar. It apparently commenced around 6500 years ago, thus before the major proliferation of such tools in the Australian archaeological record, although it has to be admitted that the dating of the Toalian is weak, and chronological priority for these tools between Sulawesi and Australia can hardly be determined with finality.[38] In Sulawesi, however, the Toalian definitely appeared prior to the Neolithic, which was associated in this island with the arrival of Austronesian-speaking populations around 3500 years ago (Chapter 8). Thus, whatever its ultimate origin, the Toalian can be considered a development associated with an indigenous hunting and gathering population in the southwestern arm of Sulawesi. Serrated bifacial points with hollow bases ('Maros Points') occur in later phases of the Toalian, but generally with pottery, hence overlapping with Austronesian settlement in the island. Only the backed tools and microliths would appear to be pre-Austronesian.

The basic Toalian technology of creating and hafting a multipurpose tool was remarkably similar to that of the backed artifact industries of Australia (Figure 5.5). Of course, it is possible that such tools were developed independently in the two regions. But given that such specific tool forms do not occur anywhere else in Southeast Asia or Australasia, except perhaps fortuitously as minor components of flake assemblages, one is tempted also to consider the possibility of some kind of contact. Against this possibility is the geographical problem of getting people, presumably by boat, across more than 1000 km of ocean without leaving any clear trace in the archaeological records of the intervening islands of eastern Indonesia, including Flores and Timor, where such tools do not occur.

However, there is a historical parallel for this situation that might make us stop and think. After AD 1750, but commencing prior to European settlement in northern Australia, Indonesian fishermen traveled annually to the Kimberley and Arnhem Land coasts to collect resources such as the sea slug (bêche-de-mer), or teripang in Malay, in demand in dried form in Chinese cuisine. They sailed to Australia with the northwest monsoon winds in the southern hemisphere summer, passing around Timor. Each year throughout the nineteenth century, a thousand or more of these fishermen sailed from the city of Makassar (formerly Ujungpandang), on the southwestern coast of Sulawesi, located centrally within the former distribution of the Toalian industry.[39] They left archaeological sites along the Kimberley coastline of Western Australia and around coastal Arnhem Land to at least as far east as the Sir Edward Pellew Islands in the Gulf of Carpentaria. These provide us with a very handy parallel for any suggested contact situation between Sulawesi and Australia, 3500 years before.[40] However, these fishermen were not the direct descendants of Toalians, as we will see in Chapter 8, so the suggested parallels are rather generalized.

Nowadays, it is not very fashionable in Australian archaeology to suggest Holocene migration or diffusion of ideas involving populations located outside the continent. But such suggestions were made in two influential and very thorough reviews of backed artifacts in both Sulawesi and Australia published in 1985.[41] Movement from Sulawesi to Australia is one possibility, and the reverse is another, as suggested by van Heekeren in 1972.[42] Heekeren also noted that southwestern Sulawesi has a great deal of cave art, including hand stencils and paintings of animals, that resemble similar rock art in Australia. He preferred cultural diffusion from Australia to Sulawesi rather than migration as the explanation, in sympathy with the general rather negative perspective on migration that existed during the 1970s.

Basically, we have an impasse in understanding these Sulawesi–Australia relationships. Independent innovation, cultural diffusion, and population migration can all be suggested to explain the lithic similarities, using selected aspects of the evidence. Dingoes necessarily required human contact for their transference to Australia, and if they arrived around 3500 years ago they must have traveled in boats, given that an Austronesian linguistic and population presence in Sulawesi was well underway by this time (Chapter 8). Can the linguistic record reveal anything further?

Linguistic Prehistory during the Australian Holocene

It is necessary first to point to one archeological and linguistic correlation that might be of immense consequence. Figure 5.6 indicates that the backed artifacts discussed earlier, and a separate category of bifacial points, have complementary distributions that are virtually identical to the distributions of the two fundamental linguistic divisions that exist within Australia, except for the top of Cape York Peninsula.

The deepest of these linguistic divisions in date of origin is the group of about 20 or so language families in tropical northern Australia termed *Non-Pama-Nyungan*. The apparent lack of imagination in the name is a direct reflection of the deep diversity of this group of families, as opposed to the much more widespread and nondiverse single family that has been termed *Pama-Nyungan*. The Non-Pama-Nyungan languages carry about 90% of the linguistic diversity within Australia according to Nicholas Evans (2003), yet occupy only the northward-flowing monsoonal river basins of the Northern Territory and the Kimberleys. Their distribution overlaps remarkably with that of bifacial points.

The other recorded languages of Australia, occupying the eastern highlands and all of the central and western deserts (but not Tasmania, for which we have very limited linguistic information), belong to the single Pama-Nyungan family. The name draws on the words for 'person' in Cape York (*pama*) and the southwest of Australia (*ñungar*). Pama-Nyungan languages are far less diverse than Non-Pama-Nyungan languages, and neighboring languages often share between 20 and 60% of their basic vocabulary.[43] Pama-Nyungan languages are fairly homogeneous in grammatical structure, but lexical sharings are often geographically uncoordinated, and there is much semantic flux in word meanings. A coherent subgrouping structure is very hard to establish, which suggests either a rapid initial spread over a large area, or simply a relatively high degree of crosscutting linguistic diffusion aided by multilingualism. No Pama-Nyungan isoglosses overlap deeply with languages in the Non-Pama-Nyungan region, except along linguistic boundaries, suggesting that significant interaction between these two major linguistic groupings was always very limited (Evans 2005). The environmental border between the monsoonal river basins to the north with their Non-Pama-Nyungan languages, and the rest of mainland Australia to the south with its Pama-Nyungan languages, appears to have been very significant. The Pama-Nyungan languages correlate in distribution very closely with the backed artifacts, except that such artifacts are absent in the northern part of the Pama-Nyungan-speaking Cape York Peninsula and the Torres Strait Islands (Figure 5.6).

Linguistic explanations for the wide extent of Pama-Nyungan languages are varied. Linguist Bob Dixon has suggested that linguistic diversification since the initial colonization of the continent reflects local interaction and borrowing, not language spread or migration. This view interprets the Pama-Nyungan family as a result of tens of millennia of *in situ* interaction and does not recognize the existence of a genetically constituted Pama-Nyungan language family at all. Neither does it explain, however, why the Pama-Nyungan and Non-Pama-Nyungan languages should show so few signs of any ancient shared ancestry, an observation emphasized by current phylogenetic analyses, or why the explanation through interaction used for Pama-Nyungan does not work for the Non-Pama-Nyungan languages, which never underwent such processes of convergence [44]

Common historical development is a major issue here, since if Pama-Nyungan can be shown to be a genetic family of languages, with a reconstructable protolanguage and a coherent geographical nesting of subgroups, radiating outwards from a putative region of origin, then some degree of population migration becomes a mandatory requirement, given the historical observations about language family movement made in Chapter 2. Dixon's view is that Pama-Nyungan is not a true genetic family, and hence carries no history of radiation. Mark Clendon (2006) takes a similar view, regarding Pama-Nyungan as a result of a repopulation of postglacial Australia from various linguistically diverse easterly refuge regions, a process commencing around 13,000 years ago. This suggestion of mixed ancestry means that Pama-Nyungan is not a valid family, but a result of superficial convergence through contact.

Against this view of continuous local interaction and flux over very long periods of time, many linguists today regard Pama-Nyungan as a valid and relatively young family, with a history of speaker dispersal and a protolanguage with more than 50 reconstructions, especially pronouns.[45] According to Nicholas Evans (1988: 105–6):

> Somehow we will have to explain an explosive, relatively recent expansion of Pama-Nyungan over seven-eighths of the continent…some sort of pervasive cultural change, accompanied by the spread of a new language, seems the most likely explanation.

The problem, of course, is to explain how this happened. Why were the Pama-Nyungans not simply absorbed into indigenous populations and why did their languages not just disappear? We are back again with questions of face-to-face interaction between demographically equal groups of hunter-gatherers, unless it can be shown that some regions were empty prior to Pama-Nyungan arrival or that the Pama-Nyungans had some decisive demographic or technological advantage over their contemporaries.

The use of backed blades and geometric microliths to create a more efficient hunting technology could imply the latter possibility, especially if the dingo was involved as well. Although such tools apparently occurred in eastern Australia in very small numbers before 3500 years ago, the rapid jump in their popularity around this time is very striking. Equally striking is the situation amongst the Non-Pama-Nyungans, who at a similar date moved to a use of bifacial points (Clarkson 2007). Was this really all coincidental? Or are we witnessing a situation of quite sharp cultural divergence?

Most Australian linguists now regard Pama-Nyungan as a true and relatively young language family, with a history of linguistic expansion commencing somewhere between 3000 and 5000 years ago. For instance, O'Grady and Fitzgerald (1997) regard it as being a little less diverse than the major Finno-Ugric subgroup of the Uralic languages, hence originating between 3500 and 4500 years ago. Patrick McConvell has long advocated a migration explanation for Pama-Nyungan, sourcing it to a linguistic homeland close to the southeastern side of the Gulf of Carpentaria and seeing it as related to the proliferation of backed artifacts.[46] Nicholas Evans and Rhys Jones (1997: 417) took a similar view in terms of date and homeland, but suggested a rather different and more complex explanation:

> …in which new technology [i.e. backed artifacts] was spread in association with a particular set of rituals, with initiates being inducted in Pama-Nyungan as they learnt new ceremonies and new tool-making techniques, and linguistic expansion being driven by ceremonial prestige and changed patterns of spouse-exchange as Pama-Nyungans demanded payment in wives for their sons, leading to the export of Pama-Nyungan to new households. Underlying the social innovation of new ceremonies and wider alliances were advances in food technology that allowed large gatherings to be fed for reasonably long periods.

This explanation does require the continuous movement of at least some Pama-Nyungan-speaking males, even if language shift is a major part of the equation. McConvell is in favor of more inclusive population movement and points to a number of individual cases of Pama-Nyungan language spread in relatively recent times. My own view falls quite close to that of McConvell, and has changed little since I first expressed it in 1997:

> Could it be that the Pama-Nyungan languages are the result of an actual dispersal of people…so rapid and extensive that it has led to a rake-like rather than a tree-like arrangement of subgroups in time and space? If some form of ancestral Pama-Nyungan was spread this way about 4000 years ago through many parts of Australia (perhaps more slowly into regions already quite densely settled, such as the Murray valley), then a large number of populations might have differentiated rapidly thereafter to produce very localized linguistic subgroups… (Bellwood 1997: 133–4)

Who Were the Ancestral Pama-Nyungans?

An explanation for the Pama-Nyungan languages, dingoes, and the proliferation of backed artifacts in Australia can legitimately be built around a concept of migration, although much of the evidence, admittedly, is rather faint. On the positive side we have dingo origins in Asia and the distributional and chronological data on the backed tools and microliths, which appeared before Austronesian settlement in Sulawesi. We also have the reconstructed prehistories of the relatively new Pama-Nyungan and much more ancient Non-Pama-Nyungan language families. The Pama-Nyungan languages show no clear phylogenetic affinity with any Non-Pama-Nyungan ones. On the negative side, however, we have no supporting biological evidence from Sulawesi, and the pre-Austronesian languages of that island are extinct.

If early Pama-Nyungan speakers had dogs that were useful for hunting and a well-developed technology of backed and microlithic artifacts, they could have had an edge against indigenous Australian groups with less specialized lithic technologies. The one group to withstand pressure from Pama-Nyungans were the Non-Pama-Nyungans, by virtue of their bifacial point and edge-ground axe technology. The latter had been used in this region, but nowhere else in Australia, since before the last glacial maximum. The Pama-Nyungan population then borrowed and spread the edge-ground axe technology southwards about 3000 years ago into the rest of mainland Australia.[47]

Can we infer that the early Toalians of Sulawesi included some elements of the ancestral Pama-Nyungan population in cultural, linguistic, and genetic terms? Did some founders travel by boat across the quiet equatorial seas to enter the Gulf of Carpentaria about 3500 years ago? Did they follow a similar route to the *teripang* fishermen of historical times, bringing as domino-effect baggage their dogs and a knowledge of outrigger canoe construction that would have reached Sulawesi with Austronesian settlers?[48] A small founder group of hunter-gatherers could have rapidly developed into a large spreading population, but only if conditions were right.

Some genetic and anthropometric evidence might be significant here. A telling observation has been made that a specific Y chromosome haplotype underwent a major expansion about 4000 years ago from a northeast Australian source region (Kayser et al. 2001). That source could have been close to Cape York and the likely homeland of the Pama-Nyungan languages. The authors specifically associated the expansion with a movement of backed tools and dogs. Much earlier, Joseph Birdsell (1967) documented differences in living body measurements between the people he termed *Carpentarians*, located mainly in the northern region occupied today by the Non-Pama-Nyungan languages, and *Murrayians*, represented by indigenous populations in southeastern Australia. Birdsell's hypotheses revolved around a *trihybrid* history of Australians that has gone out of fashion today, but it is possible that living Carpentarians and Murrayians represent the respective descendants of the earlier Non-Pama-Nyungan and Pama-Nyungan populations. Perhaps modern biologists need to look at some of these old data again in a fresh light.

Indeed, some genetic fresh light might have been shone on the problem by a new claim for gene flow from southern India to Australia at about 4000 years ago, although this claim has not met with eager acceptance from Australian prehistorians, and the data analysed are drawn only from living populations, not ancient ones.[49] Given that Toalian populations no longer exist as they did 4000 years ago, these new genetic data can only hint at a possibility of population movement at this time. But the hint is interesting, nevertheless.

In my view, the conjunction of circumstances that we can see in late Holocene South Sulawesi and Australia, in the distributions and dates for stone artifacts and dogs/dingoes, for the arrival in Sulawesi of Austronesian-speaking populations, and especially in Australia for the different histories of the Pama-Nyungan and Non-Pama-Nyungan language groupings, is a very striking conjunction indeed. Perhaps it is all too good to be true from a viewpoint of pure coincidence alone. Mid-Holocene Australia was a place of extremely dynamic change. We might have to reckon with the possibility that Australian cultures on the eve of European arrival, rather than being isolated continuations of Australian cultures at 40,000 years ago, were in fact remarkable products of cross-cultural hunter-gatherer energy.

Notes

1. These pre-LGM dogs/tame wolves identified in Europe, the Levant, and the Altai might not have been directly ancestral to modern domesticated dogs, whose ancestors were probably domesticated much later from Middle Eastern or southern Chinese wolves (VonHoldt et al. 2010; Ovodov et al. 2011; Ding et al. 2012).
2. Keinan and Clarke 2012 estimate a world population of five million at 8000 BC, prior to the rise of food production.
3. Gamble et al. 2005; also Housley et al. 1997.
4. See further discussion of Neolithic migration into Europe as traced by ancient DNA in Chapter 7.
5. Holdaway and Porch 1995; Haberle and David 2002; Lourandos and David 2002; Clarkson 2007.
6. Rankama and Kankaanpää 2008; Conneller et al. 2013.
7. Ruhlen 1987: 64; Abondolo 1998.
8. Holman et al. 2011 offer a younger date for Proto-Uralic (without Yukaghir) of only 3200 years. Blažek 2013b.
9. Ruhlen 1998; Kari and Potter 2010.
10. Goebel et al. 2008; Kitchen et al. 2008; Kari and Potter 2010.
11. Holman et al. 2011 give 4200 years for Athapaskan-Eyak, and 8500 years for 'Nuclear Na-Dene'.
12. Reich et al. 2012.
13. Matson and Magne 2007, 2013.
14. Fortescue 1998; Friesen 2013. Paleoeskimo populations are termed 'Tuniit' by McGhee 2005.
15. Rouse 1986; Fortescue 1998; McGhee 2005; Friesen 2013. Rowley-Conwy and Layton 2013 suggest that hunting of musk oxen might have been one reason behind the migration.
16. Lucier and VanStone 1992; Harry and Frink 2009.
17. Pitulko 1993, 2003. Zhokov Island at that time would have been part of mainland Siberia since it lies on the continental shelf that extends to almost 80°N, beneath the shallow East Siberian Sea.
18. Fortescue 1998, 2013.
19. Balter 2012a; Fortescue 2013.
20. Dugmore et al. 2007; Friesen and Arnold 2008; Friesen 2013.
21. Max Friesen (pers. comm.) informs me that the first recorded meeting between Europeans and indigenous Americans took place at L'Anse aux Meadows in northern Newfoundland ('Vinland') around AD 1000, although this did not involve Thule Inuit.
22. McGhee 2005: 54–5; Palsson 2008.
23. Funder et al. 2011 note that northern Greenland sea-ice reached a mid-Holocene minimum about 6000 years ago, so perhaps this assisted the Paleoeskimo colonization, although sea-ice apparently increased around the same time at Ellesmere Island.
24. Kuper and Kröpelin 2006; Kröpelin et al. 2008; Hildebrand and Grillo 2012.
25. Garcea 2006.

26. Di Lernia and Gallinaro 2010 discuss rock art; Jordeczka et al. 2011 discuss pottery.
27. Kuper and Kröpelin 2006; Huysecom et al. 2009; Jordeczka et al. 2011.
28. Breunig and Neumann 2002; Gifford-Gonzalez 2005.
29. Kuper and Kröpelin 2006; Brooks et al. 2009; Marshall and Weissbrod 2011.
30. Ehret 2002a, 2002b, 2011, 2013. Holman et al. 2011 give an age of almost 7000 years for Proto-Nilo-Saharan.
31. Heyer and Rocha 2013, using data published in Tishkoff et al. 2009. See also Campbell and Tishkoff 2010.
32. Thiel 1987; Soares et al. 2011.
33. The mtDNA haplogroup E genetic evidence claimed by Soares et al. 2008 to indicate a 'critical role' for postglacial climate change in shaping the origins of modern Island Southeast Asians accounts for only 15% of the mtDNA lineages currently represented there. I have no quarrel with the findings of this report as data, but in their abstract the authors make the statement, in my view without any genetic or archaeological foundation, that "global warming and sea-level rises at the end of the Ice Age, 15,000–7000 years ago, were the main forces shaping modern human diversity in the region." The argument is repeated by Barker and Richards 2012.
34. Lourandos and David 2002.
35. Hiscock 2008, 2013b. For charts of relative population size derived from archaeological and radiocarbon data, covering regions of both tropical and temperate Eastern Australia, see Hiscock 2008: Figure 12.6; David and Lourandos 1997.
36. On backed blade distributions and chronology see Mulvaney 1985; Hiscock and Attenbrow 1998; Clarkson 2007.
37. Savolainen et al. 2004; Larson et al. 2013.
38. On the Toalian, see Glover and Presland 1985; Bellwood 2007a: 193–6.
39. Macknight 1976, 2008, and pers. comm.
40. The Yolngu people of northeastern Arnhem Land (Figure 5.6) also have traditions about more ancient visitors who perhaps came from Indonesia (Meehan 1990; McIntosh 2008), but so far there is no specific archaeological evidence for contact apart from that referred to in this chapter. Other explanations for these traditions have also been suggested (Macknight 2008:144).
41. Glover and Presland 1985; Mulvaney 1985.
42. Van Heekeren 1972: 125.
43. Dixon 1980; Evans 2003.
44. See Dixon 1980, 1997. Dediu and Levinson 2012 discuss a lack of phylogenetic unity in the Australian languages as a whole.
45. McConvell and Bowern 2011; Bowern and Atkinson 2012; and see chapters in Bowern and Koch 2004.
46. McConvell 1990, 1996, 2010, 2013. Holman et al. 2011 offer an age of 4300 years for Proto-Pama-Nyungan based on lexical similarity calculations.
47. Clarkson 2007 notes that bifacial points become very frequent in Northern Territory archaeological sites around 3000 years ago.
48. Outrigger canoes existed in Cape York at European contact and have always been assumed to reflect contact with New Guinea, which I do not dispute. But the original source of such canoes amongst Austronesian-speaking peoples lay far to the west.
49. Pugach et al. 2012, discussed rather negatively by Brown 2013.

Chapter 6
The First Farmers and Their Offspring

The previous three chapters of this book examined the hunter-gatherer migrations that led to the hominin and modern human colonizations of virtually all habitable regions of the world, except for the remotest islands. Now, in the final four chapters, we turn to the dominance of food production as the major stimulus for migration, from about 10,000 years ago until the present day. Food production underpinned dramatic population growth and migration across all continents and oceans during the Holocene, giving rise to many of the major language families and ethnolinguistic populations that existed on the eve of the colonial era, in all regions where food production was possible. This chapter introduces the topic of food production in prehistory, and the following chapters examine consequent developments in the Old and New Worlds, respectively.

What impact on world history, and on the patterns of diversity in humans, can we attribute to the human ability to *produce food* rather than harvest it from the wild? In this chapter, I wish to introduce the concept of food production and to explain how it has led, on many occasions within the past 10,000 years, to the migrations of many of the direct ancestors of the indigenous agriculturalist populations of the world. It also led to the spreads of many of the world's major language families. The major issues to be discussed concern where and when food production began, why it developed in certain regions and not others, and what impact it had on human population sizes and densities. Since my emphasis is on human migration, I will not be especially concerned with theoretical debates about why food production developed in the first place.[1]

Many terminological issues arise in the definition of food production. *Agriculture* can serve as a generalized term for it, with reference to both plants and animals. Different kinds of food production include multicrop *gardening*, tree-crop *arboriculture*, and ruminant *pastoralism*, as well as open field (Latin *ager*, Greek *agros*) agriculture in which single stands of crops are produced, all utilizing varying combinations of rainfall and/ or irrigation to ensure production. Agriculture also has two separate components, one being the human activity patterns that we term *cultivation* and *animal husbandry*, and the other being the impacts of these activities, via both unconscious and conscious selection, on the animals and plants themselves. These impacts result in genetic change, the foundation of what we term *domestication*. The first farmers obviously cultivated wild plants (by practicing *pre-domestication cultivation*) and captured or tamed wild animals.

First Migrants: Ancient Migration in Global Perspective, First Edition. Peter Bellwood.
© Peter Bellwood. Published 2013 by John Wiley & Sons, Ltd.

The domesticated phenotypes of these species developed later, often several millennia later, allowing for the full course of domestication to take place.

Where and When Did Food Production Begin?

The most important homelands of food production, as revealed in the archaeological record in both the Old and New Worlds (Figure 6.1 and Figure 9.4), were located in tropical monsoonal or warm temperate latitudes, with strong seasonality in their rainfall distributions. This is because seasonality was necessary for the annual (as opposed to perennial) growth cycle that characterized most of the major domesticated cereals and legumes (podded plants such as beans and peas), and even many tubers. An annual growth habit still characterizes the major crops that feed us today. Annual plants use their relatively large seeds or tubers as food storage organs for the season of dormancy. Hence, they provide more food for their human exploiters than do small-grained perennial species. The majority of the agricultural homelands to be discussed in the following chapters, but not necessarily *all* of them (the New Guinea Highlands, for instance, are equatorial and nonseasonal), exist because of their climatic seasonality. They also exist because of their fortunate roles as homelands of the major domesticated plants and animals. The latter, mostly ruminants kept for food, milk, and wool, were species that were behaviorally amenable to human taming and management (Diamond 2002).

In terms of chronology (Figure 6.2), the Fertile Crescent of southwestern Asia had priority as the world's first agricultural homeland, with mixed farming of domesticated plants and animals around large sedentary settlements in existence by about 7500 BC, following a gestation period of about 2000 years. The Fertile Crescent was followed about 5000 BC by central China, following a similar gestation period, and later again by other regions such as sub-Saharan Africa, New Guinea, Mesoamerica, and northwestern South America. In all of these regions, we can see evidence for increasing population density and social complexity starting at various times during the first half of the Holocene.

We might ask why agriculture did not begin earlier, for instance, during the last interglacial, or even during the initial warming conditions that occurred after the last glacial maximum, after 18,000 years ago (Chapter 4). After all, if food production could have commenced after 16,000 BC, rather than after 9000 BC, the global consequences described in the following chapters would surely have been very different. Perhaps there were incipient attempts towards food production, especially during the archaeological phase known as the Natufian (11,500–9500 BC) in the Middle East (Hillman et al. 2001). But they were not successful, and there may be a good reason why not.

Between 10,800 and 9600 BC, most of the world underwent a phase of dramatic cooling known as the Younger Dryas, an episode of renewed glaciation thought by some climatologists to have been caused by a massive inrush of cold glacial meltwater from North America into the Atlantic Ocean. Apparently, the Younger Dryas itself was just too cold for continuing success in any prior development of plant domestication, as was the last

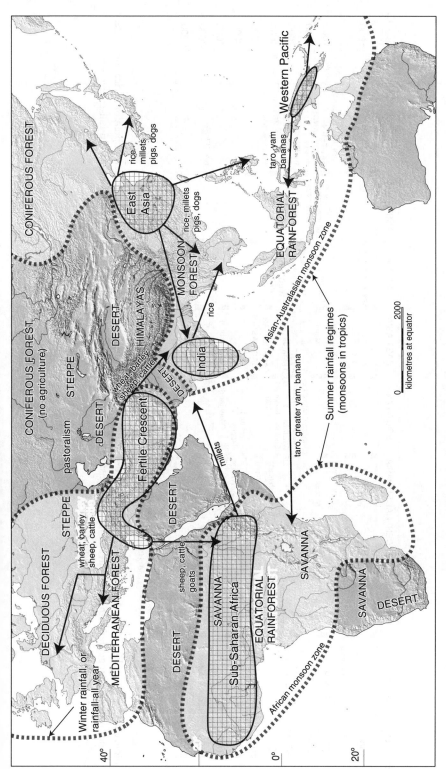

Figure 6.1 The homelands of agriculture in the Old World (unbroken lines and cross-hatching), with the regions (broken lines) of summer rainfall climate in Asia and Africa, and winter rainfall in the Middle East and around the Mediterranean. This figure shows that the expansions of the East Asian, African, and Fertile Crescent agricultural complexes were each constrained by the imperatives of their climatic homelands. Also shown are the less expansive western Pacific and South Asian agricultural complexes. Arrows refer to significant plant and animal transfers out of or between the zones in prehistoric times. For the New World, see Figure 9.4. Background map by Multimedia Services, ANU, details added by the author.

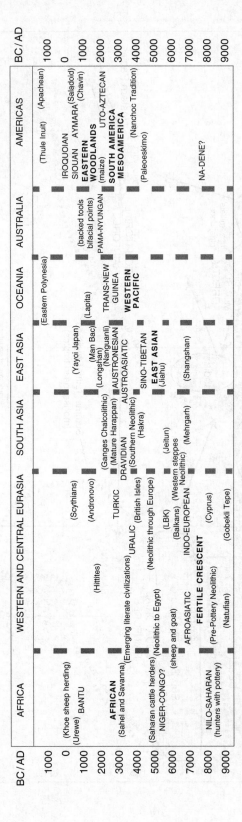

Figure 6.2 Chronological chart to show the inceptions of domesticatory agriculture in the various homeland regions (earlier pre-domestication phases are not indicated), together with likely dates of initial expansion of selected language families, hunter-gatherer as well as agriculturalist. Pertinent archaeological sites and cultures are also noted.

glacial maximum itself (Richerson et al. 2001). The very rapid emergence into warm conditions after the Younger Dryas was therefore a very major facilitator for population growth and ultimately the development of agriculture in many regions (Feynman and Ruzmaikin 2007). It was not, however, a universal *cause*. Had it been, then agriculture would have started at the same time everywhere. It most certainly did not do this.

Why Did Food Production Develop in Some Places, but Not Others?

We might ask why the developments in western Asia and China were so important, so early in time, and so rapid in terms of population growth. The distributions of the wild ancestors of the most important domesticated plants and animals provide the background to answer this question. Jared Diamond has noted that a disproportionate number of large-seeded annual grass species, such as the wheats (two species initially, emmer and einkorn) and barley, together with several important legumes such as lentils, peas, and broad beans, originated in western Asia, as did most of the world's major ruminant meat sources, especially cattle, pigs, sheep, and goats.[2] It is thus hardly a coincidence that western Asia has the world's oldest evidence for food production, a lead supported by the results of decades of intensive archaeological research. The cattle and pig (bovid and suid) genera have additional species distributed quite widely in various parts of the Old World, such as zebu cattle in India, and banteng cattle and Celebes pig in Indonesia. Some of these species also contributed genes to present-day domesticated stocks. In comparison with West Asia, however, most other regions contained fewer domesticated species of such importance in the world today, although some, such as China, Mesoamerica and the central Andes, came fairly close.

The remainder of the earth's surface is mostly occupied by regions in which such major species were either absent altogether, or only represented in ones or twos. Europe had native oats and rye, both India and northern sub-Saharan Africa had native rice and millet species. But in these regions we have no evidence for *completely* independent developments of food production in prehistory. In the case of New Guinea, where food production did develop indigenously, the emphasis was purely on fruits and tubers, with no cereals or domesticated animals prior to the introduction of the pig and dog from Indonesia about 3000 years ago.

In this regard, individual species of domesticated plants and animals have originated in many parts of the world unconnected with the centers of early food production. The existence of a locally domesticated plant or animal need not imply a completely indigenous origin of food production since people could use local resources to emulate developments that originally occurred elsewhere. Larson et al. (2007) have demonstrated this for pigs in central Europe. Early domesticated Neolithic pigs were introduced before 5500 BC from the Middle East, but their ancient mtDNA profiles soon became replaced by those of local European suid lineages, to the extent that the one-time existence of the original Fertile Crescent domesticated pigs can today only be detected from the study of their ancient DNA. Any assumption that there was an independent focus of pig domestication in Europe, separate from that in the Fertile Crescent, would be incorrect.

In terms of the totality of human behavioral evolution over the past two million years, the development of food production was dramatic, as the famous prehistorian Gordon Childe realized so clearly with his concept of a Neolithic Revolution (e.g., Childe 1936). But in fine grain it was not so fast, and the road from incipient to full-scale food production often took two millennia or more, especially where cereals were involved (Fuller 2007). A few comments about the possible behavioral mechanisms behind domestication, especially in the Middle East and China, and especially of cereals and legumes, are needed here since they will explain why food production was not just the result of a few years of intentional experimentation. It will also help to explain why the migrations of food-producing populations occurred often several millennia after the first tentative steps towards food production (Bellwood 2009a).

Postglacial plant collectors must initially have harvested morphologically wild cereal grains or legume pods while they were still unripe, in order to beat the problem of shattering.[3] Perhaps they sun-dried the harvest and then separated grains from chaff by pounding and winnowing, followed in the Middle East by further grinding on stone mortars to produce flour. The relatively gritty flour so produced was then baked into bread or cakes. But in China, the whole grains were boiled into gruel or porridge using pottery, a commodity not invented until the end of the Neolithic in the Middle East. Eventually, perhaps nudged by a desire to produce more food, people in both of these areas began to plant some of their reproductively-viable harvested grains. It would have been at this point that human selection towards the domesticated forms began, slowly but surely. Intentional planting in new lands away from former wild stands was a crucial element, since it minimized the danger of backcrossing and swamping of selected forms by the dominant wild population, especially for outcrossing as opposed to self-fertilizing species.[4]

Cereal domestication occurred because there was always a small minority of plants in any stand of wild cereals that carried a recessive gene that stopped them from disarticulating and scattering their seeds. Somehow, humans had to increase the proportion of these nonshattering plants in their crops in order to commence the domestication process. They could never have done this if they had only harvested and eaten slightly immature grain, year after year, without planting. There would have been no selection. They had to change their habits slightly so that they harvested some grain when it was ripe. Any delay in the date of harvesting, for whatever reason, until well into the rather long ripening period for wild cereals, would have presented for collection and replanting some of those rare mutant ears or panicles that could not disperse by themselves.

Planting in new fields would then have allowed these rare nonshattering variants to increase in frequency, hence an inexorable, if rather slow, rise of human domesticated food production and population size during these early but crucial millennia. Nonshattering and synchronously ripening cereals and legumes are the backbone of any agricultural system, since they allow efficient harvesting and hence higher yields. The process was doubtless subject to many stops and starts, as planted nonshattering grains could always backcross with shattering wild forms, thus sending the process back to the starting line. Some domestication trajectories came to feeble ends, apparently the case with rye in northern Syria during the Younger Dryas (Hillman et al. 2001). But eventually, domesticated nonshattering cereals with synchronous ripening, loss of dormancy and increased grain size began to dominate archaeological assemblages. By 7500 BC in the Middle East and 4500 BC in central China, the domestication process had advanced to the stage where truly domesticated food production, as opposed to pre-domestication cultivation of morphologically wild species, was well underway.[5]

The developments of food production in Africa and the Americas perhaps occurred in similar fashion to West Asia and China with respect to the domestication of cereals and legumes, although somewhat later in time. In Mesoamerica, maize might have been used initially by hunters and gatherers as a sugar source for making maize beer (from the stalk, like sugar cane), prior to the increase in cob size that eventually turned it into the staple cereal of the prehistoric Americas (Chapter 9).[6] This large-cob stage was only reached about 4000 years ago, this being one reason why the maize-dependent American civilizations were more recent in time than their Old World counterparts, with villages initially appearing about 2000 BC or later in Mesoamerica.

Finally, it is interesting to note that many populations never developed food production beyond a very minimal level, particularly in marginal environments. Bruce Smith has termed this 'low-level food production', and naturally these populations did not grow in numbers or spread. Neither did the many ethnographic hunter-gatherer populations who engaged in wild resource management yet never moved into food production, such as the acorn-exploiting and food-storing Californians described by Kat Anderson. Furthermore, the ancestors of even the most successful of the early farming populations subsisted from low-level food production for one or two millennia as the systematic production of fully domesticated species developed. Smith again gives a good example of this from the Eastern Woodlands of the United States, where some native seed-bearing plants were domesticated from about 4000 years ago, prior to the widespread growing of maize during the first millennium AD (Chapter 9). The level of agricultural dependence in any given situation is therefore a significant issue for demographic growth and population expansion.[7]

Food Production and Population Expansion

Food production allowed humans to live at significantly higher population densities than hunting and gathering. For instance, Walker and Hamilton (2011) estimate that a 10% increase in agricultural dietary dependence will result in a 50% rise in expected population size. In most regions of the world, except for those with only marginal productivity, the growth in numbers amongst early farmers developed hand in hand with settled life and increased birth rates.[8] Settlements grew in size as villages replaced the temporary camps of many hunters and gatherers, with the result that marriage networks could now shrink in geographical extent, as long as each settlement contained members of more than one exogamous lineage or clan. From the mobile territorial patterns of hunters and gatherers grew more fixed and localized ethnicities as more and more people packed into smaller and smaller, yet more productive, territories. Warfare grew apace, with increasing settlement sizes in western Asia, China, and Mesoamerica, reflecting in part a desire for safety in numbers.[9]

One of the most important factors in the growth in size of food-producing populations was settlement sedentism, or living in one place all year round as opposed to moving constantly within a seasonal cycle, as do many hunters and gatherers. Year-round residence in one place in the landscape is a very well-known inducement to an increasing birth rate and to increasing demands for food from the immediate vicinity of a settlement. Mothers do not need to carry children over such long distances or so frequently if they are sedentary, and if they have access to animal milk or cereal gruel they can wean their children earlier, and hence conceive more frequently.[10] All-year-round settlement sedentism is extremely difficult to demonstrate from the archaeology of prehistoric hunter-gatherer populations. But rising postglacial and pre-Neolithic human population densities certainly increased human residential group sizes. They also increased archaeological settlement sizes in key regions for later agricultural development, such as the Levant and central China.

In western Asia, many villages had attained 10 or more hectares in size by 7500 BC, with close-packed rectangular houses, populations in the thousands, granaries for storing cereals, and a growing dependence on a fully agropastoral economy.[11] China was entering a similar stage of development well before 5000 BC. Such villages, or better perhaps townships, sometimes had defensive walls, of stone in the case of Neolithic Jericho in Palestine (circa 8500 BC), or of stamped earth in the case of the urban enclosures of the Longshan and Liangzhu cultures of central China (circa 3000 BC). Others apparently relied on their concentrated human biomass to repel competitors.

However, vigorous settlement growth soon met its limitations, especially in technological circumstances that lacked wheeled transport and the easy ability to move large amounts of food from the countryside into growing towns. In both the Middle East and China, as well as in Neolithic Europe, we see distinct rises and falls in the average and maximum sizes of settlements over time, implying real and unyielding limits to the numbers who could subsist from small pieces of food-producing territory, especially in the virtual absence of sanitation. Environmental degradation can be clearly identified in parts of the late Neolithic Middle East (Chapter 7), and some populations appear to have suffered periodic episodes of social and economic collapse. Such collapses were perhaps important as inducements to migration.

The environmental stresses caused by increasing human populations during the Neolithic were doubtless rather minor compared to those in recent historical periods and today. But one of the most significant paleoclimatic observations may be that by William Ruddiman (2003, 2005), who postulates that the world's current high carbon dioxide levels can be traced ultimately to forest clearance starting with early agriculture in Eurasia about 8000 years ago. Ruddiman also traces the beginnings of a similar increase in methane levels to the commencement of wet-field rice farming in eastern Asia about 5000 years ago. Neolithic populations, therefore, appear to have laid the foundations of the global warming by greenhouse gases that causes us so much angst today.

For early food producers, there would have been two rather opposed ways of dealing with the problem of rapid growth in population size. An intensification of food production, by applying more labor to a given piece of land in order to extract more food to feed more people, was one of them. Most of the early civilizations invested in irrigation and landscape transformation through terracing, fallowing, manuring, raised field construction, and other labor-intensive techniques. Some tribal populations did this too, as for instance in the remarkable agricultural landscapes of the ethnographic New Guinea Highlands. We can also envisage such a process in some Neolithic societies, in particular amongst the early Neolithic wet-field rice growers in the Yangzi Valley (Bellwood 2011b). People who engaged in such intensive activities would hardly have wanted to migrate and leave all their investment behind for others to take over, unless adverse environmental circumstances intervened.

However, other groups of people might have seen many advantages in migration. These would have included younger offspring of farmers who missed out on inheritance of significant rights to land, people in impoverished circumstances who simply had no land at all, and people in surrounding regions who faced impact from the population instability generated by growth in the more central farming regions. Some of the latter might still have been hunters and gatherers in the early millennia of agricultural development, perhaps induced to adopt farming themselves and then to spread if they were able to survive the pressures towards assimilation imposed by the adjacent and growing populations of food producers.

From this perspective, the expansions of early food producers involved two kinds of people – members of the food-producing societies themselves, and neighbors impacted by domino effects.[12] In real life, because of propinquity, both groups might have been very closely related in cultural and genetic terms, which is why it can be so difficult to pick apart the exact population composition of migration situations that existed many thousands of years ago. In my view, the food producers themselves were the instigators of the demographic growth and of most population expansion, and also the main contributors to the migrating populations in terms of their genes, material culture and language (Bellwood 2005a). But some adjacent hunter-gatherer populations might eventually have become circumscribed into borrowing or developing their own systems of food production as a result of domino effects.

There is another interesting and more mutualistic possibility for situations of contact between farmers and hunter-gatherers. Farmers utilized far less of any given landscape than mobile foragers, unless they indulged in a great deal of foraging themselves. Because of this, farmers and foragers in many ethnographic situations were able to establish relatively stable exchange networks, at least for a while. The farmers exploited small areas of crop-producing land, while the foragers exploited the rest of the landscape and exchanged hunted meat or forest products with the farmers. Such situations existed until recently in parts of Island Southeast Asia, for instance in forested regions of interior Borneo and northern Luzon.[13] Unfortunately, however, as farmer populations increased and cleared more land for agriculture, so the prospects for hunter-gatherer survival as independent societies would have decreased, often catastrophically.[14] In the case of ancient food producer expansions, we cannot be sure that farmers and foragers would always have set up such balanced and stable networks of interaction for very long.

For many years, archaeologists were able to ignore demographic growth amongst early food producers because of an almost universal belief that farmers were not as healthy as contemporary forager populations, sometimes to such a degree that one must wonder why they bothered to develop farming at all.[15] Nowadays, we have increasing evidence that many early farming populations close to frontiers of expansion were in general healthy and well-supplied with food, at least in terms of a number of recent bioanthropological studies from different regions of the world.[16] They also had high 'Neolithic Demographic Transition' birth rates according to demographer Jean-Pierre Bocquet-Appel.[17] Even the crops enjoyed a kind of honeymoon, as Dark and Gent (2001) point out for Europe, before pests and diseases discovered how to attack them too.

But those who remained in large and growing settlements in the interiors of the agricultural zones, facing a lack of hygiene and a consequent threat of disease, increasing levels of intergroup hostility, and environmental degradation as cropping intervals decreased, were not so lucky. As Jared Diamond (1997) has noted, many epidemic diseases such as smallpox, tuberculosis, measles, influenza and whooping cough originated with our Old World commensal or domestic animals, and all flourished amongst crowded human populations. This was perhaps where the focus of poor health was concentrated. The first farmers were healthy, their crowded descendants increasingly sick.

The evidence for population expansions that depended upon developed forms of food production can be clearly read through a number of recurrent observations from archaeology and linguistics. Some of the first farmers in regions such as Europe, sub-Saharan Africa, Southeast Asia, and Oceania (excluding New Guinea) created very homogeneous and widespread cultural landscapes, far more extensive than many of the more regionalized cultures that followed, and far more extensive than could possibly have been created without some degree of population movement. Even Gordon Childe (1936: 86) noted this for the European Neolithic long ago. Migration in some form is undeniable, and we examine many examples in the following chapters. It appears also that many of the agriculturalist language families spread from home-land regions located either within, or closely clustered around, the archaeologically defined homelands of agriculture. I return to these issues in the next section, since I have absolutely no hesitation in stating that these geographical correlations were not coincidental (Diamond and Bellwood 2003).

One potential driver of migration that I do not invoke very frequently in this book is climate change. I have no doubt that autonomous climate change (i.e., climate change caused by natural forces, not human action) has been of tremendous importance in human history, especially for people who lived in zones of environmental fragility or sharp ecological transition.[18] Climatic fluctuations also opened doors for hominin migration during the Pleistocene into Eurasia and the Americas. Postglacial warming allowed the world's present investment in agricultural production to develop, as I have stressed earlier. But I am more interested in proximate causes for migrations, and while allowing climate change a major role as a facilitator of human action, I find it difficult to attribute to it a role as a prime or sole cause of any *specific* Holocene migratory situation outside the high Arctic or Saharan regions, at least not on the scale of the food producer migrations considered in the following chapters. My focus will be on human enterprise and demography as the essential factors.

The *Neolithic*

It is necessary at this point to put the world's early agricultural phases into some perspective with a discussion of Neolithic-related terminology. In Africa and Eurasia, the agricultural phases of prehistory everywhere in the latitudes where food production (including pastoralism) could exist are generally termed 'Neolithic' by archaeologists, implying originally the presence of pottery and ground stone, an absence of metallurgy, and nowadays for most authors the presence of food production. However, the term 'Neolithic' is not used in New Guinea, where developments were completely separate from Asia until very recently, and nor is it used in Japan. Neither does it tend to be used in most regions beyond the range of food production, although it turns up here and there in circumstances where pottery was present in the archaeological record of hunter-gatherers. For instance, in early Holocene Vietnam, nonagricultural cave and shell midden dwellers are often referred to as early Neolithic by some authors (but not by me – see Chapter 8) because of a presence of potsherds and edge-ground stone tools.

The term 'Neolithic' is also not used in the Americas, where prehistoric food production was again (as in New Guinea) completely independent in origin by virtue of the fact that it could not possibly have spread from Asia with available crops through Arctic Siberia or Alaska. A sea route for early farmers is also ruled out by the simple observation that American crops, domesticated animals, and recorded languages, except for Eskimo-Aleut and Na-Dene, were completely unrelated to those in Asia. American archaeologists often use the term 'Formative' for early agricultural phases in Mesoamerica and the Andes, although the term 'Early Agricultural' is now being used more and more in parts of North America, for instance in the southwestern United States.

In fact, the term 'Neolithic' has some very awkward definitional problems, because of the sheer number of situations that do not fit the classical definition in one way or another. Neolithic populations in the Fertile Crescent managed without pottery for about 3000 years after the appearance of pre-domestication cultivation, circa 10,000 BC, mainly because preparation of their staple cereals focused on a grinding of (mostly wheat) flour to make bread, rather than using unground porridge-like products that need to be cooked in water in pots. Most New Guinea Highland farmers never used pottery at all, except in a few situations of contact with coastal pottery-using peoples. On the other hand, late Palaeolithic hunters and gatherers in eastern Asia and Japan used pottery widely, as did some recent groups in Alaska and northern Canada, but did not practice agriculture. Andamanese hunters and gatherers also made very simple pottery in ethnographic times.[19]

The upshot of this is that pottery making and usage was not exclusively a marker of the Neolithic and its successors, even though we can state with firm assurance that the bulk of the pottery in the world archaeological record was made by food-producing populations. Polished stone tools were more universal than pottery in association with early agriculture, occurring in New Guinea and the Americas as well as the Old World, but recent discoveries in Japan and Australia also include edge-ground stone axes that date back almost 40,000 years (Chapter 5). So grinding was not an absolute Neolithic marker either, even though we can guarantee again, as with pottery, that any randomly picked up fully polished stone axe from the earth's surface will have a far greater chance of having been made by a farmer than a hunter.

What, therefore, was the Neolithic? I will define it as having the following attributes, albeit not always all of them together (particularly in situations where the archaeological record is only poorly known):

1. Botanical and zoological evidence for food production, commencing in homeland regions from the earliest stages of pre-domestication cultivation and animal taming, via a phase of low-level food production, through to an increasing dependence on domesticated resources that sometimes had sufficient demographic impact to drive migrations.

2. A roster of crops and animals that could serve as a portmanteau biota (Crosby 1986: 89), untied to narrow parameters of day length, temperature, or rainfall seasonality, and capable of being propagated in environments sometimes quite different from those of the homeland region.

3. Evidence for sedentary settlements and increasing population density. Within 3000 years of the beginnings of food production in the Fertile Crescent and China, some people were living in villages/towns that covered tens, even hundreds of hectares, often defended against competitors. Such very dense populations would not have always been in a position to migrate freely themselves, except perhaps as refugees, especially when constrained by investments in intensive production and the demands of elites. But their actions might well have caused others to migrate through the operation of domino theory.

4. A continuing interest in hunting and gathering, as well as fishing, as necessary.

5. In general, but not always, the presence of baked earthenware pottery and polished stone tools, plus other technological items such as looms and spindle whorls for weaving.

6. In general, an absence of metallurgy, although some of the earliest food producers in the Fertile Crescent used artifacts of hammered copper and gold, and the earliest farmers much later in northern India had cast copper tools (and thus are generally referred to as Chalcolithic). The Bantu migrations in Africa were also fuelled to a degree by a use of iron tools.

7. Increasing signs of an interest in exotic and status items (e.g., jade in China, massive stone ritual and burial structures together with gold in the Fertile Crescent and Europe), as we might expect in situations where social status was gradually becoming more defined as population density increased.

Food Production as the Driving Force of Early Agriculturalist Migration

The driving forces generated by the major food production complexes of the Old and New Worlds had huge repercussions in Holocene human prehistory, repercussions that continue today. Throughout their time spans, these complexes have been fuelled by a remarkably small number of astoundingly productive domesticated crops and animals (Diamond 1997). A world without wheat, barley, rice, peas, beans, millets, yams, cattle, sheep, pigs, goats and chickens would be a hungry world indeed, given our present population size. These are all Old World species, but we must also thank the New World for maize, potatoes, manioc, squashes, other kinds of beans, llamas, alpacas and turkeys. And let us not forget (again) our best friend the dog, possibly domesticated initially in the temperate Eurasian Upper Palaeolithic more than 30,000 years ago, yet also eaten as a meat staple in many ancient societies.

However, the New World animals never came close to Old World species in total meat production, and the New World had far fewer productive cereal species than the Old. Some believe this might be one reason why American farming dispersals were never as large and widespread as those of the Old World, and the civilizations there much younger in time. This circumstance was magnified by the geographical shape of the American continents, which are greatly constricted and circumscribed in some of their most fertile tropical latitudes in central America.

The fact that so few plant and animal species had such a massive impact in the human domesticated economy means that their homelands stand out in the archaeological record as places of singular importance. These homelands, and their food production complexes, were literally the driving forces behind the unfoldings described in the next few chapters. Four key homelands were of profound importance, simply because of the huge significance of the crops and animals that they produced in domesticated form. They fuelled some of the greatest food producer migrations in Holocene prehistory. Another four were of more localized importance, in that their trajectories of population growth only really expanded when certain crops, especially major cereals such as wheat, rice and maize, were introduced from elsewhere.

The four big regions in terms of food production, virtual behemoths of global development in early agriculture, were the following (see Figure 6.1 and Figure 9.4):

1. *The Fertile Crescent of Western Asia* (Chapter 7). Here we find the origins of wheat, barley, sheep, goats, pigs, cattle, and certain podded legumes such as peas, broad beans and lentils. The food production system that developed here spread with human migration, between roughly 8500 and 3000 BC, to regions characterized mainly by winter rainfall regimes. These included the Middle East to as far as northwestern India, the Mediterranean, temperate Europe, the central Asian steppes and semi-deserts, and North Africa. The system eventually reached its limits as a total complex (ignoring deserts and high mountains) against the monsoon climates of sub-Saharan Africa and those of South and East Asia, also against the Arctic climates of northern Eurasia. However, many of its component crops and animals traveled much further before the colonial era – sheep and goats

through Africa, wheat and barley into central and southwestern China and the Ganges Basin – albeit without substantial human migration.

2. *The Yellow and Yangzi Basins of China* (Chapter 8). Here we find the origins of short grain (subspecies *japonica*) rice, foxtail and common millet, soybean, pigs and chickens, indigenous cattle, and let us not forget the silkworm. This food production system spread to and beyond the limits of the Asian monsoon, with human migration, between 4000 and 1000 BC, in a complementary fashion to that from the Fertile Crescent. It traveled westwards to overlap with the Fertile Crescent complex in northern India, western China and Tibet, where both rice and wheat were grown, but never really extended beyond these regions into central Asia. *Japonica* rice-growing populations eventually settled most of Southeast Asia, but Island Southeast Asian and Pacific Island food production complexes were also heavily influenced by the development of tuber and fruit horticulture in the New Guinea region. As with the Fertile Crescent, certain crops naturally spread further, without significant migration, in later prehistory, especially rice to western Asia and the Mediterranean, and tubers and bananas to sub-Saharan Africa.

3. *Northern sub-Saharan Africa* (Chapter 9). Here we find the origins of certain yam species, a West African species of rice, and several species of millet (especially pearl millet, finger millet and sorghum). The origin region for all these crops is rather wide, extending from West Africa across to Ethiopia, and the main crops were perhaps domesticated between 5000 and 3000 years ago. They spread with human migration through all the monsoonal regions of sub-Saharan Africa, reaching their limits in the Kalahari Desert and the small area of Mediterranean climate in southwestern Africa, neither region penetrated by crop-growing populations, as opposed to sheep pastoralists, in prehistory. The millets also spread to India and Pakistan around 4000 years ago, presumably by transference across the Indian Ocean. The tropical African food production system received a sharp boost, perhaps around 2000 years ago, when bananas and taro were introduced from Southeast Asia, presumably by sea voyagers reaching the East African coast from Indonesia. Eurasian sheep, goats, and cattle were introduced much earlier, around the sixth millennium BC from the Levant, with humped cattle also being transferred later from South Asia to East Africa.

4. *Mesoamerica* (Chapter 9: mainly Mexico and Guatemala). Here we find the origins of maize, some species of beans and squashes, tomatoes, capsicum (chili pepper), avocado, and turkeys. Other crops such as sweet potatoes, other capsicums (peppers) and *Xanthosoma* (an aroid, like taro) were probably domesticated further south, in northern South America. The Mesoamerican hearth was the main source for the maize, beans and squash triumvirate that began to spread widely with human migration after 2000 BC, first to the US Southwest and the Andes, and later (during the first millennium AD) without detectable population migration into the eastern United States. As with the western Pacific, however, the Mesoamerican complex, and the other American food production complexes generally, were not such great drivers of human migration as their Old World counterparts, owing basically to their lesser levels of energy production and to geographical circumscription.

In the aforementioned four regions, food production was responsible for some very considerable episodes of human farming and language family migration, as we will see in Chapters 7–9. The other four regions had less migratory impact in human history, and their Holocene food production complexes only spread seriously after the introductions of highly productive and externally domesticated cereal or animal species. They are as follows:

1. *Western Pacific* (Chapter 8), including New Guinea (especially the Highlands). Here we find the origins for varieties of sugarcane, yams, taro and bananas, mostly after 4000 BC. Other crops such as breadfruit, coconut, sago palm (many species) and canarium nut originated in the tropical lowlands of Island Southeast Asia and western Oceania. There is currently some discussion, but few hard data, as to whether these crops were also domesticated in Island Southeast Asia before the Neolithic, since soft fruits and tubers leave few traces in the archaeological record. This food production system dominated subsistence in the Pacific islands, since rice never spread during prehistory beyond Indonesia and the Mariana Islands, and it was associated with initial human migration into the islands of Oceania beyond the Solomons. However, major migrations into Oceania only began after elements of the Chinese food production system were introduced, especially rice into Indonesia, with domesticated pigs and dogs (Chapter 8).

2. Another possible region of early food production, of less certain date and migratory significance, existed in *South Asia* (Chapter 7), where Indian long-grained rice (*Oryza sativa indica*) was originally domesticated, as well as several species of millet, grams and legumes, cotton, zebu cattle and water buffalo. However, it is possible that *indica* rice domestication was triggered by an earlier arrival in the Ganges basin of domesticated East Asian rice, *Oryza sativa japonica*, from the Yangzi basin of China. In Neolithic times, South Asia sent out few migrants to neighboring regions, and none at all to Southeast Asia, although the cultural impact of this region increased dramatically with the spreads of Indic traders and religions (Buddhism and Hinduism) after 300 BC.

3. *The central Andes* and adjacent coastal regions of Peru (Chapter 9) provided the origins for the chenopod seed-bearing plant *quinoa*, jack beans, white potatoes, sweet potatoes and cotton, together with llama and alpaca for meat, wool and pack transport. It is possible that some of the Amazonian language families originated close to the Andes, particularly Arawak, Panoan and Tucanoan, and in the Andes themselves the Aymara and Quechua families underwent considerable expansion, mostly within the past 3000 years. However, much of the Andean expansion followed the introduction and widespread consumption of maize after 2000 BC. The Amazonian expansions were perhaps tied to the domestications of manioc and sweet potato.

4. *The Eastern Woodlands of the United States*, especially the Ohio, Mississippi, and Missouri Valleys, also witnessed some local domestication of native seed-bearing crops after about 4000 years ago, but it is difficult to see any clear indications of population spread here until the appearance of maize during the first millennium AD. Siouan and Iroquoian expansions appear to have occurred mainly after the widespread consumption of maize began.

In the following three chapters, each of these regions of early food production will be dealt with in turn. Many other regions of the late hunter-gatherer world no doubt witnessed minor but independent trends towards food production in the generous climatic and environmental conditions of the Holocene, but I will stress again that my concern in this book is with human population migration, rather than independence, or otherwise, of agricultural origins. My main observation is that most of the significant food producer migrations of the Holocene were driven by a small number of very productive subsistence complexes that were based on the exploitation of relative small sets of productive domesticated plants and animals. It has been these complexes that have underpinned much of the structure of global prehistory during the Holocene, at least in the agricultural latitudes.

Notes

1. On theories to explain the origins of food production, see Bellwood 2005a, especially Chapters 2 and 3; Zeder 2006.
2. See Diamond 1997, 2002, 2012.
3. Domesticated crops, both cereals and legumes, differ from wild ones in that they do not shatter when ripe (i.e., disperse their seeds) and so are easier to harvest. The grains are looser and easier to thresh from their encasing hulls, and domesticated crops tend to ripen synchronously – important for any kind of bulk harvesting using sickles. They also lose their need to remain dormant in the ground for part of the year, as determined in the wild by changing day lengths and rainfall distributions, and so can be transferred to new environments in which different seasonal patterns of rainfall can occur. Domesticated crops, and animals, thus formed a transportable 'portmanteau biota' (Crosby 1986) for early food-producing populations, helpful indeed for forming new settlements in new landscapes.
4. Kislev et al. 2004; Allaby et al. 2008; Jones and Brown 2008.
5. Weiss et al. 2006; Balter 2007; Fuller 2007; Willcox et al. 2008; Fuller et al. 2009.
6. Smalley and Blake 2003; Webster 2011.
7. See Smith 2001, 2011; Anderson 2005; Rowley-Conwy and Layton 2013.
8. Bocquet-Appel and Naji 2006; Bocquet-Appel 2011.
9. LeBlanc 2003; Rosenberg 2003.
10. Vigne 2008: 186 points out that an increasing demand for ruminant milk might have been an essential factor behind cattle and goat domestication.
11. Kuijt and Goring-Morris 2002; Kuijt 2008. Circular granaries with raised wooden floors first appeared during the PPNA in the southern Levant: see Kuijt and Finlayson 2009.
12. A domino effect is "the theory that a political event etc. in one country will cause similar events in neighbouring countries, like a row of falling dominoes" (*Concise Oxford*). An example of a domino effect from the recent colonial past would be the effect of European settlement on the indigenous peoples of the United States, many of whom were either translocated west by force beyond the best agricultural lands of the eastern United States, or sometimes chose to move by themselves as European settlers occupied their ancestral lands. The artist George Catlin 2004, original 1841 witnessed and described much of this from first hand observations on the Mississippi and Missouri Rivers in the 1830s.
13. Peterson 1978; Sellato 1994.

14. Eder 1987 and Headland 1997 discuss striking examples of this problem from the Philippines, where Agta survival in Luzon is still threatened by forest removal and land development in the Sierra Madre.
15. Cohen and Armelagos 1980; Larsen 2006.
16. Eshed et al. 2004; Oxenham and Tayles 2006; Pinhasi and Stock 2011.
17. Bocquet-Appel 2011: S498 estimates that average birth rates in the Pre-Pottery Neolithic Levant increased from 4.5 to 10 per woman over a 2500 year period between about 9000 and 6500 BC. This is quite incredible growth, although increasing death rates would have slowed down the net rate of increase after a few centuries.
18. See, for instance, the study by Zhang et al. 2011 on the causal significance of climate change in large-scale human crises in preindustrial Europe and the Northern Hemisphere.
19. Dutta 1978; Cooper 1985. See Lucier and VanStone 1992 on recent Eskimo-Aleut pottery making.

Chapter 7
The Fertile Crescent Food Production Complex

This chapter examines the Holocene expansions of archaeological complexes, language families and human populations that emanated from the Fertile Crescent region of agricultural development centered on the Middle East. Beyond the Fertile Crescent, these expansions encompassed Europe, central Asia, the northern part of the Indian Sub-continent, and North Africa. They met their limits in climates too cold for agriculture to the north, and in the deserts and monsoon climates that dominated much of Africa and southern and eastern Asia. These population expansions required many millennia to reach their limits, in each case with some very considerable cultural and genetic transfor-mations along the way. But the results can be read to imply the workings of internally conjoined processes fuelled by developments in food production and consequent popula-tion growth. In the Fertile Crescent, the early fortunes of the Indo-European and Afroasiatic language families were linked directly to these agriculturalist (including pastoralist) migrations, as less directly were the fortunes of the Dravidian languages of Peninsular India and the Turkic languages of central Asia.

The Fertile Crescent food production complex eventually spread to become roughly coterminous with the pre-AD 1500 distributions of the Indo-European and Afroasiatic language families, and with those human populations who reveal clear Western Eurasian ancestry in their genes. There is, of course, considerable variation across these popula-tions. Northern Indians are visually distinguishable from northern Europeans, just as Ethiopians are visually distinguishable from Arabs and Israelis. Cultures and peoples met and mixed in multiple circumstances, and natural selection and genetic drift were doubtless very busy over the millennia. But the shared threads of historical causation remain clear, despite all the real-world complexity of actual on-the-spot human behavior.

Although the Western Eurasian phenotype evolved biologically long before the appearance of agriculture, its ultimate distribution has certainly involved a large amount of agriculturally induced population expansion during prehistoric times. Other popula-tions, such as early Turkic, Dravidian, and possibly Yeniseian speakers, whose descen-dants reveal rather less Western Eurasian ancestry in their genes, were also very strongly impacted by the spread of Fertile Crescent domesticated animals and pastoralism.

Fertile Crescent agro-pastoralism had already spread over much of the Middle East by the end of a formative *pre-domestication* phase of early food production that lasted

First Migrants: Ancient Migration in Global Perspective, First Edition. Peter Bellwood.
© Peter Bellwood. Published 2013 by John Wiley & Sons, Ltd.

perhaps 2000 years, between about 9500 and 7500 BC. This phase culminated after 7500 BC with the dominance of fully domesticated crops and animals. Many of the largest Neolithic villages of the region reached maximal extents around this time. Indeed, many settlements were abandoned or shrank in size soon thereafter, a situation that implies considerable pressure on food and other resources. It is debatable whether this pressure was due to human impact, autonomous climate change, or a combination of both, but the fact remains that many human groups in the Middle East began to face resource stresses as human population densities peaked. One result was that populations began to spread after 7000 BC with their cultural resources and languages, westwards through Europe and eastwards into northern India and towards central Asia. By 5000 BC, farming populations had reached Egypt, Sudan, and Ethiopia. By 3000 BC, much of the expansion was already over, but the Fertile Crescent complex of food production and technology has lived on until today as one of the most significant in world history. After all, it also fuelled the eventual European settlements of Australia and the Americas.

Agricultural Origins in the Fertile Crescent

The Fertile Crescent was the region of origin for the domesticated wheats, barley, certain legumes (especially peas, broad beans and lentils), sheep, goats, pigs and taurine (non-humped) cattle. Geographically, it curves around like a boomerang to the north of the Syrian Desert, from southern Israel to the head of the Persian Gulf, enclosed to its north and east by the various mountain ranges of Turkey and the Zagros Mountains of western Iran. To the west it approaches the Mediterranean Sea (Figure 7.1). The climate is generally warm temperate with a strong winter rainfall peak and a hot, dry summer. The major cereals and legumes that were domesticated here were adapted to grow during the winter rainfall season, and this was a major determining factor in the ultimate distribution of what is here termed "the Fertile Crescent food production complex."

The first developments in food production predictably occurred in riverine and lacustrine settings in this dry region, especially along the Jordan, upper Euphrates, and upper Tigris rivers. There is little evidence for any strong maritime orientation, although it must be remembered that the sea remained well below its present level until 5000 BC, so any early Neolithic sites on the Mediterranean and Black Sea coasts will now be deeply drowned (indeed, the remains of a few have been discovered on the sea bed).

Within this large area, archaeological knowledge is rather varied in quality, not always aided by current political and humanitarian crises. Botanical and zoological data (see Figure 7.1) indicate that the wild ancestors of the most important domesticated crops and animals overlapped in distribution in a relatively small region of alluvial and 'hilly flanks' terrain, located in the northern Levant and southeastern Anatolia.[1] The distribution does not mean that the whole Fertile Crescent agro-pastoral complex evolved entirely in this region, and many of the major species were probably cultivated or tamed initially in more than one place.[2] The important point is that many component parts of a very powerful system of food production eventually came together as a whole, linked by communication and population expansion. By 7500 BC, the whole of the Fertile

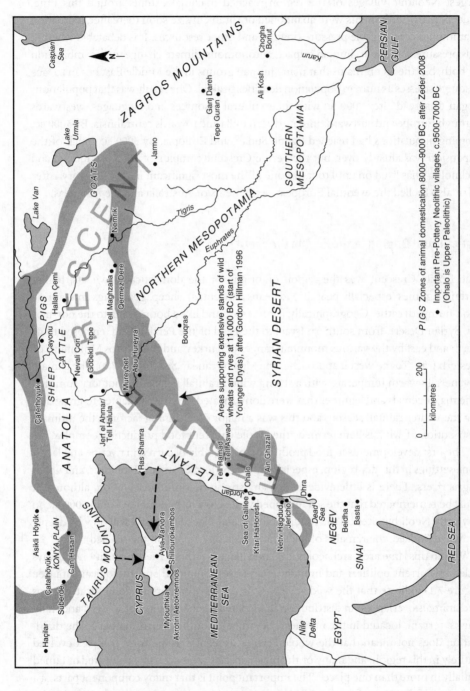

Figure 7.1 The Fertile Crescent: likely zones of cereal and animal domestication, and some major Pre-Pottery Neolithic sites.

Crescent had evolved interlaced production complexes that stretched from Israel to central Anatolia, and from the eastern Mediterranean to western Iran. These were capable of fuelling some of the most important human migrations of the past 10,000 years, through vast areas of northern Africa, central and southern Asia, and Europe.

According to current understanding, the northern Levant and southeastern Anatolia comprised the most formative region in the development of pre-domestication cultivation and animal husbandry, mainly between 9500 and 7000 BC. However, it is important to remember that the oldest evidence for exploitation of wild cereals in the Fertile Crescent actually comes from the site of Ohalo, far to the south and now submerged under the Sea of Galilee. At Ohalo, the waterlogged conditions preserved evidence for the grinding of wild emmer and barley grains to make flour, associated with the remains of six oval hut floors with plant straw bedding.[3] Remarkably, this site was occupied during the last glacial maximum, and so preceded any evidence for cereal domestication by over 10,000 years. But it does drive home the observation that the whole Fertile Crescent probably witnessed a number of small independent and local innovations that later became melded into a regional and very powerful economic whole.

The fusion of cereal and animal species into a domesticated economy occurred gradually during the two successive Pre-Pottery Neolithic (PPN) phases termed PPNA and PPNB, before the common use of earthenware pottery. During the PPNA, 9500–8500 BC, the economy seems to have been mainly one of pre-domestication cultivation but increasing settlement size. The PPNB (8500–7000 BC) saw domesticated plants and animals eventually dominate the food production economies of massive settlements, with human and animal populations in the thousands. Mean site sizes in the central and southern Levant increased through the duration of the PPN from 1 to about 10 ha. Two-storeyed houses made an appearance in the PPNB, with increasing evidence for communal grain storage. According to available survey records, new settlement foundation events in the northern Levant and upper Euphrates Valley increased during the course of the PPN from under 10 to between 40 and 70 per millennium. While there is a great deal of regional variation in such figures, it is clear that the core region of the Fertile Crescent underwent massive growth in population size and density, particularly during the PPNB. At least a ten-times multiplication of human population can be suggested through the two successive PPN phases.[4]

Another very important factor contributing to human population increase during this period was the consumption of milk from cows and goats, and the consequent selection within human populations for a lactase gene that allowed the carbohydrates in milk to be hydrolyzed into energy-providing glucose and galactose. Lipid residues in pottery indicate use of milk in Anatolia by at least the end of the PPNB. Jean-Denis Vigne discusses a number of indications, including age-at-death profiles for female animals, that suggest ruminant milk was exploited as early as the middle PPNB. Without the lactase gene for lactose digestion, now widespread in those parts of the western Old World (including North Africa) where milk is consumed regularly, milk had to be boiled or consumed as cheese, ghee, or yoghurt, or presumably not consumed at all.[5]

All of these newly domesticated sources of food, unavailable in such quantities to previous Paleolithic and Mesolithic hunter-gatherer populations, meant that human populations and settlement sizes increased in unison. They also meant that human society itself became considerably more complex than during the Paleolithic. From about 9000 BC onwards, the Fertile Crescent witnessed the construction and carving of some truly remarkable and monumental architectural creations, the first in world history. This was the beginning of the technological road that led to the Great Pyramid, the Royal Tombs of Ur, Persepolis, the Parthenon, Angkor Wat, and indeed the Empire State Building. Nothing like it had happened during the Paleolithic, even allowing for some wonderful cave art in Aurignacian, Solutrean, and Magdalenian Europe. The so-called Neolithic Revolution in the Fertile Crescent was not just a revolution in the production of food and textiles, but also a revolution in the whole creative process that we see behind later human civilization in the western Old World. Of course, civilizations evolved independently elsewhere, particularly in China and parts of the Americas, but the driving technology of our modern world still has some of its deepest foundations located firmly in the Fertile Crescent.

To make my point, I will mention two monumental PPNA sites in the Fertile Crescent that I have had the good fortune to visit, both with construction commencing at about 9000 BC. Both rank as the oldest monuments of their kind in the world. One is the Neolithic *tell* (archaeological mound) of Jericho in the Jordan valley, with its massive stone defensive wall at least 4 m high, rock-cut external ditch, and 8 m high circular solid masonry tower with an internal staircase. While opinions differ on function (defense against enemies seems most likely to me, but flood defense and 'ritual' usage are also possible), the Jericho PPNA monument is a very impressive piece of construction, a first in world prehistory.

The second site is Göbekli Tepe, located on what is today a rather barren ridge top above the Balikh drainage basin (a tributary of the Upper Euphrates) near Sanliurfa in southeastern Turkey. Göbekli is rather incredible because of its massive T-shaped limestone and possibly anthropomorphic pillars, up to 5 m high, decorated with bas-relief carvings of somewhat menacing animals (lots of curved beaks and claws) and possible images of roofed houses. These pillars were set around the insides of circular or oval stone-walled enclosures that were sometimes partly sunk into the ground, generally with two larger free-standing T-shaped pillars in the middle. The pillars weigh up to 10 tonnes, and were erected at Göbekli during two major building phases. Similar T-shaped pillars are known to occur at five other archaeological sites in the vicinity, and apparently might exist in the hundreds across a large region of the northern Levant.

Opinions differ about Göbekli Tepe. The regional economy was supported by continuing hunting as well as by the feeding of legumes to husbanded pigs and sheep, together with some kind of pre-domestication cereal and legume cultivation, as at the contemporary Syrian Euphrates site of Jerf el Ahmar. But were the structures on the site itself for communal or residential use? Why the interest in carving male human and animal genitalia, and potentially dangerous beasts?[6] I find such questions difficult to answer, but the interesting point is that this site did not emphasize the 'mother goddess' element of female fertility, which clearly became much more of a driving force in the superstitions of the established PPNB and Pottery Neolithic farmers who much later occupied western and central Anatolia, the Levant, southeastern Europe and Pakistan, after 7000 BC. The very first food producers in Anatolia, it seems, were not very interested in mother goddesses.

By the end of the PPNB, and during the following PPNC and Pottery Neolithic (7000 BC onwards), the production system that powered the Fertile Crescent Neolithic was beginning to show some signs of strain. The southern Levant, in particular, has low rainfall, and the warning signs first appeared here in the form of a widespread episode of site abandonment at the end of the PPNA (circa 8500 BC), for instance at Jericho. More widespread site abandonment or shrinkage occurred after 7000 BC, extending into the northern Levant and Anatolia, even though some of the largest PPN villages of the region reached maximal extents around this date.[7] The overall situation implies considerable pressure on environmental resources. Switches away from arable farming towards pastoralism occurred widely at this time, and many authors take the view that an apparent climatic downturn around 6200 BC contributed greatly to the situation (e.g., Sherratt 2007; Bar-Yosef 2011, 2012).

If we examine the larger picture, it becomes clear that final Pre-Pottery and Pottery Neolithic cultures began to spread outwards from the Fertile Crescent around 7000 BC, westwards into Europe, and eastwards into Pakistan and central Asia. Movement into North Africa perhaps did not occur until 2000 years later, so the whole process was therefore not particularly rapid. Peripheral regions such as northern Europe and northern India were only reached after the passage of about 4000 years. These spreads carried Fertile Crescent crops, animals and cultural resources, doubtless including languages. In an agronomic sense, the whole complex eventually reached its prehistoric limits in the summer-rainfall (monsoon) climates of sub-Saharan Africa and Asia beyond the Indus. These monsoon climates were not suited to wheat or barley production since both evolved as winter crops and would have required irrigation if grown during the dry monsoon zone winters. The West and the East, Occident and Orient, have thus had their separate agronomic foundations since at least 10,000 years back in time.

Two major questions arise before we move further to examine the expansions beyond the Fertile Crescent. Firstly, did one monolithic economy and cultural complex spread over such a vast area, or were there many constantly differentiating variants? The answer here supports the latter situation, given that the spreads themselves eventually reached their limits after many millennia of interaction with other populations. Neolithic material culture hardly remained identical all the way from the Euphrates to England or India. As we will see, many periods of stasis occurred during the expansions, sometimes for a millennium or more. Many regions reveal a considerable survival of Mesolithic populations within the Neolithic matrix. So, while a distinct and archaeologically identifiable food production system drove this expansion, it also became refracted by time, space and context into many regional variants.

Secondly, we might ask if the expansion of the Fertile Crescent economy was accompanied by an expansion of genetically and culturally related Neolithic populations, or was it due in each region simply to adoption by Mesolithic hunter-gatherers? The answer is clearly population expansion with admixture, not just in terms of the patterning in the linguistic and genetic data, but also because the archaeological cultures of the initial migration phases are generally much more unified over regions much larger than those occupied by their immediate successors. Food production did not merely spread through a static web of indigenous Mesolithic populations.

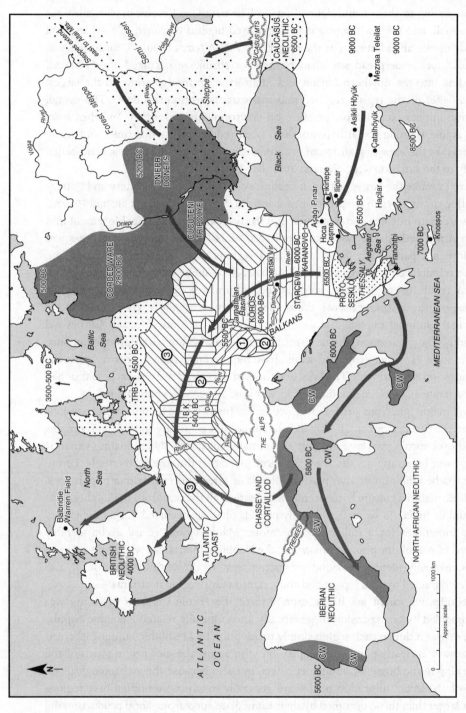

Figure 7.2 The expansion of Neolithic cultures from the Fertile Crescent into Europe. Archaeological cultures are in capitals with dates. (1) LBK origin region in western Hungary; (2) early LBK expansion; (3) later LBK expansion; CW Cardial Ware. Modified from Bellwood

Neolithic and Chalcolithic Expansion Beyond the Fertile Crescent

Anatolia and Southeastern Europe

One of the initial population movements from the Fertile Crescent traveled across Europe, eventually reaching Britain and southern Scandinavia by 4000 BC. The movement was essentially two-pronged, utilizing the Danube to the north of the Alps and the Mediterranean coastlines to the south, with an ultimate meeting between these two separate colonizing population streams in France (Figure 7.2). The Neolithic cultures of Greece and the Balkans originated from the Levant or Anatolia. But as the expansion progressed across Europe it often paused, particularly as it filled the alluvial Carpathian Basin of Hungary, the source of the Linearbandkeramik (LBK) culture that occupied the fertile loess (windblown glacial era) soils of much of northern Europe.

Pauses also occurred along the far western and northern coastlines of Europe, where more rugged environmental conditions and firmly entrenched maritime Mesolithic populations provided some resistance to Neolithic settlers. Research on ancient diet from the analysis of stable isotopes in human bone shows clearly that there was a marked shift from freshwater and marine to terrestrial diets across the Mesolithic to Neolithic transition in most of Europe, except in coastal regions such as the Baltic coast and Portugal, where fishing continued and where long-term Mesolithic survival is well attested.[8]

In Anatolia itself, the initial expansions of early food-producing populations reached central Anatolia from the upper Tigris and Euphrates valleys during the PPNB, about 8000 BC. Pottery had already come into use by the time the movement reached the Aegean seaboard of Turkey, about 6500 BC.[9] Many changes occurred during this west-ward movement. In particular, the monumental stone buildings so typical of eastern sites such as Göbekli Tepe, Nevali Çori and Çayönü were replaced in central Anatolia by clustered rectilinear room complexes of mud brick. In these central Anatolian sites, such as the famous 12 ha Çatal Höyük on the Konya Plain (7400–6000 BC), ritual para-phernalia and burials occurred within and under the floors of many of the rooms, rather than being concentrated in separate public buildings. This situation has led Mehmet Özdoğan (2011a) to ask if the colonization process was relatively egalitarian, owing to the absence of elaborate cult and prestige paraphernalia. Did it perhaps involve founder groups with relatively poor prospects of inheriting land and status at home, in search of chances to escape hierarchy, maybe even oppression (Chapter 6)?

Beyond the Konya Plain, the westward colonization process became multipronged. Off the Asian mainland, the island of Cyprus was the first to be reached, initially it would seem by hunters, and certainly by boat. Perhaps they crossed the shortest sea distance of 90 km from southern Anatolia, although the exact source is unknown and will now be under the sea. By 9500 BC, the first Cypriots were hunting an extinct species of pygmy hippopotamus, together with deer and pigs that had presumably been transported from the mainland. Ayia Varvara, dated to soon after 9000 BC in the interior of the island, has a PPNA-type microlithic tool kit and pig bones, but no charred plant remains, so its exact economic status is uncertain.[10]

However, Cyprus was certainly supporting a full Neolithic economy with strong Levantine and Anatolian PPNB affinities by 8400 BC, evidenced at sites such as Mylouthkia and Shillourokambos. A veritable Noah's Ark of pigs, cattle, goats, sheep, dogs, foxes, fallow deer, mice, and cats (to catch the mice in granaries?) was in residence by this time, all non-native to Cyprus and transported from the mainland. This menagerie alone should be enough to convince us that boat building and ocean navigation skills were relatively efficient. Some of these animals, especially the fallow deer, must have traveled as deliberately transported wild species, and mice can easily stow away on boats. Others, particularly goats, were apparently domesticated on Cyprus from introduced wild forebears. The sheep and cattle were incipiently domesticated, or at least deliberately bred, when they arrived, and might have been used for their milk as well as their meat. Einkorn wheat underwent rapid increase in grain size on the island by 7500 BC, suggesting that the isolation of Cyprus from wild cereal habitats on the mainland might have played a role in promoting successful cereal domestication there.

Continuing population growth in the Fertile Crescent led to more dramatic movements starting around 7000 BC, particularly with the developments of full domestication economies and pottery usage. These were directed through western Anatolia into the Aegean islands and mainland Greece, and northwestwards through Thrace into the Balkans. They were multiple, and sometimes cross-cutting. The spreading farmers had to adapt to changing environments in moving from the drier east to the wetter west of Anatolia, then onwards into the Balkans and the lower Danube, dealing with increasing forest and higher rainfall. This led to gradual architectural shifts away from the agglomerated sun-dried mud brick dwelling structures characteristic of central Anatolia towards the free-standing one- or two-roomed wattle and daub houses found in northwest Anatolia, Thrace and the Balkans. The need to make such adaptations apparently slowed down the rate of population spread, and it has been suggested that there was an agricultural standstill on the Konya plain for 1500 years to prepare for the successful movement, circa 6500 BC, into the forests of western Anatolia.[11]

In recent years, it has become clear that Crete was reached about 500 years before the rest of the Greek mainland, with preceramic colonization dated to 7000 BC at Knossos. A separate Pottery Neolithic movement reached mainland Greece a little later, about 6500 BC, either from western coastal Anatolia or directly by sea from the Levant. With it came red slipped or burnished pottery, sometimes impressed, and a fully domesticated repertoire of Fertile Crescent cereals, legumes, and animals. This tradition probably played a formative role in the eventual Neolithic settlement, after 5800 BC, of the Mediterranean coastline of southern Europe, from the Adriatic to Iberia, by people who made a variety of impressed pottery termed Cardial Ware.[12]

The Neolithic settlement of the Balkans, and ultimately northern Europe, also stemmed from Anatolia, probably via Thrace and up the west coast of the Black Sea towards the lower Danube. This movement occurred in two successive phases – an earlier with monochrome pottery and a later with red-slipped and painted pottery, often white-on-red. These traditions traveled with many other distinctive artifacts that link the whole complex back into central Anatolia. Some of the most widely reported items are pottery cult vessels with three or four legs, bone spoons and hooks, baked clay spindle whorls, pottery stamps, and pottery female figurines.[13] The initial spread of the monochrome pottery tradition reached Thrace around 6500 BC, but the succeeding spread of the painted pottery (circa 6200 BC) appears to have been more rapid and widespread, leading into the red-slipped and painted pottery traditions that developed right through the Neolithic Balkans, from Thessaly northwards and westwards into the Carpathian Basin of Hungary. Population expansion was perhaps enhanced when the former freshwater Black Sea was suddenly flooded around 6200 BC by an inrush of sea water from the Mediterranean, over its Bosporus sill.[14] There is little evidence from the Black Sea itself to suggest a major emigration at this time since any relevant archaeology is now deeply drowned, but the possibility is intriguing.

As in western Asia, the establishment of the Fertile Crescent Neolithic economy in southeastern Europe was associated with rapid population growth. As an example, Neolithic site numbers in some regions of Thessaly increased by a factor of 5 within a few centuries, giving rise to a network of settlements averaging 2 ha in size spaced less than 3 km apart. This is quite striking, especially in light of an almost complete lack of previous Mesolithic settlement in the same area. The Fertile Crescent domesticated animals and plants were also introduced into many regions of Europe with a high degree of homogeneity, despite variations to north and south of the Alps.[15] Ancient mtDNA analysis has revealed that both the domesticated cattle and pigs were initially of Fertile Crescent rather than local European genetic origin.[16]

Neolithic Migration Beyond Greece and the Balkans

The huge radiocarbon database available to modern archaeologists (from no less than 735 sites in Pinhasi et al. 2005) leaves no doubt that Neolithic economies spread through most of temperate Europe between 6500 and 4000 BC (Figure 7.2).[17] Those who followed the Mediterranean route reached Iberia and parts of North Africa by about 5500 BC, leaving a trail of village settlements with stamped Cardial Ware pottery of apparently Anatolian ultimate inspiration.[18] These people were interspersed here and there with surviving Mesolithic populations, but clear signs of interrelationship between Neolithic and Mesolithic populations are rare in Europe, except in rugged and mountainous regions such as the Iron Gates gorge on the Danube, and peripheral regions of central and northern Europe (Alps, Scandinavia, Baltic) where food production diminished due to short growing seasons.[19] One recent suggestion is that Neolithic people might have carried serious zoonoses (diseases derived from domesticated animals) such as smallpox, which, if correct, would have given them a survival advantage over Mesolithic populations who lacked immunity (Holtby et al. 2012).

The movement up the Danube valley reached the Carpathian Basin by about 6000 BC. The fertile alluvial soils of the Danube and its tributaries here allowed considerable demographic growth to occur as a foundation for a further advance. This took place with incredible speed, within a century or so either side of 5400 BC, over the glacial windblown loess soils that occupy much of the European landscape north of the Alps. This cultural advance has become known as the *Danubian* or *Linearbandkeramik*, and its immediate origins appear to have been in the Körös culture of the Tisza Valley, in the northern part of the Carpathian Basin. The LBK spread rapidly westwards with its characteristic longhouses to reach the Paris Basin, while other culturally-related groups spread eastwards towards the lower Danube in Romania.[20]

The LBK economy was based on permanent field cultivation of emmer and einkorn wheat, and common millet (*Panicum miliaceum*), together with husbandry of Fertile Crescent lineages of cattle, pigs, sheep and goats. It is likely that a simple ard (a plow that scratches a furrow rather than turns the soil over) was used by this time for plowing, although there is no good evidence for cattle traction. However, cattle appear to have been milked, giving an all year round food and infant weaning supply that undoubtedly would have fuelled further population growth. Indeed, new evidence for a presence of milk fat in what appear to be perforated LBK pottery strainers, used to separate milk curds from whey, attest a likely presence of cheese making (Salque et al. 2013).

Roughly 2000 villages, each consisting of several longhouses up to 45 m in length, perhaps two-storeyed for dwelling and storage, have been reported across the whole LBK region. They held populations living at densities of 8.5 persons/km² in the settled areas, although much of the landscape was taken up by unoccupied buffer territories that doubtless served to keep untrusting populations apart.[21] The loess soils of northern Europe were sufficiently fertile to allow permanent cropping every year, fertilized by animal droppings, rather than requiring shifting cultivation with long fallows. Amy Bogaard (2004: 161) has observed that the rapidity of the LBK spread can hardly have resulted from a trail of soil exhaustion and desperation for new land. It was probably driven by rapid demographic growth – more people, every generation, required more land to maintain an acceptable level of food supply.

Life during the LBK appears to have been no fun for the fainthearted, especially during the later phases of the culture at about 5000 BC. With continuous population growth, violence seems to have been increasing in the western LBK regions in Germany, Belgium and France. Many villages were defended by ditches and timber palisades, and several have rather gruesome evidence for violent death and even cannibalism.[22] Strontium analyses on human bone suggest that many people, both male and female, traveled widely during their lifetimes (e.g., Price et al. 2001), but such travel was perhaps not always voluntary.

A major observation about the LBK is that it was a boom and bust phenomenon. Stephen Shennan (2008) points out that the early LBK followed a founder rank enhancement model, as outlined in Chapter 2, in which the first settlers in the best locations increased their status above that of less lucky latecomers. In the good times, LBK populations seem to have been growing by a massive 2.7% per annum. By 5000 BC, the LBK boom was over and sites were rapidly being abandoned, as subsequently in the later Neolithic in Denmark, Holland, Belgium and the British Isles.[23] Early Neolithic populations were clearly prone to establishing unstable population trajectories in the geomorphological and climatic conditions north of the Alps. However, it is not known if the reasons for decline were connected with overexploitation of resources with increasing population size, autonomous climatic deterioration, or factors of ideology and warfare-related retribution.

The end of the LBK around 5000 BC was associated with a standstill in the pace of further migration, until about 4000 BC. A Neolithic culture with cereal production, ard plowing and dairying known to archaeologists as the TRB (Trichterbecker or

Funnel-Beaker Culture) then spread from Germany into southern Scandinavia and Poland. The Neolithic developed a little earlier in western France, apparently from a mixture of Cardial, LBK, and indigenous Mesolithic resources.[24]

The same economy that characterized the TRB also reached the British Isles by 4000 BC, with a full range of cereals, use of the ard and dairying. Mark Collard and colleagues (2010) suggest that the oldest dates indicate a two-pronged Neolithic settlement of Britain from northern France, separately into southwestern England and central Scotland. Ireland was apparently settled at about the same time from Brittany.[25] In the Western Isles of Scotland, early Neolithic forest clearance and soil erosion attest to the impact of the first farmers, and multihectare complexes of early Neolithic stonewalled fields occur in western Ireland. Several British sites of this date have produced carbonized cereal remains in association with large rectangular houses. Some, such as the 4000 BC house at Balbridie in northeastern Scotland, resemble possible LBK prototypes. At Warren Field in Aberdeenshire, wheat and barley were grown around a similar 20×9 m hall built of oak timbers, situated amongst stands of hazel in a landscape cleared locally of oak trees.[26]

These examples suggest serious attention to food production, although cereal production declined sharply in Britain during the latter part of the Neolithic and Early Bronze Age, as in the later stages of the central European LBK.[27] Despite this, the archaeological evidence for the beginning of the Neolithic in the British Isles is sharp and without signs of any major Mesolithic contribution.

In continental Europe, the commencement date for the Neolithic becomes later as one moves northwards into colder climates. There is also increasing evidence in these regions of a significant Mesolithic role in adopting agriculture. Mesolithic communities in Denmark and around the Baltic Sea adopted pointed-based pottery before farming actually arrived amongst them. The Lithuanian Neolithic commenced around 3400 BC, here with an interesting focus on the hardy common millet that also dominated agriculture on the Eurasian steppes and in northern China. Further west, on the north Polish coast, farming started around 4000 BC, but much further north in Finland there were no fully agricultural populations until about AD 1000. By this date, the agricultural colonization of Europe was essentially complete.[28]

The Steppes and Central Asia

So far, the spread of the Fertile Crescent food-producing economy has been followed westwards and northwards through Europe between 7000 and 4000 BC. To the east, the archaeological record is not so detailed. The region concerned is a vast one, flanked to the north in Siberia by nonagricultural coniferous forests and tundra, and to the east by the mountains and deserts of central Asia and the monsoon climates of India and China. The zone of most interest for migration studies is the 1000 km wide belt of steppe grassland that runs unbroken through 50° of longitude, from north of the Black Sea to the Altai and Sayan Mountains. The steppe also extends, but with different populations and cultures, beyond these mountains into Mongolia and the Manchurian Plain of northern China.[29]

The western and central steppes, from the Black Sea to the Altai, played a crucial role throughout later history in the migrations of Scythian (presumably Indo-Iranian) and Turkic-speaking populations. The better-watered western (or Pontic-Caspian) steppes supported Neolithic and Bronze Age populations with cattle and some crop production, but the drier central steppes were not very favorable environments for crop agriculture, except in oasis or riverine situations. Here, pastoralism with horses, sheep, and goats at higher altitudes, became the main economies from the late Neolithic (circa 3500 BC) and Bronze Age into historical times.

The Neolithic and Bronze Age in the western steppes are rather intransigently associated by many authorities with the issue of Indo-European linguistic and population origins. I return to this issue subsequently. But here we might ask to what degree the steppes actually witnessed migration, as opposed to interaction between populations who were essentially indigenous, an issue raised recently by Michael Frachetti.[30]

To the north of the Black Sea, the western steppes were settled by farmers from eastern Europe, mainly after 6000 BC and initially from Starçevo and Çris sources in the Balkans, who moved eventually as far east as the Dnieper River. There are also suggestions that indigenous Mesolithic hunters and gatherers here adopted pottery making before the Neolithic populations arrived. Later migrants (circa 5000 BC) also spread into the western steppes from Cucuteni and Tripol'ye sources east of the Carpathians (Figure 7.2). The Neolithic cultures of the western steppes were supported by a full agro-pastoral economy with wheat, barley, cattle and sheep, plus use of the ard and perhaps cattle traction, with the important additions of both common and foxtail millet.[31]

Further east, into central Asia proper, Neolithic cultures became more localized in expression, possibly with largely indigenous population components. Most that lie east of the Dnieper and across to the southern Urals reveal little or no evidence for crop production. Sheep and cattle pastoralism, with domesticated horses and wheeled vehicles, developed widely here after 3500 BC, although the horses were probably not commonly ridden until late in the second millennium BC. They seem to have been domesticated initially in the western steppes, initially as a source of meat and milk, and prior to the appearances in the central steppes of domesticated sheep and cattle.[32]

Did Neolithic populations also enter central Asia from the south as well as from the west? The Caucasus Mountains do not offer an easy route northwards from Armenia, and still harbor deeply indigenous Caucasian language families that do not relate to either the Turkic or Indo-European families. An early Neolithic archaeological assemblage with clear Fertile Crescent links spread into western Armenia after 6500 BC (Kushnareva 1997), but not further north. So, significant Neolithic migration from the south into the Pontic or Caspian steppes seems unlikely. Much later in time, according to Herodotus, Scythians crossed the Araxes River from the south to enter the western or Pontic steppes, but this probably happened after 1000 BC, by which time people commonly rode horses.

To the east, between the steppes to the north and the mountains that extend south of the Caspian Sea towards the Hindu Kush, there lies what is today a rather forbidding desert (Kyzyl Kum, Kara Kum). Climatic records suggest that this region was quite well watered prior to 6000 BC, like the Sahara and Arabia (Chapter 5). The Kel'teminar culture was established here by 6000 BC, around former oases and river courses east of the Caspian and Aral Seas. It has associated pottery, lithic blades and geometric microliths, but Kel'teminar pottery shows no connections with Neolithic pottery in Iran or Pakistan. This suggests that the population might have been of indigenous origin. Agriculture only made a tentative appearance in Kel'teminar contexts after 2000 BC, and beforehand the economy seems to have been based on hunting and gathering, with a possible pastoral component.[33]

South of the Kel'teminar culture towards northern Iran the situation was rather different. The best evidence in recent years for Neolithic penetration northwards comes from the village site of Jeitun, located on the Kopetdag piedmont of southern Turkmenistan, east of the southern Caspian. Jeitun faced northwards from Iran into the territories of the Kel'teminar hunters and gatherers, but seems never to have impinged directly upon them. The area was settled about 6100 BC by Neolithic colonists who arrived with a tradition of painted pottery from Iran and founded a farming village of about 30 mud brick single-roomed houses. Their economy was based on wheat, barley, herded goats and sheep; the latter fed partly on cereal by-products as fodder. This was a time of relatively good rainfall in the Kopetdag, about 150 mm higher than now, so the settlement flourished for about 500 years. Perhaps these people invested in irrigation farming, but they apparently went no further into central Asia.

Much later, an agro-pastoral economy with sheep and goat herding (and rarer horses and cattle) spread eastwards into the Pamir, Tien Shan, and Altai Mountains, but there is no reason to link this especially with the much earlier Jeitun. Frachetti has recently termed this region the 'Inner Asian Mountain Corridor' and suggests an indigenous development of sheep and goat pastoralism here by about 3500 BC, backed up by some cultivation or importation of wheat, barley and common millet.

The overall archaeological picture for the central Asian steppes and Transcaspian deserts is not particularly supportive of prehistoric passage by Indo-Europeans heading to Iran and India, or indeed of much prehistoric migration at all. Future research will have to deal with the possibility that the steppes themselves, especially east of the Aral Sea, supported indigenous populations who developed their own forms of agriculture and pastoralism after 4000 BC. Today, we know the descendants of these steppe Neolithic populations as the speakers of Turkic and Yeniseian languages, with Mongolian and Tungus speakers to the east (Figure 7.6). The Turkic- and Yeniseian-speaking peoples have been totally ignored in all of the archaeolinguistic debates about Indo-Europeans in late prehistoric central Asia. Now might be a good time to give them more recognition and I return to them in the linguistic section to follow.

Iran, Pakistan, and South Asia Beyond the Indus

The Zagros Mountains of western Iran have a Neolithic as early as anywhere else in the Fertile Crescent, but in the relatively dry climatic conditions it was dominated by animal husbandry rather than crop production (Charles 2007). A Pottery Neolithic is well attested in northern Iran by at least 6300 BC, but so far little is known about a PPN in the eastern part of the country. Nevertheless, further to the east again, perhaps by circa 7000 BC, PPN settlers had traversed northern Iran to found the site of Mehrgarh on the Kachi alluvial plain, about 150 km southeast of Quetta in Baluchistan (Figure 7.3).[34] This region lies towards the eastern limit of the winter rainfall zone, and Mehrgarh itself provides a remarkable beacon-like outpost close to the eastern limit of Fertile Crescent Neolithic expansion.

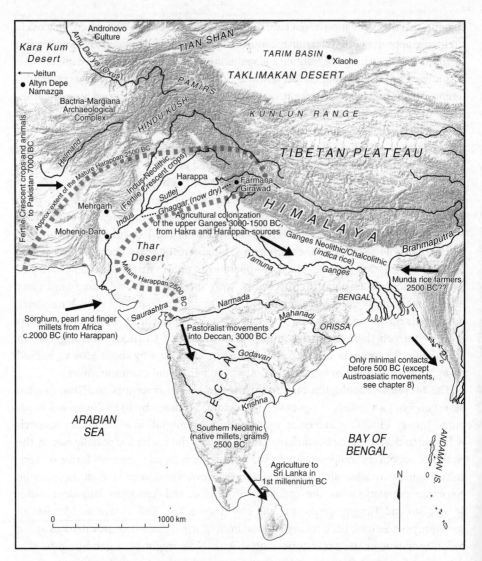

Figure 7.3 The spread of food-producing economies through South Asia, focusing especially on the movements of Fertile Crescent plants and animals. Background map by Multimedia Services, ANU, details added by the author.

The basal Preceramic Neolithic levels of Mehrgarh have mud brick constructions of 2, 4, 6, or even 10 small rectangular doorless rooms, similar to those of some agglomerated PPNB settlements in the Fertile Crescent. There is also a large cemetery with over 340 burials and a microlithic industry like that of Jeitun and the Kel'teminar culture, different from contemporary PPNB projectile point industries in the Fertile Crescent and perhaps a clue to an indigenous element in the population. Bitumen-hafted sickle blades indicate cereal harvesting, and grain impressions in mud bricks show that barley was the dominant crop, with wheat and dates present as well. In the lower levels, there were no domesticated animals, even though sheep and goats were domesticated towards the end of the preceramic phase, together with the native Indian humped cattle (*zebu*, or *Bos indicus*) that rapidly came to dominate the animal economy. Bones of the native South Asian water buffalo occur as well, but it is unclear if this animal, so fundamental to the rice farming economy of later South and Southeast Asia, was also domesticated in preceramic Mehrgarh. It most probably was by Harappan (Indus Valley Civilization) times, after 3000 BC.

South Asia beyond the Indus presents a very interesting arena for the spread of food production. Archaeobotanist Dorian Fuller has recently made a case for mid-Holocene independent domestications of *indica* rice in the Ganges Basin, and of native small millets and legumes in Saurashtra and the southern Deccan.[35] However, these developments seem not to have led to any significant demographic or cultural change amongst the Mesolithic communities who occupied India down to about 3000 BC, presumably because of low crop productivity under pre-domestication circumstances.

After 3000 BC, the upper and middle Ganges Basin was extensively settled by village-dwelling and copper-using agriculturalists of Indus and ultimately Fertile Crescent origin. These groups mixed downstream with separate populations of Neolithic rice agriculturalists, already in place, the latter perhaps a mixture of both indigenous and Mainland Southeast Asian origin (Chapter 8). The crops and animals introduced by these separate western and eastern groups of immigrants, especially the Fertile Crescent species and the East Asian millets and rice, stimulated the levels of food production and population growth required to create village-dwelling Neolithic cultures to as far east as Orissa and Bengal by 2000 BC.

A likely explanation for all of this focuses on no less than three major linguistic expansions of food-producing populations into South Asia, to which I return later, as well as the development of one of the world's greatest ancient urban and even perhaps literate civilizations. This was the Chalcolithic Harappan (or Indus Valley) civilization of Pakistan and northwestern India, dated in its Mature phase to between 2600 and 1900 BC.[36] Its direct roots in Pakistan can be traced to about 3700 BC, the date for the commencement of the Early Harappan or Hakra Phase (Kenoyer 2009). Hakra origins before this date are a little difficult to determine since much of Pakistan, and especially Baluchistan, has been off limits for archaeological research in recent years, as have Iran and Afghanistan. So it is difficult to demonstrate exactly how Hakra was related to the much earlier Preceramic Neolithic culture of Mehrgarh. However, the Chalcolithic painted pottery of Anau IA, Namazga I and Altyn Depe in southern Turkmenistan is of particular interest for its possible Hakra parallels, since it also dates to about 4000 BC and may well have belonged to a tradition that extended back to Neolithic Jeitun.[37] The Hakra Phase could thus have had quite deep roots in regions to the west of the Indus Valley, especially in southern Turkmenistan and Afghanistan.

The Mature Harappan was firmly grounded in a Fertile Crescent food production economy, with the addition of African millets (sorghum, pearl millet, finger millet) after 2000 BC in the southern regions of Saurashtra and Gujarat. By 1500 BC, the Harappan was in decline in the core region of the Indus Valley, a process that led to the eventual abandonment of many large cities such as Mohenjo-Daro and Harappa. This decline could have led to some refugee movements southwards and eastwards towards the Ganges Valley. For many years it was the widespread view of linguists and archaeologists that it also reflected the initial Indo-European migration into South Asia, thus rendering the Indus Civilization as an alien and extinct entity in the context of modern India and Pakistan. But the archaeological record of Harappan decline in the Indus Valley itself has never revealed any obvious connection with the widely claimed origin for these Indo-European invaders in the Pontic steppes or central Asia. In my view, supported linguistically on pages 161–3, the Harappan decline had nothing whatsoever to do with any Indo-European arrival in Pakistan or India, since this language family had already been present there for several millennia beforehand.

In recent years, there has been a rapid growth in the archaeological record in northwestern India and the upper Ganges Basin, particularly concerning the Early and Mature Harappan phases in Haryana and Rajasthan. Many sites here contain the same kind of red pottery with simple black or white painted designs that characterized the Hakra Phase in the Indus region itself, together with such Early and Mature Harappan features as a use of pottery kilns, pressure-flaked blades, simple copper tools, use of cattle and human figurines, urn burials of children, stone walled rectangular-roomed houses with plastered floors, and even citadel-like fortifications in Harappan style. In Haryana, between the Yamuna River and the former (now dry) Ghaggar tributary of the Indus, no less than 350 Harappan sites have been reported (Shinde et al. 2008). Many, like Girawad and Farmana, have Early Harappan basal layers that contain copper and gold artifacts, as well as painted and incised pottery related to that of the Early Harappan in the Indus Valley itself. In addition, the Post-Harappan cultures of the upper and middle Ganges Basin, especially the Ochre Colored and Black and Red Ware complexes, have clear Early and/or Mature Harappan antecedents. Indeed, sites related to the Hakra Phase reach virtually as far east as Delhi, and can be identified as the foundations beneath a great deal of the Neolithic and Chalcolithic archaeology of the upper and middle Ganges Basin, from 3000 BC onwards.

The situation suggests to me that there was a gradual movement downstream within the Ganges Basin, between 3000 and about 1500 BC, of westerly Chalcolithic populations of Hakra and Early Harappan cultural inspiration. These people mingled with easterly Neolithic populations, perhaps of separate lower Gangetic or Southeast Asian origin, who were already established there and already growing rice (Figure 7.3). The latter populations would have been at their highest densities in the downstream wet monsoonal regions of Orissa, Jharkand, Bihar and Bengal, rather than in the drier upper Ganges Basin. It is precisely in these downstream areas that Austroasiatic (Munda) speakers still exist in greatest numbers today (Anderson 2008).

The Ganges Basin, therefore, has a Neolithic record that started about 4000 years later than that in the Indus, reflecting the shift from winter rainfall climates in the west, suitable for wheat and barley, into monsoon climates in the east with summer rainfall, suitable for rice and millets. Early farmers with a Fertile Crescent economy who settled around 3000 BC in the upper Ganges Basin from the Indus would have had to irrigate their wheat and barley crops if they grew them during the winter, the most suitable season for their germination and growth. For Neolithic agriculturalists, this was an issue of considerable significance, and the eventual passage of the Fertile Crescent economy from the Indus into the Ganges Basin overcame one of the greatest potential barriers in the history of this food-producing complex.

Linguistic History and the Spread of the Fertile Crescent Food Production Complex

Now that we have examined the spread of the Fertile Crescent food-producing economy from its origins to its eventual limits in Eurasia, it is necessary to turn to the linguistic and later to the biological disciplines to see how they contribute to resolving major issues of Eurasian prehistory during the Holocene. Linguistically, the spotlight is on the histories of the Indo-European, Turkic and Dravidian language families. It will be apparent that each of the three major disciplines – archaeology, linguistics, and human biology – provides plentiful evidence in support of population expansion from the Middle East during the Neolithic. They offer far less support for putative expansions into Europe and South Asia originating in the Asian steppes.

Perspectives from Indo-European

The Indo-European family tree can most accurately be reconstructed if both living and extinct languages are taken into account, the latter including the very important Anatolian and Tocharian subgroups, once located in Turkey and Xinjiang (western China), respectively. Indo-Europeanists are very lucky to have epigraphic and historical data on these two extinct subgroups, because if they did not, no homeland reconstructions for the family as a whole would carry conviction. Without these data there would be unrecognized bias, exactly as there has been for many years behind the hypothesis that the homeland of the Indo-European family was located in the Pontic steppes north of the Black Sea, or even further east in the Urals. This hypothesis, already referred to in the archaeological section earlier, predates in its origin the discovery of Anatolian and Tocharian and is based only on surviving languages. It lacks a convincing basis in the pattern of Indo-European subgroup differentiation (Figure 7.4).

What was this pattern of differentiation? As Ruth Mace and Claire Holden (2005) point out, the ancestral languages within the Indo-European subgroups must have spread out from a common homeland region. The famous statement "sprung from some common source, which, perhaps, no longer exists" was coined by Sir William Jones in Calcutta in 1786 for Greek, Latin, 'Gothick', 'Celtick', Sanskrit and Old Persian, all within the Indo-European family (Pachori 1993: 175). The same idea was already apparent to Johann Reinhold Forster in 1774 for what we now term Austronesian languages (Chapter 8). A current family tree for Indo-European is presented in Figure 7.5. This takes extinct subgroups into account, and indicates clearly that Proto-Indo-European (the oldest traceable residue of linguistic words and meanings shared across the family) existed around 8500 years ago, using historical linguistic calibrations to

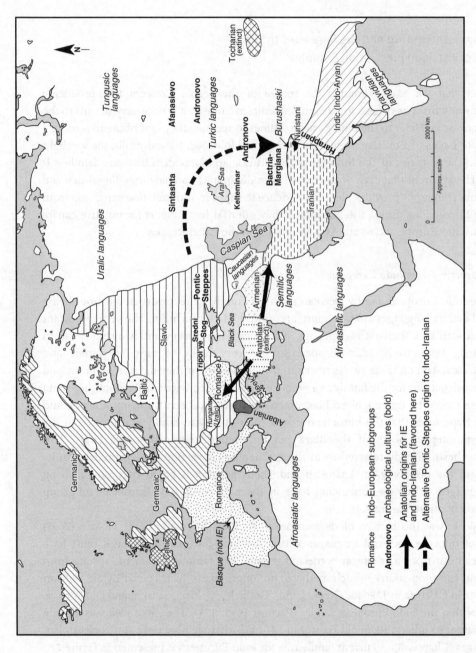

Figure 7.4 The distributions of the Indo-European subgroups at AD 1500, with selected central Asian archaeological cultures (in bold) that have featured in debates about Indo-Iranian origins. Original drawn by Multimedia Services, ANU, as Bellwood

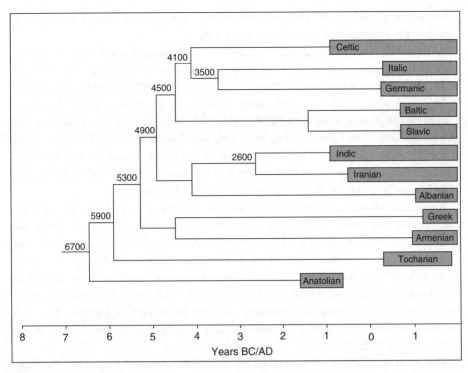

Figure 7.5   A family tree with estimated divergence dates (in millennia BC) for the subgroups within the Indo-European language family, constructed by Bouckaert et al. 2012 using statistical methods from evolutionary biology. Redrawn by the author and published courtesy of Quentin Atkinson, University of Auckland.

estimate time depths.[38] Its homeland was within the region where the historical Anatolian languages were spoken, prior to their replacements by Hellenistic and Byzantine Greek.

The Indo-European homeland was thus in Anatolia, perhaps eastern or central, as agreed by a majority of modern linguists and as demonstrated by many computational subgrouping analyses.[39] Dolgopolsky also points out that Proto-Indo-European reveals loans from Semitic and Kartvelian (Caucasus) languages, thus implying a location at least close to Anatolia and the Levant, rather than north of the Black Sea. Some even suggest that long-extinct and very poorly understood languages such as Minoan (Crete) and Etruscan could also have had origins within Proto-Indo-European, thus representing spreads older than those represented by recorded subgroup distributions.[40]

Also in support of a homeland in Anatolia, Gamkrelidze and Ivanov (1995) note that the reconstructed Proto-Indo-European vocabulary reflects a presence of mountains, thus apparently ruling out the steppes (but perhaps not the Urals), and also ruling out coastal regions since there was no term for sea.[41] The Proto-Indo-European lexicon includes terms associated with agriculture, for instance the scratch plow or ard, a term for sowing seeds, possible terms for wheat, barley and flax, and for stockbreeding of sheep, goats, pigs and cattle. Other important reconstructions include terms for milking, wool, weaving, and a term associated with rotary motion. Proto-Indo-European was therefore the vocabulary of a food-producing society.

As far as the recorded subgroups themselves are concerned, early separations soon after that of Anatolian itself involved early forms of Greek, Albanian and Armenian, all located in regions adjacent to Anatolia, and also the extinct Tocharian subgroup.[42] Indo-Iranian also occupies a fairly early position in the tree, whereas the major European subgroups – Balto-Slavic, Germanic, Italic (including the Romance languages derived from Latin), and Celtic – originated more recently. However, Indo-Aryan (or Indic) proper, as a major subgroup of the larger Indo-Iranian, only spread through the Ganges Basin after 2000 BC, much later than the ancestors of the Himalayan Indo-Iranian languages in the Dardic and Nuristani subgroups.

The Indo-European dispersal in the first instance was the result of demographic growth and migration by Neolithic populations who were of ultimate Anatolian origin, albeit with considerable admixture with native Mesolithic populations in some parts of Europe. For instance, early Indo-European speakers in Europe borrowed many still-existing river names from native populations, precisely as we would expect from parallels in more recent colonial era contexts. Even as late as Roman times, many *potentially* non-Indo-European languages survived in pockets of Europe (few were recorded in sufficient detail for certainty), just as non-Indo-European Basque still survives today in the Pyrenees.[43]

The most prominent proponent of an Anatolian Neolithic origin for the Indo-European language in recent years has been archaeologist Colin Renfrew, in a series of books and papers published since 1973.[44] The main strength of Renfrew's approach is that he has tried to bring together perspectives from archaeology, linguistics, and genetics, and takes what is essentially a population-based and demographic approach to explaining the Neolithic. As he has stated, the European archaeological record has no evidence for widespread migrations at the end of the Neolithic, which is the accepted timing for the Pontic Steppes migration theory. But, most certainly, it did at the beginning of the Neolithic.

In recent years, there have been several major proponents for the opposing Pontic Steppes hypothesis of Indo-European migration. Marija Gimbutas (e.g., 1985, 1991) brought the whole issue to the forefront by favoring a spread of early Indo-European-speaking and patriarchal nomadic pastoralists from the steppes of Ukraine and southern Russia, in three or four successive waves, between 4500 and 2500 BC. Utilizing horse-drawn wagons and constructing 'kurgan' burial mounds, these Yamnaya (Pit-Grave) invaders are suggested to have rapidly replaced the hypothetical matriarchal and goddess-centered Neolithic societies of Europe, especially north of the Alps from the Rhine to the Urals, and in the Balkans, but more slowly along the Mediterranean coastline. Gimbutas believed that these Neolithic Europeans descended from local Paleolithic populations.

These views, with modification, have had other champions in recent years, including James Mallory and David Anthony.[45] The latter has held firmly to the idea that words for wheel, draft pole, axle, and 'convey in vehicle' are all indeed genuine Proto-Indo-European reconstructions, and he locates the origins of the language family and its speakers to the east of the Dnieper river in the Sredni Stog and Yamnaya cultures, dated to circa 4300–2500 BC. These people are claimed to have moved westwards into Europe after 3000 BC, spreading Indo-European languages through a process of elite dominance rather than large-scale immigration.

There has been much debate over whether or not the Proto-Indo-Europeans really knew the use of the wheel and horse-drawn cart or chariot. They may well have known the horse, but this animal occurred in the wild in Anatolia, and there is no evidence for its domestication prior to 3500 BC. As for wheeled carts, they are known archaeologically on the Pontic and Caspian steppes and in Mesopotamia from around 3500 BC onwards, but terms for concepts such as wagon and axle are not known in Proto-Anatolian and are therefore not legitimate Proto-Indo-European reconstructions (Clackson 2000). Parpola (2008) suggests that wagon-related terms were late innovations in the sequence of Proto-Indo-European dissolution into separate subgroups, and that many were extensions of existing terms, with modified meanings. He offers the later Tripol'ye culture of eastern Europe (4000–3400 BC) as a possible source for wheeled vehicles.

Another mainstay of the Pontic Steppes hypothesis has long been the idea that the Anatolian languages were not indigenous to Anatolia. Indeed, David Anthony (2007) suggests that they were introduced into Anatolia from the Pontic Steppes. The Hittites and other Anatolians entered history in cuneiform documents dating to 1900 BC found at Kanesh (Kultepe) in central Turkey. At this time, they were flanked to the east by (non-Indo-European) Caucasian-speaking peoples such as the Hatti and Hurrians. But the documented presence of non-Indo-European languages in some regions of Anatolia does not mean that the Anatolians themselves were all immigrants, any more than the documented presence of English in Australia in 1788 implies that all Aboriginal populations were immigrants. Historical documents, or absence thereof, need have no relationship to migration at all.

The route of Indo-European language spread which has perhaps caused most debate in recent years is surely that of the Indo-Iranian languages, and especially of the lower-order subgroup within Indo-Iranian traditionally termed Indo-Aryan. Here I follow linguist Paul Heggarty (2013) and relabel this subgroup *Indic*, given the rather unfortunate history of the term *Aryan* during the twentieth century. For both the Indo-Iranian and the Tocharian languages, there are many who still argue for a Pontic and Asian steppes homeland, secondary in time to that for the Indo-Europeans as a whole.[46] However, subgrouping evidence for a steppes source for Indo-Iranian is lacking, and suggested borrowings into Uralic languages perhaps reflect Indo-Iranian excursions from the south rather than a homeland in the north. The archaeological cultures in the western steppes that are claimed to be affiliated with early Indo-Iranians,[47] including the Yamnaya, Afanasievo, Sintashta (southern Urals) and Andronovo cultures, had stamped and incised pottery, wheeled vehicles, and pastoral/horse-using economies quite unrelated to the painted pottery and undoubtedly agricultural complexes reported from Neolithic, Chalcolithic and Bronze Age southern Turkmenistan, Iran, Pakistan and northern India.[48] As discussed on pages 163–5, I prefer to associate them with ancestral speakers of Turkic or Yeniseian languages. There seems little archaeological evidence for southward movement from the steppes into Indo-Iranian territory prior to the Andronovo culture of the second millennium

BC, far too recent in time to explain the first Indo-Iranians and very different in content from the contemporary Bactria-Margiana, Iranian, and Harappan archaeological complexes to the south.

The two Tocharian languages were only distantly related to Indo-Iranian, and given their isolated location in Xinjiang it must be assumed that at one time there were ancestral Tocharian speakers further west, now presumably replaced by Indo-Iranian and Turkic speakers, unless a true leap-frogging movement occurred over intervening terrain. Tocharian speakers had *perhaps* reached Xinjiang by at least 2500 BC, if we can judge from the recent discovery of both western and eastern Eurasian mtDNA but predominantly western Eurasian NRY lineages in some of the famous clothed 'Caucasoid' mummies from the Tarim Basin (Taklamakan Desert), especially from the Xiaohe cemetery (2500–1500 BC: located on Figure 7.3). The Xiaohe mummies were associated with wheat, millet, cattle, sheep and goats that flourished under better-watered oasis conditions than those of the present.[49]

The Dardic and Nuristani languages of the Himalayas, especially Bargani, are also considered by some linguists to be coordinate with the Indo-Iranian subgroup. This raises the possibility that other Indo-European groups outside Tocharian and Indo-Iranian proper once existed more widely in the region.[50] Furthermore, Čašule (2010) has recently suggested that the Burushaski language, normally considered to be completely unrelated to Indo-European, is actually of quite early Indo-European origin. If this is correct, and it is not accepted by all linguists, it could place the ancestral speakers of Burushaski in the Himalayan region long before the radiation of the Indo-Iranian languages. We only have a direct record of the latter in central Asia and the Himalayas during the first millennium BC, in the form of historically recorded Saka, Choresmian, Sogdian and Bactrian. Čašule also suggests that Burushaski could represent one of the oldest splits in the history of the whole Indo-European family, on a similar level to that of the Anatolian languages.

These observations underline the point that that the Vedic and Sanskrit languages need not have represented the initial Indo-European-speaking settlement in the Indian Subcontinent. Instead, the spreads of these languages at a time of early state development, during and after the creation of the Rig-Veda epic (circa 1500–1000 BC), perhaps erased many unrecorded Indo-European predecessors. My assumption, therefore, is that the initial Indo-European language movement into Iran, Pakistan, and northern India dated back quite deeply into Chalcolithic or even Neolithic times. Indeed, I see no reason why the initial Neolithic occupants in this region, such as those at Jeitun and Mehrgarh I at about 6500–6000 BC, should not have been early Indo-European speakers as well. Serious archaeological research will be required to solve problems of continuity or otherwise in the Neolithic–Chalcolithic sequence of these Indo-Iranian regions, not easy in the current social and political unrest that afflicts this area. However, Neolithic and Chalcolithic Iran and Pakistan must also have contained non-Indo-European languages in the Elamite and Dravidian families (Southworth and McAlpin 2013), so we may never know exactly what were the linguistic affiliations of any specific archaeological sites of this age in the Indo-Iranian borderlands. But, that is no reason to bring in the first Indo-European languages to South Asia as recently as 1500 BC.

There is an interesting corollary to this reconstruction, for it implies that the Harappan urban civilization of the Indus River and its tributaries, extending into northwestern India by 2500 BC, housed large populations of Indo-Iranian (early Indic) speakers.[51] The Harappan symbol system (was it a mnemonic notation or a script?) thereby becomes the oldest attested Indo-European *potential* writing system on record, predating Hittite and Linear B Greek by almost 1000 years. It is perhaps not surprising, therefore, that Jonathan Kenoyer (2009) has traced the origins of some Harappan symbols into Hakra Phase sites in Pakistan, early in the fourth millennium BC.

The Possible Significance of the Turkic and Yeniseian Languages in Central Asia

It is necessary to return to the central Asian steppes in order to consider the role of the Turkic and Yeniseian languages in the prehistory of this region. I have stated earlier that the Indo-Iranian languages within Indo-European are most unlikely to have had a steppe origin, although they undoubtedly had a widespread presence in the steppes during the first millennium BC. River names such as Don, Dnieper, and Dniester in the western steppes are of Indo-Iranian origin, and we know from Herodotus that Scythians, presumed by some linguists to have been speakers of Iranian languages, existed there in the mid-first millennium BC. However, ancient Indo-Iranian place names are apparently rare in central Asia proper, east of the Caspian, and river names are especially resistant to change.[52] This is hardly supportive of an ancient and widespread Indo-European presence there before the expansion of the Turkic languages.

The indigenous people of early Holocene central Asia, as the creators of the first steppe Neolithic cultures, were in my view not Indo-Europeans (or Indo-Iranians) at all, but speakers of ancestral Turkic and Yeniseian languages. These people have been generally ignored in reconstructions of central Asian prehistory on the assumption that all the migrations of Turkic speakers occurred only after AD 400, out of a Mongolian or nearby central Asian homeland. But the modern Turkic languages (Figure 7.6), like modern Indo-European languages, possibly have deeper layers of prehistory erased by these more recent migrations. Proto-Turkic in central Asia is estimated by Peter Golden (1998: 68) to date from before 3000 BC, so a great deal of central Asian archaeology summarily attributed to 'Indo-Europeans' or 'Indo-Iranians' is equally likely to have been Turkic handiwork.[53] Just as likely might be Yeniseian handiwork, given the linguistic evidence discussed in Chapter 5, in connection with Na-Dene, that these languages were widespread in central Asia before 2000 years ago.

In this regard, a series of major steppe and Transcaspian Bronze Age cultures dating to the late third and second millennia BC, such as Sintashta and Andronovo, are in my view likely to have been associated with Turkic and/or Yeniseian speakers, or possibly even Uralic speakers. In the absence of relevant written documentation, it is perhaps impossible to demonstrate this with great conviction. But these pastoralist cultures with their horse gear and wagons, distinctive styles of pottery, and kurgan burials show no connections whatsoever with the Chalcolithic to Iron Age developing urban cultures of Iran and South Asia. Yet they belong to a time when we know that

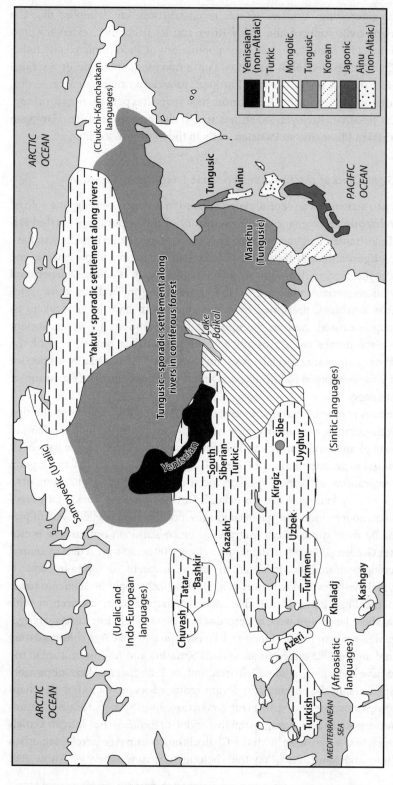

Figure 7.6 Map to show the likely generalized distributions of the Altaic languages prior to the recent expansions of Russian and Chinese. The boundaries are approximate and do not accurately reflect current distributions, especially for the Tungusic, Mongolic, and some Turkic languages that are spoken today only in small enclaves. Also shown is the recorded distribution of the Yeniseian languages, discussed in Chapter 5, from Kari and Potter 2010, Map B. Background map by Multimedia Services, ANU, using data from Ruhlen 1987.

Indo-Iranian speakers with their urban and agricultural traditions must already have been widely present in the Indus and upper Ganges Valleys.

West Eurasian Genetic and Population History in the Holocene

Can evidence from bioarchaeology and human genetics support the aforementioned archaeological and linguistic interpretations for the expansion of the Fertile Crescent agro-pastoral complex, at least to western Europe, on the one hand, and northern India, on the other? During the early 2000s, mtDNA phylogeographers were using molecular clock calculations to claim that most living Europeans carry indigenous Paleolithic or Mesolithic mtDNA haplogroups. This finding rendered insignificant the impact of any Neolithic migration from Anatolia or the Levant, and much emphasis was placed on postglacial colonization from the presumed refuges in southern Europe that were discussed in Chapter 5.[54] It was also widely assumed, as explained by Barbujani and Chikhi (2006), that the molecular clock mutation dates calculated for these haplogroups corresponded to the actual migration dates for the ancestral carriers. No firm reason was ever given to support this assumption, and the molecular clock dates in themselves carried very large ranges of error.

Contrary to these mtDNA molecular clock interpretations, other perspectives have since led to a more favorable approach towards the importance of Neolithic migration into Europe. Mathematical modeling of Mesolithic and Neolithic population histories has generally supported its significance.[55] Ancient DNA analysis is allowing geneticists to examine the genetic profiles of ancient people, a very important development since they are no longer entirely dependent on samples from the living, many millennia after the events in question. The Y-chromosome has also come into prominence in recent years as a champion for Neolithic immigration, at least by males, from western Asia into Europe and North Africa.[56]

Christopher Gignoux and colleagues (2011) have also examined the density of mutation events through time in the whole genomes of mtDNA haplogroups, using the assumption that a major increase in population will increase the frequency of mutation. Their results imply considerable population growth amongst ancestral agricultural as opposed to hunter-gatherer populations, especially during the spreads of food production through Europe, Southeast Asia and sub-Saharan Africa. For Europe, rapid population growth commenced in molecular clock terms around 5700 BC, close to the beginning of the LBK Neolithic in the Carpathian Basin. Although this approach does not necessarily identify the growing populations as immigrant or indigenous, it does reveal that haplogroups identified specifically as descending from Late Paleolithic and Mesolithic populations declined in numbers during and after the cold conditions of the Younger Dryas (11,000–9600 BC).

Perhaps the most thought-provoking observations on human genetic history in recent years have come from the study of ancient DNA.[57] In European prehistory, this approach came to prominence in 2005, when mtDNA results from a central European

Neolithic (LBK) population were published with the unexpected conclusion that the lineages represented were neither derived entirely from preceding local Mesolithic populations, nor were they directly ancestral to the majority of modern Europeans. Mystery reigned for a short time, but more ancient DNA results are now available from Spain, France, Germany, Sweden, Austria and Hungary that help to clarify the situation. Unfortunately, none have yet come from the Fertile Crescent itself. But the recent European analyses reinforce the deep separation between Mesolithic and Neolithic populations in Europe, and in most cases between Neolithic and modern populations, with the interesting proviso that a small degree of Paleolithic and Mesolithic mtDNA heritage is still represented in the modern European population as a whole. How to explain this?

Marie-France Deguilloux and collaborators (2012a) interpret these new ancient DNA results as indicating leap-frog migration by small Neolithic populations, emanating in the first instance from the Fertile Crescent or Anatolia, hopping through and over existing European Mesolithic groups, with rather little initial mixing between the two. Most initial Neolithic populations were therefore immigrants, extending along both the Danube and Mediterranean routes westwards and continuing into northwestern Europe. Strontium analyses of the bones of LBK people indicate that they were highly mobile, although this does not mean they or their immediate ancestors all traveled hundreds or thousands of kilometers during their lifetimes directly from the Fertile Crescent. Given that the temperate European Neolithic took over 3000 years to unfold, it is not surprising that a number of mtDNA haplogroups common in the LBK population were not necessarily drawn directly from the contemporary Near East at all, although the absence of ancient DNA from this region must mean uncertainty. However, these mtDNA lineages were not Mesolithic in origin, and it is very unlikely from modern genome studies that they came from the Eurasian steppes. Instead, the Neolithic pioneers of Europe, with their rapidly increasing population sizes,[58] probably generated several new haplogroups themselves within European territory as they paused, grew in numbers, and reformulated, often for several centuries, between migratory pulses.

An interesting observation that follows on from this leap-frogging scenario is that, after the Neolithic populations themselves became established, so the rate of admixture with surrounding formerly Mesolithic populations increased. This is perhaps because some of the latter were adopting agriculture and so increasing their own populations around the fringes of the agricultural expansion, hence increasing the all-round likelihood of population contact. The structure here probably resembled that of recent colonial instances of migration in Australia or the Americas, albeit with less adverse initial impact on the indigenous groups. As noted previously, a very similar trajectory occurred with the import of Neolithic domesticated pigs from the Near East into Europe. The first domestic pigs, according to ancient DNA analysis, carried mtDNA haplogroups of Near Eastern origin. But by at least the fourth millennium BC their DNA had become swamped by that of local and formerly wild European pigs.[59]

The aforementioned reconstruction of European Neolithic prehistory from ancient DNA is supported by recent developments in yet another branch of human biology, the study of the skeletons of the actors themselves. The most recent and informative of these studies, using craniometric data, suggest again that European Neolithic populations spread from a southeast European or Near Eastern origin by processes of demic diffusion and leap-frogging, initially with little gene flow with Mesolithic populations.[60] But, as suggested by the ancient DNA, populations with Mesolithic genetic heritage continued to exist on the Baltic and Atlantic fringes of the continent, and the descendants of these populations eventually contributed to the genetic makeup of modern Europe.

The ancient DNA record of Neolithic expansion is so far confined mainly to Europe, at least within the limits of the Fertile Crescent agro-pastoral complex. Fewer detailed studies are available for regions east of the Fertile Crescent. In the case of South Asia, mtDNA data on living populations support a high degree of indigenous haplogroup origin, especially in the south of the subcontinent, whereas NRY data give stronger support to links with western Asia and Europe, especially for the Indic-speaking populations in the north.[61] The NRY data also reveal a very sharp separation between Indian and East Asian populations, the latter including the Tibeto-Burman and Munda (Austroasiatic) speakers of northeastern India (discussed further in Chapter 8), who share with East and Southeast Asians a predominance of NRY haplogroup O.[62] Few people crossed the rugged terrain between India and Burma in prehistoric times, apart from the Austroasiatic-speaking ancestors of the Munda and Khasi peoples of northeastern India, who entered that region from Southeast Asia. Even in the Palaeolithic (Chapter 3), this forested region appears to have formed a potential barrier during interglacial climatic phases. The Hindu-Buddhist traders who carried Indic cultural influences to Southeast Asia from 2500 years ago more likely traveled by sea, and only small numbers of these ever settled permanently in their trading locations.

The genetic history of South Asia has been revealed most clearly by whole genome research. As with the NRY and mtDNA data, this also shows very clearly that the modern populations of Pakistan and northern India, especially the Indic-speaking caste populations, are closely related to populations located in the Middle East and Europe. Southern Indian Dravidian-speaking populations, on the other hand, carry more indigenous genetic profiles, albeit with considerable influence from the north. For instance, autosomal SNP (single nucleotide polymorphism) data suggest that Indic speakers introduced between 50 and 70% of the modern genome of northern Indians from western Eurasian sources, but only ~40% of the southern (mostly Dravidian-speaking) genome. Likewise, identification of two major South Asian ancestry components from SNPs reveals one focused in northern India and linked to western Asia and the Caucasus, the other focused in southern India, essentially indigenous to the subcontinent.[63] Both of these ancestry components have calculated ages greater than 1500 BC according to admixture modeling, and so predate the Rig-Veda and the end of the Mature Harappan.

Unfortunately, South Asia does not have a great deal of informative skeletal information that reflects on ancient migrations, but dental metric data suggest a degree of continuity in northwestern South Asia from Neolithic Mehrgarh through to Chalcolithic and early historical populations.[64] While the craniometric and dental evidence is not strong, there is no obvious instance of significant population replacement in Pakistan and northwestern India from the time of Neolithic Mehrgarh (7000 BC) onwards.

Peninsular Indian Archaeology and Dravidian Linguistic History

As stated previously, a climatic divide between winter and summer rainfall marked the passage of the Fertile Crescent economy from the Indus into the Ganges Valley. A similar divide marked the passage from the Indus southwards into Peninsular India, since this was also a monsoonal region. The Neolithic populations of this region, beyond Maharashtra, essentially cultivated indigenous millets and grams, with occasional occurrences of West Asian wheat and barley, and later rice. In southern India, pottery-using cattle pastoralists with millets and grams established themselves in Karnataka by 3000–2500 BC, evidently from a northwesterly origin in the general region of Rajasthan, Gujarat and Maharashtra. The migration of the bearers of this complex may well have taken place down a central zone of open grassland through the Deccan Peninsula, and agriculture appears only to have reached densely forested Sri Lanka around 1000 BC.[65] The descendants of these Neolithic migrants speak Dravidian languages today.

From a linguistic perspective, the immediate Dravidian homeland was located in the northwestern part of the present distribution of the family, also in Gujarat or Rajasthan, according to the presence there and perhaps also in Sind of a Dravidian place-name substratum. These regions today are occupied by Indic speakers. The most recent statement of Dravidian linguistic origins, by Frank Southworth and David McAlpin, derives the family ultimately from even further west on the Iranian Plateau, where it shared a very remote common ancestry with the ancient Elamite language of Iran. Proto-Dravidian speakers later spread, after 3000 BC, with an ancestral agricultural and pastoral vocabulary that included terms for cattle, sheep and goats, pottery, grain processing, and possibly some form of plow, but no specified cereals.[66] The spread thus occurred with dominant pastoralism and small-scale (presumably millet and gram) cultivation, at roughly the same time as the ancestral Indic speakers were migrating along a more northerly route from the Indus into the Ganges Basin (Figure 7.3).

In contradistinction to the interior grassland route suggested above, an important linguistic detail about the early Dravidian movement through Maharashtra into Karnataka, revealed clearly by Southworth's (2005) discussion of Dravidian place names, is that it was essentially focused on the Konkan coastal plain of western India, rather than on the Deccan Plateau itself. The interior uplands, if we take the place name evidence seriously, were settled by Indic speakers who might indeed have moved among pockets of Dravidian speakers, but who more likely were intruding upon an essentially Mesolithic cultural landscape of unknown linguistic affiliation. The Ganges Basin itself has never supported extensive Dravidian-speaking populations, and at 2000 BC the only other well-attested populations here, apart from Indic speakers, would have been ancestral Munda (Austroasiatic) speakers (Chapter 8).

The Dravidian language family, therefore, appears to have begun life in Iran as part of an independent linguistic macrofamily (Elamo-Dravidian) that also included Elamite. Its main distribution was created by a Neolithic migration of its ancestral speakers from the eastern edge of the Fertile Crescent into southern Pakistan and northwestern India. Its speakers became transformed economically during their movement into the dry monsoonal climate of Peninsular India, towards pastoralism on the one hand, and towards cultivation of a range of indigenous drought-resistant millets and grams on the other. The genetic profile of the Dravidian-speakers today is predominantly indigenous to South Asia, and presumably also to pre-Indo-European southern Iran.

The Spread of the Fertile Crescent Food-Producing Economy into North Africa

The final leg of expansion of the full Fertile Crescent economy to be considered runs from the Levant, via Egypt, into North Africa, a narrow region of fluctuating agricultural potential confined to the southern littoral of the Mediterranean and the Nile Valley. As discussed in Chapter 5, the southern Sahara was much better-watered than now from 9000 to 4000 BC, during the favorable monsoonal conditions of the early Holocene. At this time, Nilo-Saharan-speaking hunter-gatherer populations occupied many of the well-watered massifs, hunting cattle and other ungulates, and harvesting wild millets. The Arabian Peninsula was also wetter at that time, and pastoralist populations of Levant PPNB derivation penetrated it from the north during the early Holocene (Figure 5.4 and Figure 9.1).[67]

By the sixth millennium BC, Neolithic populations of farmers and herders from the southern Levant and Arabia were poised to cross into North Africa. The most detailed record concerning their arrival comes from Egypt, where farming villages first appeared in the Nile Valley archaeological record at about 5000 BC.[68] The development of food production in the Nile Valley and along the North African littoral began with Fertile Crescent wheat, barley, legumes, sheep, goats and cattle, brought either through Sinai or by sea across the southeastern Mediterranean. Sheep and goats might also have been introduced into Africa separately, slightly earlier and without cereals, either directly across the Red Sea from western Arabia or via Yemen and the Bab al Mandab to the Horn of Africa.

Unlike the sheep and goats, which ultimately spread through the whole of Africa (especially the sheep, which reached the Cape of Good Hope), the Fertile Crescent cereals and legumes did not initially spread beyond North Africa. They appear to have reached Ethiopia only during the first millennium BC (Hassan 2002). However, the Nile alluvium in Egypt was a perfect place for growing Fertile Crescent crops since it flooded in the autumn, just in time for the winter growing season, so winter cultivation in normal years could have occurred as the floods receded without any need during the Neolithic for elaborate irrigation works.

The date for the initial spread of farming from the Levant into Egypt is still not well established. The current date of circa 5000 BC seems late in light of the much earlier Neolithic movements from the Fertile Crescent into Europe

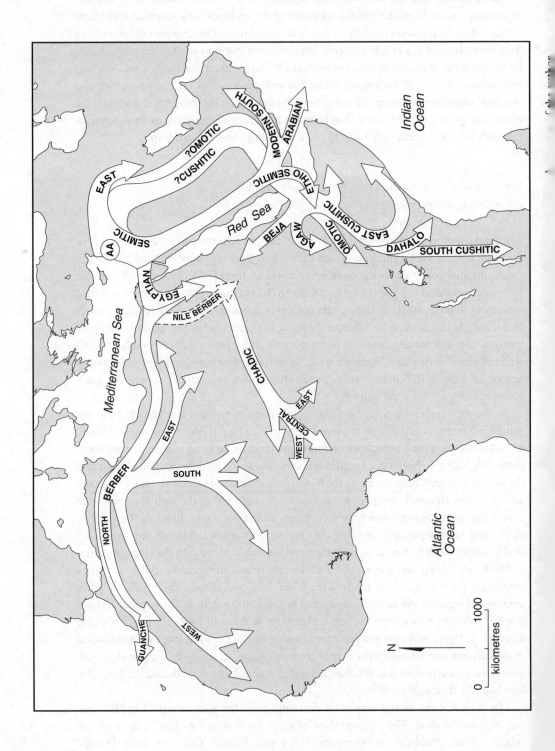

and Pakistan, not to mention the very early Holocene sea crossing to Cyprus. One explanation might be that the bed of the lower Nile was severely incised during the last glacial maximum as the river eroded down to the lower (-100 m or more) sea level, then filled with massive depths of alluvium after sea level rose in the early Holocene. If this is correct, any early Holocene settlements located close to the Nile will now be buried under tens of meters of sediment, hence virtually impossible to find.

I find it quite possible, however, that the late date could be correct. The North African littoral of Libya and Algeria also has Neolithic sites that date from 5000 BC onwards, but so far nothing earlier. If agriculture was introduced into the Nile Valley only around 5000 BC, it would fit well with the linguistic history of the Afroasiatic language family, which places Ancient Egyptian relatively late in the order of subgroup differentiation. I return to this issue subsequently.

It is also worth remembering that the Egyptian Neolithic and the great civilization that eventually developed from it were very different in cultural style and language from their contemporaries in the Middle East. One striking difference was that Egyptian Neolithic architecture focused initially on the use of timber and reeds, as opposed to the sun-dried mud bricks used almost universally from Pre-Pottery Neolithic times onwards in the Fertile Crescent. Predynastic figurines, pottery, and ornaments in Upper Egypt (i.e., south of the delta) were also very different from those in the Levant. Indeed, we know from history that by 3000 BC the Nile Valley had a remarkable culture with its own Afroasiatic language and locally invented hieroglyphic writing system. The Egyptian proto-state between 3200 and 3000 BC developed from two separate Lower (Nile Delta) and Upper (Nile valley) Egyptian kingdoms that became unified, apparently by conquest, under the early Pharaohs. Is it too much to suggest that these two Lower and Upper kingdoms were inhabited respectively by populations with ancestries predominantly of Levant and North African origin?[69]

What of Holocene linguistic expansion from the Fertile Crescent into North Africa? The Afroasiatic language family today includes languages in six major subgroups – Semitic, Egyptian, Chadic, Berber, Cushitic and Omotic (Figure 7.7). Many linguists propose an African origin, on the grounds that five of these six subgroups occur only in Africa and because the Omotic subgroup in particular appears to be genealogically well differentiated from all the others.[70] The precise location of the homeland varies a little according to author, oscillating through Ethiopia and Sudan towards the Red Sea coast. These linguists tend to regard early Afroasiatic expansion as preagricultural, although not pre-herding in the view of Chris Ehret (2002b), thus perhaps to be equated with population spread and cattle hunting/herding in the eastern Sahara consequent upon the wetter climatic conditions after 9000 BC. However, I discussed these wetter climatic conditions in Chapter 5, and there related them to early Nilo-Saharan linguistic prehistory.

Unfortunately, subgrouping evidence is not sufficiently strong to demonstrate an African origin with certainty, and Ehret (2011: 249) is only able to list two linguistic innovations that would justify placing Omotic at the base of the family tree in order to claim a northeastern African origin. Neither, it should be said, is subgrouping evidence strong enough to demonstrate a Levant origin. It seems likely that much former diversity in both western Asia and North Africa has been erased by the historical expansions of state-level and conquest languages such as Akkadian/Babylonian, Aramaic, Ethio-Semitic and Arabic. The Semitic subgroup alone, for instance, has an estimated time depth of almost 6000 years according to Kitchen et al. (2009), and many languages in this subgroup underwent very significant early historical expansions, not least into Africa during the first millennium BC in the form of ancestral Ethio-Semitic.

My own view, from a multidisciplinary perspective, is that a much earlier Levant origin for the whole Afroasiatic family, deeply within the Pre-Pottery Neolithic, fits the observed situation far better than a northeast African origin. In support, I turn to a school of linguists that bases its opinion on comparative vocabulary reconstruction. This school claims a Proto-Afroasiatic roster of plants and animals that are of Asian, not North African origin, including sheep, goat, barley and chickpea.[71] Alexander Militarev (2002) favors early agricultural correlations, which would place the initial expansion of the family well within the Neolithic in the Levant. The most recent statement from this perspective is by Vaclav Blažek (2013b), who suggests that the apparent deep separation of Omotic reflects contact-induced change within Ethiopia, and that Cushitic and Omotic were derived through an initial population movement with domesticated sheep and goats from the Levant across the Red Sea via Arabia (Figure 7.7). He also suggests that Chadic was established quite early (5000 BC?) from the Nile valley, perhaps before the end of the Saharan wet phase, and that Berber and Guanche (Canary Islands) represent a much more recent spread from the Nile, concentrated mainly in the first millennium BC. Blažek's rather tentative chronology would place the initial movement of Afroasiatic languages from the Levant to Africa in the eighth millennium BC – rather early, but still within reach of an apparent archaeological movement closer to 5000 BC.

This is by far the best available reconstruction for Afroasiatic linguistic history, similar in its explanatory power to the Anatolian homeland hypothesis for Indo-European. The family tree favored by Blažek is similar in structure to the trees favored by Ehret and Blench in its placement of Omotic and Cushitic as early separations from Proto-Afroasiatic. It differs from these views in placing the homeland in the Levant rather than Africa, but with them it supports the late arrival of farming in the Nile Valley suggested by the archaeology, by virtue of the subgrouping of Egyptian, Semitic and Berber as a secondary node within the overall Afroasiatic phylogeny. It is therefore quite possible that the first spread of sheep and goats from the Fertile Crescent agro-pastoral complex into Africa was not to the Nile Valley at all, but across the Red Sea or Bab al Mandab, quite far to the south. However, the spread of the full agro-pastoral complex of Fertile Crescent origin from the Levant into the Nile Valley still represents the first occurrence of a domesticated crop-production economy in Africa.[72]

The Fertile Crescent Food Production Complex and Its Impact on Holocene Prehistory in Western Eurasia

In summary, the Fertile Crescent complex of food production, carrying both crops and animals, spread from its Levant and Anatolian origins between 8500 and 4000 BC to its limits as a full complex in the British Isles, southern Scandinavia, the Western Eurasian steppes, Pakistan, northwestern India, and the Egyptian Nile valley. In its most complete form, with full repertoires of domesticated cereals, legumes and animals, the complex very clearly ran out of steam where winter rainfall climates met either monsoonal summer rainfall climates, or climates so cold or dry (or both) that crop production was impossible. Pastoralism was able to extend beyond these limits into the deserts and semi-deserts of central Asia and North Africa, and elements of the Fertile Crescent package spread into monsoonal northern India after 3000 BC, and into Ethiopia after 500 BC. The Longshan and Shang Chinese also obtained wheat, barley, taurine cattle and sheep via central Asia after 2600 BC. But the Fertile Crescent complex did not penetrate these surrounding regions in full form, and became watered down by admixture with indigenous domesticated crops and animals that were more suited to the changed environmental conditions. The humans, the languages, and the archaeological complexes of material culture all followed these foundation food-producing imperatives in their own expansions.

Fertile Crescent food production, based predominantly on a small set of important cereals, legumes, and ruminant animals, has therefore supported economically the bulk of the human migration profile of Western Eurasia, including North Africa, during the past 10,000 years. The population spreads that occurred between 6500 and 2000 BC led to distributions of languages, genes, and economic lifestyles from Gibraltar to Bangladesh, and North Africa to Scandinavia, that still underpin the Western World as we know it today. The only other migration episode of parallel extent, that involved this same food production complex in a later manifestation, was that of the post-AD 1500 colonial era into the Americas and Australasia. The Barbarian migrations in post-Roman Europe were almost trivial by comparison. There is very little evidence for significant Mesolithic cultural or genetic contribution to Neolithic and later populations, except perhaps in the Fertile Crescent itself where some foragers clearly became farmers, and most importantly in the mtDNA data that reflect the female side of prehistory. Everyone alive today carries some direct Palaeolithic or Mesolithic ancestry; the questions are "how much, and where was it from?"

The data outlined in this chapter are of varying reliability, and, as always, it will be easy for critics to find minor loopholes that might, with considerable exertion, be blown up in an attempt to refute the whole reconstruction. But I am confident that the picture outlined is becoming more and more supported by the scientific literature, and that the strongest anti-migrationist views are no longer tenable. All explanations concerning the prehistoric human past are a compromise between what often appear to be conflicting data sets, and the only way to establish these explanations is to hold them up against a constant flow of new information.

Notes

1. As described by Hillman 1996; Lev-Yadun et al. 2000; and Zeder 2008, 2011. Fuller et al. 2011a suggest that domestication occurred all over Fertile Crescent, rather than in just one small core area.

2. For example, Allaby et al. 2008 for crops; Naderi et al. 2008 for goats.

3. Nadel et al. 2004; Piperno et al. 2004; Weiss et al. 2004. See Verhoeven 2011 on the lengthy evolution of the Neolithic in the Middle East.

4. For pre-domestication grain cultivation in the PPNA northern Levant (circa 9000 BC) see Willcox and Stordeur 2012. Communal grain storage is discussed by Kuijt 2008, Willcox et al. 2008, and Kuijt and Finlayson 2009. Goring-Morris and Belfer-Cohen 2008 discuss site numbers through time. Eshed and Galili 2011 document an almost 50% increase in the birth rate according to cemetery data from the Natufian to the PPNB in Israel.

5. Evershed et al. 2008 (Anatolia); Vigne 2008. Arredi et al. 2007; Thomas et al. 2013 and Cordain et al. 2012 discuss the importance of lactose digestion.

6. See the recent discussions of Göbekli Tepe by Hodder and Meskell 2011; Banning 2011; Dietrich et al. 2012; Schmidt 2012; and by various authors in *Current Anthropology* 53:125–9, 2012. On the Göbekli Tepe economy, see Neef 2003; Grupe and Peters 2011. The site has evidence for brewing, as well as wild cereal consumption. Willcox et al. 2008; Willcox 2012; Willcox and Stordeur 2012 discuss the Jerf el Ahmar economy. Byrd 2005 discusses early Fertile Crescent villages in general, and see also Finlayson et al. 2011 for an important new PPNA settlement discovered in southern Jordan, south of the Dead Sea.

7. Site abandonment during the course of the Pre-Pottery Neolithic is discussed by Kohler-Rollefson 1988; Akkermans and Schwartz 2003: 110–2; Bellwood 2005a: 65–6; Simmons 2007; Özdoğan 2008; Goring-Morris and Belfer-Cohen 2011.

8. Schulting 2011 discusses this dietary change in general, and Craig et al. 2011 point out that fishing on the Baltic coasts continued from Mesolithic into Neolithic times, as one would expect.

9. On the Turkish Neolithic see Düring 2011; Özdoğan 2007, 2011a, 2011b.

10. See Simmons 2004, 2008; Manning et al. 2010a. Vigne et al. 2011 discuss Neolithic animals in Cyprus. Colledge and Conolly 2007; Lucas et al. 2011; and Asouti and Fuller 2012 discuss cereals.

11. Schoop 2005. The two conference volumes edited by Lichter 2005 and Gatsov and Schwartzenberg 2006 contain a wealth of information on Anatolia and the Balkans during the Neolithic. See also Özdoğan 2007, 2008, 2011a, 2011b, 2013. See also Roodenberg and Alpasan-Roodenberg 2008 for an excellent description of the sites of Ilıpınar and Menteşe in northwest Anatolia, both settled by immigrant farmers after 6400 BC.

12. Neolithic Crete and Greece are discussed by Broodbank and Strasser 1991; Hansen 1992; Perlès 1999, 2005; Efstratiou 2005; Kyparissi-Apostolica 2006; Valamoti and Kotsakis 2007.

13. These items are described by Schwartzenberg 2005, 2006; Özdoğan 2008: Figures 7–13. See also Anthony 2010.

14. Turney and Brown 2007 suggest that this was due to the collapse and melting of the Laurentide Ice Sheet (Figure 4.1), and consequent rapid sea level rise.

15. Coward et al. 2008.

16. See Rowley-Conwy 2004a; Benecke 2006; Coward et al. 2008; Sherratt 2005 on the reality of 'packages'. Scheu et al. 2008; Ajmone-Marsan et al. 2010 and Larson et al. 2007 discuss cattle and pig genetics.

17. Maier 1996; Colledge and Conolly 2007; Coward et al. 2008; Pinhasi 2013.

18. Punctate-stamped decoration of this type is found as early as 6500 BC in Anatolian sites such as Mezraa-Teleilat (Upper Euphrates) and Aşağı Pınar (Thrace) (personal observations, courtesy of examining collections with Mehmet Özdoğan).

19. For Portugal see Zilhão 2000, 2001, 2011. Farmer to hunter-gatherer relations in Neolithic northern Europe are discussed by Keeley 1992; Rowley-Conwy 2011.

20. For the LBK see Bogucki 2003; Kaczanowska and Kozlowski 2003; Coudart 2009; Burger and Thomas 2011.

21. Zimmermann et al. 2009.

22. For instance, up to 1000 individuals at Herxheim in Germany; Boulestin et al. 2009. See also Golitko and Keeley 2007.

23. On the LBK trajectory see Shennan 2008, 2009; Shennan and Edinburgh 2007. The founder rank enhancement model has recently been documented archaeologically at the site of Vaihingen in Germany (Bogaard et al. 2011).

24. On the TRB see Solberg 1989; Robinson 2007; Linderholm 2011. For France see Gronenborn 1999; Jochim 2000.

25. For the British Isles see Mills et al 2004; Rowley-Conwy 2004b, 2011; Copley et al. 2005; Stevens 2007; Brown 2007.

26. Tipping et al. 2009.

27. Stevens and Fuller 2012.

28. Rimantiené 1992 and Taavitsainen et al. 1998 discuss Lithuania and Finland.

29. See Telegin 1987; Dergachev 1989; Levine et al. 1999; Anthony 2007, 2010; Kuzmina 2007; Monah 2007; Frachetti and Benecke 2009; Frachetti et al. 2010; Frachetti 2012; Pinhasi and Heyer 2013.

30. Frachetti 2012; Lawler 2012.

31. Common millet *P. miliceum* is reported from pre-5000 BC Neolithic sites in both China and Western Eurasia, but there are no reported occurrences so early in central Asia. It is unclear if this species was domesticated twice, or only once, and spread by trans-Asian contact (Hunt et al. 2008).

32. Warmuth et al. 2012. Outram et al. 2009 report that some Botai (Kazakhstan) horses were also bridled, so riding is a possibility, even at 3500 BC.

33. On Kel'teminar and Transcaspian climatic records see Boroffka 2010; Harris 2010. Because the Kyzyl Kum was more humid than now between 6000 and 3000 BC, one wonders if evidence for sporadic Neolithic plant cultivation will one day be discovered there. For Jeitun see Harris 2010.

34. On Mehrgarh see Costantini 2007–8; Jarrige 2007–8a, 2007–8b.

35. Fuller 2011, 2013.

36. My views on South Asian Holocene prehistory are given in Bellwood 2005a: 86–95, 2007–2008, 2009b.

37. On Anau and Altyn Depe see Masson 1988; Hiebert 2003; Kohl 2007: 218.

38. This tree is from Bouckaert et al. 2012. For similar calculations see Forster and Toth 2003; Gray and Atkinson 2003; Mace and Holden 2005; Atkinson and Gray 2006.

39. For other computational analyses of Indo-European family trees see Warnow 1997; Ringe et al. 1998, 2002; Rexova et al 2003; Fortunato 2008; Bouckaert et al. 2012.

40. Dolgopolsky 1987, 1993. Merritt Ruhlen 1994: 181–94 presents a very readable account of Indo-European origins. On Minoan and Etruscan as early Indo-European languages, see Renfrew 1998; Drews 2001. Ghirotto et al. 2013 present genetic data supporting ancestral connections between Tuscan and Anatolian populations 5000 years ago, suggesting an early arrival of Etruscan in Italy.

41. References on the Proto-Indo-European vocabulary include Beekes 1995; Gamkrelidze and Ivanov 1995; Watkins 1998; Comrie 2002.

42. On the early separations of Greek and Armenian see Serva and Petroni 2008. Tocharian is recorded as two languages spoken between AD 500 and 700 in the Tarim Basin of Xinjiang,

western China, and written as Buddhist literature in Brahmi, one of the alphabetic scripts of Aramaic origin that developed in northwestern South Asia after the conquests by the Persian Empire and Alexander the Great (Lane 1970).

43. See Vennemann 1994 and Kitson 1996 on European river names, also the papers in Andersen 2003 for debate on substrate languages. Wiik 2000 and Strade 1998 discuss Uralic substrates beneath Indo-European subgroups, especially Germanic, Baltic, and Slavic.

44. See especially Renfrew 1987, 1989, 1992a, 1992b, 1999, 2000, 2001, 2002; and also Krantz 1988 for a similar perspective. Since the early 1990s, Renfrew (e.g., 1991) has been applying his ideas to farming dispersal in general. In Renfrew 2000, he was the first to use the term 'language/farming dispersal model'.

45. Mallory 1989, 1997; Anthony 1990, 1995, 2007.

46. For example, Parpola 1999; Witzel 2003; Anthony 2007; Kuzmina 2007; Parpola 2008. For Tocharian, we have far less of an archaeological record than for Indo-Iranian. Blažek and Schwartz 2008 derive it from the steppes and southern Urals, via the Afanasievo culture of the Altai region at 3500–2500 BC, entering the Tarim Basin around 2000 BC.

47. For instance, by Witzel 2003, Anthony 2007, and Kuzmina 2007.

48. Hiebert 1994; Lamberg-Karlovsky 2002: 74; Kohl 2007, 2009.

49. Cox and Hammer 2010; Li et al. 2010. The Xiaohe information is a personal communication from Prof. Yo-ichiro Sato, Research Institute for Humanity and Nature, Kyoto. Mallory and Mair 2000 discuss the Tarim Basin mummies in general, and favor Tocharian affinities for the older ones.

50. See discussions of Bargani in Cardona and Jain 2003; Witzel 2003. Blažek and Hegedüs n.d. use glottochronological calculations to suggest that Nuristani split from Indo-Iranian around 2700 BC. Blažek n.d. suggests that Burushaski is related to Yeniseian and Na-Dene languages (see Chapter 5), and is not Indo-European.

51. The Harappan probably housed some Dravidian-speaking populations as well, given that Dravidian place names extend as far northwest as Sind in Pakistan, a region well within the Harappan sphere of cultural influence (Southworth 2005; Southworth and McAlpin 2013).

52. On Indo-Iranian placenames see Mallory and Mair 2000: 106; Witzel 2005.

53. For Turkic, see Vovin 2013.

54. For the mtDNA phylogeographic perspective on the European Neolithic, see Richards 2003; Wells 2006; Soares et al. 2010.

55. See, for instance, Chikhi et al. 2002; Dupanloup et al. 2004; Belle et al. 2006.

56. See Forster and Renfrew 2011. The most common NRY lineage in western Europe, for instance, is stated by Balaresque et al. 2010 to be of Holocene and presumably Neolithic Near Eastern origin, although other interpretations have also been offered (Myres et al. 2011; Busby et al. 2012). Other recent papers on the spreads of NRY haplogroups, especially J, from the Levant and Anatolia into southeastern Europe include Chiaroni et al. 2008; King et al. 2008; Battaglia et al. 2009; Lacan et al. 2011.

57. References for this section include Haak et al. 2005, 2010; Bramanti et al. 2009; Malmstrom et al. 2009; Deguilloux et al. 2011; Gamba et al. 2012; Lacan et al. 2011; Pinhasi et al. 2012; Skoglund et al. 2012; Thomas et al. 2013. Battaglia et al. 2009 argue that the first Mediterranean Neolithic (Cardial) populations carried Mesolithic mtDNA haplogroups from the Balkans. Sampietro et al. 2007 claim direct Neolithic to modern continuity in northern Spain.

58. Gignoux et al. 2011; and see Moreau et al. 2011 for a recent example of very rapid population growth along an expanding wave front of colonization – French Canada after 1686.

59. Larson et al. 2007.

60. Brace et al. 2006; Pinhasi and Cramon-Taubadel 2009; Cramon-Taubadel and Pinhasi 2011.

61. References for this section include Quintana-Murci et al. 2004 (mtDNA); Cordaux et al. 2004a, 2004b (mtDNA and NRY); Bastos-Rodriguez et al. 2006 (microsatellites); Li et al. 2008; Reich et al. 2009; Majumder 2010 and Metspalu et al. 2011 (whole genome data).

62. For a graphic illustration see http://www.scs.illinois.edu/~mcdonald/WorldHaplogroups-Maps.pdf. See also Cordaux et al. 2004c; Kumar et al. 2007.

63. Reich et al. 2009; Metspalu et al. 2011.

64. Hemphill et al. 1991; Hemphill 2009.

65. Fuller 2011 discusses the South Asian archaeobotanical record.

66. Southworth 2005: 288–312 (place-name substratum); Southworth and McAlpin 2013. Southworth 2009, 2011 discusses the Proto-Dravidian agricultural vocabulary.

67. For eastern Arabia, see Uerpmann et al. 2009.

68. For a summary of the Egyptian Neolithic see Gilbert 2013.

69. See Hassan 1988, Shirai 2005 and Gilbert 2013 on links between the Levant and Egypt.

70. Recent examples include Ehret 2002a, 2011; Ehret et al. 2004 (with reply by Bellwood 2004); Blench 2006; Kitchen et al. 2009; and see other references in my *First Farmers* page 209. The present-day widespread distribution of Semitic languages in North Africa does not reflect *in situ* descent directly from the earliest history of this family since Arabic spread very widely after the seventh-century Arab conquests. The ancestors of the more diverse Ethiopic (or Ethio-Semitic) languages, also in the Semitic subgroup, spread from Arabia during the second millennium BC. These spreads probably erased much older diversity, both in North Africa and Arabia.

71. See references in Bellwood 2005a: 209–10; Blažek 2013a. Vaclav Blažek (pers. comm.) also regards traces of deeply shared ancestry (Nostratic hypothesis) between Afroasiatic and Elamite as particularly important for placing the Afroasiatic homeland in the Levant.

72. For NRY lineage spreads from western Asia into North Africa during the Holocene, see Arredi et al. 2004, 2007; Luis et al. 2004 (Egypt). Modern North African mtDNA profiles resemble those in the Levant rather than sub-Saharan Africa. Soares et al. 2010 note that North Africa shows a substantial reduction in genetic diversity compared to sub-Saharan Africa, as would be expected if ancestral immigrants had entered the region from the Levant during the Holocene.

Chapter 8
The East Asian and Western Pacific Food Production Complexes

In this chapter, we examine the two very different food production complexes that developed independently of each other in East Asia and western Oceania. The first commenced in the Yellow and Yangzi basins, with the eventual domestications from indigenous wild forebears of short-grained rice, foxtail and common millet, soybean, and pigs. This complex played a major role in the origins of the Sino-Tibetan, Altaic, Austroasiatic, Austronesian and Tai language families, and its carrier populations today occupy virtually all of eastern Asia and Oceania, except for Melanesia and Australia. Like the Fertile Crescent, these two valleys in central China have together formed one of the most significant regions for demographic expansion in Holocene world history. Reference is also made to incipient and seemingly indigenous plant domestication in Japan.

The second quite separate route to plant domestication developed in the western Pacific, especially in highland New Guinea. This involved varieties of sugarcane, yams, taro, bananas, other tree and tuber crops, and lacked domestic animals and cereals. The fertile valleys of the New Guinea Highlands, a core region for these developments, played a major role in the origins of the Trans New Guinea (Papuan) language family and its speakers. This complex also had a significant impact on food production in eastern Indonesia and throughout Oceania.

Agricultural Origins in the Yellow and Yangzi Basins of East Asia

In East Asia, a monsoon-climate agricultural complex was under incipient development by 7000 BC. In the Yellow valley and northeast China, it was initially based on broomcorn millet (*Panicum miliaceum*) and foxtail millet (*Setaria italica*). In the middle and lower Yangzi valley, it was initially based on short-grained rice (*Oryza sativa japonica*). Pigs were the main domesticated animal in both regions, often fed on millets in the north. Pottery usage occurred in both valleys from the late Paleolithic onwards, since the husked grains of these cereal crops were normally cooked by boiling, most efficiently in earthenware pots. As in the Fertile Crescent, early East Asian populations practiced a kind of pre-domestication cultivation that

First Migrants: Ancient Migration in Global Perspective, First Edition. Peter Bellwood.
© Peter Bellwood. Published 2013 by John Wiley & Sons, Ltd.

utilized morphologically wild cereals, with full dependence on domesticated rice and millets developing gradually between 7000 and 4500 BC (Figure 8.1).

As also in the Fertile Crescent, the considerable population growth on these huge riverine plains led to rapid increase in settlement numbers and areas of human occupation. Large villages up to 15 ha in size were common by 5000 BC, especially in the Yangshao culture along the Yellow River. The largest settlements were up to 200 ha in size by Longshan times, circa 2500 BC, many with hundreds of house floors and human burials in large cemeteries.[1] Many of these settlements had enclosing ditches with stamped earth inner defensive walls, raised earthen platforms, storage pits, ground-level houses in the north, and sometimes elongated pile dwellings in the swampy riverine terrain of the south. The records indicate a possible 50-fold increase in population along the middle and lower courses of the Yellow and Yangzi rivers between 7000 and 2000 BC.

Not surprisingly, rice and millet cultivating populations eventually spread throughout southern China and Mainland Southeast Asia, encircling the Himalayas and extending well into India. Other populations migrated at the same time through Island Southeast Asia into the Pacific, eventually (as Malagasy and Polynesians) migrating more than halfway around the world. Yet others spread northwards, carrying millet and rice cultivation to Korea and northeast Asia. Today, almost one half of the world's population owes a good part of its origin to the expansion of the East Asian food production complex, as does close to the other half (excluding sub-Saharan Africans and Native Americans) to the spread from the Fertile Crescent.

In the past, it was generally considered that the Yellow and Yangzi valleys underwent their own separate transitions to food production. But new research has shown that the middle and lower courses of both rivers and their intervening tributaries, despite their rather different crops (hardy dryland millets in the north, wetland rice in the south), formed essentially one internally linked region of development. This is clear from the high level of artifact similarity between the oldest agricultural assemblages in China, located in both the Yellow and Yangzi basins and in the Huai valley between them. It is especially clear at Jiahu in the Huai valley, where a Yellow River artifact assemblage, virtually identical to that from the site of Peiligang to the north, occurs in combination with a Yangzi River rice economy.[2] This need not mean that just one small population group was responsible for the whole of the East Asian Neolithic. Indeed, this would be most unlikely in light of the very large degree of ethnolinguistic diversity that appears to have emanated from this region. But there were some very significant regional linkages.

At present, paleobotanical evidence suggests that common (or broomcorn) millet in the north was the first crop in China to reach a status defined as 'domesticated', generally with a nonshattering habit, but there are still unresolved issues with chronology that render this matter uncertain.[3] As with the Fertile Crescent, it is best not to jump to conclusions about one region or another being first. It needs also to be remembered that central China was considerably warmer than now during the early Holocene, so the wild ancestors of both rice and the millets would have grown considerably north of their present ranges. Wild rice today grows only in southern China and Southeast Asia, but in 7000 BC it was growing up to and even slightly north of the Yangzi.

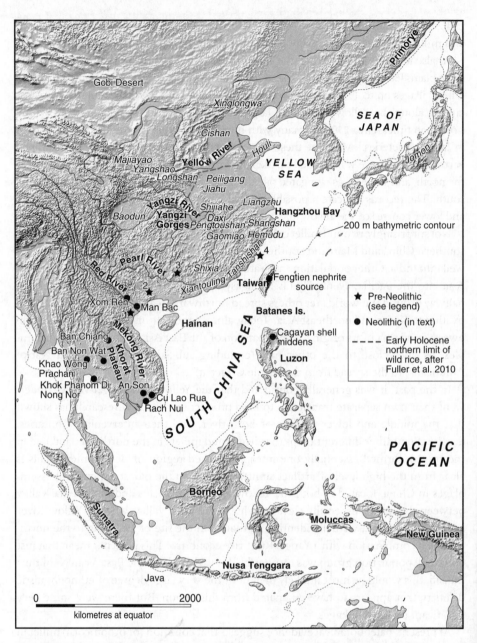

Figure 8.1 The Neolithic in China and Southeast Asia. The stars indicate pre-Neolithic sites in Southeast Asia with combinations of shell middens, contorted or sitting burials, coarse pottery, and no evidence for food production. They include (1) Da But and Con Co Ngua in northern Vietnam; (2) Dingsishan and Dayan Cave near Nanning in Guangxi; (3) Zengpiyan in Guilin, Guangxi; and (4) a site on Liang Island in the Matsu Islands off Fujian (Taiwan). Individual Neolithic sites are not shown for China since there are so many, but major cultural groups referred to in the text are labeled in italics (not all are contemporary). Background map by Multimedia Services, ANU, details added by the author.

If we examine East Asian Holocene prehistory as a whole, with migration in mind, then it becomes clear that the two great riverine plains of central China, the Yellow and the Yangzi, formed the combined source of a considerable quantity of population movement to north and south, just as they did when Qin and Han dynastic rulers forged the Chinese Empire around 2000 years ago. Broomcorn and foxtail millet tended to move north, although millets are now being found widely in Southeast Asian Neolithic sites, especially in Thailand and Vietnam. Rice tended to move south, although many of the Neolithic cultures along the Yellow River have some rice remains from a very early date, especially in Shandong Province near the warmer eastern seaboard. Indeed, the region between the two great rivers appears to have had a predominance of rice during the early Neolithic, as at Jiahu, followed by an increase in millets around 4500 BC during Yangshao times, perhaps reflecting a drier mid-Holocene climate. There was then a shift back towards rice in the Longshan period, around 3000 BC.[4] From linguistic reconstructions, the ancestral Chinese have certainly known both crops since the origin period of the Sino-Tibetan language family.

Migrations from the Yellow River Basin

The archaeological record traces the presence of the East Asian millets in Neolithic cultures in northeastern China by at least 6500 BC, as at Xinglongwa in Inner Mongolia. They were carried further into the Korean Peninsula and Pacific coastal Russia (Primorye) by 3500 BC. At about the same time, millet farmers from the Yellow River (Majiayao culture) reached northern Sichuan Province and the Chengdu Plain on the upper Yangzi, later spreading into Tibet by 2000 BC. This East Asian agricultural complex did not spread much further into central Asia because of the dry and cold climate, and also because of competition from pastoral economies of westerly steppe derivation with their Fertile Crescent crops and animals. Interestingly, millets were replaced by rice prior to 2700 BC during the Baodun phase on the Chengdu Plain of Sichuan, signaling stronger relations by this time with rice-growing populations in the middle and lower Yangzi.[5]

The Neolithic millet economies that spread up the Yellow River, and southwestwards into Sichuan and the Himalayas, were probably carried by human population movements, most probably by early speakers of Sino-Tibetan (including Tibeto-Burman) languages. However, this is not so clear for crop movements to the north of the Yellow River. The Neolithic of Inner Mongolia and Manchuria, with its cultural sequence from Xinglongwa to Hongshan, was quite different in its pottery and jade artifact forms from the Peiligang, Yangshao and Dawenkou assemblages of the Yellow River. This suggests that millet cultivation in the northeast of China involved an indigenous population, one likely ancestral to the modern speakers of Tungusic (including Manchu) and Mongolian languages, both completely unrelated to Sino-Tibetan (Figure 7.7). Japanese and Korean are also very distantly related to Tungusic and Mongolian, as part of the so-called Altaic superfamily, introduced in chapter 7. My main conclusion here would be that early farming in northeastern China was both indigenous in a population sense and yet linked with regions to the south in an agricultural sense.

What of Japan? These islands offer an early agricultural situation in which migration was apparently not involved at all, since an indigenous population of foragers, arboriculturalists and low-level cereal cultivators remained in place from the late Pleistocene until almost 2000 years ago. Japan remained free of intensive continental domination until the arrival from Korea of wet rice farming, new pottery styles, and bronze and iron working during the Yayoi phase in the first millennium BC.[6] The plant subsistence complex of the preceding Jomon phase (14,000 to 500 BC), with soybean, barnyard millet (*Echinochloa esculenta*), beans, acorns, chestnuts, walnuts, and occasional finds of rice, was clearly associated with some degree of food production.[7] But this crop complex and its attached human populations appear never to have spread outside Japan, or even beyond Okinawa or the Kurile Islands.

Japan, therefore, offers us an interesting example of a small but seemingly independent development of food production, with a range of cereals and tree crops similar to those domesticated in China. Jomon material culture and settlements, especially in the Middle Jomon (circa 3000 BC), were quintessentially Neolithic in terms of fine pottery, polished stone tools, large village settlements, and actual DNA and grain size evidence for plant domestication. But current indications are that the level of production was less intensive than in the great river valleys of China. Prehistoric Japan does not stand as a source of external migration, but rather became a recipient of population during the Yayoi phase.[8]

Migrations from the Yangzi Basin – Mainland Southeast Asia

The spread of food production southwards was more complex than northwards in terms of human numbers and ethnolinguistic repercussions. It accompanied ancestral Tibeto-Burman, Austronesian, Austroasiatic, Tai and Hmong-Mien populations to the far reaches of both Mainland and Island Southeast Asia, and around the Himalayas (Figure 8.2). Within all of this linguistic complexity we can recognize two macro-scale shifts of human population. One traveled southwards and westwards into Mainland Southeast Asia, Tibet, and northeastern India. The other traveled offshore via Taiwan and the Philippines into Island Southeast Asia and the Pacific Islands (Figure 8.3). I focus first on the Asian mainland migrations.

The first issue to consider is that of where and how rice was initially domesticated since this was the major crop south of the Yangzi, although often found with foxtail millet. Because of the importance of Asian rice (*Oryza sativa*) in the world today, it has been exceptionally well studied by agronomists, geneticists and archaeobotanists. Current genetic evidence suggests only a single domestication of *Oryza rufipogon*, the perennial ancestor for *Oryza sativa japonica* (the Asian short-grained and sticky rices), in or close to the Yangzi basin.[9] *Oryza sativa indica* (long-grained rice) was domesticated from an annual forebear in South Asia, initially perhaps independently of *japonica* and probably in the Ganges and Brahmaputra valleys (Figure 7.3). However, the emergence of *indica* as a major domesticated crop involved hybridization with *japonica*, which was probably carried into northern India by early Tibeto-Burman and Austroasiatic speakers around 2500–2000 BC. The Yangzi basin was thus the most likely source of domesticated rice in the first instance.

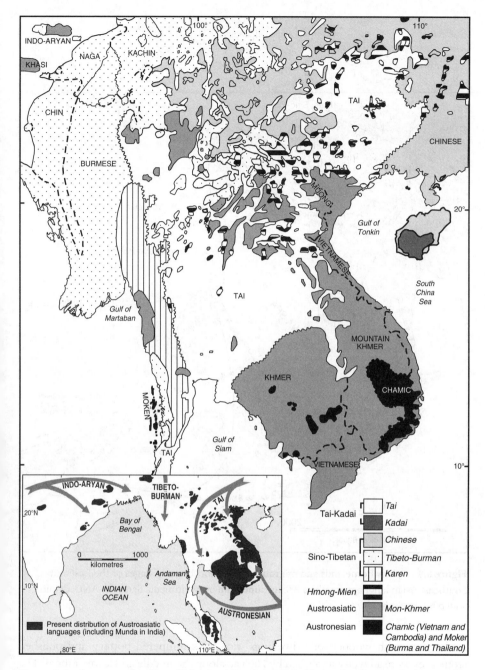

Figure 8.2 Language families of Mainland Southeast Asia. Drawn by Carmen Sarjeant and by Multimedia Services, ANU. Reproduced by permission of Paul Sidwell (see Sidwell 2013).

The archaeobotanical record from the Yangzi basin indicates a fairly long development from pre-domesticated to domesticated *japonica* rice production, occurring between roughly 7000 and 4000 BC. In terms of associated archaeology, village

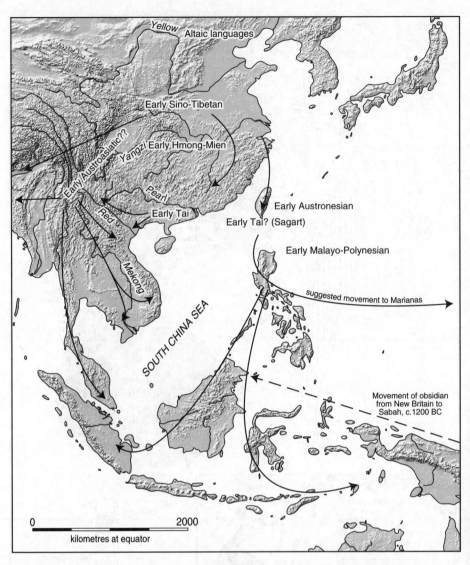

Figure 8.3 Likely homelands and migration routes for the early stages of the East and Southeast Asian language families. Background map by Multimedia Services, ANU, details added by the author.

settlements with wooden pile dwellings, rice husk tempered pottery and polished stone axes were all well established by 7000 BC along the middle and lower Yangzi. The rice at this early date was still morphologically wild, but exploited through pre-domestication cultivation and threshing. The 7000 BC pottery at Shangshan in Zhejiang, for instance, contained processed chaff, not just unprocessed grains or stalk fragments. Similar evidence, including residue analysis of pottery fabrics as well as stable isotope dietary analysis of human bone, indicates contemporary rice consumption at Jiahu in the Huai Valley.[10]

After Jiahu and Shangshan, further archaeological evidence for increasingly intensive rice exploitation comes from several waterlogged sites in northern Zhejiang. These have produced some remarkable assemblages that include dug-out canoes, wooden paddles and agricultural tools, foundations of pile dwellings, many other items reflecting high skills in carpentry, and richly decorated pottery traditions. The proportions of morphologically domesticated *japonica* rice in these sites increased over time, and by 4600 BC accounted for perhaps 30% of a regional plant food diet that also included wild acorns, water chestnuts, foxnuts and possibly domestic pigs.[11] By 4000 BC, the rice-growing inhabitants of this region were investing labor in constructing slightly sunken wet fields, linked to settlements of considerable and growing size. By the third millennium BC, this trend attained almost urban proportions in some Liangzhu sites, with increasing areas of wet rice fields along the lower Yangzi. It is perhaps no coincidence that the major spread of population from southern China into Southeast Asia took place during this specific millennium of very high population growth.

However, this increasing investment in rice cultivation and the population growth that resulted from it did not occur in a completely stable environment. Central China was warmer then than now, and perhaps wetter, which is why rice domestication commenced so far north of the present range of wild rice. Also, a very major change occurred during this time in the level of the sea. Between 9500 and 5000 BC, there was an early Holocene rise in global sea level of 60 m as a result of glacial melt water release. This converted the 700 km wide Pleistocene coastal plain of eastern China into a shallow sea dotted with many offshore islands (Figure 8.1). It created a situation in which rice cultivation in riverine and coastal wetlands was growing in intensity just as those wetlands were disappearing (or had already disappeared) beneath the rising sea.[12] In addition, periodic episodes of climatic cooling, documented for instance at circa 4200 and 2200 BC, would also have had a strong impact since rice along the latitude of the Yangzi was growing so close at that time to the northern edge of its range.[13] These conditions might be thought conducive to rice farmer migration, although the stresses were probably not universal.

The Neolithic spread south of the Yangzi occurred mainly between 3000 and 2000 BC, by which time the *japonica* rice grown in the Yangzi basin itself had developed a substantially domesticated status.[14] As the rice was moved south, there was probably increasing investment in dryland systems of cultivation, these being more transportable than labor-intensive systems of wet rice cultivation, which would also have been held back by the inertia of high land values.[15] Prior to 3000 BC, many regions south of the Yangzi were still occupied by hunter-gatherer populations, best known from cave sites and a small number of open air shell middens in the southern Chinese provinces of Guangxi, Jiangxi and Hainan. They also occur in the Matsu Islands off the coast of Fujian, and in northern Vietnam (Bacsonian or Da But culture, see Figure 8.1). These hunter-gatherers made coarse grit-tempered pottery that is dated from the late Pleistocene onwards, and buried their dead without grave goods in distinctive flexed, contorted or sitting postures, unlike later Neolithic populations who generally preferred an extended supine burial posture and supplied prolific grave goods, especially pots.

There is no evidence for any form of food production in these pre-Neolithic sites. One suggestion by Tracey Lu is that the pots were used to cook shellfish, perhaps with the unconscious advantage of reducing the danger of parasitic infection from schistosomiasis. Domestic dog bones occur in mid-Holocene contexts at Dingsishan in Guangxi, but there are no records of domestic pig. Wild animals, tubers and nuts were hunted and collected, and lithics tools include both edge-ground and fully ground adzes. The Dingsishan shell midden in southern Guangxi, covering about 0.5 ha and dated to before 3000 BC, had a cemetery with at least 130 tightly flexed burials, suggesting quite a large population at this time.[16]

These pre-Neolithic populations survived right into Neolithic times (circa 2000 BC) in northern Vietnam, and certainly contributed some genes to the later populations of Mainland Southeast Asia. Craniometrically, however, they were Australo-Melanesian in their affinities and so cannot be seen as the major ancestors for any extant Mainland Southeast Asian non-Negrito populations. Everywhere, apart from northern Vietnam, the Neolithic was preceded only by pebble and flake industries, sometimes with edge-grinding, with no clear archaeological continuity between the two phases. Indeed, many non-limestone regions of Mainland Southeast Asia have no identified pre-Neolithic archaeological record at all, reflecting if not a total absence of human population, at least a very low density.

As for the southwards movements of the farmers themselves from central China, two main routes are apparent.[17] One went up the southern tributaries of the middle Yangzi and then down the Pearl to the coastline of Guangdong. The other went from the lower Yangzi down the Zhejiang coastline to Fujian and Taiwan. The rice-growing Neolithic cultures that appear to have had the largest roles behind these southerly expansions include the Tangjiagang, Daxi, and Shijiahe in the middle Yangzi, and the Hemudu, Majiabang, and Liangzhu in the lower Yangzi, dating in combination between 5000 and 2500 BC (Figure 8.1). Most well-dated Neolithic sites in the south with rice or millet are younger than 3000 BC, thus belonging to a time when Shijiahe and Liangzhu population sizes in the Yangzi were very large. Examples include Tanshishan near Fuzhou in Fujian Province, 75 km inland now but near the sea when inhabited about 3000–2300 BC, and Shixia, a 3 ha site with rice and jade working in northern Guangdong. Both show links, especially the Shixia jades, with the Liangzhu culture. The contemporary Xiantouling culture of coastal Guangdong had middle Yangzi links, particularly with the Daxi and Gaomiao cultures, but it is not clear at present if Xiantouling and Gaomiao were associated with food production (the Daxi people grew rice). Certainly, agriculture was not widespread in southern China much prior to 3000 BC, perhaps 2000 years after the transition to domestication in the Yangzi valley itself.

Crossing the border into Mainland Southeast Asia, the Neolithic record commenced generally around 2000 BC and current information comes from four geographical regions. These are the lower Red River and adjacent regions of northern Vietnam (Phung Nguyen culture), the Vam Co and Dong Nai drainages just north of the Mekong in southern Vietnam, the Khorat Plateau in northeastern Thailand, and the Chao Phraya Valley and environs in central Thailand. The archaeological record from these sites is prolific, so only a brief outline can be given here.[18]

A number of authors have recently pointed out that the earliest pottery from these sites shows a great deal of regional similarity in surface decoration, extending from the Malay Peninsula up into the southern provinces of China, especially Yunnan.[19] This decoration, especially on footed presentation vessels, emphasized horizontal bands of geometric or curvilinear motifs filled with punctate or dentate stamping, or fine comb incision. Associated with this pottery are sometimes extended burials in large cemeteries, a wide array of polished stone adzes and shell body ornaments, bones of domesticated pig and dog,[20] and carbonized and phytolith remains of *japonica* rice and foxtail millet. Coastal sites like Khok Phanom Di in central Thailand and Rach Nui in southern Vietnam have prolific evidence for maritime resource exploitation, especially along mangrove shorelines.

Because the known sites are not absolutely contemporary it is difficult to see universal parallels in pottery decoration between them, but the assemblages as a whole reveal considerable congruence. The early Neolithic pottery of northern Vietnam, Guangdong and Guangxi is closely related, especially in the dominance of carved paddle-impression. This northern expression is likely to have been connected with the early migrations of Tai speakers. A likely homeland for Proto-Tai, or Proto-Kra-Dai in the terminology of Weera Ostapirat, is located in the southern Chinese provinces of Guangxi, Guangdong and Hainan, together with northern Vietnam.[21] On the other hand, the early Neolithic pottery of southern Vietnam is closely related to that of the Khorat Plateau sites in Thailand, all these sites linked by the Mekong drainage system and its tributaries.[22] This more southerly expression was perhaps connected with the early migration of Austroasiatic speakers, ancestors especially of the Khmers, Vietnamese, and many small tribal populations scattered over the mainland of Southeast Asia into northern India. Let us now examine these Southeast Asian linguistic populations in more detail.

Early Rice and the Linguistic Record

The oldest Yellow and Yangzi Neolithic cultures enshrine the ancestry of not just Sinitic-speaking peoples, but the common linguistic roots of many other populations in East and Southeast Asia, plus Oceania. Thus, while the Yangshao culture along the Yellow River could conceivably be ancestral to the Han Chinese, so the contemporary Neolithic cultures of Fujian and Taiwan could be associated with early Austronesian speakers. As just noted, those of Guangdong and Guangxi could be associated with early Tai speakers, and of the Mekong Valley with early Austroasiatic speakers. However, these oldest Neolithic cultures long predated the precipitation of any sharply defined modern ethnolinguistic identities. This is sometimes a difficult concept to get across to modern audiences, who react with puzzlement when told that many Southeast Asian cultures appear to have had ultimate origins in southern China about 4000 years ago. People find it hard to think of 'China' as ever having been anything other than just like modern China – full of people speaking Chinese languages, looking like Chinese and presumably identifying in some way as Chinese or Han across an unchanging ethnic landscape.

However, a voluminous historical record informs us that Han Chinese populations have spread over most of what is now China south of the Yangzi only within the past 2500 years. In a way, the Chinese were once the ultimate 'stay-at-homes' of the East Asian Neolithic revolution, just as the ancestral Semitic speakers stayed at home in the Levant, and ancestral Formosan (Austronesian) speakers stayed at home in Taiwan. It is absolutely essential to understand that Han Chinese ethnic identity has not always been coincident with the geographical distribution of the Chinese people today, even less so with the piece of geographical space that today is called China.

The possible homelands and spreads of the major language families of Southeast Asia are delineated in Figure 8.2 and Figure 8.3. All of them (Austronesian, Austroasiatic, Tai, Hmong-Mien, and Sino-Tibetan with Tibeto-Burman) have reconstructable proto-vocabularies that suggest an early and deep acquaintance with rice and its exploitation. In the cases of Tibeto-Burman and Austronesian, there was also a knowledge of foxtail millet.[23] In Proto-Austronesian there is evidence for a familiarity with both wet and dry rice, as well as with transplantation techniques. Linguist Laurent Sagart favors a dual origin for rice vocabularies, one involving inland Austroasiatic dispersal down the Mekong and Irrawaddy, the other involving coastal China from southern Shandong south to Hainan and Taiwan (Sino-Tibetan, Austronesian, and Tai). The ultimate source for both vocabularies would presumably have been in the middle and lower Yangzi Valley, where only Sino-Tibetan languages are spoken today.

The rather submerged distribution of the Austroasiatic language family today means that it no longer has a precisely reconstructable homeland. Diffloth and van Driem suggest an origin close to the Bay of Bengal or the Brahmaputra valley. Sidwell and Blench favor a Mekong Basin origin, and Sagart favors the Yangzi.[24] This wide range of linguistic opinion raises a question. Has the evidence for an Austroasiatic homeland been entirely erased by the expansions of Sinitic, Khmer, Vietnamese, Tai and Burmese, rendering a once-widespread language family now just a shadow of its former self?[25] Sagart suggests this explanation in his quest for a middle Yangzi origin. Conversely, was Austroasiatic dispersal the result of a domino effect, with populations of ultimate Yangzi origin introducing rice cultivation to an ancestral Austroasiatic linguistic population located outside the Yangzi Basin, possibly somewhere in Mainland Southeast Asia, which then expanded further in its own right? Either scenario is quite possible.

The archaeological record can never prove or disprove linguistic homeland and migration hypotheses such as these, but it can render some more likely than others. Given the archaeological record, the Yangzi would certainly have an edge as a significant linguistic homeland for both rice vocabularies and rice-growing populations over the Mekong or the Bay of Bengal. Neither of these last two regions reveals any evidence for outward Neolithic population spread, although research coverage is still poor. I would not be at all surprised if ancestral Austroasiatic speakers spread from the middle Yangzi southwards through Mainland Southeast Asia, or if they imposed their language domino-wise on a separate hinterland population, who thereupon joined the process of expansion. Likewise, we would have a very favorable linkage between the archaeological and linguistic records if ancestral Tai and Austronesian spread from north to south down the eastern coast of China, respectively towards northern Vietnam and Taiwan.

Given the obvious importance of the Yangzi and Yellow rivers in the rise of food production and consequent population growth in eastern Asia, could it be possible that all major language families of the region, including Austronesian, developed first along or somewhere near these two major rivers? The suggestion is also raised by Sagart (2011), especially for Austroasiatic, Sino-Tibetan and Austronesian. He also sees the last two as related in the form of a Sino-Austronesian macrofamily. There is no absolute linguistic proof for these suggestions and perhaps there never will be, but it is important also to remember the domino factor referred to earlier. My suspicion here is that the ultimate homelands of the major language families of Southeast Asia, such as Austronesian, Tai and Austroasiatic, were not located directly along the courses of the Yangzi or Yellow rivers themselves, where increasingly sedentary populations were intensifying production in the direction of emergent Chinese early civilization. Rather, they were located in regions slightly more peripheral. These regions could have been either just to the north, such as Shandong where Sagart (2005a, 2008) locates his Proto-Sino-Austronesian, or just to the south, where we might one day locate the origins of Austroasiatic.

Genetics, Human Biology, and the East Asian Mainland during the Holocene

The biological history of East and Mainland Southeast Asia is rapidly becoming clearer due to cranial morphometric and ancient DNA analysis. These analyses add time depth to the observations made by comparing purely modern or historical populations. In Chapter 4, I discussed the origins of the Australo-Melanesians, the original late Pleistocene colonists of early modern human Southeast Asia, extending to Australia, New Guinea and the Solomon Islands, around 50,000 years ago. The modern indigenous peoples of New Guinea, much of Island Melanesia and Australia descend fairly directly from these early settlers, albeit with many local population movements through time, such as that postulated to explain the Pama-Nyungan language family of Australia in Chapter 5. This deeply indigenous genetic descent is clear from mtDNA and NRY studies, which show that Australian and New Guinea peoples share haplogroups of Pleistocene Asian origin, especially within mtDNA haplogroups M and N and NRY haplogroups C and K.[26] Southeast Asian populations in the hunter-gatherer Negrito population group, especially in West Malaysia and the Andaman Islands, have similarly deep-seated haploid genetic profiles (Endicott 2003).

New research by Hirofumi Matsumura and colleagues on skull morphometrics from Neolithic cemeteries in China and Mainland Southeast is giving us a much clearer view of how the indigenous Australo-Melanesian populations, who originally occupied all of Southeast Asia and apparently southern China, contributed to the rise of the Neolithic. The pre-Neolithic shell midden builders and pottery makers of southern China and northern Vietnam, referred to earlier, were of Australo-Melanesian cranio-facial morphology. So too were the Hoabinhian and Bacsonian cave dwellers of Mainland Southeast Asia, and also the pre-Neolithic populations of Island Southeast Asia, especially from caves in Borneo and Java.[27]

Recent results from the Neolithic cemetery at Man Bac in northern Vietnam, using both skull morphometrics and ancient DNA, reveal a population dating from circa 2000 BC that lived right on the cusp of Neolithic expansion southwards from Guangxi and Guangdong. The cemetery records precisely how immigrating Asian rice farmers shared their settlement with indigenous Australo-Melanesian hunters and gatherers. Man Bac has a cemetery of about 100 individuals, with a very high infant to adult ratio suggesting high population growth, fuelled in part by rice growing according to the large densities of rice phytoliths in the site.[28] The majority of the inhabitants were close to modern East Asians in craniofacial morphology, and a minority resembled Australo-Melanesians. Most identified ancient mtDNA was from East Asian haplogroups D and G, but a few people carried the indigenous Southeast Asian haplogroup F. Unfortunately, it has been difficult to match specific crania with specific mtDNA results since most of the latter came from individuals with incomplete crania, and most complete crania contained no surviving DNA. However, these two morphologically and genetically distinct populations were clearly interacting since they were buried together, even though both sets of crania can be separated statistically, suggesting that genetic blending at Man Bac had not yet proceeded very far.

As Matsumura and colleagues 2011: 169-70 point out:

> Man Bac may be an example of one of those extremely rare archaeological snap shots of a population in transition; a somewhat cosmopolitan mix of indigenous inhabitants tracing their origins back to the Hoabinhian and new comers with a genetic heritage located outside of the region. The eventual outcome of this integration was a new population that contributed to the modern Southeast Asian morphology.

Analyses carried out by Matsumura on other Mainland East Asian Neolithic cemetery populations, such as that from Hemudu in Zhejiang (circa 4500 BC), and from An Son in southern Vietnam (circa 1500 BC), suggest that these populations were also basically similar to modern East Asians, but with some surviving Australo-Melanesian features, especially in tooth morphology.[29]

What else do we know about the ancestry of modern agricultural populations in East and Southeast Asia, especially from modern DNA distributions? As discussed in Chapter 7, Gignoux and colleagues (2011) have examined the density of mutation events through time in whole mtDNA genomes. Their results indicate that considerable population increase occurred in Mainland Southeast Asia around 2500 BC, especially in mtDNA lineages that can be associated with agricultural populations. This suggests rapid population growth during the Neolithic, something also clearly visible from the archaeological record, as in contemporary Longshan and Liangzhu contexts in central China.

East and Mainland Southeast Asians, apart from the Negrito populations, are also fairly closely related in terms of their NRY lineages, especially within haplogroup O. Furthermore, mtDNA analyses of modern populations suggest a degree of Holocene migration southwards down the Malay Peninsula. Stephen Oppenheimer associates this with southwards gene flow into the Senoi agricultural population of interior West Malaysia, who derive around half of their mtDNA from shared ancestry with the indigenous Negrito Semang, and the other half from the north.[30] There is also a small amount of aDNA research on skeletons from Neolithic Thailand that has related them most closely to modern speakers of Austroasiatic rather than Tai languages.[31] This is expected, since the Tai linguistic radiation into what is now Thailand occurred only in the past millennium. Neolithic and Bronze/Iron Age populations in Thailand presumably spoke mostly Austroasiatic languages.

Island Southeast Asia and Oceania

The East Asian food production complex eventually came to dominate many of the northern and western islands of Southeast Asia as a result of migration out of southern coastal China into Taiwan around 3500 BC. This was followed by a crossing from Taiwan into the northern Philippines around 2200 BC (Figure 8.4).[32] The complex underwent considerable transformation after 1500 BC in the eastern islands of Indonesia, with the loss of rice and millet cultivation[33] and a switch to tree and tuber crops such as bananas, coconuts, breadfruit, taro and yams. Some of these were of Island Southeast Asian and western Pacific origin, and they lead us into the western Pacific food production complex, which evolved quite independently of that in East Asia. The western Pacific complex contributed to the major migrations by Austronesian-speaking populations into Oceania after 1300 BC, culminating after AD 800 in the colonization of the remotest islands of eastern Polynesia.

The most important economic players in the genesis of this western Pacific agricultural complex were the ancestors of the indigenous Papuan-speaking populations of New Guinea and adjacent islands. The New Guinea highlands, in particular, form a unique environment in world terms, being well watered, high in altitude, equatorial in climate (hence without marked rainfall seasons), and well protected by mountain walls from external population intrusion. They are also high enough in altitude to be malaria-free, an important consideration given the evidence for the rather disastrous effects of malaria in some Southeast Asian lowland Neolithic societies, as well as in lowland regions of Indonesia and Melanesia today.[34] The New Guinea Highland archaeological record indicates that people there were cultivating bananas, taro and perhaps sugar cane by at least 4500 BC. But no cereals or domesticated animals were present, so levels of productivity compared to those in China were quite low.[35]

There is no genetic or linguistic evidence that suggests significant Holocene population expansion from New Guinea towards Asia, unlike the huge body of evidence that points to movement the other way. But, as far as the western Pacific as a whole is concerned, the genetic and cultural contributions from western Melanesia were quite dramatic. Within New Guinea itself and adjacent islands, the New Guinea Highland variant of the western Pacific food production complex probably gave rise to the radiation of the early Trans New Guinea languages, which ultimately came to dominate most of the island, especially the interior.[36] Although many coastal New Guinea and Melanesian island populations today speak Austronesian languages as a result of language shifts in prehistory, the modern populations themselves, especially in

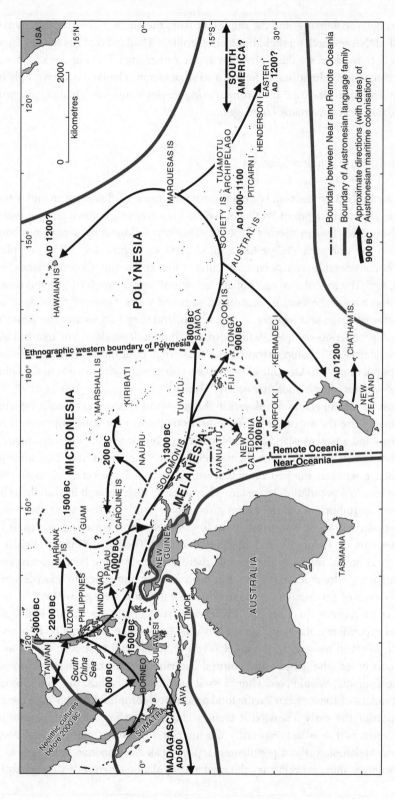

Figure 8.4 Holocene population movements through Island Southeast Asia and across Oceania, according to archaeological and comparative linguistic data. This map is also published in Bellwood 2013. Original by Multimedia Services, ANU.

southeastern Indonesia, and in the Solomon, Vanuatu and New Caledonia island groups, are genetically of mainly indigenous Melanesian origin.[37] We return to this issue later, since there was also a degree of Melanesian genetic input into the genomes of Polynesians, who are otherwise a population very clearly of Asian rather than Melanesian origin.

As for as the initial outflow of Neolithic populations off the Asian mainland into Island Southeast Asia, an agricultural way of life with pottery, stone adzes, rice, millets, pigs and dogs had spread southwards by 3500 BC, through the coastal provinces and offshore islands of southern China, to reach Taiwan. A long pause in migration then occurred in Taiwan until around 2200 BC, when the archaeological record reveals the commencement of a spread of related cultural complexes, with red-slipped and often stamped pottery, domestic animals, and similar kinds of stone and shell artifacts, through the Philippines into Indonesia and the islands of the western Pacific. This migration reached Guam by 1500 BC and western Polynesia (Tonga and Samoa) by about 900 BC.

Important discoveries related to the earliest Neolithic way of life in Island Southeast Asia have recently been excavated at Nanguanli in southwestern Taiwan, associated with the Dabenkeng phase of Taiwan prehistory. Rescue excavations here into waterlogged deposits 7 m below ground level, dating between 3000 and 2500 BC, have produced pottery with cord-marked, red-painted and red-slipped decoration, stone bark cloth beaters, perforated slate projectile points, shouldered stone adzes, baked clay spindle whorls, tanged shell reaping knives, and shell bracelets and earrings. Found with these artifacts were complete dog burials, pig bones, and carbonized grains of *japonica* rice and foxtail millet. The Dabenkeng complex was introduced decisively into Taiwan about 3500 BC, replacing a very sparse flaked stone assemblage known as the Changbinian, associated with earlier hunter-gatherer settlement.

In Neolithic Taiwan, there is very good evidence for considerable population growth between 3500 and 2000 BC, with a 20-fold increase in site numbers during this period in one region near Taipei. There was also a 20–30 times increase in total site area, with individual sites reaching a maximum extent of 60 ha. Similar data are available for eastern Taiwan, indicating that the period from 3500 to 2000 BC was one of considerable growth throughout the island.[38] It is striking that the movement of Neolithic populations from Taiwan into the northern Philippines, at around 2200 BC, coincided with such a high population density in Taiwan. It also coincided with some potential evidence for landscape degradation, especially in the Penghu Islands that lie between Taiwan and Fujian.[39] A desire for new agricultural land emerges as a possible motive, fuelling further migration.

Beyond Taiwan, the Neolithic settlement of the Philippines is well recorded in the archaeology of the Batanes Islands and the Cagayan Valley in the north of the country. Finely cord-marked pottery of a type dated to before 1500 BC in southern Taiwan occurred first, in Batanes only, then red-slipped pottery of southern Taiwan ancestry replaced the cord-marked and spread into Luzon.[40] Taiwan jade occurs in Neolithic sites in both Batanes and the Cagayan Valley, imported from the Fengtian source near Hualian in eastern Taiwan. The Cagayan sites have red-slipped punctate and dentate stamped pottery which is difficult to trace to any particular source in Taiwan, but this type of decoration occurs in Dabenkeng contexts at Nanguanli and also has very distinctive parallels in Yangzi basin Neolithic complexes such as Daxi (circa 4000 BC).

South of the Philippines, archaeological traces of Neolithic expansion during the middle and late second millennium BC have been found in a number of rock shelters and open sites in Malaysian Borneo, Sulawesi, eastern Java, Timor, and the northern Moluccas.[41] These sites contain occasional evidence for rice, with mostly undecorated red-slipped pottery and polished stone adzes. The archaeological record has many gaps, but it is possible that two cultural streams might have been involved in the movement southwards from the northern Philippines. An eastern one with mainly plain red-slipped pottery and a diminishing reliance on rice eventually entered the Moluccas and Nusa Tenggara (the Lesser Sundas). A western one, via Palawan and western Borneo, ultimately reached Sumatra and Java with paddle-impressed pottery and continuing rice cultivation (Figure 8.3 and Figure 8.4). But for the moment this is merely supposition, as additional field archaeology is required in these regions.

The Colonization of Oceania

In Micronesia, the first settlers to reach the Mariana Islands were evidently derived directly from the Philippines, according to parallels in the earliest red-slipped and stamped pottery in these two regions.[42] They also perhaps took rice (but not pigs or dogs) with them, which would have been the only occasion this crop was transported into Oceania. The open-sea crossing to the Marianas from the Philippines, at least 2300 km, justifiably ranks as the first crossing of this distance known in Oceanic or even world cultural history, given that the archaeological record so far fails to indicate any other route except for the most direct one. The Palau Islands were settled about 1000 BC, but they reveal no direct archaeological links with the earliest Marianas assemblages. The other islands of southern Micronesia, especially the Carolines (mostly atolls), were settled after 500 BC since the coral reefs responsible for atoll formation did not provide habitable land above the Holocene sea level until this time (Figure 8.4).

Between 1350 and 900 BC, Neolithic colonists in Island Melanesia (excluding New Guinea) and western Polynesia (Tonga, Samoa, and adjacent islands) left an extremely clear-cut trail of sites belonging to the Lapita cultural complex (Figure 8.5).[43] In New Caledonia, Vanuatu, Fiji, Tonga and Samoa, Lapita marked the first documented human settlement. Of course, the more westerly islands from New Guinea out to as far as the Solomons had already been long settled by pre-Neolithic indigenous populations, some practicing horticulture or arboriculture, but these groups did not use pottery or keep domesticated animals before Lapita times. Interestingly, early Lapita sites have never been found on New Guinea itself, although there are a few sherds from the northern coast and some new discoveries of rather late Lapita sites on the southeastern coast (McNiven et al. 2011). Lapita settlers appear to have had preferences for coastlines with fringing coral reefs and lagoons, and such environments were rare around most of New Guinea proper due to rapid rates of uplift along the narrow northern coastline and the rapid alluvial sedimentation in the vast swamplands in the south.

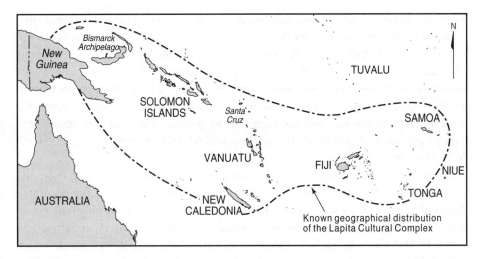

Figure 8.5 The distribution of Lapita sites in Oceania. This map has also been published in Spriggs 2013, and is reproduced with the permission of Matthew Spriggs.

This impressive Lapita migration involved Neolithic populations whose archaeological origins have long been assumed to be in eastern Indonesia. However, the closest parallels in terms of decorated pottery and shell fishhooks occur much further north, in the just-discussed Cagayan Valley sites in the Philippines and in the Mariana Islands. One current view[44] is that an identifiable population movement occurred from the Philippines, via the Marianas, and directly south into the Bismarck Archipelago, the latter serving as the immediate homeland of Lapita within Melanesia. From the Bismarcks, subsequent movements prior to 1000 BC must have gone west into eastern Indonesia, generally avoiding New Guinea itself but carrying black volcanic obsidian from sources in the Bismarck Archipelago to as far west as Sabah in northern Borneo (this movement is indicated in Figures 8.3 and 8.4). At the same time, groups possibly moved the other way, from eastern Indonesia to the Bismarcks (again avoiding New Guinea), although the only evidence for this at the moment appears to be linguistic and not archaeological.

Lapita pottery is well known for its decoration, often red-slipped, with horizontal zones of intricately incised and dentate-stamped rectilinear, curvilinear and even anthropomorphic motifs, the latter perhaps indicating the concern with ancestors common to all Austronesian speaking populations. Late Lapita pottery tended to have simpler designs. Dentate stamping faded in popularity after 750 BC in favor of plain ware in western Polynesia, although other styles of incised, appliqué, and carved paddle-impressed pottery continued until late prehistory in some Melanesian archipelagos and parts of coastal New Guinea. Apart from pottery, other items of Lapita material culture similar to those found in contemporary sites in the Philippines and eastern Indonesia included stone and shell adzes, and a range of shell ornaments including beads and arm rings. Lapita shell fishhooks, however, find their closest ancestral parallels in the Marianas.

Lapita village settlements, in some cases of stilt houses over shallow lagoons, averaged about 1 ha in size (maximum 7–8 ha) in coastal and small offshore island locations. Economically, Lapita was based on a mix of horticultural and maritime subsistence, but without rice or other cereals. Plant remains from waterlogged sites in the Bismarck Archipelago include taro, coconut, candlenut, pandanus, canarium nuts and bananas, most exploited by pre-Lapita indigenous populations in western Melanesia. Pigs,[45] fowl and dogs were all present in Lapita sites, although not all sites or island groups have yielded the same results. Lapita settlers were initially distracted away from their domesticated food supplies by prolific wild resources (littoral and avian) in the areas they colonized, until these became reduced through extinction and local extirpation.

Beyond Melanesia, Lapita colonists reached Tonga and Samoa in western Polynesia by about 900 to 850 BC (Burley and Dickinson 2010). As in Melanesia, the decorated forms of Lapita pottery lasted for only a few centuries, eventually turning into a plain ware of increasing thickness before the eventual demise of pottery in Samoa and southern Micronesia by AD 300. Without rice, Polynesians did not need pots in which to boil their food, and managed instead with earth ovens and open hearths. Together with the earlier losses, prior to reaching Oceania, of rice and millet, loom weaving, and the associated clay spindle whorls for spinning fibers, this eventual loss of pottery-making suggests bottleneck cultural simplification as small groups pushed ever further east, gradually losing contact with their more complex homeland cultures and leaving behind aspects of cultural knowledge.

Nevertheless, although Polynesians might well have lacked rice, pottery, and woven cloth, they (or some of their immediate ancestors) reversed cultural simplification in a very impressive way by inventing the double sailing canoe, a remarkable construction that allowed the discovery and planned colonization of islands located thousands of kilometers over the horizon. Indeed, double canoes could have aided the much earlier colonization of the Mariana Islands from the Philippines, although this form had been replaced by double outrigger canoes in Island Southeast Asia by historical times. Polynesians also developed complex forms of terraced-field and canal-fed taro irrigation, as well as dry stone platform monuments, massive carved stone statues (on Easter Island), and palisaded earthwork fortifications, the latter reaching an apogee in Maori New Zealand (Bellwood and Hiscock 2013).

The settlement of the islands of central and eastern Polynesia – the Marquesas, Societies, Cooks, Australs, Tuamotus, Hawaiian Islands, Easter Island, New Zealand, and many others – occurred after a long migratory pause in western Polynesia. None were settled before AD 700, and most not until after AD 1000 (Wilmshurst et al. 2011). Easter Island with its famous stone statues was long thought to have been first settled almost 2000 years ago, but recent research has brought this date forward to circa AD 1200. Why the rapid spread into eastern Polynesia occurred after such a long pause in Tonga and Samoa is not clear, but many Oceanic atolls were still below sea level until as recently as 1000 years ago, hence making some sea crossings much longer. However, eastern Polynesia was not the only region of Oceania to see quite intensive seaborne colonization around AD 1000, since many atolls and formerly settled high islands in Melanesia and southern Micronesia were also settled at this time by a process of reverse 'Polynesian Outlier' migration, assisted in its general east to west direction by the prevailing trade winds.[46] These movements led to replacement or assimilation of earlier Malayo-Polynesian-speaking resident populations in many cases.

Apart from the settlement of the Mariana Islands and eastern Polynesia, another extraordinary feat of long-distance colonization carried Austronesians across the Indian Ocean westwards to Madagascar and the Comoro Islands (the latter now Bantu-speaking), probably in the mid-1st millennium AD. Madagascar itself was evidently reached by colonists from southern Borneo, perhaps with Malay- or Javanese-speaking leaders, presumably during the existence of a Sumatra-based early Indic kingdom known as Srivijaya. Interestingly, the most recent evidence in support of an Indonesian origin for the Malagasy comes from genetics and linguistics.[47]

Why did all this island migration come about? Simply looking for new islands for agricultural land or other resources does not explain everything, given the huge sizes of many of the islands of Southeast Asia, even now underpopulated in some remote equatorial areas. Periodic increases in the frequencies of westerly winds could have encouraged sailing to the east (Anderson et al. 2006), but this factor is unlikely to have started and maintained the whole migration process. My preference is for founder rank expansion, based on those younger sons and their families, able to found only lineages of junior rank at home, who sought to found new senior lines through the colonization of new territories. The genealogically ranked societies of Micronesia and Polynesia provided ideal circumstances for this process to operate.

But one question remains. Why did the spurts of migration occur when they did? The history of Neolithic migration into Oceania clearly occurred in two rather explosive phases, one dating to 1500–1000 BC, the other to around AD 1000–1200. It is almost as if the first migration became exhausted in the face of increasing interisland distances, and the second then depended on some lucky travel-related advantage. Increased incidence of winds blowing from the west, the invention of the double canoe, even the emergence of atolls above sea level can all be suggested as promoters of the second push into Polynesia, but I find none of these very convincing in themselves. The answer might be pure chance. Perhaps no one was lucky enough to find new land and return home to tell the tale after western Polynesia was settled about 900 BC. Someone else might have been much luckier on a chance voyage eastwards around AD 1000, and the floodgates opened. Founder rank enhancement reigned anew, at least for a while. This would also explain why the later voyages took place not just over vast distances into eastern Polynesia, but also over much shorter Polynesian Outlier distances back westwards and northwards into Melanesia and southern Micronesia. It might have been the social desire to find new land that was revolutionary, if short-lived, and not just the means of doing it.

The History of the Austronesian Language Family

Of all human ethnolinguistic dispersals prior to AD 1500, that of the Austronesian-speaking peoples was the most extensive. It can be related directly to the archaeological spread of Neolithic populations through Island Southeast Asia and the Pacific, as described earlier. Austronesian-speaking founder populations eventually migrated

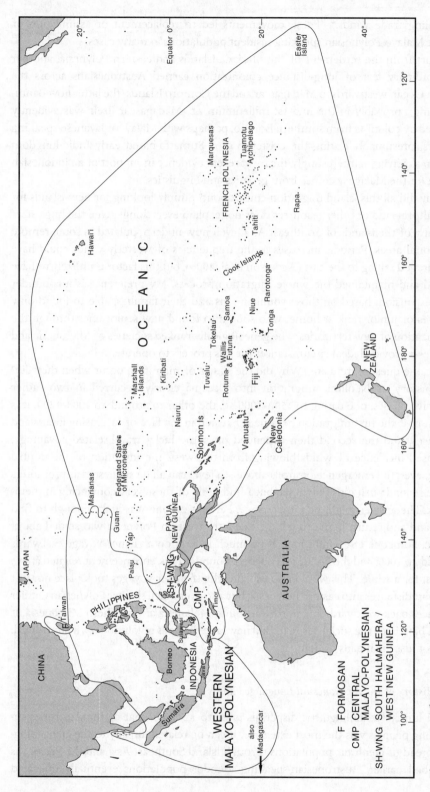

Figure 8.6 The Austronesian languages and their major subgroups, as classified by linguist Robert Blust (also published in Blust 2013). Map production by Multimedia Services, ANU.

through more than 210° of longitude, to as far as Madagascar, Easter Island and New Zealand, through an astounding west to east 22,000 km spread of ocean and islands (Figure 8.6). The whole dispersal required more than 4000 years for completion.[48]

Today, there are more than 1000 Austronesian languages, making it the second-largest language family in the world in number of languages, after the Niger-Congo family of Africa. The language family first crystallized in Taiwan, where several of its most deeply rooted subgroups still exist today. But the most remarkable observation made about Austronesian languages is that all languages outside Taiwan, from Madagascar right across Island Southeast Asia to Polynesia, belong to only *one* sub-group, termed Malayo-Polynesian by the linguist Robert Blust.[49] This subgroup is sufficiently homogeneous to support a hypothesis of extremely rapid initial settlement of the Philippines, Indonesia, and Island Melanesia, down to and including the phase of Lapita colonization, a hypothesis supported very strongly by the archaeological record and associated radiocarbon dates. Islands such as Madagascar, those of eastern Polynesia, and Micronesia beyond the Mariana and Palau Islands took much longer to reach, according to both the linguistic and the archaeological perspectives.

Comparative linguistic reconstructions make it very clear that the earliest identifiable Austronesian speakers in Taiwan (Proto-Austronesians) were agriculturalists of immediate southern Chinese origin who grew foxtail millet, sugarcane and rice, together with some tubers and fruits. They made canoes and rafts, probably used sails, and lived in timber houses.[50] They kept pigs and dogs (chickens are uncertain, and unattested archaeologically before Lapita times), used bows and arrows, had some form of loom (backstrap?) for weaving, and made pottery. They did not cast copper or smelt iron. In archaeological terms, these were Neolithic societies with a material culture similar to that of many Pacific Island Austronesian communities who survived without knowledge of metallurgy until European contact.

Because the Philippines are tropical, whereas most of Taiwan and southern China are temperate, the earliest Malayo-Polynesian-speaking settlers who arrived in the Philippines after 2000 BC would have found new crops such as breadfruit, coconut and bananas to add to their food supplies. Yams and aroids (*Colocasia* and *Alocasia* taro) were also certainly cultivated by this time, as presumably was sugarcane. In the prevailing equatorial, ever-wet and nonseasonal climates of the southern Philippines and Indonesia, these indigenous fruits and tubers came to dominate the economy that spread into the Pacific beyond the Solomons, and rice and millet faded from popularity. Some of these tree and tuber crops might have been domesticated earlier in New Guinea and adjacent regions, as related earlier, and carried westwards into Indonesia by Papuan-speaking populations. It is also possible that some were domesticated in pre-Austronesian times in Island Southeast Asia (Donohue and Denham 2009), although so far no archaeological evidence has come forward in support of this suggestion.

Indeed, the pre-Neolithic archaeological record in Island Southeast Asia generally suggests a presence of only very small scattered populations of hunter-gatherers, whose records survive mostly in the form of flaked stone tool assemblages in caves. Shell fishhooks have been claimed from pre-Neolithic contexts in Timor, but they remain unique so far across the whole of Island Southeast Asia at this time level.[51]

Given the exiguity of pre-Neolithic occupation in these islands, it is not surprising that the progress of Austronesian colonization was rapid and linguistically dominant.

One of the factors that distinguishes Island from Mainland Southeast Asia in linguistic terms is that only Austronesian language are spoken in the islands, beyond the Papuan-speaking regions in and close to New Guinea. The Southeast Asian mainland has, on the contrary, seen many episodes of linguistic overlay, with Austroasiatic tribal languages now submerged beneath various layers of Tai, Tibeto-Burman, Khmer, and Vietnamese. Although it has been argued that other languages, especially Austroasiatic, were spoken widely in Island Southeast Asia before the arrival of Malayo-Polynesian speakers (e.g., Blench 2010), there is no convincing archaeological, linguistic, or place-name evidence to give this opinion much credibility. If Austroasiatic languages were once widespread, one would have to ask why and how they were entirely replaced by so many small and tribal Austronesian languages, given that the process of Austronesian expansion was certainly not associated with state authority. Of course, non-Austronesian languages of some kind must have been spoken in Island Southeast Asia before the arrival of Austronesian languages, but they were more likely affiliated with Papuan languages than with mainland Austroasiatic.

Moving now into Oceania, most linguists accept that the protolanguage of the Oceanic subgroup of Malayo-Polynesian, that includes all the Pacific Island Austronesian languages apart from Chamorro (Marianas) and Palauan, originated during Lapita times and most probably in the Bismarck Archipelago. The emergence of Proto-Oceanic has long been considered a result of population movement from Halmahera and the western tip of New Guinea into the Bismarcks, where a small degree of borrowing from Papuan languages occurred (Pawley 2007). But the archaeological evidence for links between these regions is not strong at all, far weaker than the Lapita archaeological links with the northern Philippines and Marianas. The number of linguistic innovations that link Halmahera with Oceanic languages is also rather few (Blust 1993). These could reflect later contacts, albeit quite early in relative date, rather than relationships defined at the very point of initial settlement.

Indeed, the present-day Malayo-Polynesian subgroup patterning might not reflect directly the very first years of colonization at all. This is because people at that time of significant migration, around 1500 to 1000 BC, were still speaking a relatively coherent Proto-Malayo-Polynesian language, essentially then still a single language, just as modern British, Australians and North Americans still speak inter-comprehensible versions of English.[52] Linguistic subgroups take time to emerge, and need a fair number of uniquely shared innovations if they are to be identified at all. This situation implies that the first Malayo-Polynesian-speaking migrants to travel beyond the Philippines could have gone in several directions at the same time – to Borneo, eastern Indonesia, and the Mariana Islands, for instance – with their inter-comprehensible versions of Proto-Malayo-Polynesian. It might not be possible to identify evidence for such contemporary movements purely from comparisons of the linguistic subgroups that exist today.

The spread of the early Malayo-Polynesian languages and their speakers through the Philippines, Indonesia, and into the western Pacific during the latter part of the second millennium BC can therefore be traced in both the linguistic and the archaeological records. The flow was slowed sometimes by an existing presence of other non-Austronesian agricultural populations, especially by Austroasiatic speakers on the Asian mainland who grew rice, and around coastal New Guinea. Otherwise, the Malayo-Polynesian dispersal was only impeded by scattered hunter-gatherers, or by no people at all beyond the Solomon Islands. Beyond Tonga and Samoa in western Polynesia, settled by 900–850 BC, ever-increasing ocean expanses within Polynesia intervened to slow the migration process down, for almost two millennia. As indicated by the archaeological record, most of eastern Polynesia was not colonized before AD 1000.

The eventual result of all this migration, spread through 4000 years from Taiwan to eastern Polynesia, was that the Austronesian and Malayo-Polynesian-speaking populations formed the most widespread ethnolinguistic group in the world prior to AD 1500. Laurent Sagart (2005b) has also suggested a Taiwan or northern Philippine ultimate origin for the Tai language family, as a cousinly subgroup to Malayo-Polynesian (Figure 8.3). This is most interesting but difficult to assess archaeologically, owing to the relative lack of Neolithic information from the key Chinese provinces of Hainan, Guangdong and Guangxi, the provinces in which most other linguists locate Tai origins. Early Neolithic links in artifact assemblages between Taiwan and the Pearl Delta region of Guangdong have been suggested by Tsang Chenghwa (2005: 71), but the archaeological record at this stage is too thin to allow any real testing of Sagart's hypothesis for the Tai languages.

Biological Anthropology and the Austronesians

Possession of an Austronesian language need not mean shared biological identity. Austronesian speakers in the Philippines, Indonesia, and the western Pacific are extremely varied genetically, ranging from Asian to Melanesian in their DNA affinities. As Johann Reinhold Forster asked in 1774, "What occasions the inhabitants of O-Taheitee to be so much distinguished from the Mallicolese?"[53] Philippine and western Indonesian populations are mainly of recent Asian descent, but Philippine Negritos (Agta, Aeta) are not, yet they also speak Austronesian languages as a result of language change in prehistory (Reid 1994). Likewise, many Austronesian languages are spoken in and around New Guinea by populations who certainly are not of recent Asian descent, but who have shifted from Papuan to Austronesian languages in the past. One of the attractions of early Malayo-Polynesian dialects as spoken around 1500 BC would have been that they were remarkably inter-comprehensible over vast areas. This could have made bilingualism or even language shift attractive options for some indigenous populations of Island Southeast Asia and western Oceania, doubtless linguistically diverse after at least 40,000 years of prior settlement.

In recent years, geneticists have offered much insight into this admixture phenomenon, which was apparent not only to Forster but also to the famous naturalist Alfred Russel Wallace in the mid-nineteenth century. In the last few years, a great deal of new information has come from an analysis of the autosomal genome across many populations in Southeast Asia and Oceania. The results of these new analyses confirm that Asian populations penetrated Island Southeast Asia in large numbers between 2000 and 1000 BC, admixing increasingly towards the island of New Guinea with native Melanesian peoples, who still occupy the latter island almost exclusively. Beyond New Guinea and Melanesia, however, Asian populations were the main colonizers of the uninhabited islands of Micronesia and Polynesia.

Genetic research into Island Southeast Asian and Oceanic peoples came to many dead ends in the late twentieth century owing to a dependence on mtDNA and very error-prone molecular clocks. In one case it was claimed that Polynesians were unrelated genetically to other Austronesian speakers in Taiwan and most of Island Southeast Asia, and evolved in mtDNA terms in the remote Paleolithic of eastern Indonesia, about 17,000 years ago.[54] Such historical reconstructions are untenable in the light of archaeological and linguistic data, and require impossible explanations based on language and culture shift through trade and other unlikely processes. They also require a complete disjunction between population and language history.

The current picture, focusing on the most recent analyses of whole genome autosomal DNA, together with considerations of both NRY and mtDNA data, is summarized by Murray Cox (2013). He refers to the new methods that use multiple ancestry-informative markers, drawn from across the human genome, as the 'gold standard'. Cox's general summary of the situation amongst Austronesian speakers is that Formosans carry an entirely Asian autosomal ancestry, whereas amongst Polynesians it is around 80%. Conversely, amongst western Pacific populations in and around New Guinea, including both Papuan and Austronesian speakers, the percentage of overall Asian autosomal ancestry drops to about 20%. Within Indonesia itself, a major shift from Asian to Melanesian genotypes occurs across the region between Bali and Flores, with a rise in Melanesian ancestry from almost zero in Bali to 50% in Alor, near Timor.[55]

This picture of genetic admixture between populations of Asian and Melanesian origin through Indonesia is given very strong support by an important new genetic study that uses whole-genome data from modern groups located along the Sunda island chain and in Borneo.[56] The results indicate significant levels of population migration from the north and west into eastern Indonesia, dated by an autosomal molecular clock to around the second millennium BC. This is in excellent agreement with inferences based on Austronesian languages and archaeology. The results underline the great impact of Austronesian migration from Taiwan and the Philippines into Borneo, Sulawesi, and the Indonesian islands to the west of Bali and Lombok. They also underline how significant has been the indigenous western Pacific population in the prehistory of the eastern regions of Indonesia and the Pacific Islands. Forster and Wallace sensed the same result from their observations so long ago.

This new genetic perspective naturally gives considerable importance to Austronesian migration through Island Southeast Asia. However, this need not mean that huge numbers of colonists were sailing constantly forth in their canoes, unlike the recent European shipborne colonizations of Australia and the Americas. It is likely that actual colonizing groups were quite small in numbers, as many geneticists suggest, but then expanded very rapidly once they found new and fertile terrain to support their large families. The more females in the colonizing parties the better. The same situation is being revealed by genetic research into the European Neolithic (Chapter 7).

Finer detail is available for the genetic makeup of individual regions. Western Indonesian populations carry mtDNA and NRY haplogroups that were evidently brought in by Neolithic migrants from the Asian Mainland, in some cases via Taiwan (e.g., NRY haplogroup O). Eastern Indonesian populations carry more indigenous Melanesian haplogroups, as expected, but also carry a large number of Asian haplogroups derived via Neolithic Taiwan. Eastern Indonesia might also have been the source of the specific mutation in mtDNA haplogroup B that was carried almost to 100% fixation by early Polynesian migrants as a result of extreme founder effects.[57] This is the 'Polynesian motif', B4a1a1a, recently identified from ancient DNA as the main haplogroup amongst the first New Zealand Maoris (Knapp et al. 2013). Polynesians otherwise acquired little of their genetic ancestry from Melanesia, apart from some of their Y-chromosomes, and in the early years of colonization there may have been relatively little genetic admixture between the two populations, explaining why the archaeological signature from Lapita seems to suggest long-distance leap-frogging towards the east over regions already settled by Papuan populations (Sheppard 2011). A recent craniofacial analysis also support a Polynesian ancestry firmly in Southeast Asia rather than Melanesia, albeit with some regional variation that might be mainly a reflection of founder effects (Buck and Vidarsdottir 2012).

The haploid lineages, however, do suggest one interesting point about Oceanic colonization. Polynesians and eastern Indonesians carry mtDNA that is mainly of Asian female derivation, although the occurrence is not quite 100%.[58] On the other hand, the NRY distribution amongst Polynesians and eastern Indonesians reveals a greater presence of indigenous male Melanesian haplogroups, albeit still with strong evidence for NRY and autosomal links between Polynesians and some Formosan groups such as the Amis.[59] These results have suggested to some geneticists that Austronesian migration involved large numbers of Austronesian-speaking women of Asian genetic origin, who founded local lineages and thereafter stayed matrilocally at home, sometimes attracting husbands from outside communities. Some of these husbands in the western Pacific were perhaps drawn from indigenous Papuanspeaking communities.

The Austronesian situation is unusual if compared to the Eurasian and African patterns discussed in Chapters 7 and 9. The Neolithic migrations of farmers in Eurasia and in Bantu-speaking Africa appear to have been associated more with Y-chromosome (male) than mtDNA (female) transference by the initial farming groups. MtDNA haplogroup distributions in these regions incorporate high levels of female admixture from populations of indigenous hunter-gatherer descent, and ancient DNA in the case of Europe tells us that much of this admixture took place long after the Neolithic migrations actually took place. This rings a small warning bell for me as far as the Pacific region is concerned, because the idea that many of the Austronesian migrant males were of indigenous local western Pacific descent, but most of the women were Asian, makes little sense if applied to the migration situation itself. After all, it is difficult to imagine why women would wish to migrate into new territories, and men not, in the context of small-scale and sea-borne Neolithic societies.

It seems far more likely to me that the differing male and female patterns apparent in both haploid and autosomal markers amongst modern Austronesians relate to population movements and intermarriage during the whole of prehistory, over a period of 3500 years, and may not have much significance for understanding the actual foundation migrations themselves. It is very likely, for instance, that Melanesian populations, especially males, spread genetically through Melanesia, to as far as Fiji, long after Lapita times, simply through continuous processes of small-scale but gradually compounding movement. Similar movement might well have occurred from New Guinea westwards into eastern Indonesia. A good example is given by Lansing et al. (2011) of how women in certain Austronesian-speaking communities in Timor still marry Papuan-speaking men at a rate greater than the converse.[60]

The East Asian and Western Pacific Food Production Complexes and Their Impacts on Holocene Prehistory

To summarize, the East Asian food production complex gave rise to a human population equally as numerous, widespread, and significant in world affairs as that of the Fertile Crescent. It commenced its expansion a little later than that from the Middle East, spreading into Southeast Asia mainly after 2500 BC. Its origins involved two large river valleys in what is now central China with differing crop complexes – millets in the north and rice in the south – but with considerable cultural overlap in their archaeological records. This situation also resembles that in the Fertile Crescent, with its local regions contributing to an overarching whole. As with the Fertile Crescent spreads into Europe, North Africa and Pakistan, the long-distance spreads from China only happened three or four millennia after the beginnings of pre-domestication plant cultivation and animal management in the homeland areas themselves.

There were some interesting differences between the two food production complexes, however. The East Asian one remained almost entirely within the monsoon and trade wind zones with summer rainfall. Its early spreads were clearly constrained by changes in latitude, day length and temperature, both to the north and towards the equator in the south. The Fertile Crescent complex, by comparison, spread in a more longitudinal fashion, predominantly west and east, and found its major friction zone in terms of changing rainfall seasonality as it entered the monsoon zone in India.

Like the Fertile Crescent complex, the East Asian one also gave rise to a number of widespread language families and human populations, with DNA characteristics that are only now being revealed to us as the science of genetics begins to investigate and compare whole genomes. The western Pacific complex gave rise to settled Papuan-speaking populations and Trans New Guinea languages in and adjacent to New Guinea. It also contributed a great deal in terms of crops and DNA to the Austronesian colonization of the Pacific Islands. But the western Pacific complex did not spread very far west or north of New Guinea, and was not initially involved with any cereals or domestic animals. Nascent agriculture also developed in Jomon Japan, but with no apparent impact on regions beyond these islands.

In Chapter 5, I discussed the Pama-Nyungan linguistic spread through most of Australia as a possible domino effect of the arrival of the East Asian food production complex and its attached populations in central and eastern Indonesia. I do not wish to push this opinion too far since it its verification lies essentially beyond the limits of present data. But, if correct, then Australia also had a late prehistory with relevance for the subject matter of this chapter.

Finally, it is interesting that relatively few elements of the East Asian food production complex spread into the Pacific Islands themselves. Pigs and dogs traveled there, as eventually did domestic fowl, but neither cattle, rice, nor millet entered Oceania, except for a possibility of rice in the Marianas. We perhaps owe this situation to the presence of the Western Oceanic food production complex and its carrier populations in New Guinea and adjacent islands, acting as a kind of gatekeeper and source of friction for Malayo-Polynesian-speaking populations moving around 3500 years ago from Island Southeast Asia into the Pacific Islands.

However, it is apparent linguistically that many of the major fruits and tubers taken into the Pacific were already known to early Malayo-Polynesian speakers in the Philippines, so they were not just adopted from western Pacific sources. Indeed, there is no clear evidence that Malayo-Polynesian speakers adopted any of their major crops from Papuan speakers in the New Guinea region. Most might have entered the economy much further north, in the Philippines for instance. Nevertheless, the human populations and their languages eventually made the trip from Taiwan to Polynesia, even if the production system that initially fuelled this population movement underwent many changes, not least being the abandonment of rice cultivation as people entered the world of small and far apart Oceanic islands. The main reasons for abandoning rice and millet might have been the constraints imposed by a fully equatorial climate in Indonesia and Melanesia, rather than simply the presence of an indigenous western Pacific population with its own well-adapted system of food production.

My final conclusion, as for Chapter 7, is that the primary cultural driver of all of this Holocene migration and interlaced population growth in Eurasia was food production itself, including the domesticated plants and animals and the ways by which they were created by human management rather than hunted and collected from the wild. The same conclusion holds for Africa and the Americas, to where we travel next.

Notes

1. For general archaeological descriptions, see Liu 2004; Yang 2004; Cohen 2011.
2. Yan 2004; also Cohen 2011; Zhang and Hung 2013. See also Zhang et al. 2012 for common millet and rice together at Tanghu, a little north of Jiahu, at 5800 BC.
3. See Fuller et al. 2009, 2010, 2011b; Zhao 2011. Lu et al. 2009 and Bettinger et al. 2010 favor common millet as the oldest domesticated cereal in China. Cohen 2011 has reservations.

4. Much of this material is published only in Chinese, but I owe some of these comments to information from Deng Zhenhua and Jin Guiyun, received at conferences in Yuyao and Beijing in 2011.

5. On Sichuan see Zhang and Hung 2010; D'Alpoim-Guedes 2011. Lee 2011 discusses Korea, and Kuzmin et al. 1998 discuss early millet cultivation in Primorye.

6. There is not space here to discuss Yayoi migration to Japan, but see Hudson 1999, 2013 for archaeology; and Lee and Hasegawa 2011 for a linguistic perspective.

7. On botanical evidence for Jomon domestication see Sato et al. 2003; Matsui and Kanehara 2006; Crawford 2011.

8. On Jomon and Yayoi NRY genetics see Hammer et al. 2006; Adachi et al. 2011. Jomon populations carried NRY haplogroup D from mainland Asia into Japan circa 20,000 years ago (Chapter 4). Yayoi ancestors brought in NRY haplogroup O from China via Korea after 3000 years ago.

9. Zhao 2010; Molina et al. 2011. The history of rice domestication is presented from paleo-botanical samples by Fuller et al. 2009, 2010, 2011b; Zhao 2011; and see also many current papers on early rice-related archaeology, linguistics and genetics in the journal *Rice* 4(3–4): 2011. A genomic study of the origins of *O. rufipogon* by Huang et al. 2012 sources rice domestication to the middle Pearl valley of Guangdong, contradicting the prolific archaeological record for a Yangzi origin presented here. But the study only accessed available modern wild rice samples and did not take Holocene climate change into account. Ancient DNA from Neolithic wild rice samples along the Yangzi, where *O. rufipogon* does not grow today, will be necessary for more realistic conclusions.

10. Zhao 2010 for Shangshan; for Jiahu see McGovern et al. 2004; Hu et al. 2006.

11. On the northern Zhejiang Neolithic sites see Zong et al. 2007; Fuller et al. 2009; Liu et al. 2007.

12. Bellwood 2011b. Smith et al. 2011 discuss the sea level change; Nakamura 2010 and Rolett et al. 2011 the Chinese coastline. See Carson 2011 for similar effects in Micronesia.

13. Chen et al. 2005; Li et al. 2009; Liu and Feng 2012.

14. General references for this section include Bellwood 2005a, Chapter 6; Bellwood 2005b, 2006, 2007b; Fuller et al. 2010; Zhang and Hung 2008, 2010, 2012, 2013. Fuller defines domesticated rice as essentially non-shattering, with grain size increase playing a lesser defining role.

15. Bellwood 2011b.

16. References for pre-Neolithic southern China include Lu 2010; Higham et al. 2011a; Zhang and Hung 2012, 2013.

17. Zhang and Hung 2008, 2010, 2012, 2013.

18. For general surveys, see the chapters in Glover and Bellwood 2004. For Man Bac, see Oxenham et al. 2011. For An Son, see Bellwood et al. 2011a; Piper et al. 2012 (Rach Nui is not yet published). For the Thailand sites, see Higham 2002, 2013 for general surveys, and Higham and Thosarat 2004 (Khok Phanom Di); Higham and Kijngam 2010 (Ban Non Wat); Weber et al. 2010 (Khao Wong Prachan and fostail millet); Castillo 2011. Cristina Castillo informs me that all analyzed rice samples from Neolithic contexts in Mainland Southeast Asia are so far morphometrically of the *japonica* subspecies. *Indica* rices did not spread through Southeast Asia until after 2500 years ago.

19. For example, Higham and Thosarat 1994; Higham 2002; Rispoli 2007; Wiriyaromp 2010.

20. Dogs were apparently bred for eating at An Son in southern Vietnam (Piper et al. 2012). Neolithic cattle are only reported so far from sites in Thailand and it is unclear to what extent they were domesticated.

21. Ostapirat 2005.
22. Sarjeant 2012a, 2012b.
23. Zorc 1994; Sagart 2003; Ferlus 2010; Ratliff 2010; Wolff 2010; Bradley 2011; Diffloth 2011.
24. Sagart 2005a, 2008, 2011; Diffloth 2011; van Driem 2011; Sidwell and Blench 2011; Sidwell 2013.
25. Khmer and Vietnamese are of course Austroasiatic languages, but during their state-level spreads since AD 800–1000 they doubtless erased many smaller tribal linguistic relatives.
26. Hudjashov et al. 2007; Stoneking and Delfin 2010; Oppenheimer 2011; Cox 2013.
27. See chapters in Majid 2005; Matsumura et al. 2008a, 2008b, 2011; Matsumura and Oxenham 2013.
28. See Bellwood and Oxenham 2008 on Man Bac demography. The rice phytolith data are a personal communication from Tetsuro Udatsu, Miyazaki University, Japan.
29. Bellwood et al. (2011a) for An Son; Matsumura pers. comm. for Hemudu. Brown 1999 has noted that anatomically East Asian populations first became widespread in China during the Neolithic, not before.
30. Hill et al. 2007a; Oppenheimer 2011. These authors use a molecular clock to claim that most of the southward migration was caused by early Holocene drowning of the Sunda Shelf, but I have given my views on this hypothesis on page 112 and regard it as totally unfounded.
31. Lertrit et al. 2008. See also Oota et al. 2001 for preliminary aDNA results from the Malay Peninsula.
32. Bellwood 2011a, 2013; Bellwood et al. 2011b.
33. The abandonment of cereal cultivation on the route towards Oceania perhaps reflected day-length sensitivity in the early cultivars, the ever-wet equatorial climate, and lack of interest in growing cereals amongst Papuan-speaking farmers accustomed to vegetative reproduction of tubers (Bellwood 2011b; Hsieh et al. 2011). Even today, rice cultivation does not flourish near the Equator in Indonesia.
34. See Tayles 1999 for Khok Phanom Di in central Thailand. Malaria causes a very high infant death rate.
35. On New Highlands agricultural prehistory see Denham 2005, 2011. This region had no indigenous pigs, and no domesticated ones before 1000 BC: see Bellwood and White 2005; O'Connor et al. 2011b.
36. Pawley 2005.
37. Less so in Fiji than further west – see Wollstein et al. 2010.
38. Hung 2005; Liu 2007: 55.
39. The sandy and windswept Penghu Islands reveal a very sharp decline in site numbers around 2000–1500 BC, after which they appear to have lacked subsequent occupation until the Chinese historical period, within the past 1000 years (Tsang 1992). There is a possibility here that colonization by a Neolithic rice-growing population led to such high levels of population growth and deforestation that these islands were actually abandoned for a long period.
40. Bellwood and Dizon 2005, 2008; Hung 2005; Hung et al. 2011.
41. Bellwood 2007a, 2011a.
42. Hung et al. 2011; Carson et al. 2013; Carson 2013. See Blust 2000a for linguistic evidence that the Marianas were settled from the Philippines and that the first settlers carried rice. For debate on the Philippine–Marianas connection, see Hung et al. 2012; Winter et al. 2012.

43. Kirch 1997, 2010; Summerhayes 2010; Sheppard 2011; Spriggs 2011, 2013.

44. Bellwood 2011b; Carson et al. 2013.

45. Pigs are interesting because there appear to have been two routes of introduction into Island Southeast Asia in terms of mtDNA haplogroups, one via Taiwan into the Philippines, another directly from Mainland Southeast Asia through southern Indonesia into the Lapita complex (Larson et al. 2010).

46. Carson 2012. The island of Lanyu (Botel Tobago) off southeastern Taiwan was also resettled by migrants from the Batanes Islands at about the same time.

47. Adelaar 1995; Serva et al. 2011; Cox et al. 2012. Burney et al. 2003 review radiocarbon dates for human activity and extinct megafauna on Madagascar, noting a sharp decline in the latter after 1700 years ago, presumably due to human arrival. A recent report of cut marks on bones from a cave in northwestern Madagascar suggest a possible human presence much earlier, around 2000 BC (Gommery et al. 2010), but no cultural materials are reported.

48. For Austronesian linguistic family trees and the tempo of overall dispersal using linguistc data, see Gray and Jordan 2000; Gray et al. 2009. Polynesians certainly reached South America (page 211), but never settled there in large numbers or established languages.

49. Informative general surveys of Austronesian linguistic history include Blust 1995, 2009; Pawley 2002; and the section by Malcolm Ross in Bellwood et al. 2011b, which also discusses the linguistic innovations that define the Malayo-Polynesian subgroup of Austronesian. Donohue and Denham 2010 unconvincingly relate the whole process of Austronesian spread into Island Southeast Asia to language shift.

50. Linguists usually assume that early Formosans did not use sails because of the apparent lack of a reconstructable word with this meaning in Proto-Austronesian (Wolff 2010: 886). But Andrew Pawley 2007 reconstructs *layaR* for Proto-Austronesian *sail*, a word still used as *layar* in modern Indonesian and Malay. As Pawley and Pawley 1994: 360 pointed out, such uncertainties might reflect lack or loss of information from the few remaining Formosan languages, rather than a real absence.

51. O'Connor and Veth 2005.

52. Of course, these are kept inter-comprehensible nowadays by modern forms of mass communication. But linguistic unity could still have been retained for several centuries amongst mobile Neolithic societies. In 1769, according to the English Captain James Cook, Maoris and Raiateans (from an island near Tahiti) were still able to communicate fairly well, after at least 500 years of prior separation.

53. Modern Tahiti, and Malakula in Vanuatu. Both populations speak Oceanic (Austronesian) languages. Quoted from Thomas et al. 1996: 175.

54. Oppenheimer and Richards 2002 present this position, which is still held by some geneticists (Hill et al. 2007b; Soares et al. 2011). The molecular clock data, in this case for the mtDNA 'Polynesian motif' (haplotype B4a1a1a), have been doubted by Cox 2005, who regards the motif as purely Holocene in age and most likely associated with Austronesian migration from Taiwan.

55. Data for these statements are given by Friedlaender et al. 2008; Kayser et al. 2008; Mona et al. 2009; Cox et al. 2010; Karafet and Hallmark 2010; Tabbada et al. 2010; Wollstein et al. 2010; Xu et al. 2012; Tumonggor et al. 2013; and by Geoffrey Chambers in Bellwood et al. 2011b. Lansing et al. 2011 discuss the social factor of matrilocality and its possible role in the genetic patterning.

56. Xu 2012; Xu et al. 2012. Another study of mtDNA and autosomal data by Jinam et al. 2012 suggests that many western Austronesians, especially in Malaysia, Java and Borneo, carry

Paleolithic mtDNA lineages of Mainland Southeast Asian origin. This may be so, but their conclusion that Austronesian migration required two completely separate movements, one from Mainland Southeast Asia through West Malaysia between 30,000 and 10,000 years ago, and another through Taiwan between 7000 and 5000 years ago, is completely at odds with the archaeological and linguistic records. It also contradicts recent contributions by other geneticists and correlates mtDNA mutation ages directly with major episodes of human migration. The results are more likely to reflect long histories of population mixing, rather than two distinct episodes of ancient migration.

57. As Loftus and Cunningham 2000: 257 state: "A female who has only one surviving daughter has only a 2% chance of contributing her mtDNA to a population 100 generations later." In small founder populations, differential fecundity could have caused dramatic reductions in the number of mtDNA lineages present in future generations. Early Polynesian women with B4a1a1a for some reason clearly had more children during the early generations than women who carried other haplogroups. With each new settlement, a higher proportion of B4a1a1a would have characterized the population, until eventually the proportion reached 100% in some islands.

58. Late prehistoric human remains with Melanesian mtDNA haplogroup Q1 have recently been identified in the Gambier Islands (Mangareva) in French Polynesia (Deguilloux et al. 2012b).

59. Kayser et al. 2008; Cox et al. 2010; Mirabal et al. 2012.

60. The island of Timor contains both Malayo-Polynesian and Papuan-speaking populations.

Chapter 9
The African and American Food Production Complexes

In this final chapter, we examine the later Holocene migrations of food-producing societies and their languages in Africa and the Americas. In Africa, these include the dispersals of Nilo-Saharan and Niger-Congo-speaking pastoralists and farmers, following the earlier hunter-gatherer colonization of the green Sahara described in Chapter 5. The major indigenous language family of sub-Saharan Africa, Niger-Congo, has been associated with food production since 2500 BC and spread widely after that date with migrating agro-pastoral populations in tropical West Africa. The main Bantu expansion itself, between 1000 BC and AD 1000, was by far the most remarkable in the Niger-Congo family in its extent and relative rapidity, and was on a par in this regard with the major language family dispersals of Eurasia, such as those of Indo-European and Sino-Tibetan.

In the prehistoric Americas, food production developed in several source regions in Mesoamerica, the Andes, and the greater Mississippi Basin. It eventually spread through latitudes between about 45 °N and 35 °S, roughly between Montreal and Buenos Aires. American food production remained rather limited in productivity compared to the Old World, until the spread of maize as a staple within the past 4000 years. Few language families in the Americas extended over areas as large as their major Old World counterparts, but Uto-Aztecan, Quechua, Arawak and Tupian all appear to have spread with early food production, especially with maize and manioc.

The developments and spreads of food-producing populations in both sub-Saharan Africa and the Americas occurred significantly later than those out of the Fertile Crescent and China. It is possible to argue that two major thresholds had to be crossed before significant success was attained in each case – iron working in sub-Saharan Africa, and maize cultivation in the Americas.

As in Eurasia, the major food-producing plants of Africa and the Americas were domesticated in seasonally dry tropical to warm temperate regions, where cereals, legumes and tubers developed the annual energy-storing habits that led to large seed and tuber size, exactly as in the Fertile Crescent and East Asia. Africa was a source of a native species of rice (*Oryza glaberrima*) and several important millets, especially pearl millet (*Pennisetum glaucum*) and sorghum (*Sorghum bicolor*). Mesoamerica produced maize, and

First Migrants: Ancient Migration in Global Perspective, First Edition. Peter Bellwood.
© Peter Bellwood. Published 2013 by John Wiley & Sons, Ltd.

various species of squash and beans. The Andes and their lowland environs produced other seed-bearing plants, and tubers such as potato, sweet potato and manioc.

Both Africa and the Americas, however, were relatively lacking in indigenously domesticated animal species.[1] African societies benefited greatly from introduced Fertile Crescent sheep and goats, although many of the cattle herded and perhaps domesticated in the early Holocene Sahara might have carried indigenous North African DNA.[2] Donkeys were also domesticated around 4000 BC from the African wild ass, presumably in Egypt.

Nevertheless, despite the fame of its splendid mammal fauna, sub-Saharan Africa did not produce any significant species of domesticated animal. Neither did the Americas, where domestic animals were restricted mainly to dogs (brought in from Asia by Paleoindians), turkeys (Mesoamerica and US Southwest), guinea pigs, and the camel-like llamas and alpacas used for meat, wool, and pack transport (Andes). Llamas and alpacas certainly became important in the central and southern Andes, but were never exported to other regions of the Americas.

Neither sub-Saharan Africa nor the Americas developed intensive forms of food production until around 4000 years ago, several millennia later than parallel developments in the Fertile Crescent and East Asia. Given that food production was very widespread in China by at least that time, one might ask why it never spread from there to the Americas. Apart from the American sweet potato in prehistoric Eastern Polynesia, together with a possibility of coconuts of Philippine origin in central America, there was no significant exchange of domesticated crops or animals between the two hemispheres at any time during the Holocene.[3] This was, no doubt, partly because any land-based spread of agriculture from Asia to America would have had to go via Beringia, where agriculture was impossible, and any sea crossing within Chinese agricultural latitudes would have had to traverse the whole Pacific Ocean, 12,000 km wide at the latitude of Japan and the Yangzi River.

I make this statement in full awareness of the literature stretching back over the past century or more on Transpacific contacts, and I have no doubt that contact did occur on rare occasions, especially between Eastern Polynesia and South America. Much iconography and architecture in Formative and Classic Mesoamerica resembles aspects of Hindu iconography and architecture in Asia, and I find this very interesting, if a little inexplicable. But the bottom line remains – no crops or domesticated animals were transferred between the Asian mainland and the Americas in prehistory, or indeed the other way, apart from dogs. Furthermore, if we exclude ancestral Na-Dene and Eskimo-Aleut speakers, no language families, archaeological complexes or significant human populations ever moved between the two hemispheres during the Holocene, in either direction. Transpacific contacts were contacts, not migrations.

Food Production in Sub-Saharan Africa

The likely source regions for the major indigenous domesticated crops and animals in Africa are shown in Figure 9.1. We look to the northern fringes of sub-Saharan Africa for the domestications of African yams, groundnuts, oil palm, the West African species

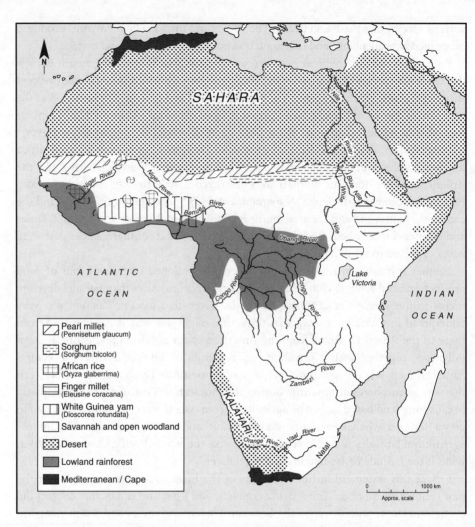

Figure 9.1 The present-day vegetational and climatic regions of Africa, with crop homelands suggested by botanist Jack Harlan (modified from Bellwood 2005a, Figure 5.1). Original map by Multimedia Services, ANU, modified by the author.

of rice (*Oryza glaberrima*), and millets (especially pearl millet and sorghum). The region spans the Sahel zone of grassland and the savanna zone of parkland to its immediate south, between the Sahara Desert proper and the rainforest, and extends from Mauritania across to Sudan. The two major indigenous populations involved in these developments were the ancestors of today's Nilo-Saharan and Niger-Congo-speaking peoples, in the east and west of the Sahel and savanna zones, respectively. Other crops were domesticated in the highlands of Ethiopia, including finger millet (*Eleusine coracana*), the banana-like enset (*Musa ensete*), and tef (*Eragrostis tef*, a cereal).

In Chapter 5, I examined the postglacial colonization of the Sahara by hunter-gatherers, perhaps in many cases early speakers of Nilo-Saharan languages, taking advantage of better Holocene climatic conditions to hunt, fish, and harvest wild grasses (Figure 5.4). During the course of the Holocene, these Nilo-Saharan populations transformed themselves into cattle pastoralists, certainly by 5000 BC, and it was with this economy that they spread south around 2500 BC towards East Africa, as the Sahara returned to forbidding desert. By this time, the Nilo-Saharan populations were already flanked in Ethiopia and the Horn of Africa by speakers of Afroasiatic languages presumably ancestral to the Cushitic and Omotic subgroups. As discussed in Chapter 7, it was the ancestors of these Afroasiatic-speaking populations who introduced the earliest economy of food production from the Levant into northeastern Africa, around 6000 BC. Nilo-Saharan speakers probably adopted domesticated cattle, sheep and goats from Afroasiatic sources as they began to move southwards towards Uganda and northern Kenya. However, bovine diseases spread by the tsetse fly would have stopped progress in this direction beyond the Serengeti Plain. Cattle were not taken successfully below 10° S until early in the first millennium AD (Figure 9.2).[4]

The first evidence for a presence of domesticated animals in the Sahara commenced around 6000 BC, perhaps a little earlier than along the North African coast or in the Nile Valley in Egypt. Sheep and goat bones, for instance, occur soon after 6000 BC in a number of sites in southern Egypt and the eastern Sahara.[5] Cattle appear to have been domesticated a little later, with the best evidence coming not from bones but from evidence for milking, recently revealed in lipid residues in pottery dated to 5000 BC from Takarkori rock shelter in southwestern Libya (Dunne et al. 2012). Genetic evidence reviewed by Cordain et al. (2012) also points to a similar antiquity for the coalescence of a gene for lactase persistence (the ability to digest cow's milk) amongst indigenous northern African populations. The lactase persistence gene was probably important also in Africa owing to its apparent ability, via a diet high in milk products, to suppress malaria. However, there is a remarkable falloff in the dates for cattle in archaeological sites in the southwestern Sahara, with a first appearance here only around 2000 BC.[6] Cattle were evidently not an important species in the early history of the Niger-Congo speakers, to whom we now turn.

West Africa and the Niger-Congo-Speaking Populations

In the western Sahel and savanna, the trajectory towards food production appears to have involved indigenous crop species, especially African rice and pearl millet. Domesticated sheep, goats and cattle were introduced about 4000 years ago, presumably by movement from the north or east. As noted earlier, there was no prior tradition of hunting or herding cattle in this region, and the sheep and goats must have arrived via the mediation of Afroasiatic-speaking populations. However, West Africa in general, from the rainforest northwards into Mauritania and Mali, reveals a separate course of cultural development from the central and eastern Sahara during the later Holocene. A quite different population would appear to have been implicated.

Archaeologically, the most common assumption is that some Saharan herder populations moved south owing to increasing climatic desiccation after 4000 BC, triggering the domestication of indigenous pearl millet, a process that was well underway by 2500 BC according to dated archaeobotanical evidence from sites in Mauritania, Burkina

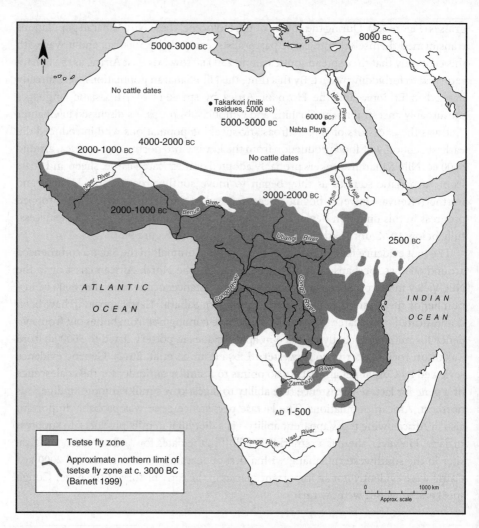

Figure 9.2 Dates for the spread of cattle in Africa, with the approximate northern boundary of the tsetse fly zone at 3000 BC (Barnett 1999) and the distribution of that zone today (modified from Bellwood 2005a, Figure 5.3). Original map by Multimedia Services, ANU, modified by the author).

Faso, Ghana and Mali.[7] The Kintampo culture of Ivory Coast and Ghana was associated with pearl millet production and the raising of cattle, sheep and goats by 2000 BC, and ranks as the oldest complex in West Africa with a putatively Neolithic material culture, with pottery, polished stone and food production. However, evidence for the domestication of African rice, native to the Niger River region, does not occur until about 2000 years ago, nor for sorghum until this date further to the east.

This late date for the acquisition of domesticated characteristics for sorghum, such as non-shattering habit and an increase in seed size, is a little puzzling. We know that African sorghum, pearl millet and finger millet appeared in India and Pakistan as domesticated crops in late Harappan times, around 2000 BC. This means that either older domesticated samples of sorghum are waiting to be discovered in Africa, back to at least 2000 BC, or this crop was carried to South Asia in pre-domesticated form and domesticated there. One reason why the African millet species were so slow to acquire domesticated characteristics (increased seed size, non-shattering habit) is that they are mostly wind- rather than self-pollinated, thus subject to constant back-crossing with wild plants. So it is quite possible that they underwent very long periods of pre-domestication cultivation in Africa, during which their presences in the archaeological record could be rather fugitive.

Consequently, the archaeological record does not yet allow claims for agriculture or animal domestication anywhere in West Africa before 2500 BC. The main episode of Bantu migration from a presumed homeland in the northern Cameroon grasslands, southwards and eastwards to reach Natal, did not occur until after 1000 BC. Neither is there good evidence for agricultural settlement in the West African equatorial rainforest until about 1000 BC, when evidence for pit storage of oil palm appears in the site of Tchissanga on the coast of the Republic of Congo, actually just south of the rainforest border. As reviewed by Klieman (2003), the rainforest proper holds little direct evidence for farming before 1000 BC, and Robertshaw (2013) points out that agricultural populations would not have been widespread in the rainforest until iron became available, perhaps around 500 BC. Claims for very early (2500 BC) occurrences of phytoliths of Southeast Asian bananas in West African sites have not withstood careful scrutiny. Therefore, the African equatorial rainforest is actually very similar to the Southeast Asian equatorial rainforest, in the sense that agricultural populations penetrated very late in time, remained low in density, and probably never settled far away from riverbanks.[8]

However, the Niger-Congo language family in its West African region of origin contains a very large number of differentiated subgroups that probably represent a considerable passage of time. This origin was probably located amongst the early Holocene pottery-using grain collectors discussed on pages 109–11, distributed at about 10° N from Gambia across to Mali and Nigeria.[9] Like the early Nilo-Saharans further east, the early Niger-Congo speakers also took advantage of wetter early Holocene conditions to spread through the westerly Sahel and savanna regions abandoned by human populations during the last glacial maximum. Ehret gives Proto-Niger-Congo a date of 9500 BC, and Blench opts for 5000 BC, both basing their dates partly on glottochronological estimates.[10] Both Ehret and Blench see the bow and arrow as a likely propeller of early Niger-Congo migration, and there is no need to invoke any kind of agricultural production at this early stage.

Linguists and archaeologists seem to be in agreement that the real beginnings of Niger-Congo agricultural expansion did not occur until the third millennium BC, in accord with the aforementioned dates for domesticated pearl millet in the Sahel and savanna.[11] By this date, according to Klieman, ancestral Bantu vocabulary reconstructions, probably localized to the borderlands between rainforest and savanna in Cameroon, indicate a familiarity with yams, gourds, oil palm nuts, castor beans, black-eyed peas, groundnuts, dogs, goats, guinea fowl, pottery, and basketry.[12] Millets were presumably present too, at least somewhere in the vicinity.

After 1000 BC, the linguistic record attests to the initial diversification and spread of the Bantu languages proper, a subgroup of what Ehret (2013) terms the East

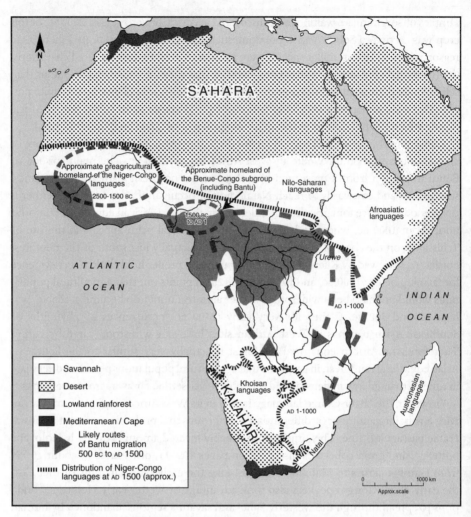

Figure 9.3 Generalized directions of Bantu migration between 500 BC and AD 1000, with archaeological dates (on the map) for the appearance of pearl millet, from Manning et al. 2010b. Base map by Multimedia Services, ANU, modified by the author.

Benue-Congo languages (the Benue is an eastern tributary of the Niger River). The Bantu languages in turn have Western and Eastern subgroups, and the Eastern Bantu-speaking populations began to spread first through the wooded grassland country from northern Cameroon to Lake Victoria. They then spread south from Lake Victoria to settle vast regions of eastern and southern Africa in a very short time (Figure 9.3). The linguistic record does not reveal an exact chronology, although it is clear that the Bantu languages are so closely related that very rapid spread is the only answer to explain them.

The dating for Bantu migration comes from archaeology. The migrations in eastern Africa are traceable through what David Phillipson (2005) has termed the Chifumbaze pottery complex, with an early Urewe variant in the vicinity of Lake Victoria dated to about 500 BC. Iron working appeared in Urewe contexts, and the main spread southwards was accompanied by a village farming complex with cattle, sorghum, pearl and finger millet, these crops being well suited to the relatively dry climatic conditions of eastern Africa. Sheep, goats and chickens were initially rare or absent, and cattle eventually became dominant in Bantu animal husbandry. The migration might have been assisted in wetter tropical regions by the acquisition, perhaps during the first millennium AD, of Southeast Asian bananas, taro and greater yam, although these crops remained more important in the forested regions to the west. Like the linguists, archaeologists recognize separate western and eastern streams to the Bantu migration, with the western one tending to cross the continent from west to east. However, it should be remembered here that the Bantu languages of eastern Africa belong to the Eastern rather than the Western Bantu subgroup, so there is no linguistic support for any major movement across the southern part of the continent from west to east.

By AD 300, the Eastern Bantu had reached Natal in far southern Africa. It is clear that other Western Bantu-speaking populations spread at some point southwards through the rainforest into Angola, but the precise chronology and extent of this movement is uncertain. Linguistic dating suggests this commenced around 1000 BC, but some recent genetic evidence indicates that indigenous hunter-gatherer populations probably survived quite widely in Angola until the thirteenth century AD, after which time they were replaced genetically by immigrant Bantu-speaking groups.[13]

The Eastern Bantu migrations thus commenced around 500 BC and were nearing completion within less than one millennium.[14] The distance covered was more than 3000 km from north to south, from the tropics into the temperate zone. Ultimately, the Bantu were stopped only by the change to a winter rainfall Mediterranean climate in Natal, and by the Kalahari Desert in the southwest. They did not come into contact with Dutch colonists in South Africa until around 1760, so European colonization was not a significant factor in stopping movement until this time. The Bantu migration, assisted by the working of iron for tools, was one of the greatest ethnolinguistic spreads in world history, given that Bantu speakers today number 240 million people and speak somewhere between 450 and 650 different languages, all with a common and rather recent shared origin.[15]

Genetic evidence also indicates a very strong demographic profile for the Bantu (as opposed to indigenous hunter-gatherer) populations throughout the unfolding of their ancestral migration. Gignoux et al. (2011), for instance, use mutation rates within whole mtDNA genomes to suggest that sub-Saharan African populations increased dramatically in numbers around 4500 years ago. This is, of course, a date well within the range of early agriculture right across northern sub-Saharan Africa, although it is a little early for the main Bantu migrations themselves. Tishkoff et al. (2009) provide autosomal genetic data that strongly support the existence of Niger-Congo-speaking populations as a significant and expansive node within the sub-Saharan population as a whole. Heyer and Rocha (2013), using the Tishkoff database, comment on the relative genetic homogeneity of the Bantu speakers in particular, and show how their spread must have led to considerable incorporation of indigenous hunter-gatherer mtDNA via unions between Bantu men and indigenous women, whereas the reverse is not attested.

Finally, what can be said about the Holocene prehistory of the indigenous populations who inhabited sub-Saharan Africa before the incursions of pastoralists and farmers? The descendants of these populations exist today as the Khoe-San hunters and sheep herders of southern Africa, together with hunter-gatherer groups such as the Hadza and Sandawe in Tanzania and the Pygmies of the West African rainforests. These populations have a distinctive and partially shared genetic profile. The first two speak related languages with click consonants that belong to the Khoisan (or Khoesan) language macrofamily in southern Africa. Pygmies nowadays all speak Niger-Congo languages, but like the Southeast Asian Negritos they probably underwent language shift in prehistoric times. The Dahalo of Kenya also once spoke a Khoisan-type language, but today speak a Cushitic language. Many southern Bantu languages reveal traces of click-language substrate influences, for instance Xhosa, as do some Cushitic languages in Kenya.

These indigenous hunter-gatherers are considered by many geneticists to preserve some of the root DNA profiles of modern humanity across the world, as discussed in Chapter 3. This does not make them any more *ancient* than anyone else; it just means that they have occupied their ancestral homeland for longer than anyone else. The Bantu migrations of course replaced most of these populations in central and eastern Africa, but we know that the Khoisan groups and the Pygmies share a unique and common but very ancient ancestry apart from other human groups.[16]

Around 2000 years ago, the Khoe-speaking populations of South Africa adopted sheep herding from a source that was clearly north of the Zambezi River. This source has long been considered to have been amongst Bantu-speaking populations, but NRY genetic comparisons of modern Tanzanian populations and Khoe pastoralists indicate that non-Bantu people, or at least some males, also migrated south around 2000 years ago. Genetically, it appears that there may have been a Nilo-Saharan (Southern Nilotic) source population for this migration, but linguistic data suggest a group more closely related to the present-day Khoisan languages.[17] This movement appears also to have had a genetic influence on the Hadza and Sandawe Khoisan-related people of Tanzania. Needless to say, there are no linguistic traces of such a far southerly extension of Nilo-Saharan languages, but this sheep-carrying migration obviously preceded the main Bantu spread. It could therefore have been linguistically overwhelmed outside the area occupied by Khoisan languages today.

The African Food Production Complex in Perspective

A still-common perspective on African prehistory is that it started in a big way in terms of human evolution, but then faded during the Holocene in competition with the rest of the world created by its many successful emigrants into Eurasia and eventually Australia and the Americas. Egypt normally escapes this fate by being treated as a world unto itself. I hope in the previous discussions of Africa, in Chapters 5 and 7, as well as in this chapter, that this continent comes through instead as a region of remarkable Holocene migratory activity.

To recap the main developments, we witnessed first the hunter-gatherer colonization of an early Holocene greening Sahara, devoid of human life until after 10,000 BC. Then, Africa's first firmly attested food production was introduced around 6000 BC, by immigrant Afroasiatic speakers from the Levant. This led ultimately to the rise of Egyptian civilization, to a contemporary spread of pastoralism around the fringes of a rapidly drying mid-Holocene Sahara, and to the development of agriculture in the Ethiopian highlands. Nilo-Saharan populations apparently (the evidence is mostly linguistic) adopted pastoralism from Afroasiatic speakers and some migrated south into Uganda and Kenya. As the desert became less habitable after 4000 BC, populations along the Sahel and savanna fringes of the Sahara took the first steps towards developing indigenous African agriculture, a product of the summer monsoon pattern of rainfall. The resulting spread of Niger-Congo-speaking farmers was probably just commencing by 2500 BC, and by 500 BC the greatest migration in recent African prehistory, that of the Bantu speakers, was heading south. By AD 300, the Bantu had spread over 3000 km, from Lake Victoria to Natal.

All of Africa was affected by these movements, even the southern hunters and gatherers, some of whom adopted sheep herding about 2000 years ago and many of whom much later lost their lands to Bantu farmers. The Pygmies of the rainforest adopted Niger-Congo languages. While the Khoe-San hunters of the Kalahari are often stated to be the only ones to have retained the genomes, languages, and material lifestyles of their ancestors via an unbroken line of local inheritance that goes back into the Pleistocene, there are some who also doubt this.[18] Perhaps few populations can live in a state of total isolation for over 10,000 years.

While Afroasiatic populations introduced agriculture and animal husbandry to northeastern Africa, they did not spread very far to the south of the Sahara. As in Asia, where the winter rainfall to monsoon climatic divide kept western and eastern Eurasians apart for several millennia (and still does so today), so also in Africa the fluctuating northern boundary of the African monsoon kept apart Afroasiatic and Niger-Congo speaking populations. Nilo-Saharans straddled the boundary, and the Ethiopian highlands were environmentally unique enough to go their own way, just like New Guinea within the Indo-Pacific region. The monsoon boundary was perhaps the greatest environmental determinant of African agricultural history, backed of course in the north by the mighty Sahara, the gateway into the continent from all regions north or east, except for seaborne visitors such as Austronesians.

Holocene Migrations in the Americas

Although individual plants and animals were domesticated in many different temperate and tropical regions of the Americas, some quite early in the Holocene, only four genuine foci of early farming development and consequent population growth, and potential out-migration, can be identified today. These are the central Andes and adjacent Pacific coastal lowlands, western Amazonia, Mesoamerica (northwestern

Figure 9.4 The main homelands of crop domestication in the New World. Sources are listed in Bellwood 2005a, Figure 8.1, with the addition of data from Piperno 2011a, 2011b. Base map by Multimedia Services, ANU, modified by the author.

Mexico to El Salvador), and the middle Mississippi, lower Missouri and Ohio basins of the eastern United States (Figure 9.4). Not all of the domesticated plants and animals of the Americas necessarily originated in just these regions and no others, but it was in these regions that the earliest identified systems of agricultural dependence developed, together with the earliest complex societies.

However, while the archaeological evidence from these regions is often very detailed, there are problems due to the immense colonial era impact on language distributions, especially through depopulation in regions such as temperate South America and the eastern United States. There is also relatively little genetic information that reflects directly on recent time periods. Most genetics research emphasis so far has naturally been on understanding the initial Paleoindian colonization from Siberia.

In my *First Farmers*, I proposed a small number of archaeology and language family correlations for Mesoamerica and the eastern United States, but found few data available for South America. Specifically, I suggested that the major Mesoamerican early agricultural language families – Otomanguean, Mixe-Zoquean, and Mayan – had been constrained from expansion by geographical circumscription within what was essentially a very narrow isthmus between desert to the north and rainforest to the southeast. I also proposed that early Uto-Aztecan speakers had been able to break out and to migrate after 2000 BC from northern Mesoamerica into the US Southwest, with an economy involving irrigated maize cultivation. I also suggested that early Siouan and Iroquoian speakers spread initially in the Eastern Woodlands with the development of indigenous plant cultivation after 2000 BC, but more widely after maize became widespread in eastern North America during the middle to late first millennium AD.[19] I still hold the aforementioned views today.

However, it is necessary to emphasize that very large areas of North America never received any agricultural settlement at all during prehistory, especially down the western side of the continent, including California. Large areas of the eastern United States beyond the range of the native crops (see Figure 9.8) were also apparently without food production until the arrival of maize. Most of these agriculturalist language family dispersals were relatively restricted compared to the extents of the major Old World language families, even though Uto-Aztecan itself eventually covered about 30° of latitude, from central America to Idaho.

This northwards movement by the early Uto-Aztecans is also interesting for another reason. It led in southern California and the arid Great Basin of Nevada and Utah to a partial switch into management of wild resources, rather than full agriculture, a process that tends to reverse what many regard as the more normal direction of cultural evolution from hunting and gathering towards greater levels of food production. This northward spread of the Numic-speaking Uto-Aztecans illustrates how farmers might frequently have become hunter-gatherers in situations where farming was less efficient than foraging or downright impossible for climatic reasons. Such situations occurred in southern New Zealand, some interior regions of Borneo, and possibly parts of Amazonia.[20] Migration processes sometimes carried people far beyond the limits of their existing agricultural economies, whether consciously or not.

As in the Old World, so the New World also reveals widespread homogeneity in material culture at times when we might suspect that migration was important. The Early Paleoindian colonization era, with its Clovis and other point types, is an excellent example. The Early Paleoindian era was followed by regional diversification in cultural style during the long millennia of the Late Paleoindian and Archaic periods, commencing around 11,000 BC. With the rise of agriculture after 2000 BC, wide expanses of homogeneous cultural style formed again during the Early Agricultural or Formative phases of New World archaeology, as noted many years ago by James A. Ford.[21]

The Central Andes

In the central Andes, the first hints of agriculture and settled village life can be traced to a number of fertile lowland valleys in both forested southern Ecuador and arid

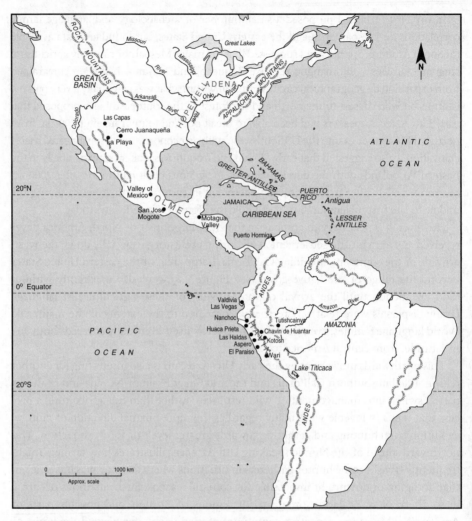

Figure 9.5 Archaeological sites and major complexes in the Americas, as discussed in the text. Base map by Multimedia Services, ANU, modified by the author.

northern Peru. Good examples come from the Valdivia sites in lowland Ecuador, and from sites of the Nanchoc Tradition in the drier Zaña Valley, at an altitude of 450 m in northern Peru (Figure 9.5). In both these locations, early attempts at cultivation involved Andean crops such as *quinoa* (a grain-bearing chenopod), *achira* (a tuber), squash, beans, manioc, guava, sweet potato and cotton, many of nonlocal immediate origin. This suggests a considerable amount of plant transfer from one region to another by early low-level food producers.[22] Further evidence comes from the excavation of houses and sometimes small villages in both regions, with claims for furrowed fields and small irrigation canals dating back as far as 4200 BC in the Zaña Valley.[23] However, as the Zaña Valley investigators note, such finds do not appear in adjacent valleys and it is still difficult to understand their full significance. As emphasized by Dolores Piperno, developments towards low-level food production, many of a pre-domestication nature, were occurring in various regions of northwestern tropical South America and Mesoamerica from quite early in the Holocene.[24]

The very prolific archaeological record for northern Peru suggests that significant population growth was restricted until agriculture became firmly established by around 2500 BC. At this time, some very impressive adobe and stone monumental constructions began to appear in the valleys of northern and central Peru.[25] The locking together of a food production system capable of supporting large populations clearly did not occur until several millennia after the initial attempts at plant cultivation, exactly as in Old World regions such as the Fertile Crescent and China. In Peru, these large sites belong to the Late Preceramic and Initial periods (the latter distinguished by a presence of pottery and maize) that together lasted between 2500 and 900 BC. They are often associated with substantial evidence for food and textile production, with obligatory irrigation in the arid lowland valleys. Mark Cohen (1977: 164) has suggested a 15–20 times population increase between 2500 and 1750 BC from site surveys in a small coastal region of central Peru.

By 2000 BC, much of the impetus for cultural growth also incorporated the Andean highland regions to as far south as Lake Titicaca, where potatoes, guinea pigs and llamas were first domesticated. Maize became widespread in Ecuador and northern Peru around 2000 BC, but the possible explanations for the spread of this Mesoamerican cereal into South America are complex. Was it transferred initially from Mexico to Peru as a kind of sugarcane, or was it spread as a plant already with a large ear (the maize cob) full of edible grain? The sugar in its stalk could have been used initially for making *chicha* beer, but maize could hardly have increased human population sizes by very much if used only in this way. However, as a plant with edible grain, the ancestor of modern sweet corn, maize would have had tremendous dietary significance.[26] Maize cobs have been directly C14-dated to about 2000 BC from the site of Huaca Prieta on the north coast of Peru (Dillehay et al. 2012), but since the cob sizes are not given in the available report the situation remains unclear. Consistent reports over many years suggest a presence of maize phytoliths at about 5000 BC in the Las Vegas sites in Ecuador, even earlier in Panama,[27] but maize has never been found in pre-2000 BC Late Preceramic sites with good botanical preservation in Peru.

The Late Preceramic and Initial Periods were perhaps the first in Peruvian prehistory within which we can search usefully for the origins of an extant and widespread Andean language family. By 1000 BC, after a millennium of sustained population growth during the Initial Period, increasing evidence for warfare and site abandonment suggests that some degree of social and environmental collapse might have occurred, especially along the north Peruvian coast. Following this period of instability, there appears to have been a reformulation of the whole system during the mid-first millennium BC in terms of a region-wide horizon of religious cult, art, and interaction named after the site of Chavin de Huantar in the northern highlands of Peru. Chavin is conveniently situated on an extreme upper branch of the Marañon tributary of the Amazon, and also close to the Callejon de Huaylas that drains into the Pacific. This was clearly a good location for any culture that wished to spread its influence, both within the Andes and eastwards into the fringes of Amazonia. Chavin has recently come into prominence as a likely source complex for the two major language families of the central Andes, Quechua and Aymara.

In my *First Farmers*, I had little to say on the histories of the Quechua and Aymara speakers who dominate large areas of Ecuador, Peru and Bolivia today, and obviously have done so for a very long time. However, there has been a recent flurry of attention to this issue, led by linguist Paul Heggarty and archaeologist David Beresford-Jones.[28] The essence of their argument is that some version of a farming dispersal hypothesis accounts best for the Quechua and Aymara migrations, focused on circumstances of identifiable population growth and cultural coherence within the archaeological record. However, it appears that neither Quechua nor Aymara have time depths suffi-ciently long to intersect with the Late Preceramic or Initial periods, although this does not rule out older undocumented language dispersal at this time. Early Aymara, with a slightly greater time depth from extant languages than Quechua, is stated by these authors to have been carried south from around 500 BC out of an Early Horizon (Chavin-related) homeland in north-central Peru, moving towards Bolivia, where most Aymara languages are spoken today. During the expansion process, which might have been fuelled to a degree by maize cultivation, Aymara had a contact-induced impact on an early Quechua group of languages still located in central Peru.

The early Quechua speakers then took their turn to spread from central Peru during the middle to late first millennium AD, in connection with the spread of the Middle Horizon cultural tradition centered on the site of Wari, near Ayacucho, with its expan-sive political and religious activities. In the process, Quechua speakers spread south to overlay the previous dispersal of Aymara in many regions. One form of Quechua was adopted many centuries later by the Incas and Spanish as the lingua franca of their successive empires – the ancestral Inca, initially, were perhaps Puquina or Aymara speakers. Interestingly, neither Aymara nor Quechua speakers seem to have spread very far north from central Peru in pre-Inca times (Quechua probably reached Cajamarca), and unrelated languages were retained by groups such as the Chimu in northern Peru. Quechua did spread into Ecuador during Inca times, just as it spread far south of Bolivia into northern Chile and Argentina, but in this case with imperial conquest and some degree of population translocation.

In 2008, a seminar on Archaeology and Language in the Andes was organized in Cambridge, wherein many different opinions on these issues were proposed, especially by linguists.[29] It is clear that no consensus yet exists, and some authors find it easy to reverse the aforementioned order, having Quechua before Aymara, and other variations. My view is that such issues can only be sorted out from the perspective of a major theory such as the early farming dispersal hypothesis. Multidisciplinary vision will be required.

Amazonia

The Andes and Upper Amazonia are locked together by a remarkable network of rivers, tributaries of the greater Amazon system, that often penetrate far through the

Andes mountains to rise quite close to the Pacific Ocean. Even the inhabitants of Chavin de Huantar would have passed Manaus and Santarem if they happened to travel downstream far enough from their homes. For this reason, I have always found it difficult to regard the Andes and Amazonia as totally unrelated worlds. Many of course have long agreed. Betty Meggers and Clifford Evans long ago related some of the earliest Amazonian pottery to sites such as Valdivia in Ecuador, Puerto Hormiga in Colombia, the Initial Period sites of northern Peru, and the site of Tutishcainyo in the upper Ucayali valley of eastern Peru.[30] Indeed, many Initial Period sites are located down the eastern side of the Peruvian Andes, especially in the montane forest between 1500 and 3700 m, where they formed part of a north-to-south interaction zone along the western edge of upper Amazonia.[31]

Links between the Andes and Amazonia were, therefore, quite possible and indeed very likely in prehistory. But it must be remembered that Amazonia offers to human colonists a very different lowland and riverine environment than does the Andes, with equatorial wet rainforest in its western parts, and slightly more seasonal and drier evergreen forest to the east and south.[32] Tubers such as manioc and sweet potato were more significant than maize in most regions, and agriculture and villages were very much concentrated along the *varzea* regions of fertile new alluvium that flank some (but not all) of the major rivers. Also, there are no linguistic links of significance today that cross through the high Andes into Amazonia in the vicinity of Peru or Ecuador, and neither is there evidence for any in the past. Amazonia has its own distinctive language families and populations – Arawak, Carib, Tupí, Panoan, Tucanoan, Macro-Jê (see following text). Quechua and Aymara speakers never appear to have attempted to colonize the lowlands east of the Andes ranges, and Amazonian populations never seriously penetrated the other way.

The archaeology of Amazonia has received a significant boost in recent years, with the oldest evidence for agriculture now coming from the upper valley of the Madeira River and its tributaries that drain the eastern slopes of the Andes below Lake Titicaca. These rivers pass through the Brazilian provinces of Acre and Rondônia, as well as northern Bolivia, and supported prehistoric systems of raised fields constructed from swamps, with anthropogenic (manured and cultivated) soils, canals and mounds, believed to date back as far as 2500 BC in some locations, prior to the regional appearance of pottery.[33] This region of southwestern Amazonia is also regarded as the botanical homeland for manioc, peanuts, and a species of squash, and as we will subsequently it was also the most likely homeland for the dispersal of the Tupí languages. Similar lowland raised field complexes are reported from upper Amazon tributaries in Colombia and Ecuador, raising the possibility that the beginnings of farming in Amazonia as a whole actually began around its western fringes, adjacent to the Andes. Elsewhere in Amazonia there are few traces of agriculture and large villages until around 1000 BC.[34]

In most regions of Amazonia, archaeologists have attempted to trace the spreads of the major language families, to be described later, through the distributions of certain kinds of pottery. There is a general consensus that Arawak-speaking populations tended to prefer incised and modeled pottery, while Tupí speakers preferred

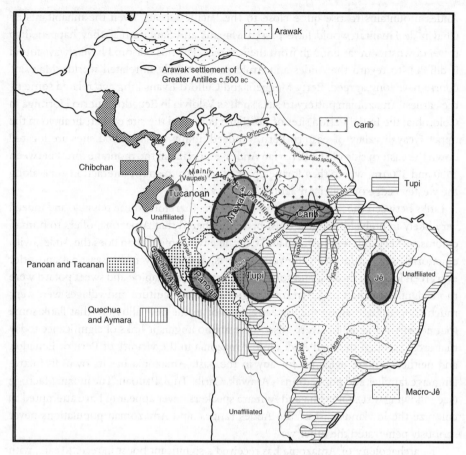

Figure 9.6 The eight major language families of South America and their possible homelands. The distributions are approximate and relate to the period before AD 1500 (many regions are Spanish- and Portuguese-speaking today). This map was prepared by Clive Hilliker and Peter Bellwood, and has also been published in Aikhenvald 2013.

polychrome styles.[35] However, the possibility should be borne in mind that the initial expansions of these language families might have begun before pottery came into use and were hence preceramic, as is quite possible also in the Andes and Mesoamerica.

As far as the Amazonian language families are concerned, I will limit the following discussion to the three most widespread: Tupí, Carib, and Arawak, the latter also spread through the Caribbean Islands (Figure 9.6). Sixty percent of the Amazonian and all the indigenous Caribbean languages have disappeared since Europeans arrived, so this makes linguistic history a little elusive. The surviving pattern is very much a mosaic, with speakers of unrelated languages living side by side in many areas, although it is possible that much of this patterning reflects refugee activity since the arrival of European settlers with their unquenchable demands for land. Nevertheless, Amazonia both today and in the recent past has interesting complexes of what Michael Heckenberger (2013) has termed 'pluri-ethnic' villages. Well-known situations occur along the Xingu River, and in the rather celebrated case of the Vaupes region of lowland Colombia, different linguistic groups even engage in obligatory linguistic exogamy – each person is required to marry a person from a different but coresident linguistic group. In such situations, social pressures tend to ensure that languages remain separate and do not pidginize, although there is limited lexical and much deeper grammatical borrowing.[36] Despite the existence of many localized cases of language shift in recent Amazonian ethnography, most linguists, and I suspect most archaeologists, regard the prehistoric dispersals of the major language families as reflections of actual, linguistically conjoined, population movement rather than language shift alone, although the latter explanation is sometimes adopted.[37]

The ages of the Amazonian families are rather difficult to estimate from linguistic data, but a new set of calculations based on measures of lexical similarity suggest that the Arawak family is in excess of 4000 years old, Tupí about 3600 years, and Carib, Panoan and Tucanoan only about 2500 to 2000 years old.[38] The Macro-Jê family of southern Brazil has a much greater antiquity and presumably represents former hunter-gatherers who adopted agriculture (many were still hunter-gatherers at contact) and essentially remained in place, surrounded by migrating Tupí-Guarani speakers who have managed to surround the whole Brazilian Highland region, reaching Rio de Janeiro around 2000 years ago and eventually the latitude of Buenos Aires.[39]

The Tupí homeland, indeed, is likely to be southwestern Amazonia, in the neighborhood of the upper Madeira river and its tributaries, where the early manioc cultivation described earlier was developed from about 2500 BC onwards. The majority of the Tupí linguistic subgroups exist in this area,[40] and the possibility arises that manioc cultivation was one of the main driving forces behind their spread. Recent genetic data on microsatellites and protein markers also suggests that the ancestors of the modern Tupí-speaking population could have originated in the Rondônia region.[41]

The Arawak homeland was also located in western Amazonia, according to a recent phylogeographic study of the basic lexicons of Arawak languages, perhaps on the upper Amazon and Negro rivers a little to the north of the Tupí homeland.[42] Heckenberger identifies the Arawak diaspora as associated with lowland riverine farmers who practiced wetland management and constructed raised fields. He sees their main spread as occurring between 500 BC and AD 500, associated with an incised-rim style of pottery.[43] Their settlement of the Caribbean islands around 500 BC will be described later, and by AD 800 they had also reached the upper Xingu river in southeastern Amazonia. These Arawak-speaking migrants carried an economy based on cultivation of manioc, sweet potato and maize, and a social system based on concepts of inherited hierarchy with chiefs and founder-rank enhancement. Heckenberger specifically compares the Arawak diaspora with the Bantu and Austronesian cases discussed in previous chapters, and it also accords with my own model of early farming dispersal.

The Carib are harder to pin down, although the linguistic evidence gives them an eastern Amazonian origin, on subgrouping grounds perhaps close to the lower Amazon itself. Heckenberger defines both the Tupí and the Carib diasporas as associated with upland shifting agriculture rather than the kind of lowland riverine-based farming that characterized the Arawak speakers. Archaeological sites that can be related to Carib speakers, with incised and punctate pottery, are known by AD 500–1000 from the Orinoco valley, the Guianas and the Santarem region,[44] but their eventual migrations did not extend as far as those of the Tupí or Arawak. The latter, indeed, can be credited with undertaking the most significant ethnolinguistic colonization of the Caribbean Islands, to which we now turn.

The Caribbean Islands

The islands of the Caribbean (West Indies) comprise three major archipelagoes: the Greater Antilles (Cuba to Puerto Rico); the Bahamas chain to the northeast (with the Turks and Caicos Islands); and the Lesser Antilles to the east of Puerto Rico from the Virgin Islands southwards to Trinidad (Figure 9.5). The larger islands are intervisible, but the Caribbean Islands as a whole, apart from Trinidad and Tobago, are not visible from adjacent points on the mainland (Venezuela, Mexico, Florida). Access was always by sea and initially required a crossing out of sight of land.

So far, there is no indication that Paleoindian settlers reached the West Indies. Current surveys of the archaeology of these islands indicate that Archaic hunter-gatherers arrived first, sometime between 5000 and 2500 BC (Fitzpatrick 2006). The initial colonization was accompanied by an extinction horizon similar to that on many Pacific islands, in this case involving flightless owls, sloths, seals and bats. Sites of this era occur in the Greater Antilles, apart from Jamaica, and a few also occur in the Lesser Antilles to as far south as Antigua. The Lesser Antilles would in many cases have been too small and resource-limited to have supported permanent preagricultural settlement, as with very small islands in Eastern Indonesia and Oceania. It is possible that they were only utilized on a temporary basis. The origins of these initial preceramic settlers are uncertain, although Keegan and Wilson suggest the Yucatan Peninsula of Mexico and Belize.[45] Callaghan (2001) has noted the ease of boat travel from Venezuela to Puerto Rico, but using data from the ceramic era rather than the Archaic.

The first appearance of agriculture in the West Indies is documented from Puerto Rico, where evidence for manioc, sweet potato, maize and early pottery appeared by 1300 BC.[46] But the main ceramic phase, termed the Saladoid and associated with painted, modeled, incised and punctate pottery, spread through the Greater Antilles between 800 and 500 BC. Given that the Greater Antilles were occupied by Arawak-speaking people (called Taino) when Columbus arrived, it is generally agreed that this Saladoid movement, from multiple locations on the northern coast of South America, incorporated the major part of their ancestry. Saladoid populations also spread into the Lesser Antilles, most probably from the north rather than the south according to Keegan, apparently commencing from Puerto Rico around AD 200. However, Hofman and colleagues also suggest a Saladoid movement from Tobago to Grenada at about 400 BC.[47] In addition, jadeite axes of likely Guatemalan origin (Motagua Valley) discovered in Saladoid stone workshops on Antigua, dating between AD 250 and 500, suggest yet another route of contact, across 3100 km of land and sea.[48]

Finally, within the Caribbean, the Bahamas were settled from Cuba and Dominica around AD 700–1000, and the Turks and Caicos soon after. The Lesser Antilles were also subject to incursions by Carib speakers, mostly male, in late prehistory. These formed a group known historically as the Island Caribs, from whom the Caribbean Sea took its name. Bermuda has no reported prehistoric settlement.

Mesoamerica

In Mesoamerica, as in the Andes, there was a long preceramic phase of low-level food production that occupied much of the early Holocene, especially involving the initial domestication of maize, a development currently located to altitudes above 500 m in the Balsas Basin of Michoacan and Guerrero, more or less due south of the modern location of Mexico City (Valley of Mexico). By 5000 BC, there are suggestions that slash-and-burn cultivation of maize was occurring in the Gulf and Pacific coastal regions of Mexico and in the central Balsas Basin, although there are as yet no signs of any significant growth in population or settlement complexity at such an early date. It was soon after this time, however, that the earliest preserved maize cobs started to accumulate size changes towards the larger domesticated Formative Period varieties of the second and first millennia BC.[49]

As in Ecuador and Peru, the development of full domestication-based agriculture that utilized maize as a productive and increasingly large-cobbed cereal did not occur in Mesoamerica until after 2000 BC. By 1800 BC, large villages with pottery, baked clay human figurines, rectangular pole and thatch houses, earthen platforms and bell-shaped storage pits were beginning to develop in fertile inland valleys and along tropical coastlines, through an extensive region that stretched from the Valley of Mexico, Oaxaca and Chiapas eastwards to Costa Rica.[50] Furthermore, maize cobs are reported to have doubled in length between 1300 and 1000 BC in the Soconusco region of Chiapas (Rosenswig 2006).

These Early Agricultural and Formative developments in Mesoamerica laid the foundations for the expansions of the Otomanguean, Uto-Aztecan, Mixe-Zoque and Mayan language families, with the first-listed having the greatest time depth, perhaps by virtue of being located very close to the most likely region of maize domestication in the Balsas Basin. Recent calculations of ages from lexical similarities between languages within these families give roughly 6500 years for Proto-Otomanguean, 4000 for Proto-Uto-Aztecan, but closer to only 2500–1500 years for Mixe-Zoque and Mayan.[51] This suggests that early Otomanguean speakers spread first. But quite how far is not clear since this family nowadays has a rather restricted distribution circumscribed and overlain by the other families, especially by the expansion of the Nahua language within the Uto-Aztecan family, the lingua franca of the fifteenth-century Aztec Empire. All of these linguistic families, according to vocabulary reconstructions, were spoken by populations who were familiar with agricultural practices, and especially the growing of maize, together with various other crops such as sweet potatoes, tomatoes, manioc, beans and squashes. Linguist Cecil Brown (2010b) reconstructs the domestications of these and many other crops between 7000 and 2000 years ago using linguistic dating methods, in the earliest instances in interior basins such as the Balsas as well as in the highlands of Mesoamerica.

A second phase of linguistic expansion might have occurred during the Olmec phase of extensive stylistic and ritual homogeneity that developed during the first millennium BC. This extended from an apparent heartland in the Isthmus of Tehuantepec, towards the Valley of Mexico to the west and eastwards to as far as El Salvador. In chronology and overall extent, the Olmec phase corresponded to Chavin in Peru as a kind of secondary reformulation of a landscape of cultural integration that had developed a millennium or more earlier. The major ceremonial centers of the Olmec were located near the Gulf coast in Veracruz and Tabasco, and Olmec iconography was generally absent in the Maya region and northern Mesoamerica. This makes it very unlikely to have been connected with the early histories of the Mayan and Uto-Aztecan-speaking populations, but Mixe-Zoque and certainly some intermediate Otomanguean expansion might well have been associated with it.

One general conclusion here would be that the early Otomanguean, Mixe-Zoque and Mayan speakers existed in a situation of strong mutual circumscription, hemmed in together within the narrow isthmian region of central America. Likely suggestions for their homelands are discussed in a recent survey by Jane Hill (2013) and focus on Oaxaca and Puebla for Otomanguean, the Guatemalan Highlands or the Gulf of Honduras for Mayan, and the narrow Isthmus of Tehuantepec for Mixe-Zoque (see Figure 9.7).

Northern Mesoamerica, the Southwestern United States, and the Uto-Aztecans[52]

One major Mesoamerican language family remains – Uto-Aztecan. This was the one that eventually spread the furthest, from El Salvador to Idaho, over a distance of virtually 5000 km and on a scale that one can truly compare with many Old World spreads such as Bantu and Sino-Tibetan. But first I must explain that there are two opposed viewpoints on the origins of Uto-Aztecan-speaking maize farmers. One view sees them as indigenous to the US Southwest, as former hunter-gatherers who adopted maize agriculture from Mesoamercia as a result of cultural diffusion. The other view, which I favor, brings them northwards into the Southwest from somewhere close to the homeland of domesticated maize in Mesoamerica. No one disputes the botanical status of Mesoamerica as the homeland of maize, given that *teosinte*, the wild ancestor of maize, only grows there. But a majority of North American archaeologists have always believed in the first option, that domesticated maize was not carried into the Southwest by migrating Mesoamericans, but rather by cultural exchange alone. Many American linguists have supported this view by claiming that the Uto-Aztecan language family did not originate in Mesoamerica, but in the United States.

The most recent claim for an indigenous Southwestern origin proposes a mid-Nevada Great Basin origin for the Uto-Aztecan family, which was carried southwards by hunter-gatherers around 6900 BC as a response to a wetter climate. Eventually, after 2100 BC, their descendants adopted maize cultivation as the migration progressed into northern Mexico, and then spread the maize cultivation back into the Southwest

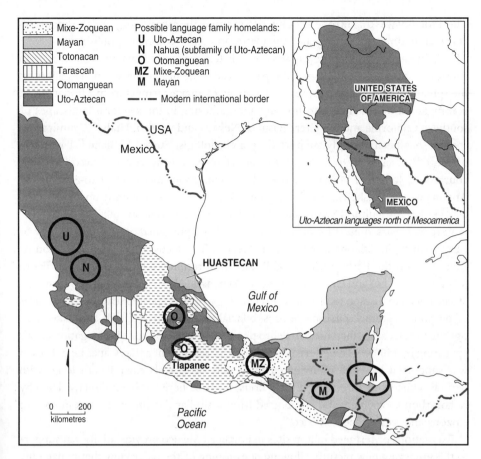

Figure 9.7 The major language families of Mesoamerica and the US Southwest and their likely homelands. Based on a map by J. Kathryn Josserand and Nicholas A. Hopkins on the web site of the Foundation for the Advancement of Mesoamerican Studies, Inc., at www. famsi.org/map/linguistic.html. This map has also been published in Hill 2013, and is reproduced here with the permission of Jane Hill. Map drawn by Multimedia Services, ANU.

through cultural diffusion.[53] The reason for locating Proto-Uto-Aztecan in the Great Basin centers on an unwillingness to accept that cognates for maize-related vocabulary items exist in sufficient numbers to support an agriculturalist status for Proto-Uto-Aztecan. It is also based on the observation that Proto-Uto-Aztecan had no reconstructed term for pinyon nut. These nuts did not grow naturally in the Great Basin during the early Holocene, which at that time lay north of their limit. Therefore, it is suggested that Uto-Aztecan must have originated there (Merrill et al. 2009).

The opposing view, which I favor with linguist Jane Hill, is that maize farming spread north from Mesoamerica into Arizona with existing farmers, speakers of early Uto-Aztecan languages, about 4000 years ago. A version of this view was originally presented by Kimball Romney from a linguistic and ethnographic perspective in 1957, and then supported from an archaeological perspective by Michael Berry in 1985.[54]

The difficulty was that no one attempted to examine the archaeology and the linguistics at the same time, until I broached the matter in a short comment published in 1997.[55] The significance of this approach was immediately recognized by Hill, whom I met on a visit to Tucson in 1999. During the past decade, she has published many papers on the spread of Proto-Uto-Aztecan as a language of maize farmers from Mesoamerica, accompanied by a switch into hunting and gathering in the semiarid landscapes of southern California and the Great Basin of Nevada and western Utah.[56] A similar perspective has been strongly supported by archaeologist Steven LeBlanc.[57] I was also privileged to see some very impressive archaeology on my visit to Tucson in 1999, courtesy of Jonathan Mabry. My overall opinions about maize and Uto-Aztecans in Arizona were published in detail in my *First Farmers*, and subsequently updated for the Jack Harlan Agricultural Symposium held in Davis, California, in 2008.[58]

In recent years, quite a lot of new data have been published on the archaeology of early farming in Arizona and northern Mexico. The focus in the Tucson region of Arizona is on the Early Agricultural Phase, until recently defined by the San Pedro (circa 1300-500 BC) and Cienega (500 BC-AD 1) phases. New results from the Congress Street Locus in Tucson (Rio Nuevo Archaeology Project) push back the appearances of pit houses, storage pits, maize cobs, bifacial points, incised sherds and baked clay figurines even earlier than the San Pedro phase, to about 2100 BC, with irrigation canals appearing by 1500 BC. The 3.6 ha San Pedro phase settlement at Las Capas near Tucson was supported by 11 ha of irrigated fields and two canals each 1.1 km long, with periodic clusters of three to five field houses. Maize here has been directly dated by radiocarbon to 2000 BC, and is reported from a similar date in other sites in eastern Arizona and western new Mexico.[59]

Excavations of terraced hilltop sites in northern Mexico provide additional support to this emerging new picture, allowing questioning of the older view that maize only spread into the Southwest as a minor supplementary resource via forager adoption. Whether or not these earliest farmers *depended* on maize for their subsistence is not so clear, and much will depend on how one defines dependence. But the crop appears to have become ubiquitous in the archaeological record by at least 1300 BC at Cerro Juanaqueña in northern Chihuahua. In this site, it supported a 10 ha defensible and terraced hilltop settlement with circular hut foundations and storage pits. The 550 surveyed terraces averaged 52 m² in area and were lined with 8 km of stonewalling. The maize itself is thought to have been grown together with amaranth mainly in the valley bottom below the site. The contemporary site of La Playa in Sonora also had at least 35 ha of fields and irrigation canals, revealed by aerial photography, with roasting pits for maize and a large cemetery.[60]

As Bruce Huckell and colleagues have pointed out for southeastern Arizona, low-level food production would not have been viable without irrigation in such a dry environment. This is an extremely important observation that militates against casual hunter-gatherer adoption of maize farming. Huckell emphasizes the significance of irrigation for growing maize ears that measured at this time up to 8.4 cm long and 2.9 cm in diameter, and that were stored in pits capable in some sites of holding up to 10,000 cobs – sufficient to feed several people for a whole year. A contemporary increase about 4000 years ago in the rate of stream aggradation in southern Arizona also suggests to me a strong human impact through tillage and vegetation clearance, although the recent tendency amongst Southwestern archaeologists has been to relate this to autonomous climate change. Overall, the data suggest a rapid spread of maize across the Southwest, reaching the Four Corners region by 2000 BC and the Rio Grande basin by 1400 BC. In some of these situations, there was clearly a substantial dependence on maize production within the diet.[61]

However, as with all good ideas, there are many who do not agree that these early farmers lived in sedentary settlements supported by intensive maize farming.[62] The sites are often claimed to contain noncontemporary occupation units such as pits and house floors, indicating mobile and small populations of people engaged in low-level food production rather than large sedentary village populations. In addition, the storage pits are claimed to have been inefficient for maize storage, until large pottery vessels came into use during Hohokam times after AD 150. The corn cobs are still relatively small. In debates such as this, archaeologists will inevitably place themselves along a continuum of opinion, favoring explanations between low-level food production at one end as opposed to serious dependence on irrigated maize at the other, and the data themselves will be malleable in terms of interpretation. In my view,[63] even if food production in the Early Agricultural Phase in the Southwest at 2000 BC was associated with undeveloped storage technology, relatively small maize cob size and lack of full sedentism, the question still remains – can it have been associated with a spread of food producers from Mesoamerica, or not? The ubiquity of maize in many sites and the associated irrigation and pit storage technologies are sufficient to convince me that substantial food production occurred, and that it was fundamental in the expansion of Uto-Aztecan-speaking maize farmers northwards from Mesoamerica into the US Southwest around 4000 years ago.

But where did these migrants originate? The two parallel Sierra Madre mountain ranges of northern Mexico and the lower-lying terrain between them, between the Tropic of Cancer and about 30° N, are extremely dry and contain almost no archaeological evidence except for a relatively late penetration of maize farming into Tamaulipas in the east. How was maize farming able to spread through such a dry area? Merrill et al. (2009) avoid the issue by suggesting that the people of Las Capas and Cerro Juanaqueña carried no traceable cultural links with Mesoamerica, preferring to see them as indigenous hunter-gatherers who adopted maize agriculture by diffusion from the south, perhaps during a period of increased rainfall. I find this hard to accept.

Unfortunately, as Steven LeBlanc (2008, 2013) also discusses, there is little genetic evidence that can adjudicate the migration issue. Malhi et al. (2003) have identified a small amount of male migration into the Southwest from Mesoamerica from Y chromosome data, and this has recently been supported by more NRY research by Kemp et al. (2010). Male migration is thus likely, but female migration traces within mtDNA might have been obscured by more recent population expansions, making the extraction of ancient DNA from Early Agricultural Phase skeletons a major priority. Jane Hill (2006) notes that men were generally responsible for agricultural activities in ethnographic Uto-Aztecan societies, so perhaps early farming males frequently took female partners from indigenous forager communities. However, identification of ancient mtDNA from saliva in preserved chewed quids and blood on women's aprons also suggests a possible movement of mtDNA lineage A from Mesoamerica into the Southwest (LeBlanc et al. 2007).

In my view, the clinching evidence that maize farmers and Uto-Aztecan languages spread northwards together comes from linguistic research. The meticulous comparative subgrouping reconstructions by Jane Hill indicate that early Uto-Aztecan speakers were maize farmers with at least ten linguistic reconstructions for maize-related terms (squash and beans apparently traveled later).[64] They probably used pottery, and were in contact with early Otomanguean speakers in central Mexico, who might have transmitted the knowledge of maize and pottery to them. Furthermore, the earliest phases of subgroup differentiation occurred amongst Southern Uto-Aztecan languages, rather than Northern. This implies that the language family originated in Mesoamerica, perhaps even as far south as Queretaro or Toluca, rather than in the southwestern United States. Hill (2013) places the homeland close to the Tropic of Cancer in western Mexico and offers a date close to 4000 years ago for the early stages of Uto-Aztecan dispersal. This is paralleled by the independent calculation of 4000 years for Proto-Uto-Aztecan by Holman et al. (2011), which fits well with the archaeological record.

My view is that the Uto-Aztecan languages could not possibly have spread over such a vast area, from Mexico through the Southwest, then with hunter-gatherers on to the Great Plains (the Comanche), and to as far north as Idaho, unless they were carried by existing speakers. Archaeologically, this population can best be identified initially with maize farmers spreading in search of alluvial farmlands through the semidesert terrains of northern Mexico and southern Arizona. Some eventually found cultivable alluvial land in quantity in the tributaries of the Gila river in southern Arizona, and it is these people who have recently come to light through the archaeological record. Their descendants continued further, spreading maize farming and mixing to varying degrees with indigenous foragers to become the Anasazi, Mogollon and Fremont peoples of Southwestern archaeologists (Matson 2002). Eventually, many of them switched into resource managing (but not food-producing) economies in the dry regions of eastern California, the Great Basin and the southern Great Plains (Hill 2002), although many agricultural activities such as irrigation and broadcast sowing remained within their cultural traditions. Some southern Great Basin populations, such as the Southern Paiute and Chemehuevi of Nevada and Utah, were actively irrigating fields of corn, beans and squash after Europeans arrived, but it is unclear if this was a prehistoric tradition or a result of colonial era contact.[65]

Some of the so-called Eastern Basketmakers of the Mogollon highlands in New Mexico and southern Colorado are considered to have been indigenous foragers who adopted farming from incoming (presumably Uto-Aztecan-speaking) agricultural populations to their west and southwest.[66] However, these later adjustments do not overturn the basic model of initial farmer spread.

The Eastern Woodlands

The traveler and artist George Catlin (2004: 55) was particularly interested in population movements amongst Native Americans in the US Midwest during his journeys there in the 1830s. He commented:

Large parties who are, straying off in pursuit of game, or in the occupation of war, are oftentimes intercepted by their enemy; and being prevented from returning, are run off to a distant region, where they take up their residence and establish themselves as a nation…

Catlin was traveling on the Missouri River when he made this observation, amongst Indian populations who had recently spread on to the Great Plains from the east as mounted buffalo (bison) hunters, the horse having been reintroduced into the Americas by the Spanish. In this way, a number of populations who spoke Siouan and Algonquian languages, many with prior agricultural traditions, appear to have been attracted on to the Plains for their hunting prospects from the seventeenth century onwards. Some of the Siouan groups would certainly have left agricultural traditions behind.[67]

In chapter 5, I described the migrations of the Eskimo-Aleut and Athapaskan hunter-gatherer populations, each covering vast distances from west to east and from north to south, respectively. As the aforementioned quotation from Catlin will suggest, these were not the only hunter-gatherer migrations to follow those of the Pleistocene First American pioneers. The speakers of Algonquian languages also spread very widely through Canada and the northern United States, from a possible Great Lakes homeland, to give rise to such widely dispersed populations as the Blackfoot of Alberta and Montana, the Cree and Ojibwa of the Canadian Shield, the native peoples of the Eastern Seaboard to as far south as North Carolina, and possibly even the remarkably distant Yurok and Wiyot of north coastal California, the latter reflecting an 'Algic' migration that occurred about 5500 years ago according to recent linguistic calculations. Algonquian proper (without Yurok and Wiyot) does not have a great linguistic time depth, possibly only 3500 years, and its protolanguage has no terms for maize, beans, or squash agriculture, although it is possible that former terms for native crops to be discussed subsequently could have been lost as these crops fell out of use.[68] Adoption of the bow and arrow from ancestral Inuit is another suggestion for Algonquian expansionary success.[69] Although I attempted to link early Algonquians with Eastern Woodlands agriculture in First Farmers, the fact remains that over 90% of the recorded Algonquian distribution lies outside the recorded geographical range of the relevant crops. So, even if some southeastern Algonquians became farmers after 4000 years ago, this explanation for expansion cannot cover the whole language family.

Such migrations as those of the early Algonquians must, under hunter-gatherer circumstances, have carried actual human populations – language shift alone would be a most unconvincing explanation. Even Catlin (2004: 385) spoke of tribes being "often carried from one end of the Continent to the other, or from ocean to ocean." While he gives no actual example of such an astounding migration, it is clear that many of his informants had in mind some remarkable traditions, whether exaggerated or not. The Pre-Algonquians (with ancestral Yurok and Wiyot) did indeed spread from coast to coast, from Nova Scotia to California, but certainly not within a single episode of movement.

The other major Eastern Woodland language families were more deeply associated with food production than Algonquian. They include Muskogean,

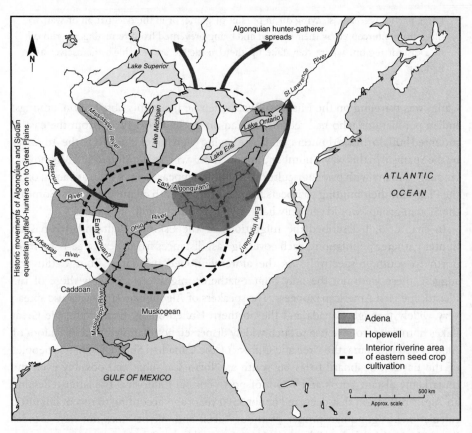

Figure 9.8 The Eastern Woodland crop complex of the United States, together with possible homelands for the Algonquian, Iroquoian and Siouan language families. Distributions of the Adena and Hopewell burial mound and ceremonial complexes are also shown. Modified from Bellwood 2005a, Figure 10.13. Original map by Multimedia Services, ANU, modified by the author.

Iroquoian, Siouan and Caddoan (Figure 9.8).[70] The early dispersal histories of the Iroquoians and Siouans (with less certainty for Muskogean and Caddoan) were in all likelihood associated with a very important indigenous agricultural tradition in the Eastern Woodlands, underway by 2500 BC. This involved a number of native seed plants, including a chenopod (*Chenopodium berlandieri*), a native squash, marsh elder (*Iva annua*), and sunflower.[71] None of these crops originated in Mesoamerica or the US Southwest, so their domestication was indigenous, and the Eastern Woodlands are well separated from these regions by the agriculturally marginal southern Great Plains and the arid lands of northeastern Mexico and southwestern Texas. Prehistoric farmers, if they really wanted to migrate from Mesoamerica to the Mississippi, would probably have needed to travel by sea across the Gulf of Mexico. There might indeed have been some prehistoric contact via this route, but that populations never migrated this way in large numbers is rendered clear by the observation that no languages of ultimate Mesoamerican origin were recognizably established in North America (i.e., traceable through comparative linguistic methods). The only exception is the Uto-Aztecan family, but this was confined to the western United States.

The Eastern Woodland agricultural tradition was quite restricted in extent, mainly around the region where the Ohio, Missouri, and Mississippi rivers converge, spreading east towards the Appalachians and west towards the eastern edge of the Great Plains. South of 34° N and down the Atlantic coastline it appears that no agriculture was present before the arrival of maize, a crop that first made a tentative appearance in the eastern United States around 2000 years ago and then became dominant at various times in different regions between AD 500 and 1000.[72] Neither were the native crops ever present around the Great Lakes or to their north, even though maize itself reached Ontario by AD 500. The native cropping system, according to Bruce Smith, was low-level in productivity and never led to significant population increase, although those who practiced it were certainly involved in the construction of many of the complexes of earthen mounds of the Adena and Hopewell cultures that occur in the Ohio valley and adjacent areas (Figure 9.8).

The main changes in Eastern Woodlands archaeology after the development of the indigenous seed crop tradition occurred with the spread of maize farming, most rapidly around AD 700–1000, across the Mississippi towards the eastern Plains, into eastern Texas, and northwards towards its limits around the Great Lakes, Ontario, and New York State.[73] According to one seventeenth-century authority, the Iroquoian-speaking Hurons of Ontario were then eating maize every day, and it supplied 80% of their food.[74] Recent phytolith analyses have revealed that maize and squash were present over 2000 years ago in New York, but the maize varieties available at that time were probably being grown hard against their climatic limits.[75] One suggestion by Dean Snow is that the Medieval Warm Period (circa AD 900–1300), that assisted the migrations of the Thule Inuit along Arctic latitudes of Canada (Chapter 5), also opened the door for a considerable expansion of maize agriculture northwards and probably lay behind the main expansion of Iroquoian speakers from Pennsylvanian origins into Ontario and the Saint Lawrence valley.[76] However, the Iroquoian family as a whole (with Cherokee) existed long before this, perhaps around the eastern fringes of the Eastern Woodlands agricultural complex prior to the arrival of maize.

It is worth noting that neither Iroquoian nor Siouan have definite maize-related agricultural terms in their reconstructed protolanguages. If they once had terms for native Woodland crops, these must have been lost long ago.[77] The Siouan language family, like Iroquoian, has a time depth calculated by different authorities at between 3500 and 6000 years, so its origin long precedes any likely occurrence of maize agriculture.[78] Its likely homeland was somewhere close to the Ohio Valley and adjacent regions of the lower Missouri and Mississippi – indeed, close to the epicenter for the Eastern Woodland agricultural complex and close to the Mississippian cultures that existed for a few centuries prior to the arrival of Europeans. Rankin suggests that the major subgroups of Siouan were already separate by AD 200, and so an initial establishment of this family during the Early

Agricultural Phase, followed by more dramatic expansions after maize appeared, and then further expansion on to the Great Plains with horses after European arrival, seems likely. Dean Snow (2013) also favors maize-related major expansions of the Iroquoian- and Siouan-speaking populations.

The American Food Production Complexes and Their Impacts on Holocene Prehistory

Alfred Crosby and Jared Diamond have both pointed out that the New World differs from the Old in terms of its north–south (versus west–east) geographical orientation. In Eurasia, agricultural populations spread mainly east–west along latitudes, but in the Americas (and Africa too) they were obliged to move mainly across them, through more sharply differentiated climatic zones.[79] However, if one looks more carefully, the differences can become a little illusory. The main barrier to spreading agricultural complexes in Eurasia was that between the winter rainfall belt to the west and the summer monsoon rainfall belt to the east, with that barrier taking a decidedly tortuous but overall north–south course from eastern into southern Asia around the eastern edge of the Himalayas. Both Eurasia and North America also presented similar problems for farmer migration northwards because of their huge land areas in cold northern latitudes, with the only agricultural dispersal into Canada in prehistory being that of the maize-growing Iroquoians into Ontario.

The Americas also differed from the Old World because their two most important foci of early domestication were geographically quite strongly circumscribed. Mesoamerica was an isthmian bottleneck of restricted extent, hemmed in by desert and seasonal rainforest along the main routes outwards into the US Southwest and South America, respectively. The Andes, being high mountains, rendered free access from western Peru and Ecuador into the Amazon Basin a little difficult, although certainly not impossible. These geographical circumstances meant that most of the American language families that were associated with the earliest developments of farming remained limited in distribution, although the Uto-Aztecan speakers most certainly escaped the confinement in a rather impressive way. The language families of the eastern United States and Amazonia did not face such circumscription, so the speakers of the Siouan, Tupí and Arawak languages were able to spread much further once they had developed the demographic and subsistence foundations (based on maize and manioc, respectively) to support their movements.

Unfortunately, the Americas have not yet yielded much genetic evidence that can throw light on Holocene population movements, partly because of sampling difficulties and partly because the initial settlement was too recent for any deep diversification to have formed, at least outside the areas of subsequent Na-Dene and Eskimo-Aleut settlement from northeastern Asia (neither of which intersected with food production in prehistoric times). Any population expansions would generally have mixed with or replaced other quite closely related populations, as is perhaps evident from the results of recent whole genome comparisons across the Americas (Reich et al. 2012).

The most remarkable observation to conclude this chapter concerns the essential independence of the food production trajectories in the Old World, taken as a whole, versus the New World as a whole. We have two examples, each very different, of what food production can lead to in terms of cultural development and human migration. The eventual results of these differences at the hands of an aggrandizing Western civilization have been treated in a number of widely read works, for instance by Alfred Crosby (1986) and Jared Diamond (1997). Unfortunately, that was the way the balance tipped for the Native Americans, but at least we can see that our modern human world has roots of immense complexity in both hemispheres.

Notes

1. Diamond 2012 discusses why some animals but not others were domesticated.
2. North Africa had indigenous cattle populations, and mtDNA studies suggest that both they and Asian cattle contributed to African domesticated stock (Bradley and Loftus 2000; Ajmone-Marsan et al. 2010; Marshall and Weissbrod 2011: S401–2).
3. Dogs traveled from Asia to America too, but long before the Holocene (Chapter 4). Green 2005 reviews these crop transfers. On sweet potato transference to Eastern Polynesia as a 'hardy kind of yam', see Leach 2005; Barber 2010. Baudouin and Lebrun 2009 discuss genetic evidence for a late prehistoric transfer of coconuts from the Philippines to Panama, where they were observed in 1513, but the suggested archaeological links (pottery in Ecuador) are not very convincing. Storey et al. 2012 discuss the possibility of a transfer of chickens from Polynesia to South America very late in prehistory.
4. Gifford-Gonzalez 2005; Marshall and Weissbrod 2011.
5. Kuper and Kröpelin 2006; Marshall and Weissbrod 2011.
6. Brooks et al. 2009; Hildebrand and Grillo 2012.
7. Wetterstrom 1998; Breunig and Neumann 2002; Bellwood 2005a; Manning et al. 2010b; Marshall and Weissbrod 2011.
8. See Neumann and Hildebrand 2009 for doubts about early banana phytoliths; Denbow 2012 for Tchissanga.
9. Ehret 2002a, 2002b, 2011, 2013, and see Huysecom et al. 2009 for the Ounjougou site in Mali, with pottery dating to 9000 BC.
10. Blench 2006; Ehret 2013. Holman et al. 2011 give a date of only 4000 BC for Proto-Niger-Congo based on lexical similarity calculations.
11. Linguist Roger Blench 2006 sees little evidence for a spread of food production in West Africa before 2000 BC.
12. Ehret 1998; Klieman 2003.
13. Klieman 2003 for linguistics; Beleza et al. 2005 for genetics.
14. Phillipson 2005; Ehret 2013; Robertshaw 2013.
15. Holden 2002; Mace and Holden 2005.
16. Tishkoff et al. 2009.
17. Henn et al. 2008 for the genetics; Güldemann 2008 for the linguistics; Ginter 2011; Pleurdeau et al. 2012 for the archaeology. Smith 2008 believes the sheep were introduced by a Khoe migration from the northern Kalahari, rather than from East Africa.

18. Güldemann 2008 doubts such continuity, but Balter 2012c describes a new archaeological discovery that suggests that San material culture in southern Africa has an in-place antiquity of at least 44,000 years.

19. Excellent distribution maps of the Native American language families are to be found in Coe et al. 1986.

20. See Hill 2002 on this switch within Uto-Aztecan, and Bellwood 2005a: Chapter 2.

21. Ford 1969. See also the relevant chapters on the Americas in Scarre 2013.

22. Pearsall 2003; Piperno 2011a.

23. Dillehay et al. 2007; Dillehay 2011.

24. Piperno 2011a.

25. Browman et al. 2013; Moseley and Heckenberger 2013.

26. For recent commentary on early maize discoveries and the sugarcane issue, see Webster 2011. Piperno et al. 2009 and Ranere et al. 2009 dispute the sugarcane theory from a Mesoamerican phytolith perspective, suggesting that cobs were exploited from very early in the domestication sequence there.

27. Dickau et al. 2007; Piperno 2011a.

28. Heggarty and Beresford-Jones 2010; Heggarty and Beresford-Jones 2012, with many other contributor opinions; Beresford-Jones and Heggarty 2013; Heggarty and Beresford-Jones 2013.

29. Heggarty and Beresford-Jones 2012.

30. Meggers and Evans 1983; Meggers 1987.

31. Warren Church, presentation at Il Encontro Internacional de Arqueologia Amazônica, Manaus, Brazil, 12–17 September 2010. I owe much of my perspective on Amazonia to my attendance at this conference, and wish to thank Eduardo Neves for making my attendance possible.

32. The Peruvian city of Iquitos, a little south of the Equator on the Upper Amazon and 3400 km from the mouth of that river, is only 100 m above sea level.

33. Mann 2008; Piperno 2011b.

34. Neves 2008; Helen Lima, presentation at Il Encontro Internacional de Arqueologia Amazônica, Manaus, Brazil, 12–17 September 2010.

35. Noelli 1998; Heckenberger 2005; Neves 2008; Heckenberger and Neves 2009.

36. Aikhenvald 1996, 2001; Epps 2006.

37. For example, Hornborg 2005 for Arawak. Heckenberger 2005, 2013 and Heckenberger and Neves 2009 prefer migration-related explanations for Tupi and Sarawak.

38. Holman et al. 2011.

39. Heckenberger 2013.

40. Migliazza 1982; Epps 2006; Neves 2008; Heckenberger and Neves 2009; Aikhenvald 2013. Heckenberger and Neves equate the Tupí spread with polychrome pottery and date it to within the past 2000 years, although the overall archaeological and linguistic situation might suggest much earlier beginnings.

41. Eduardo Santos, presentation at Il Encontro Internacional de Arqueologia Amazônica, Manaus, Brazil, 12–17 September 2010.

42. Heckenberger 2002; Epps 2006; Walker and Ribeiro 2011; Aikhenvald 2013.

43. Heckenberger 2005, 2013.

44. Neves 2008; Heckenberger and Neves 2009.

45. Wilson 2007; Keegan 2013.

46. Keegan 2013: 378, quoting Rodriguez-Ramos.

47. Hofman et al. 2007; Keegan 2013.

48. Harlow et al. 2006. However, although the authors of this report identify Guatemala as a reasonable source, they note that as yet unknown sources in Cuba, Hispaniola, or Jamaica cannot be ruled out.

49. Maize domestication commenced from a *teosinte* background in the Balsas basin by at least 9000 years ago, according to Ranere et al. 2009; Piperno et al. 2009, 2011a; Webster 2011. Kennett et al. 2010 discuss early slash-and-burn cultivation and Benz 2006 discusses the evolution of maize in general.

50. For recent published examples, see Lesure et al. 2006; Neff et al. 2006.

51. Brown 2010b; Holman et al. 2011. Hill 2013 also reviews suggested ages and homelands for these language families. Hammond 2007 notes that villages with maize cultivation do not occur in the Yucatan Peninsula until 1000 BC. This supports the relatively late date suggested here for the initial expansion of the Mayan languages, certainly much later than for Otomanguean.

52. Some of the text in this section is modified from Bellwood 2012.

53. Merrill et al. 2009. Doubts over the linguistic argument in this article are raised by Hill 2010, Brown 2010a.

54. Romney 1957; Berry 1985.

55. Bellwood 1997.

56. Hill 2001, 2002, 2006, 2013.

57. LeBlanc 2008, 2013.

58. Bellwood 2005a: 168–74, 240–4; Bellwood 2012.

59. On these sites see Mabry 2002; Diehl 2005b; Sliva 2005; Diehl and Mabry 2006; Mabry et al. 2008:164–5; Merrill et al. 2009.

60. On these sites see Carpenter et al. 2005; Hard and Roney 2007.

61. Huckell et al. 2002; Mabry 2005; Coltrain et al. 2006; Vierra and Ford 2006. See Smith 2001 for low-level food production.

62. For example, Diehl 2005a, 2005b; Mabry 2005; Diehl and Waters 2006; Doolittle and Mabry 2006; Mabry et al. 2008; Mabry and Doolittle 2008.

63. Bellwood 2012.

64. Hill 2001, 2002, 2006, 2013.

65. Winter and Hogan 1986.

66. Matson 2002, 2007; Hill 2008; LeBlanc 2008; LeBlanc et al. 2008.

67. Snow 2013. Such groups probably included the ancestors of the Crow, Assiniboine and Teton (Siouan speakers), and the Cheyenne and Arapaho (Algonquian speakers).

68. The linguistic calculations are from Holman et al. 2011. Munson 1973 notes that Proto-Algonquian did not have terms for maize, beans or squash.

69. Fiedel 1990, 1991; Snow 2013.

70. Bellwood 2005a: 174–9, 244–51.

71. Bruce Smith 2006, 2011 has presented a number of more recent appraisals of this agricultural tradition.

72. See chapters in Staller et al. 2006; Hart et al. 2007.

73. Adair 1994; Snow 1996; O'Brien and Wood, 1998.

74. Chapdelaine 1993.

75. Hart et al. 2007.

76. Snow 1994, 1995, 2013; Fagan 2008. Martin 2008 discusses some of the archaeological complexities in interpreting Iroquoian, but does not refer to linguistic opinions.

77. Mithun 1984; Rankin 2006.

78. Holman et al. 2011 give 6000 years for Greater Siouan (with Catawba), but only 3000 years for 'Siouan proper'. Foster 1996 and Rankin 2006 suggest 3500–4000 years for Proto-Siouan.
79. Crosby 1986: 18; Diamond 1994, 1997.

Chapter 10
The Role of Migration in the History of Humanity

In this book, we have followed our ancestors, both archaic and sapient, through some very remarkable episodes of migration. Migration has been a continuous activity throughout human prehistory, but it has also been cyclical in its intensity. It has served as a distributor rather than a primary generator of human biological and cultural innovation, although there can be no doubt that any migration into a new and unfamiliar environment can alter the selective canvas within which mutation and innovation must operate. Often, we see generalized pulses or range expansions rather than actual population histories with specific details, especially in the Pleistocene, when the records are faint. During the Holocene, reconstructions can often become much sharper with the added perspective of comparative linguistics.

Successful prehistoric migrations would have required a number of important facilitating conditions. First comes opportunity through *demographic profile*; a successful migrant population must have been able to grow in numbers, although whether such growth came entirely from an increasing birth rate within or by assimilation of others from without can often be an interesting question. Obviously, growth was always from within in situations of initial colonization. Second comes opportunity through *geographical access*, usually reflecting environmental opportunity to enter a region that was previously inaccessible, whether previously occupied or not. Third comes opportunity through *technology and economy*. Early speakers of Indo-European languages would perhaps not have migrated anywhere if they were hunter-gatherers rather than Fertile Crescent farmers with a highly portable and land-hungry system of food production. Similarly, Polynesians would have gone nowhere without their boats.

To what degree was prehistoric migration a conscious process, as opposed to an unthinking reaction to some environmental imperative? In my view, the human migratory past becomes more coherent, and infinitely more interesting, if we allow our ancestors the ability to act rationally, to make decisions and choices, and to plan for the future. Human rationality can find ways around what might appear to be environmental or climatic imperatives, through the application of cultural knowledge. How far back in time we push these abilities is another matter, but they were probably present in some form two million years ago, lubricated by a rudimentary hominin language ability. We have no concrete information to the effect that we are more intelligent than our sapient ancestors at, let us say, 40,000 years ago, although the differences will surely be compounded as we go back further in time.

First Migrants: Ancient Migration in Global Perspective, First Edition. Peter Bellwood.
© Peter Bellwood. Published 2013 by John Wiley & Sons, Ltd.

In this book, therefore, I have promoted human agency rather than climatic or other environmental changes (for instance, in sea level) as the main stimulus behind any prehistoric migration. Postglacial climatic amelioration allowed food production and the migrations that resulted from it to develop, but it alone did not determine the Fertile Crescent and China as such crucial regions for early development. The crops, the animals, and their human exploiters also defined such situations, and while species distributions were climatically determined, it was not just postglacial warming that made wild wheat grow in Syria and wild rice in China. Prior long-term botanical histories also mattered.

However, I fully admit that looking for any single stimulus such as climate change or human free will to explain any situation in prehistory might be misguided. I like to think that human affairs then were just as complex in structure as human affairs today, and there are many situations in the world today that I would find very hard to understand or explain relying on just a single causal factor. Nevertheless, while simplification of complex situations can sometimes be unwarranted, simplification to some degree is necessary if one is to present a coherent account of human migration through the ages, across the whole world, without becoming buried under the minutiae, unable to see the light at the end of the tunnel.

In this book, I have tried to expose the foundations of the whole human array of biological and cultural variation, as it existed on the eve of the ancient world, the Medieval world, and the era of European colonization. I have maximized the significance of actual migrations of human populations as major creators of this array, depositing layer upon layer of human residue to build up the vast palimpsest that makes our species what it is today. Many of these layers have been almost erased, like those laid down by the Anatolian and Yeniseian language groups, or by many once-meaningful parts of the archaeological record, or in the DNA of the Neanderthals. Minor hints of such former existences survive for those of us who are willing to search hard. I have also argued strongly against ideas that relate the observed biological and cultural patterning *purely* to factors which do not involve population migration, such as gene flow, cultural diffusion or language shift, since I regard such factors as being geographically localized in their direct impacts. I certainly do not deny the significance of such reticulate processes, but I believe that a world-wide and multidisciplinary perspective is necessary if we are to understand their significances correctly.

For instance, genetic and cultural factors that have high selective value, directly related to biological fecundity or cultural efficiency (e.g., a broad pelvis, strong heterosexual inclinations, the bow and arrow, the computer), can no doubt spread from one population to another through interbreeding or communication, rather than through migration alone. But whole genomes, whole languages and whole cultures have massive *complexity*, and, more importantly from a migration perspective, massive *inertia*. Some of their component variables are able to spread independently, but the whole entities not so easily, unless the carriers of those entities choose to carry them physically via migration. The situation of cultural and genetic free-flow mixing across continents that seems to many people to characterize our world today is very much a result of cultural and especially religious freedom, technological wizardry, and mass communication. I doubt that it characterized Paleolithic or Neolithic cultures that existed at tribal rather than state levels of organization, even if some of them did invest considerable energy in trade and exchange with distant regions.

Looking at all of the data on ancient migration presented in the previous chapters, can we make any further interesting observations? The most impressive migrations in human prehistory had nothing to do with ancient states or conquering armies, but were related entirely to small tribal populations of hunters and gatherers, farmers, and fisher folk. In general, the oldest migrations appear to have gone the furthest, especially those of the Palaeolithic hunter-gatherers who discovered the previously unsettled Americas and Australia. Once the continents, apart from Antarctica, had hunter-gatherer populations in residence, then subsequent migration by further hunter-gatherers into inhabited territory was more limited in extent. The First Americans were able to migrate much further than the Na-Dene or the Eskimo-Aleuts, simply because they got there first.

During the Holocene, rapid expansion commenced again with many of the early food producing populations, such as the Indo-Europeans, Bantu and Sino-Tibetans of the Old World. These populations, by virtue of their rapid demographic growth and developing technologies, were able to penetrate vast territories formerly the preserve of hunters and gatherers. However, once these early food producer migrations reached their pre-colonial limits, in both hemispheres, the pace of migration died down. In Eurasia, most significant continental-scale migration was long over by the time of Christ, only to commence again during the colonial era after AD 1500. Even the great post-Roman migrations of Germanic and Turkic speakers led to very little population or language change, except in those few cases in which Anglo-Saxons and Vikings were able to cross sea and found thriving new settlements.

We must therefore conclude that the Palaeolithic migrations were the greatest in geographical extent. The Holocene migrations of food producers were more limited in extent than those of the first *Homo sapiens*, or even the first Eurasian hominins, even if we lump the food producer migrations all together. This is partly because very extensive regions of the earth's surface were simply impossible for the establishment of successful agriculture, whereas virtually everywhere, apart from the most hostile deserts and mountains, and the poles, could support some form of hunting and gathering. Most of these food producer migrations also occurred into regions that were already settled, hence, they faced varying degrees of resistance, as likewise did those by hunter-gatherers in similar circumstances of pre-existing settlement. Some groups of course spread much further than others, with Austronesians perhaps taking line honors because of the intervention of so much sea, not to mention the fact that all of the Pacific Islands beyond the Solomons were previously empty. Migrations into empty or relatively empty territories spread more rapidly and successfully than migrations into densely inhabited terrain, a conclusion driven home by a simple examination of the course of European colonial history since AD 1500.[1] Much always depended, of course, on the relative levels of population density and cultural complexity between indigenous and migrant groups.

Why did ancient populations commence their migrations? My instinct would be to place need for land and resources as the most common causal factor in situations of free and considered migration (not forced by war or other sources of desperation), both in the prehistoric past and in more recent history. Issues connected with land and resources would presumably also have been uppermost in the minds of those actually migrating, rather than abstract worries about climate change or trends in demographic profile, neither likely to have been obvious to prehistoric people with only rudimentary methods of recording and notation.

Why did migrations cease? Those that entered empty territory continued apace until they met environmental barriers (mountains, deserts, sea). But not even climatic limits to farming stopped all farmers from spreading onwards into lives of obligatory hunting and gathering, as in the Great Basin of North America, the South Island of New Zealand, and probably the rainforests of the deep interior of Borneo. In previously occupied landscapes, we find so often that the greatest inertia, especially in food producer migrations, was caused by admixture and assimilation. We can see this clearly when we examine biological variation across many of the Old World major language families that were spread by relatively recent population migrations in Holocene time.

For instance, northern Europeans and South Asians, who speak unequivocally-related Indo-European languages, undoubtedly owe some of their differentiating physical features to natural selection that has occurred since the original Indo-European diaspora about 8500 years ago. Such are likely to include blue eyes and light skin color in the case of northern Europeans, and darker skin color and dark eyes in the case of South Asians. After all, these features are related directly to latitudinal variations in the intensity of solar radiation, especially ultraviolet light. But it is also clear from current genetic research that much of the differentiation relates directly to a carry-over of genetic substratum from the pre-Indo-European populations of each region (Chapter 7). These pre-Indo-European populations were perhaps even more differentiated from each other, after 40,000 years of natural selection amongst their Palaeolithic and Mesolithic ancestors, than are modern northern Europeans and South Asians. As I have stressed throughout this book, migration has never been an all or nothing aspect of human behavior, with extinction the only route for the indigenous. Migration into an inhabited territory will always have involved a process of admixture. This is surely true whether we are discussing deep prehistory, or the colonial era in Australasia and the Americas.

Questions also arise concerning the sizes of ancient migrations, in terms of human population numbers. Exact figures are impossible to obtain, although relative increases in population size and density can often be plotted from the archaeological and genetic records. We must also distinguish between actual groups of migrants at any one time, as part of a single event, and the overall aggregate sizes of whole ethnolinguistic migrations, such as those of the early Bantu or Indo-Europeans from start to finish (however concepts such as 'start' and 'finish' might be defined). The early Bantu and Indo-Europeans, of course, must eventually have numbered in the tens of thousands of people, spread over huge regions and through long periods of time, involving many uncoordinated but compounded individual episodes of small group migration.

If we focus on those individual episodes of migration, then we can be fairly sure that they were originally small in population numbers in prehistoric contexts. Mass coordinated migration, such as that which led to the recent European colonizations of Australia and North America, obviously could not have occurred in prehistory. There was simply not the transport technology nor the massive bureaucracy necessary to implement such a process. However, and I believe this to be very important, while initial groups of prehistoric migrants were necessarily small, their potential for demographic growth, once they reached new and encouraging circumstances, was in many cases absolutely phenomenal. We see this in so many cases, involving both hunter-gatherers and early farmers in prehistory, as well as in many comparative historical situations, some discussed in Chapters 1 and 2.

However, lest the reader thinks that migration was the only solution to a need for land and resources in prehistory, we must not forget that many populations who felt such needs never resorted to migration at all. The alternative to a migratory solution is to intensify production, assuming one has the technological ability to engage in such a course of action. Studies of late prehistoric and ethnographic cultures in New Guinea and Oceania reveal to us quite clearly that an increasing intensity of agricultural production reduces any incentive to migrate, simply because of the increasing value of improved land and the energy invested in creating it.[2] In Chapter 8, I discussed an example of this involving early rice farmers on the fertile alluvial soils of the Yangzi Valley. Early migrant food producers were more likely to have emanated from stressed hinterland environments than core environments of plenty, often perhaps as a result of domino effects originating through the various demographic or environmental imbalances that could arise within the latter regions. This is a generalization that fits well with farmer migration out of a rather heavily exploited late Neolithic Fertile Crescent, or from the hinterland of the Yangzi and Yellow rivers down the constricted and rather barren southern coastline of China into Fujian, Guangdong and Taiwan. It is no coincidence that Fujian and Guangdong were also the main source regions for the recent historical 'Chinese diaspora', that carried so many settlers of Chinese origin into nineteenth- and twentieth-century Southeast Asia and Oceania.

Sometimes, perhaps, ancient migrants somehow beat the odds and found themselves in locations where no one could have dreamt they could go. I repeat from Chapter 9 the comment of George Catlin, concerning the Great Plains of North America in the 1830s, that groups of people could be "run off to a distant region, where they take up their residence and establish themselves as a nation." I have tended in this book to treat migrations as rational processes that reflected specific demographic, cultural, and environmental circumstances, and that traveled in likely as opposed to unlikely directions. From the viewpoint of a scientific investigator, this is undoubtedly the assumption to make, since tracing something random and inchoate in human behavior back into prehistoric time is unlikely to be a rewarding exercise. However, I will happily admit that chance must have played just as much of a role as careful planning behind the outcomes of many prehistoric migrations.

What does the future hold for migration studies in human prehistory? I suspect that developments in human genetics, both autosomal and in ancient DNA, will have a tremendous impact. So too will advances in the use of computational techniques in comparative linguistics, and in fields such as chronology, residue analysis and stable isotope analysis in archaeology and bioanthropology. But chance will always play a role in the recovery of data, given that so much has been destroyed and lost from the deep past. There will always be problems with small samples, unrepresentative samples, and sometimes misidentification. When I was writing *First Farmers*, for instance, major constructional activities in Arizona and southwestern Taiwan were bringing to light astounding remains of the activities of early farmers, revealing details of ancient life previously undreamt of. Recent excavations beneath the Bosporus in Istanbul are having a similar impact on our knowledge of many periods of the past there, including the Neolithic and the Byzantine port of Theodosius. Sadly, however, in many developing countries without strong laws to protect antiquities, similar constructional activities go unobserved by archaeologists, and archaeological records of any kind are almost nonexistent, or looted for greed and profit. The study of human prehistory should not be just a prerogative of wealthy nations, but should ideally involve the inhabitants of every country, given that the past belongs to everyone, equally. We must all share our ancestral experiences without prejudice or superiority. As members of a single species, all humans alive now are just as modern, or just as ancient, as all other humans. There are no throw-backs or remnants. All that divides us is the ceaseless current of the past.

Notes

1. Boxer 1965; Crosby 1986.
2. For excellent statements to this effect see Brown and Podolefsky 1976 for the New Guinea Highlands; Kirch 1994 for the island of Futuna in western Polynesia.

References

Abi-Rached, L., Jobin, M. et al. 2011 The shaping of modern human immune systems by multiregional admixture with archaic humans. *Science* 334:89–94.

Abondolo, D. 1998 Introduction. In D. Abondolo, ed., *The Uralic Languages*, pp. 1–42. London: Routledge.

Ackerman, R. 2007 The microblade complexes of Alaska and the Yukon. In Y. Kuzmin, S. Keates et al., eds, *Origin and Spread of Microblade Technology in Northern Asia and North America*, pp. 147–70. Burnaby: Archaeology Press.

Adachi, N., Shinoda, K. et al. 2011 Mitochondrial DNA analysis of Hokkaido Jomon skeletons. *American Journal of Physical Anthropology* 146:346–60.

Adair, M. 1994 Corn and culture history in the central Plains. In S. Johannessen and C. Hastorf, eds, *Corn and Culture in the Prehistoric New World*, pp. 315–34. Boulder: Westview.

Adelaar, K.A. 1995 Borneo as a cross-roads for comparative Austronesian linguistics. In P. Bellwood, J.J. Fox, et al., eds, *The Austronesians: Comparative and Historical Perspectives*, pp. 75–95. Canberra: Dept Anthropology, Research School of Pacific and Asian Studies, Australian National University.

Adovasio, J. and Pedler, D. 2004 Pre-Clovis sites and their implications for human occupation before the last glacial maximum. In D.B. Madsen, ed., *Entering America*, pp. 139–58. Salt Lake City: University of Utah Press.

Agusti, J. and Lordkipanidze, D. 2011 How "African" was the early human dispersal out of Africa? *Quaternary Science Reviews* 30:1338–42.

Aiello, L. 2010 Five years of *Homo floresiensis*. *American Journal of Physical Anthropology* 142, 167–79.

Aikens, C.M., Zhushchikovskaya, I. et al. 2009 Environment, ecology, and interaction in Japan, Korea, and the Russian Far East. *Asian Perspectives* 48:207–48.

First Migrants: Ancient Migration in Global Perspective, First Edition. Peter Bellwood.
© Peter Bellwood. Published 2013 by John Wiley & Sons, Ltd.

Aikhenvald, A. 1996 Areal diffusion in northwest Amazonia – the case of Tariana. *Anthropological Linguistics* 38:73–116.

Aikhenvald, A. 2001 Areal diffusion, genetic inheritance, and problems of subgrouping: a North Arawak case study. In A. Aikhenvald and R. Dixon, eds, *Areal Diffusion and Genetic Inheritance*, pp. 167–94. Oxford: Oxford University Press.

Aikhenvald, A. 2002 *Language Contact in Amazonia*. Oxford: Oxford University Press.

Aikhenvald, A. 2013 Amazonia: linguistic history. In I. Ness and P. Bellwood, eds, *Encyclopedia of Global Human Migration*. Volume 1, *Prehistory*, pp. 384–91. Malden, MA and Oxford: Wiley-Blackwell.

Ajmone-Marsan, P., Garcia, J. et al. 2010 On the origin of cattle. *Evolutionary Anthropology* 19:148–57.

Akkermans, P. and Schwartz, G. 2003 *The Archaeology of Syria*. Cambridge: Cambridge University Press.

Allaby, R., Fuller, D. et al. 2008 The genetic expectations of a protracted model for the origins of domesticated crops, *Proceedings of the National Academy of Sciences (USA)* 105:13982–86.

Allard, F. 2006 Frontiers and boundaries: the Han Empire from its southern periphery. In M. Stark, ed., *Archaeology of Asia*, pp. 233–54. Malden: Blackwell.

Allen, J., ed. 1996 *Report of the Southern Forests Archaeological Project*. Volume 1, School of Archaeology, Melbourne: La Trobe University.

Allen, N.J., Callen, C. et al., eds, 2008 *Early Human Kinship*. Oxford: Blackwell.

Ambrose, S. 1998 Chronology of the Later Stone Age and food production in East Africa. *Journal of Archaeological Science* 25:377–92.

Ambrose, S. 2001 Paleolithic technology and human evolution. *Science* 291:1748–53.

Ambrose, S. 2010 Co-evolution of composite-tool technology, constructive memory and language. *Current Anthropology* 51 (Supplement 1): S135–48.

Ammerman, A.J. and Cavalli-Sforza, L.L. 1984 *The Neolithic Transition and the Genetics of Populations in Europe*. Princeton: Princeton University Press.

Andersen, H., ed. 2003 *Language Contacts in Prehistory*. Amsterdam: Benjamins.

Anderson, D. 1990 *Lang Rongrien Rockshelter*. Philadelphia: University of Pennsylvania Museum.

Anderson, M. 2005 *Tending the Wild*. Berkeley: University of California Press.

Anderson, G., ed. 2008 *The Munda Languages*. London: Routledge.

Anderson, A. 2010 The origins and development of seafaring. In A. Anderson, J. Barrett et al., eds, *The Global Origins and Development of Seafaring*, pp. 3–18. Cambridge: McDonald Institute Monograph.

Anderson, D. and Gillam, J. 2000 Paleoindian colonization of the Americas. *American Antiquity* 65:43–66.

Anthony, D. 1990 Migration in archaeology: the baby and the bathwater. *American Anthropologist* 92:895–914.

Anthony, D. 1995 Horse, wagon and chariot: Indo-European languages and archaeology. *Antiquity* 69:554–64.

Anthony, D. 1997 Prehistoric migration as social process. In J. Chapman and H. Hamerow, eds, *Migrations and Invasions in Archaeological Explanation*, pp. 21–32. Oxford: BAR International Series 664.

Anthony, D. 2007 *The Horse, the Wheel, and Language*. Princeton: Princeton University Press.

Anthony, D., ed. 2010 *The Lost World of Old Europe*. New York: Institute for the Study of the Ancient World.

Anton, S. 2012 Early *Homo*: who, when, and where. *Current Anthropology* 53 (Supplement 6):S278-98.

Apicella, C., Marlowe, F. et al. 2012 Social networks and cooperation in hunter-gatherers. *Nature* 481:497–501.

Ardika, I. and Bellwood, P. 1991 Sembiran: the beginnings of Indian contact with Bali. *Antiquity* 247:221–32.

Argue, D., Donlon, D. et al. 2006 *Homo floresiensis*: microcephalic, pygmoid, *Australopithecus*, or *Homo? Journal of Human Evolution*, 51:360–74.

Argue, D., Morwood, M. et al. 2009 *Homo floresiensis*: a cladistic analysis. *Journal of Human Evolution* 57:623–39.

Armitage, S., Jasim, A. et al. 2011 The southern route "out of Africa". *Science* 331:453–6.

Arredi, B., Poloni, E. et al. 2004 A predominantly Neolithic origin for Y-chromosomal DNA variation in North Africa. *American Journal of Human Genetics* 75:338–45.

Arredi, B., Poloni, E. et al. 2007 The peopling of Europe. In M. Crawford, ed., *Anthropological Genetics*, pp. 380–408. Cambridge: Cambridge University Press.

Arzarello, M., Pavia, G. et al. 2012 Evidence of an Early Pleistocene hominin presence at Pirro Nord. *Quaternary International* 267:56–61.

Asouti, E. and Fuller, D. 2012 From foraging to farming in the southern Levant. *Vegetation History and Archaeobotany* 21:149–62.

Atkinson, Q. 2011 Phonemic diversity supports a serial founder effect model of language expansion from Africa. *Science* 332:346–8.

Atkinson, Q. and Gray, R. 2006 How old is the Indo-European language family? In P. Forster and C. Renfrew, eds, *Phylogenetic Methods and the Prehistory of Languages*, pp.91–110. Cambridge: McDonald Institute.

Atkinson, Q.D., Gray, R. et al. 2008 MtDNA variation predicts population size in humans and reveals a major southern chapter in human prehistory. *Molecular Biology and Evolution* 25:468–74.

Bailey, R.C., Head, G. et al. 1989 Hunting and gathering in the tropical rainforest: is it possible? *American Anthropologist* 91:59–82.

Bailey, G., Flemming, N. et al. 2007 Coastlines, submerged landscapes, and human evolution: the Red Sea Basin and the Farasan Islands. *Journal of Island and Coastal Archaeology* 2:127–60.

Balaresque, P., Bowden, G. et al. 2010 A predominantly Neolithic origin for European paternal lineages. *PloS Biology* 8 (1):e1000285.

Balloux, F, Handley, L. et al. 2009 Climate shaped the worldwide distribution of human mitochondrial DNA sequence variation. *Proceedings of the Royal Society of London, Series B* 276:3447–55.

Balme, J., Davidson, I. et al. 2009 Symbolic behaviour and the peopling of the southern arc route to Australia. *Quaternary International* 202:59–68.

Balter, M. 2007 Seeking agriculture's ancient roots. *Science* 316:1830–5.

Balter, M. 2010 Score One for hunting at Olduvai. *Science* 329:1464.

Balter, M. 2011 Was North Africa the launching pad for modern human migrations? *Science* 331:220–3.

Balter, M. 2012a The peopling of the Aleutians. *Science* 335:158–61.

Balter, M. 2012b Critics assail notion that Europeans settled Americas. *Science* 335:1289–90.

Balter, M. 2012c Ice Age tools hint at 40,000 years of Bushman culture. *Science* 337:512.

Banning, E. 2011 So fair a house. *Current Anthropology* 52:619–60.

Barber, I. 2010 A fast yam to Polynesia. *Rapa Nui Journal* 26:31–42.

Barbujani, G. and Chikhi, L. 2006 DNAs from the European Neolithic. *Heredity* 97:84–5.

Barham, L. and P. Mitchell 2008 *The First Africans*. Cambridge: Cambridge University Press.

Barker, G., Barton, H. et al. 2007 The 'human revolution' in tropical lowland Southeast Asia. *Journal of Human Evolution* 52:243–61.

Barker, G., Barton, H. et al. 2008 The Cultured Rainforest Project. *Sarawak Museum Journal* 86:121–90.

Barker, G. and Richards, M. 2012 Foraging–farming transitions in Island Southeast Asia. *Journal of Archaeological Method and Theory*. Online 6 October 2012.

Barnett, T. 1999 *The Emergence of Food Production in Ethiopia*. BAR International Series 763. Oxford: Archaeopress.

Barrett, J. 2010 Rounding up the usual suspects: causation and the Viking Age diaspora. In J. Anderson, H. Barrett et al., eds, *The Global Origins and Development of Seafaring*, pp. 289–304. Cambridge: McDonald Institute for Archaeological Research.

Bar-Yosef, O. 2011 Climatic fluctuations and early farming in west and east Asia. *Current Anthropology* 52 (Supplement 4):S175–93.

Bar-Yosef, O. 2012 From foraging to farming in Western and Eastern Asia. In P. Gepts, T.R. Famula et al., eds, *Biodiversity in Agriculture*, pp. 57–91. Cambridge: Cambridge University Press.

Bar-Yosef, O. and Bordes, J.-G. 2010 Who were the makers of the Châtelperronian culture? *Journal of Human Evolution* 59:586–93.

Bastos-Rodrigues, L., Pimenta, J. et al. 2006 The genetic structure of human populations studied through short insertion–deletion polymorphisms. *Annals of Human Genetics* 70:658–65.

Battaglia, V., Fornarino, S. et al. 2009 Y-chromosomal evidence of the cultural diffusion of agriculture in southeast Europe. *European Journal of Human Genetics* 17:820–30.

Batty, R. 2007 *Rome and the Nomads*. Oxford: Oxford University Press.

Baudouin, L. and Lebrun, P. 2009 Coconut (*Cocos nucifera* L.) DNA studies support the hypothesis of an ancient Austronesian migration from Southeast Asia to America. *Genetic Resources and Crop Evolution* 56:257–62.

Beck, C. and Jones, G. 2010 Clovis and Western Stemmed. *American Antiquity* 75:81–116.

Bednarik, R. 2008 The mythical moderns. *Journal of World Prehistory* 21:85–102.

Beekes, R. 1995 *Comparative Indo-European Linguistics*. Amsterdam: Benjamins.

Behar, D., Villems, R. et al. 2008 The dawn of human matrilineal diversity. *American Journal of Human Genetics* 82:1130–40.

Beleza, S., Gusmao, L. et al. 2005 The genetic legacy of western Bantu migrations. *Human Genetics* 117:366–75.

Belle, E., Landry, P. et al. 2006 Origins and evolution of the Europeans' genome: evidence from multiple microsatellite loci. *Proceedings of the Royal Society of London, Series B* 273:1595–602.

Bellwood, P. 1996a Hierarchy, founder ideology and Austronesian expansion. In J. Fox and C. Sather, eds, *Origin, Ancestry and Alliance*, pp. 18-40. Canberra: Department of Anthropology, Comparative Austronesian Project, ANU.

Bellwood, P. 1996b Phylogeny and reticulation in prehistory. *Antiquity* 70:881–90.

Bellwood, P. 1997 Prehistoric cultural explanations for widespread language families. In P. McConvell and N. Evans, eds, *Archaeology and Linguistics*, pp. 123-34. Oxford: Oxford University Press.

Bellwood, P. 2000 Some thoughts on understanding the human colonization of the Pacific. *People and Culture in Oceania* 16:5–17.

Bellwood, P. 2001 Early agriculturalist population diasporas? Farming, languages and genes. *Annual Review of Anthropology* 30:181–207.

Bellwood, P. 2004 Response to "The origins of Afroasiatic". *Science* 306:1681.

Bellwood, P. 2005a *First Farmers*. Oxford and Malden, MA: Blackwell.

Bellwood, P. 2005b Examining the language/farming dispersal hypothesis in the East Asian context. In L. Sagart, R. Blench et al., eds, *The Peopling of East Asia*, pp. 17–30. London: RoutledgeCurzon.

Bellwood, P. 2006 Asian farming diasporas? Agriculture, languages, and genes in China and Southeast Asia. In M.T. Stark, ed., *Archaeology of Asia*, pp. 96–118. Malden: Blackwell

Bellwood, P. 2007a *Prehistory of the Indo-Malaysian Archipelago*. 2nd edition. Canberra: ANU E Press.

Bellwood, P. 2007b Southeast China and the prehistory of the Austronesians. In Tianlong Jiao, ed., *Lost Maritime Cultures: China and the Pacific*, pp. 36–53. Honolulu: Bishop Museum Press.

Bellwood, P. 2007–2008 Understanding the Neolithic in northern India. *Pragdhara: Journal of the Uttar Pradesh State Archaeology Department, India* 18:331–46.

Bellwood, P. 2008 Archaeology and the origins of language families. In A. Bentley, H. Maschner et al.eds, *Handbook of Archaeological Theories*, pp. 225–43. Lanham: Altamira.

Bellwood, P. 2009a The dispersals of established food-producing populations. *Current Anthropology* 50:621–6.

Bellwood, P. 2009b Early farmers: issues of spread and migration with respect to the Indian Subcontinent. In T. Osada, ed., *Linguistics, Archaeology and Human Past in South Asia*, pp. 55–69. New Delhi: Manohar.

Bellwood, P. 2011a Holocene population history in the Pacific region as a model for world-wide food producer dispersals. *Current Anthropology* 52(S4):363–78.

Bellwood, P. 2011b The checkered prehistory of rice movement southwards as a domesticated cereal – from the Yangzi to the Equator. *Rice* 4:93–103.

Bellwood, P. 2012 How and why did agriculture spread? In P. Gepts, T.R. Famula et al., eds, *Biodiversity in Agriculture: Domestication, Evolution, and Sustainability*, pp. 160–89. Cambridge: Cambridge University Press.

Bellwood, P. 2013 Southeast Asian islands: archaeology. In I. Ness and P. Bellwood *Encyclopedia of Global Human Migration*. Volume 1, *Prehistory*, pp. 284–92. Malden, MA and Oxford: Wiley-Blackwell.

Bellwood, P. and Dizon, E. 2005 The Batanes Archaeological Project and the "Out Of Taiwan" hypothesis for Austronesian dispersal. *Journal of Austronesian Studies* (Taitung, Taiwan) 1:1–33.

Bellwood, P. and Dizon, E. 2008 Austronesian cultural origins: out of Taiwan, via the Batanes Islands, and onwards to western Polynesia. In A. Sanchez-Mazas, R. Blench et al., eds, *Past Human Migrations in East Asia*, pp. 23–39. London: Routledge.

Bellwood, P. and Hiscock, P. 2013 Holocene Australia and the Pacific Basin. In Scarre, ed., *The Human Past*, pp. 264–305. London: Thames and Hudson.

Bellwood, P. and Oxenham, M. 2008 The expansions of farming societies and the role of the Neolithic Demographic Transition. In J-P. Bocquet-Appel and O. Bar-Yosef, eds, *The Neolithic Demographic Transition and its Consequences*, pp. 13–34. Dordrecht: Springer.

Bellwood, P., Nitihaminoto, G. et al. 1998 35,000 years of prehistory in the northern Moluccas. In G-J. Bartstra, ed., *Bird's Head Approaches*, pp. 233–75. *Modern Quaternary Research in Southeast Asia* 15. Rotterdam: Balkema.

Bellwood, P., Oxenham, M. et al. 2011a. An Son and the Neolithic of southern Vietnam. *Asian Perspectives* 50:144–74.

Bellwood, P., Chambers, G. et al. 2011b Are "cultures" inherited? Multidisciplinary perspectives on the origins and migrations of Austronesian-speaking peoples prior to 1000 BC. In B. Roberts and M. Van der Linden, eds, *Investigating Archaeological Cultures: Material Culture, Variability and Transmission*, pp. 321–54. Dordrecht: Springer.

Benazzi, S., Douka, K. et al. 2011 Early dispersal of modern humans in Europe and implications for Neanderthal behaviour. *Nature* 479:525–8.

Benecke, N. 2006 Animal husbandry and hunting in the Early Neolithic of southeast Europe. In I. Gatsov and H. Schwartzenberg, eds, *Aegean-Marmara-Black Sea*, pp. 175–86. Langenweissbach: Beier and Beran.

Benz, B. 2006 Maize in the Americas. In Staller, Tykot, R. et al., eds, *Histories of Maize*, pp. 9–21. Amsterdam: Elsevier.

Beresford-Jones, D. and Heggarty, P. 2013 Andes: archaeology. In I. Ness and P. Bellwood, eds, *Encyclopedia of Global Human Migration*. Volume 1, *Prehistory*, pp. 410–6. Malden, MA and Oxford: Wiley-Blackwell.

Bermudez De Castro J., Martinon-Torres, M. et al. 2010 New human evidence of the Early Pleistocene settlement of Europe from Sima del Elefante site. *Quaternary International* 223–4:431–3.

Berna, F., Goldberg, P. et al. 2012 Microstratigraphic evidence of in situ fire in the Acheulian strata of Wonderwork Cave, northern Cape province, South Africa. *Proceedings of the National Academy of Sciences (USA)* 109:E1215-E1220.

Berry, M. 1985 The age of maize in the Greater Southwest. In R. Ford, ed., *Prehistoric Food Production in North America*, pp. 279–308. Anthropological Papers 75. University of Michigan: Museum of Anthropology.

Bettinger, R., Barton, L. et al. 2010 The origins of food production in north China. *Evolutionary Anthropology* 19:9–21.

Billington, R.A. 1967 *Westward Expansion*. (3rd edition). New York: Macmillan.

Bird, M., Taylor, D., et al. 2005 Palaeoenvironments of insular Southeast Asia during the Last Glacial Period: a savanna corridor in Sundaland? *Quaternary Science Reviews* 24:2228–42.

Birdsell, J. 1957 Some population problems involving Pleistocene man. *Cold Spring Harbour Symposia on Quantitative Biology* 22:47–69.

Birdsell, J. 1967 Preliminary data on the trihybrid origin of the Australian Aborigines. *Archaeology and Physical Anthropology in Oceania* 2:100–55.

Birdsell, J. 1977 The recalibration of a paradigm for the first peopling of Greater Australia. In J. Allen, J. Golson, et al, eds, *Sunda and Sahul: Prehistoric Studies in Southeast Asia, Melanesia and Australia*, pp. 113–67. London: Academic Press.

Blainey, G. 1966 *The Tyranny of Distance*. Melbourne: Sun.

Blažek, V. 2013a Levant and North Africa: Afroasiatic linguistic history. In I. Ness and P. Bellwood, eds, *Encyclopedia of Global Human Migration*. Volume 1, *Prehistory*, pp. 125–32. Malden, MA and Oxford: Wiley-Blackwell.

Blažek, V. 2013b Northern Europe and Russia: Uralic linguistic history. In I. Ness and P. Bellwood, eds, *Encyclopedia of Global Human Migration*. Volume 1, *Prehistory*, pp. 178–83. Malden, MA and Oxford: Wiley-Blackwell.

Blažek, V. n.d. Burushaski-Yeniseian: glottochronological dating of their divergence (unpublished ms).

Blažek, V. and Hegedüs, I. n.d. On the position of Nuristani within Indo-Iranian (unpublished ms).

Blažek, V. and Schwartz, M. 2008 Tocharians. *Lingua Posnaniensis* 50:47–74.

Blench, R. 2006 *Archaeology, Linguistics and the Afrian Past*. Lanham: Altamira.

Blench, R. 2010 Was there an Austroasiatic presence in Island Southeast Asia prior to the Austronesian expansion? *Bulletin of the Indo-Pacific Prehistory Association* 30:133–44.

Blum, M. and Jakobsson, M. 2011 Deep divergences of human gene trees and models of human origins. *Molecular Biology and Evolution* 28:889–98.

Blust, R. 1991 Sound change and migration distance. In R. Blust, ed., *Currents in Pacific Linguistics*, pp. 27–42. Series C-117. Canberra: Pacific Linguistics.

Blust, R. 1993 Central and Central-Eastern Malayo-Polynesian. *Oceanic Linguistics* 32:241–93.

Blust, R. 1995 The prehistory of the Austronesian-speaking peoples: a view from language. *Journal of World Prehistory* 9:453–510.

Blust, R. 2000a Chamorro historical phonology. *Oceanic Linguistics* 39:83–122.

Blust, R. 2000b Why lexicostatistics doesn't work. In C. Renfrew, A. McMahon et al.eds, *Time Depth in Historical Linguistics*, pp. 311–32. Cambridge: McDonald Institute for Archaeological Research.

Blust, R. 2009 *The Austronesian Languages*. Canberra: Pacific Linguistics.

Blust, R. 2013 Southeast Asian islands and Oceania: Austronesian linguistic history. In I. Ness and P. Bellwood, eds, *Encyclopedia of Global Human Migration*. Volume 1, *Prehistory*, pp. 276–83. Malden, MA and Oxford: Wiley-Blackwell.

Bocquet-Appel, J-P. 2011 When the world's population took off: the springboard of the Neolithic Demographic Transition. *Science* 333:560–1.

Bocquet-Appel, J-P. and Naji, S. 2006 Testing the hypothesis of a worldwide Neolithic demographic transition: corroboration from American cemeteries. *Current Anthropology* 47:341–65.

Bogaard, A. 2004 *Neolithic Farming in Central Europe*. London: Routledge.

Bogaard, A., Krause, R. et al. 2011 Towards a social geography of cultivation and plant use in an early farming community. *Antiquity* 85:395–416.

Bogucki, P. 2003 Neolithic dispersals in Neolithic riverine interior central Europe. In A. Ammerman and P. Biagi, eds, *The Widening Harvest*, pp. 249–72. Boston: Archaeological Institute of America.

Boivin, N., Fuller, D. et al. 2013 Human disperal across diverse environments of Asia during the Upper Pleistocene. *Quaternary International,* advance online January 2013.

Bolus, M. 2011 The late Middle Paleolithic and the Aurignacian of the Swabian Jura, southwestern Germany. In A. Derevianko and M. Shunkov, eds, *Characteristic Features of the Middle to Upper Paleolithic Transition in Eurasia*, pp. 1–10. Novosibirsk: Institute of Archaeology and Ethnography, Russian Academy of Sciences.

Boroffka, N. 2010 Archaeology and its relevance to climate and water level changes: a review. In A. Kostianoy and A. Kosarev, eds, *The Aral Sea Environment*, pp. 283–303. Hamburg: Springer.

Bouckaert, R., Lemey, P. et al. 2012 Mapping the origins and expansion of the Indo-European language family. *Science* 337:957–60.

Boulestin, B., Zeeb-Lanz, A. et al. 2009 Mass cannibalism in the Linear Pottery culture at Herxheim. *Antiquity* 83:968–82.

Bowern, C. and Atkinson, Q. 2012 Computational phylogenetics and the internal structure of Pama-Nyungan. *Language* 88:817–45.

Bowern, C. and Koch, H., eds, 2004 *Australian Languages*. Amsterdam: Benjamins.

Bowler, J., Johnston, H. et al. 2003 New ages for human occupation and climatic change at Lake Mungo, Australia. *Nature* 421:837–40.

Boxer, C.R. 1965 *The Dutch Seaborne Empire 1600–1800*. London: Hutchinson.

Brace, C., Seguchi, N. et al. 2006 The questionable contribution of the Neolithic and the Bronze Age to European craniofacial form. *Proceedings of the National Academy of Sciences (USA)* 103:242–7.

Bradley, D. 2011 Proto-Tibeto-Burman grain crops. *Rice* 4:134–41.

Bradley, D. and Loftus, R. 2000 Two eves for *Taurus*? Bovine mitochondrial DNA and African cattle domestication. In Blench, R. and MacDonald, K., eds, *The Origins and Development of African Livestock*, pp. 244–50. London: UCL Press.

Bramanti, B., Thomas, M. et al. 2009 Genetic discontinuity between local hunter–gatherers and central Europe's first farmers. *Science* 326:137–40.

Brantingham, P.J., Kerry, K. et al. 2004 Time-space dynamics in the early Upper Paleolithic of Northeast Asia. In D.B. Madsen, ed., *Entering America*, pp. 255–84. Salt Lake City: University of Utah Press.

Brantingham, P.J., Rhode, D. et al. 2010 Archaeology augments Tibet's genetic history. *Science* 329:1467.

Brennan, P. 1990 A Rome away from Rome. In J-P. Descoudres, ed., *Greek Colonists and Native Populations*, pp. 491–502. Oxford: Clarendon.

Breunig, P. and Neumann, A. 2002 From hunters and gatherers to food producers. In F. Hassan, ed., *Droughts, Food and Culture*, pp. 123–56. New York: Kluwer.

Brigham-Grette, J., Lozhkin, A. et al. 2004 Paleoenvironmental conditions in western Beringia before and during the last glacial maximum. In D.B. Madsen, ed., *Entering America*, pp. 29–62. Salt Lake City: University of Utah Press.

Broecker, W. 2000 Abrupt climate change. *Earth Science Reviews* 51:137–54.

Broodbank, C. and Strasser, T.F. 1991 Migrant farmers and the Neolithic colonization of Crete. *Antiquity* 65:233–45.

Brooks, N., Clarke, J. et al., 2009 The archaeology of Western Sahara. *Antiquity* 83:918–34.

Brosius, P. 1991 Foraging in tropical rainforests: the case of the Penan of Sarawak, East Malaysia. *Human Ecology* 19:123–50.

Browman, D., Fritz, G. et al. 2013 Origins of food producing economies in the Americas. In Scarre, ed., *The Human Past*, pp. 306–49. London: Thames and Hudson.

Brown, P. 1999 The first modern East Asians? In K. Omoto, ed., *Interdisciplinary Perspectives on the Origins of the Japanese*, pp. 105–26. Kyoto: International Research Center for Japanese Studies.

Brown, A. 2007 Dating the onset of cereal cultivation in Britain and Ireland. *Antiquity* 81: 1042–52.

Brown, C. 2010a Lack of linguistic support for Proto-Uto-Aztecan at 8900 BP. *Proceedings of the National Academy of Sciences (USA)* 107: E34.

Brown, C. 2010b Development of agriculture in prehistoric Mesoamerica: the linguistic evidence. In J. Staller and M. Carrasco, eds, *Pre-Columbian Foodways*, pp. 71–107. New York: Springer.

Brown, P. 2013. Of humans, dogs and tiny tools. *Nature* 494:316–7.

Brown, P. and Podolefsky, A. 1976 Population density, agricultural intensity, land tenure and group size in the New Guinea Highlands. *Ethnology* 15:211–38.

Brown, K., Marean, C. et al. 2012. An early and enduring advanced technology originating 71,000 years ago in South Africa. *Nature* 491:590–3.

Brumm, A. and Moore, M. 2012 Biface distributions and the Movius Line. *Australian Archaeology* 74:32–46.

Brumm, A., Jensen, G. et al. 2010 Hominins on Flores, Indonesia, by one million years ago. *Nature* 464:748–53.

Buck, C. and Bard, E. 2007 A calendar chronology for Pleistocene mammoth and horse extinction in North America. *Quaternary Science Reviews* 26:2031–5.

Buck, T. and Vidarsdottir, U. 2012 Craniofacial evolution in Polynesia: a geometric morphometric study of population diversity. *American Journal of Human Biology* 24:776–85.

Bulbeck, D., Raghavan, P. et al. 2006 Races of *Homo sapiens*: if not in the southwest Pacific, then nowhere. *World Archaeology* 38:109–32.

Burger, J. and Thomas, M. 2011 The palaeopopulation genetics of humans, cattle and dairying in Neolithic Europe. In R. Pinhasi and J. Stock, eds, *Human Bioarchaeology at the Transition to Agriculture*, pp. 371–84. Chichester: Wiley-Blackwell.

Burley, D. and Dickinson, W. 2010 Among Polynesia's first pots. *Journal of Archaeological Science* 37:1020–26.

Burney, D., Burney, L. et al. 2003 A chronology for late prehistoric Madagascar. *Journal of Human Evolution* 47:25–63.

Busby, G., Brisighelli, F. et al. 2012 The peopling of Europe and the cautionary tale of Y chromosome lineage R-M269. *Proceedings of the Royal Society of London, Series B* 279:884–92.

Butlin, N. 1993 *Economics and the Dreamtime*. Cambridge: Cambridge University Press.

Byrd, B. 2005 Reassessing the emergence of village life in the Near East. *Journal of Archaeological Research* 13:231–90.

Cabana, G. and Clark, J., eds, 2011 *Rethinking Anthropological Perspectives on Migration*. Gainesville: University Press of Florida.

Callaghan, R. 2001 Ceramic age seafaring and interaction potential in the Antilles. *Current Anthropology* 42:308–13.

Callaway, E. 2012 Date with history. *Nature* 485:27–9.

Cameron, D. and Groves, C. 2004 *Bones, Stone and Molecules*. Burlington: Elsevier.

Campbell, M. and Tishkoff, S. 2010 The evolution of human genetic and phenotypic variation in Africa. *Current Biology* 20:R166-73.

Cann, R., Stoneking, M. et al. 1987 Mitochondrial DNA and human evolution. *Nature* 325: 31–6.

Cannon, C., Morley, R. et al. 2009 The current refugial rainforests of Sundaland are unrepresentative of their biogeographic past and highly vulnerable to disturbance. *Proceedings of the National Academy of Sciences (USA)* 106:11188–93.

Caramelli, D., Milani, L. et al. 2008 A 28,000 years old Cro-Magnon mtDNA sequence differs from all potentially contaminating modern sequences. *PloS ONE* 3(7):e2700.

Carbonell, E., Bermudez de Castro, J. et al. 2008 The first hominin of Europe. *Nature* 452:465–9.

Carbonell, E., Sala Ramos, R. et al. 2010a Early hominid dispersals: a techbnological hypothesis for "out of Africa." *Quaternary International* 223–4:36–44.

Carbonell, E., Caceres, I. et al. 2010b Cultural cannibalism as a paleoeconomic system in the European Lower Pleistocene. *Current Anthropology* 51:539–49.

Cardona G. and Jain D., eds, 2003 *The Indo-Aryan languages*. London: Routledge.

Caron, F., d'Errico, F. et al. 2011 The reality of Neanderthal symbolic behavior at the Grotte du Renne. *PloS ONE* 6(6):e21545.

Carpenter, J., Sanchez, G. et al. 2005 The Late Archaic/Early Agricultural period in Sonora, Mexico. In B. Vierra, ed., *The Late Archaic across the Borderlands*, pp. 13–40. Austin: University of Texas Press.

Carson, M. 2011 Palaeohabitat of first settlement sites 1500–1000 BC in Guam, Mariana Islands. *Journal of Archaeological Science* 38:2207–21.

Carson, M. 2012 Recent developments in prehistory. Perspectives on settlement chronology, inter-community relations and identity formation. In R. Feinberg and R. Scaglion, eds, *The Polynesian Outliers: State of the Art*, pp. 27–48. Pittsburgh: Ethnology Monograph 21.

Carson, M. 2013 Micronesia: archaeology. In I. Ness and P. Bellwood, eds, *Encyclopedia of Global Human Migration*. Volume 1, *Prehistory*, pp. 314–9. Malden, MA and Oxford: Wiley-Blackwell.

Carson, M., Hung, H-c. et al. 2013 The pottery trail from Southeast Asia to Remote Oceania. *Journal of Island and Coastal Archaeology* 8:17–36.

Castañeda, I.S., Mulitza, S. et al. 2009 Wet phases in the Sahara/Sahel region and human migration patterns in North Africa. *Proceedings of the National Academy of Sciences (USA)* 106:20159–63.

Castillo, C. 2011 Rice in Thailand: the archaeobotanical contribution. *Rice* 4:114–20.

Čašule, I. 2010 *Burushaski as an Indo-European "Kentum" Language*. Munich: LINCOM.

Catlin, G. 2004 *North American Indians*. New York: Penguin.

Cavalli-Sforza, L.L. 2002 Demic diffusion as the basic process of human expansions. In P. Bellwood and C. Renfrew, eds, *Examining the Farming/Language Dispersal Hypothesis*, pp. 79–88. Cambridge: McDonald Institute.

Chagnon, A. 1992 *Yanomamö*. Fort Worth: Harcourt Brace Jovanovich.

Chang, K.C. 1983 *Art, Myth, and Ritual: the Path to Political Authority in Ancient China*. Cambridge, MA: Harvard University Press.

Chapdelaine, J. 1993 The sedentarization of the prehistoric Iroquoians: a slow or rapid transformation? *Journal of Anthropological Archaeology* 12:173–209.

Charles, M. 2007 East of Eden? A consideration of Neolithic crop spectra in the eastern Fertile Crescent and beyond. In S. Colledge and J. Conolly, eds, *The Origins and Spread of Domestic Plants in Southwest Asia and Europe*, pp. 37–52. Walnut Creek: West Coast Press.

Chauhan, P. 2009 Early *Homo* occupation near the *Gate of Tears*. In E. Hovers and D. Braun, eds, *Interdisciplinary Approaches to the Oldowan*, pp 49–61. Dordrecht: Springer.

Chen, Z., Wang, Z. et al. 2005 Holocene climatic fluctuations in the Yangtze delta of eastern China and the Neolithic response. *The Holocene* 15:915–24.

Chiaroni, J., King, R. et al. 2008 Correlation of annual precipitation with human Y-chromosomal diversity. *Antiquity* 82:281–9.

Chikhi, L., Nichols, R. et al. 2002 Y genetic data support the Neolithic demic diffusion model. *Proceedings of the National Academy of Sciences (USA)* 99:11008–13.

Childe, V.G. 1936 *Man Makes Himself*. London: Watts.

Childe, V.G. 1948 *What Happened in History*. Harmondsworth: Penguin.

Ciochon, R. 2009 The mystery ape of Pleistocene Asia. *Nature* 459:910–1.

Clackson, J. 2000 Time depth in Indo-European. In C. Renfrew and A. McMahon, eds, *Time Depth in Historical Linguistics*, pp. 441–54. Cambridge: McDonald Institute for Archaeological Research.

Clark, J.D., Beyene, Y. et al. 2003 Stratigraphic, chronological and behavioural aspects of Pleistocene *Homo sapiens* from Middle Awash, Ethiopia. *Nature* 423:747–52.

Clarke, D. 1968 *Analytical Archaeology*. London: Methuen.

Clarkson, C. 2007 *Lithics in the Land of the Lightning Brothers*. Canberra: ANU E Press.

Clarkson, C., Petraglia, M. et al. 2009 The oldest and longest enduring microlithic sequence in India. *Antiquity* 83:326–48.

Clarkson, C., Jones, S. et al. 2012 Continuity and change in the lithic industries of the Jurreru Valley, India, before and after the Toba eruption. *Quaternary International* 258:165–79.

Clendon, M. 2006 Reassessing Australia's linguistic prehistory. *Current Anthropology* 47:39–61.

Coe, M., Snow, D. et al. 1986 *Atlas of Ancient America*. New York: Facts on File.

Cohen, M. 1977 Population pressure and the origins of agriculture: an archaeological example from the coast of Peru. In C.A. Reed, ed., *Origins of Agriculture*, pp. 135–78. The Hague: Mouton.

Cohen, D. 2011 The beginnings of agriculture in China: a multiregional view. *Current Anthropology* 52 (Supplement 4):S273–95.

Cohen, M. and Armelagos, G., eds, 1980 *Paleopathology at the Origins of Agriculture*. Orlando: Academic.

Collard, M., Edinborough, S. et al. 2010 Radiocarbon evidence indicates that migrants introduced farming to Britain. *Journal of Archaeological Science* 37:866–70.

Colledge, S. and Conolly, J. 2007 A review and synthesis of the evidence for the origins of farming on Cyprus and Crete. In S. Colledge and J. Conolly, eds, *The Origins and Spread of Domestic Plants in Southwest Asia and Europe*, pp. 53–74. Walnut Creek: West Coast Press.

Collins, M. and Lohse, J. 2004 The nature of Clovis blades and blade cores. In D.B. Madsen, ed., *Entering America*, pp. 159–87. Salt Lake City: University of Utah Press.

Collis, J. 2003 *The Celts: Origins, Myths, Inventions*. Stroud: Tempus.

Coltrain, J., Janetski, J. et al. 2006 The stable and radio-isotope chemistry of Eastern Basketmaker and Pueblo groups. In J. Staller, Tykot, R. et al., eds, *Histories of Maize*, pp. 276–289. Amsterdam: Elsevier.

Comrie, B. 2002 Farming dispersal in Europe and the spread of the Indo-European language family. In P. Bellwood and C. Renfrew, eds, *Examining the Farming/Language Dispersal Hypothesis*, pp. 409-20. Cambridge: McDonald Institute.

Conneller, C., Milner, N. et al. 2013 Substantial settlement in the European early Mesolithic. *Antiquity* 86:1004–20.

Cooper, Z. 1985 Archaeological explorations in the Andaman Islands. *Bulletin of the Indo-Pacific Prehistory Association* 6:27–39.

Copley, M., Berstan, R. et al. 2005 Processing of milk products in pottery vessels through British prehistory. *Antiquity* 79:895–908.

Coppens, Y. 1994 East Side Story: the origin of humankind. *Scientific American* 270(5):62–9.

Cordain, I., Hickey, M. et al. 2012 Malaria and rickets represent selective forces for the convergent evolutionof adult lactase persistence. In P. Gepts, T.R. Famula et al., eds, *Biodiversity in Agriculture*, pp. 299–309. Cambridge: Cambridge University Press.

Cordaux, R., Deepa, E. et al. 2004a Genetic evidence for the demic diffusion of agriculture to India. *Science* 304:1125.

Cordaux, R., Aunger, R. et al. 2004b Independent origins of Indian caste and tribal paternal lineages. *Current Biology* 14:231–5.

Cordaux, R., Weiss, G. et al. 2004c The Northeast Indian passageway: a barrier or corridor for human migrations? *Molecular Biology and Evolution* 21:1525–33.

Costantini, L. 2007–2008 The first farmers in western Pakistan. *Pragdahara* 18:167–78. Lucknow.

Coudart, A. 2009 La maison néolithique. In J-P. Demoule, ed., *La révolution néolithique dans le monde*, pp. 215–38. Paris: CNRS.

Coward, F., Shennan S. et al. 2008 The spread of Neolithic plant economies from the Near East to northwest Europe: a phylogenetic analysis. *Journal of Archaeological Science* 35:42–56.

Cox, B. 1975 The placenames of the earliest English records. *Journal of the English Place-name Society* 8:12–66.

Cox, M. 2005 Indonesian mitochondrial DNA and its opposition to a Pleistocene era origin of Proto-Polynesians in Island Southeast Asia. *Human Biology* 77:179–88.

Cox, M. 2013 Southeast Asian islands and Oceania: human genetics. In I. Ness and P. Bellwood, eds, *Encyclopedia of Global Human Migration*. Volume 1, *Prehistory*, pp. 293–301. Malden, MA and Oxford: Wiley-Blackwell.

Cox, M. and Hammer, M. 2010 A question of scale: human migrations writ large and small. *BMC Biology* 8:98.

Cox, M., Karafet, T. et al. 2010 Autosomal and X-linked SNPs reveal a sharp transition from Asian to Melanesian ancestry in Eastern Indonesia and a female bias in admixture rates. *Proceedings of the Royal Society of London, Series B* 277:1589–96.

Cox, M., Nelson, M. et al. 2012 A small cohort of Island Southeast Asian women founded Madagascar. *Proceedings of the Royal Society of London, Series B* 279:2761–68.

Craig, O., Steele, V. et al. 2011 Ancient lipids reveal continuity in culinary practices across the transition to agriculture in northern Europe. *Proceedings of the National Academy of Sciences (USA)* 108:17910–15.

Cramon-Taubadel, N. and Pinhasi, R. 2011 Craniometric data support a mosaic model of demic and cultural Neolithic diffusion to outlying regions of Europe. *Proceedings of the Royal Society of London, Series B* 278:2874–80.

Crawford, G. 2011 Advances in understanding early agriculture in Japan. *Current Anthropology* 52 (Supplement 4): S331–46.

Crosby, A.W. 1986 *Ecological Imperialism*. Cambridge: Cambridge University Press.

Cunliffe, B. 2008 *Europe between the Oceans*. New Haven: Yale University Press.

Curnoe, D., Ji, X. et al. 2012 Human remains from the Pleistocene-Holocene transition of southwest China suggest a complex evolutionary history for East Asians. *PloS One* 7(3):e31918.

Currie, T. and Mace, R. 2009 Political complexity predicts the spread of ethnolinguistic groups. *Proceedings of the National Academy of Sciences (USA)* 106:7339–44.

D'Alpoim-Guedes, J. 2011 Millets, rice, social complexity, and the spread of agriculture to the Chengdu Plain. *Rice* 4:104–13.

Dark, K. 2002 *Britain and the End of the Roman Empire*. Stroud: Tempus.

Dark, P. and Gent, H. 2001 Pests and diseases of prehistoric crops: a yield 'honeymoon' for early grain crops in Europe? *Oxford Journal of Archaeology* 20:59–78.

David, B. and Lourandos, H. 1997 37,000 years and more in tropical Australia. *Proceedings of the Prehistoric Society* 63:1–23.

David, N., Sterner, J. et al. 1988 Why pots are decorated. *Current Anthropology* 29:365–89.

Davidson, I. 2010 The colonization of Australia and its adjacent islands and the evolution of modern cognition. *Current Anthropology* 51 (Supplement 1):S177–90.

Davidson, J. and Leach, B.F. 2001 The Strandlooper concept and economic naivety. In G. Clark, A. Anderson et al., eds, *The Archaeology of Lapita Dispersal in Oceania*, pp. 115–24. Canberra: Terra Australis.

De Azevedo, S., Nocera, A. et al. 2011 Evaluating microevolutionary models for the early settlement of the New World. *American Journal of Physical Anthropology* 146:539–62.

De Knijf, P. 2010 Population genetics and the migration of modern humans. In J. Lucassen, L. Lucassen et al.eds, *Migration History in World History*, pp. 39–58. Leiden: Brill.

Decsy, G. 1990 *The Uralic Protolanguage*. Bloomington: Eurolingua.

Dediu, D. and Levinson, S. 2012 Abstract profiles of structural stability point to universl tendencies, family-specific factors, and ancient connections between languages. *PLoS ONE* 7(9):e45198.

Deguilloux, M-F., Soler, L. et al. 2011 News from the west: ancient DNA from a French megalithic burial chamber. *American Journal of Physical Anthropology* 144:108–18.

Deguilloux, M-F., Leahy, R. et al. 2012a European Neolithization and ancient DNA: an assessment. *Evolutionary Anthropology* 21:24–37.

Deguilloux, M-F., Pemonga, M-H. et al. 2012b Human ancient and extant mtDNA from the Gambier Islands. *American Journal of Physical Anthropology* 144:248–57.

Delfin, F., Salvador, J. et al. 2011 The Y-chromosome landscape of the Philippines. *European Journal of Human Genetics* 19:224–30.

Demay, C., Pean. S. et al. 2012 Mammoths used as food and building resources by Neanderthals. *Quaternary International* 276–277:212–26.

DeMenocal, P. 2011 Climate and human evolution. *Science* 331:540–2.

Demeter, F., Shackleford, L. et al. 2012 Anatomically modern human in Southeast Asia (Laos) by 46 ka. *Proceedings of the National Academy of Sciences (USA)* 109:14375–80.

Denbow, J. 2012 Pride, prejudice, plunder and preservation. *Antiquity* 86:383–408.

Denevan, W.M. 1992 The pristine myth: the landscapes of the Americas in 1492. *Annals of the Association of American Geographers* 82:369–85.

Denham, T. 2005 Agricultural origins and the emergence of rectilinear ditch networks in the highlands of New Guinea. In A. Pawley, R. Attenborough et al.eds, *Papuan Pasts*, pp. 329–62. Canberra: Pacific Linguistics.

Denham, T. 2011 Early agriculture and plant domestication in New Guinea and Island Southeast Asia. *Current Anthropology* 52 (Supplement 4): S379–96.

Denham, T., Fullagar, R. et al. 2009 Plant exploitation on Sahul. *Quaternary International* 202:29–40.

Dennell, R. 2009 *The Paleolithic Settlement of Eurasia*. Cambridge: Cambridge University Press.

Dennell, R. and Roebroeks, W. 2005 An Asian perspective on early human dispersal from Africa. *Nature* 438:1099–104.

Dennell, R., Martinon-Torres, M. et al. 2011 Hominin variability, climatic instability and population demography in Middle Pleistocene Europe. *Quaternary Science Reviews* 30:1511–24.

Derevianko, A. 2005 The earliest human migrations in Eurasia and the origin of the Upper Paleolithic. In Derevianko, A., ed., *The Middle to Upper Paleolithic Transition in Eurasia*, pp. 5–19. Novosibirsk: Institute of Archaeology and Ethnography.

Derevianko, A. and Shunkov, M. 2005 Formation of the Upper Paleolithic traditions in the Altai. In Derevianko, A., ed., *The Middle to Upper Paleolithic Transition in Eurasia*, pp. 283–311. Novosibirsk: Institute of Archaeology and Ethnography.

Derevianko, A. and Shunkov, M. 2011 Anthropogenesis and colonization of Eurasia by archaic populations. In A. Derevianko and M. Shunkov, eds, *Characteristic Features of the Middle to Upper Paleolithic Transition in Eurasia*, pp. 50–74. Novosibirsk: Institute of Archaeology and Ethnography.

Dergachev, V. 1989 Neolithic and Bronze Age cultural communities of the steppe zone of the USSR. *Antiquity* 63:793–802.

Derricourt, R. 2005 Getting "Out of Africa": sea crossings, land crossings and culture in the hominin migrations. *Journal of World Prehistory* 19:119–32.

Détroit, F. 2006 *Homo sapiens* in Southeast Asian archipelagos. In T. Simanjuntak, ed., *Austronesian Diaspora and the Ethnogeneses of People in the Indonesian Archipelago*, pp. 186–204. Jakarta: LIPI Press.

Détroit, F., Dizon, E. et al. 2004 Upper Pleistocene *Homo sapiens* from the Tabon Cave. *Comptes Rendues – Palevol* 3:705–12.

Di Lernia, S. and Gallinaro, M. 2010 The date and context of Neolithic rock art in the Sahara. *Antiquity* 84:954–75.

Diamond, J. 1994 Spacious skies and tilted axes. *Natural History* 103(5):16–22.

Diamond, J. 1997 *Guns, Germs and Steel*. London: Jonathan Cape.

Diamond, J. 2002 Evolution, consequences and future of plant and animal domestication. *Nature* 418:700–7.

Diamond, J. 2012 The local origins of domestication. In P. Gepts, T.R. Famula et al., eds, *Biodiversity in Agriculture: Domestication, Evolution, and Sustainability*, pp. 9–17. Cambridge: Cambridge University Press.

Diamond, J. and Bellwood, P. 2003 Farmers and their languages: the first expansions. *Science* 300:597–603.

Dickau, R., Ranere, A. et al. 2007 Starch grain evidence for preceramic dispersals of maize and root crops into tropical dry and humid forests of Panama. *Proceedings of the National Academy of Sciences (USA)* 104:3651–56.

Diehl, M. 2005a Morphological observations on recently recovered Early Agricultural Period maize cob fragments from southern Arizona. *American Antiquity* 70:361–75.

Diehl, M., ed. 2005b *Subsistence and Resource Use Strategies in Early Agricultural Communities in Southern Arizona.* Anthropological Papers 34. Tucson: Center for Desert Archaeology.

Diehl, J. and Mabry, J., eds, 2006 *Rio Nuevo Archaeology Program.* Technical Report No. 2004–11 for Desert Archaeology, Tucson, Arizona.

Diehl, M. and Waters, J. 2006 Aspects of optimization and risk during the Early Agricultural Period in southeastern Arizona. In D. Kennett and B. Winterhalder, eds, *Behavioral Ecology and the Transition to Agriculture*, pp. 63–86. Berkeley: University of California Press.

Dietrich, O., Heun M. et al. 2012 The role of cult and feasting in the emergence of Neolithic communities. *Antiquity* 86:674–95.

Diffloth, G. 2011 Austroasiatic word histories: boats, husked rice and taro. In N. Enfield, ed., *Dynamics of Human Diversity*, pp. 295–314. Canberra: Pacific Linguistics.

Dillehay, T. 2009 Probing deeper into first American studies. *Proceedings of the National Academy of Sciences (USA)* 106:971–8.

Dillehay, T., ed. 2011 *From Foraging to Farming in the Andes.* Cambridge: Cambridge University Press.

Dillehay, T., Rossen, J. et al. 2007 Preceramic adoption of peanut, squash and cotton in northern Peru. *Science* 316:1890–93.

Dillehay, T., Bonavia, D. et al. 2012 Chronology, mound-building and environment at Huaca Prieta. *Antiquity* 331:48–70.

Ding, Z., Oskarsson, M. et al. 2012 Origins of domestic dog in Southern East Asia is supported by analysis of Y-chromosome DNA. *Nature* 108:507–14.

Dixon, E. 2001 Human colonization of the Americas: timing, technology and process. *Quaternary Science Reviews* 20:277–9.

Dixon, R. 1980 *The Languages of Australia.* Cambridge: Cambridge University Press.

Dixon, R. 1997 *The Rise and Fall of Languages.* Cambridge: Cambridge University Press.

Dolgopolsky, A. 1987 The Indo-European homeland and lexical contacts of Proto-Indo-European with other languages. *Mediterranean Language Review* 3:7–31.

Dolgopolsky, A. 1993 More about the Indo-European homeland problem. *Mediterranean Language Review* 6:230–48.

Donohue, M. and Denham, T. 2009 Banana (*Musa* spp.) domestication in the Asia-pacific region. *Ethnobotany Research and Applications* 7:292–332.

Donohue, M. and Denham, T. 2010 Farming and language in Island Southeast Asia; reframing Austronesian history. *Current Anthropology* 51:223–56.

Doolittle, W. and Mabry, J. 2006 Environmental mosaics, agricultural diversity and the evolutionary adoption of maize in the American Southwest. In J. Staller, Tykot, R. et al., eds, *Histories of Maize*, pp. 109–19. Amsterdam: Elsevier.

Drews, R. 2001 Greater Anatolia: Proto-Anatolian, Proto-Indo-Hittite, and beyond. In R. Drews, ed., *Greater Anatolia and the Indo-Hittite Language Family*, pp. 248–84. Washington, DC: Journal of Indo-European Studies Monograph 38.

Dugmore, A., Keller, C. et al. 2007 Norse Greenland settlement: reflections on climate change, trade, and the contrasting fates of human settlements in the North Atlantic Islands. *Arctic Anthropology* 44:12–36.

Dumond, D. 2010 The Dene arrival in Alaska. In J. Kari and B. Potter, eds, *The Dene-Yeniseian Connection*, pp. 335–46. Fairbanks: University of Alaska Fairbanks, Department of Anthropology.

Dunn, F. and Dunn, D. 1977 Maritime adaptations and exploitation of marine resources in Sundaic Southeast Asian prehistory. *Modern Quaternary Research in SE Asia* 3:1–28.

Dunne, J., Evershed, R. et al. 2012 First dairying in green Saharan Africa in the fifth millennium BC. *Nature* 486:390–4.

Dupanloup, I., Bertorelle, G. et al. 2004 Estimating the impact of prehistoric admixture on the genome of Europeans. *Molecular Biology and Evolution* 21:1361–72.

Düring, B. 2011 *The Prehistory of Asia Minor*. Cambridge: Cambridge University Press.

Dutta, P. 1978 *The Great Andamanese*. Calcutta: Anthropological Survey of India.

Dutton, A. and Lambeck, K. 2012 Ice volume and sea level during the last interglacial. *Science* 337:216–9.

Eder, J. 1987 *On the Road to Tribal Extinction*. Berkeley: University of California Press.

Efstratiou, N. 2005 Tracing the story of the first farmers in Greece. In C. Lichter, ed., *How did Farming Reach Europe?* pp. 143–54. Istanbul: Ege Yayınlari.

Ehret, C. 1998 *An African Classical Age*. Charlottesville: University Press of Virginia.

Ehret, C. 2002a Language family expansions: broadening our understandings of cause from an African perspective. In P. Bellwood and C. Renfrew, eds, *Examining the Farming/Language Dispersal Hypothesis*, pp. 163–76. Cambridge: McDonald Institute.

Ehret, C. 2002b *The Civilizations of Africa*. Charlottesville: University Press of Virginia.

Ehret, C. 2011 *History and the Testimony of Language*. Berkeley: University of California Press.

Ehret, C. 2013 Sub-Saharan Africa: lingustic prehistory. In I. Ness and P. Bellwood, eds, *Encyclopedia of Global Human Migration*. Volume 1, Prehistory, pp. 96–106. Malden, MA and Oxford: Wiley-Blackwell.

Ehret, C., Keita, S. et al. 2004 The origins of Afroasiatic. *Science* 306:1680–1.

Ellis, C. 2008 The fluted point tradition and the Arctic Small Tool tradition. *Journal of Anthropological Archaeology* 27:298–314.

Endicott, K. and Bellwood, P. 1991 The possibility of independent foraging in the rain forest of Peninsular Malaysia. *Human Ecology* 19:151–86.

Endicott, P. 2003 The genetic origins of the Andaman Islanders. *American Journal of Human Genetics* 72:178–84.

Epps, P. 2006 Language classification, language contact, and Amazonian prehistory. *Language and Linguistics Compass* 3/2:581–606.

Eriksson, A. and Manica, A. 2012 Effects of ancient population structure on the degree of polymorphism shared between modern human populations and ancient hominins. *Proceedings of the National Academy of Sciences (USA)* 109:13956–60.

Erlandson, J., Graham, M. et al. 2007 The Kelp Highway hypothesis. *Journal of Island and Coastal Archaeology* 2:161–74.

Erlandson, J., Rick, T. et al. 2011 Paleoindian seafaring, maritime technologies, and coastal foraging on California's Channel Islands. *Science* 331:1181–4.

Eshed, V. and Galili, E. 2011 Paleodemography of southern Levantine Pre-Pottery Neolithic populations. In R. Pinhasi and J. Stock, eds, *Human Bioarchaeology at the Transition to Agriculture*, pp. 403–28. Chichester: Wiley-Blackwell.

Eshed, V., Gopher, A. et al. 2004 Has the transition to agriculture reshaped the demographic structure of prehistoric populations? New evidence from the Levant. *American Journal of Physical Anthropology* 124:315–29.

Evans, N. 1988 Arguments for Pama-Nyungan as a genetic subgroup. *Aboriginal Linguistics* 1:91–110.

Evans, N. 2003 Comparative non-Pama-Nyungan and Australian historical linguistics. In N. Evans, ed., *The Non-Pama-Nyungan Languages of Northern Australia*, pp. 3–25. Canberra: Pacific Linguistics.

Evans, N. 2005 Australian languages reconsidered. *Oceanic Linguistics* 44:242–86.

Evans, N. and Jones, R. 1997 The cradle of the Pama-Nyungans. In P. McConvell and N. Evans, eds, *Archaeology and Linguistics*, pp. 385–418. Oxford University Press.

Evershed, R., Payne, S. et al. 2008 Earliest date for milk use in the Near East and southeastern Europe. *Nature* 455:528–31.

Fagan, B. 2008 *The Great Warming*. New York: Bloomsbury.

Fage, L-N. and Chazine, J-M. 2009 *Bornéo: La Mémoire des Grottes*. Lyon: Fage.

Ferlus, M. 2010 The Austroasiatic vocabulary for rice: its origin and expansion. *Journal of the Southeast Asian Linguistics Society* 3.2:61–76.

Ferring, R., Oms, O. et al. 2011 Earliest human occupations at Dmanisi (Georgian Caucasus) dated to 1.85–1.78 ma. *Proceedings of the National Academy of Sciences (USA)* 108:10432–36.

Feynman, J. and Ruzmaikin, A. 2007 Climate stability and the development of agricultural soceities. *Climatic Change* 84:295–311.

Fiedel, S. 1990 Middle Woodland and Algonquian expansion: a refined model. *North American Archaeologist* 11:209–30.

Fiedel, S. 1991 Correlating archaeology and linguistics: the Algonquian case. *Man in the Northeast* 41:9–32.

Finlayson, B., Mithen, S. et al. 2011 Architecture, sedentism, and social complexity at Pre-Pottery Neolithic A WF16, southern Jordan. *Proceedings of the National Academy of Sciences (USA)* 108:8183–8.

Fitzpatrick, S. 2006 A critical approach to ^{14}C dating in the Caribbean. *Latin American Archaeology* 17:389–418.

Fix, A. 2011 Origin of genetic diversity among Malayan Orang Asli: an alternative to the demic diffusion model. In N.J. Enfield, ed., *Dynamics of Human Diversity*, pp. 277–92. Canberra: Pacific Lingusitics.

Fogelin, L. 2007 Inference to the best explanation. *American Antiquity* 72:603–25.

Ford, J.A. 1969 *A Comparison of Formative Cultures in the Americas*. Washington DC: Smithsonian.

Forster, P. 2004 Ice ages and the mitochondrial DNA chronology of human dispersals: a review. *Philosophical Transactions of the Royal Society of London, Series B* 59:255–64.

Forster, P. and Renfrew, C. 2011 Mother tongue and Y chromosomes. *Science* 333:1290–1.

Forster, P. and Toth, A. 2003 Toward a phylogenetic chronology of ancient Gaulish, Celtic, and Indo-European. *Proceedings of the National Academy of Sciences (USA)* 100:9079–84.

Fortescue, M. 1998 *Language Relations across Bering Strait*. London: Cassell.

Fortescue, M. 2010 Yeniseian: Siberian intruder or remnant? In J. Kari and B. Potter, eds, *The Dene-Yeniseian Connection*, pp. 310–5. Fairbanks: University of Alaska Fairbanks, Department of Anthropology.

Fortescue, M. 2013 North America: Eskimo-Aleut linguistic history. In I. Ness and P. Bellwood, eds, *Encyclopedia of Global Human Migration*. Volume 1, *Prehistory*, pp. 340–5. Malden, MA and Oxford: Wiley-Blackwell.

Fortunato, L. 2008 A phylogenetic approach to the history of cultural practices. In N.J. Allen, C. Callen et al., eds, *Early Human Kinship*, pp. 189–99. Oxford: Blackwell.

Foster, M. 1996 Language and the culture history of North America. In I. Goddard, ed., *Handbook of North American Indians*, Vol 17, pp. 64–110. Washington DC: Smithsonian.

Frachetti, M. 2012 Multiregional emergence of mobile pastoralism and nonuniform institutional complexity across Eurasia. *Current Anthropology* 53:2–38.

Frachetti, M. and Benecke, N. 2009 From sheep to (some) horses. *Antiquity* 83:1023–37.

Frachetti, M., Spengler, R. et al. 2010 Earliest direct evidence for broomcorn millet and wheat in the central Asian steppe region. *Antiquity* 84:993–1010.

Freeman D. 1970 *Report on the Iban*. Athlone, London.

Friedlaender, J. 2007 Introduction. In J. Friedlaender, ed., *Genes, Language and Culture History in the Southwest Pacific*, pp. 3–9. New York: Oxford University Press.

Friedlaender, J., Friedlaender, F. et al. 2008 The genetic structure of Pacific Islanders. *PloS Genetics* 4(1):e19.

Friesen, T. 2013 North America: Paleoeskimo and Iniut archaeology. In I. Ness and P. Bellwood, eds, *Encyclopedia of Global Human Migration*. Volume 1, *Prehistory*, pp. 346–53. Malden, MA and Oxford: Wiley-Blackwell.

Friesen, T. and Arnold, C. 2008 The timing of the Thule Migration: new dates from the western Canadian Arctic. *American Antiquity* 73(3):527–38.

Fuller, D. 2007 Contrasting patterns in crop domestication and domestication rates. *Annals of Botany* 100:903–24.

Fuller, D. 2011 Finding plant domestication in the Indian subcontinent. *Current Anthropology* 52 (Supplement 4):S347–62.

Fuller, D. 2013 South Asia: archaeology. In I. Ness and P. Bellwood, eds, *Encyclopedia of Global Human Migration*. Volume 1, *Prehistory*, pp. 245–53. Malden, MA and Oxford: Wiley-Blackwell.

Fuller, D., Qin, L. et al. 2009 The domestication process and domestication rate in rice. *Science* 323:1607–10.

Fuller, D., Sato, Y-I. et al. 2010 Consilience of genetics and archaeobotany in the entangled history of rice. *Archaeological and Anthropological Sciences* 2:115–31.

Fuller, D., Willcox, G. et al. 2011a Early agricultural pathways: moving outside the 'core area' hypothesis in Southwest Asia. *Journal of Experimental Botany* 63:617–33.

Fuller, D., van Etten, J. et al. 2011b The contribution of rice agriculture and livestock pastoralism to prehistoric methane levels. *The Holocene* 21:743–59.

Funder, S., Goosse, H. et al. 2011 A 10,000-year record of Arctic sea-ice variability. *Science* 333:747–50.

Gamba, C., Fernández, E. et al. 2012 Ancient DNA from an early Neolithic Iberian population supports a pioneer colonization by first farmers. *Molecular Ecology* 21:45–56.

Gamble, C., Davies, W. et al. 2005 The archaeological and genetic foundations of the European population during the Late Glacial. *Cambridge Archaeological Journal* 15:193–223.

Gamkrelidze, T. and Ivanov, V. 1995 *Indo-European and the Indo-Europeans*. Berlin: Mouton de Gruyter.

Garcea, E. 2006 Semi-permanent foragers in semi-arid environments of North Africa. *World Archaeology* 38:197–219.

Garcea, E., ed. 2010 *South-Eastern Mediterranean Peoples Between 130,000 and 10,000 Years Ago*. Oxford: Oxbow.

Garcia, J., Martinez, K. et al. 2011a Continuity of the first human occupation in the Iberian Peninsula. *Comptes Rendus Palevol* 10:279–84.

Garcia, O., Fregel, R. et al. 2011b Using mitochondrial DNA to test the hypothesis of a European post-glacial recolonization from the Franco-Cantabrian region,. *Heredity* 106:37–45.

Garrigan, D. and Kingan S. 2007 Archaic human adnmixture. *Current Anthropology* 48:895–902.

Gatsov, I. and Schwartzenberg, H., eds, 2006 *Aegean-Marmara-Black Sea*. Langenweissbach: Beier and Beran.

Ghirotto, S., Tassi, F. et al. 2013 Origins and evolution of the Etruscans' mtDNA. *PLoS ONE* 8(2):e55519.

Gibbard, P., Head, M. et al. 2009 Formal ratification of the Quaternary System/Period and the Pleistocene Series/Epoch with a base at 2.58 ma. *Journal of Quaternary Science* 25:96–102.

Gibbons, A. 2011 Who were the Denisovans? *Science* 333:1084–7.

Gifford-Gonzalez, D. 2005 Pastoralism and its consequences. In A.B. Stahl, ed., *African Archaeology*, pp. 187–224. Malden, MA: Blackwell.

Gignoux, C., Henn, B. et al. 2011 Rapid, global demographic expansions after the origins of agriculture. *Proceedings of the National Academy of Sciences (USA)* 108:6044–9.

Gilbert, G. 2013 Levant and North Africa: archaeology. In I. Ness and P. Bellwood, eds, *Encyclopedia of Global Human Migration*. Volume 1, *Prehistory*, pp. 133–8. Malden, MA and Oxford: Wiley-Blackwell.

Gilbert, M., Jenkins, D. et al. 2008 DNA from Pre-Clovis human coprolites in Oregon. *Science* 320:786–9.

Gill, J., Williams, J. et al. 2009 Pleistocene megafaunal collapse, novel plant communities, and enhanced fire regimes in North America. *Science* 326:1100–3.

Gilligan, I. 2007 Neanderthal extinction and modern human behaviour: the role of climate change and clothing. *World Archaeology* 39:499–514.

Gilligan, I. 2008 Clothing and climate in Aboriginal Australia. *Current Anthropology* 49:487–95.

Gilligan, I. 2010 The prehistoric development of clothing: archaeological implications of a thermal model. *Journal of Archaeological Method and Theory* 17:15–80.

Gimbutas, M. 1985 Primary and secondary homelands of the Indo-Europeans. *Journal of Indo-European Studies* 13:185–202.

Gimbutas, M. 1991 Deities and symbols of Old Europe. In S. Lamb and E. Mitchell, eds, *Sprung from Some Common Source*, pp. 89–121. Stanford: Stanford University Press.

Ginter, J. 2011 Using a bioarchaeological approach to explore subsistence transitions in the Eastern Cape, South Africa. In R. Pinhasi and J. Stock, eds, *Human Bioarchaeology at the Transition to Agriculture*, pp. 107–52. Chichester: Wiley-Blackwell.

Glover, I. and Bellwood, P., eds, 2004 *Southeast Asia: From Prehistory to History*. London: RoutledgeCurzon.

Glover, I.C. and Presland, G. 1985 Microliths in Indonesian flaked stone industries. In V.N. Misra and P. Bellwood, eds, *Recent Advances in Indo-Pacific Prehistory*, pp. 185–95. New Delhi: Oxford & IBH.

Goebel, T. 2002 The 'microblade adaptation" and recolonization of Siberia during the late Upper Pleistocene. *Archaeological Papers of the American Anthropological Association* 12:117–31.

Goebel, T. 2004 The search for a Clovis progenitor in Subarctic Siberia. In D.B. Madsen, ed., *Entering America*, pp. 311–56. Salt Lake City: University of Utah Press.

Goebel, T. 2007 The missing years for modern humans. *Science* 315:194–6.

Goebel, T., Waters, M. et al. 2008 The Late Pleistocene dispersal of modern humans in the Americas. *Science* 319:1497–502.

Goebel, T., Slobodin, S. et al. 2010 New dates from Ushki-1, Kamchatka. *Journal of Archaeological Science* 37:2640–9.

Golden, P. 1998 The Turkic peoples: a historical sketch. In L. Johansson and E. Csato, eds, *The Turkic Languages*, pp. 16–29. London: Routledge.

Goldstein, D.B and Chikhi, L. 2002 Human migrations and population structure. *Annual Review of Genomics and Human Genetics* 3:129–52.

Golitko, M. and Keeley, L. 2007 Beating ploughshares back into swords: warfare in the Linearbandkeramik. *Antiquity* 81:332–42.

Golovanova, L.V., Doronichev, V. et al. 2010 Significance of ecological factoers in the Middle to Upper Paleolithic transition. *Current Anthropology* 51:655–92.

Gommery, D., Ramanivosoa, B. et al. 2010 Les plus anciennes traces d'activités anthropiques de Madagascar. *Comptes Rendus Palevol* 10:271–78.

Goring-Morris, N. and Belfer-Cohen, A. 2008 A roof over one's head. In J-P. Bocquet-Appel and O. Bar-Yosef, eds, *The Neolithic Demographic Transition and its Consequences*, pp. 239–86. Dordrecht: Springer.

Goring-Morris, N. and Belfer-Cohen, A. 2011 Neolithization processes in the Levant: the outer envelope. *Current Anthropology* 52 (Supplement 4):S195–208.

Gosselain, O. 2008 Mother Bella was not a Bella. In M. Stark, B.J. Bowser et al., eds, *Cultural Transmission and Material Culture*, pp. 150–77. Tucson: University of Arizona Press.

Graf, K. 2009 "The good, the bad, and the ugly": evaluating the radiocarbon chronology of the middle and late Upper Palaeolithic in the Enesei River valley. *Journal of Archaeological Science* 36:694–707.

Graf, K. 2010 Hunter–gatherer dispersals in the mammoth steppe. *Journal of Archaeological Science* 37:210–23.

Gray, R. and Atkinson, Q. 2003 Language tree divergence times support the Anatolian theory of Indo-European origin. *Nature* 426:435–9.

Gray, R. and Jordan, F. 2000 Language trees support the express-train sequence of Austronesian expansion. *Nature* 405:1052–5.

Gray, R.D., Drummond, A.J. et al. 2009 Language phylogenies reveal expansion pulses and pauses in Pacific settlement. *Science* 323:479–83.

Green R. 2005 Sweet potato transfers in Polynesian prehistory. In C. Ballard, R.P. Brown et al., eds, *The Sweet Potato in Oceania: A Reappraisal*, pp. 43–62. Pittsburgh: Ethnology Monograph 19.

Green, R. and Krause, J. et al. 2010 A draft sequence of the Neanderthal genome. *Science* 328:710–21.

Greenberg, J. 1987 *Language in the Americas*. Stanford: Stanford University Press.

Greenberg, J., Turner II, C. et al. 1986 The settlement of the Americas: a comparison of the linguistic, dental, and genetic evidence. *Current Anthropology* 27:477–98.

Grenville, K. 2005 *The Secret River*. Melbourne: Text Publishing Company.

Griffith, T. 1996 *Herodotus: Histories*. Ware: Wordsworth Editions.

Grine, F., Bailey, R. et al. 2007 Late Pleistocene human skull from Hofmeyr, South Africa, and modern human origins. *Science* 315:226–9.

Gronenborn, D. 1999 A variation on a basic theme: the transition to farming in southern central Europe. *Journal of World Prehistory* 13:123–212.

Groves, C. 2008 Walking with hobbits. *Australasian Science* (March 2008) pp. 16–8.

Groves, C. 2013 Hominin migrations before Homo sapiens: out of Africa – how many times? In I. Ness and P. Bellwood, eds, *Encyclopedia of Global Human Migration*. Volume 1, *Prehistory*, pp. 18–25. Malden, MA and Oxford: Wiley-Blackwell.

Grupe, G. and Peters, J. 2011 Climatic conditions, hunting activities and husbandry practices. In R. Pinhasi and J. Stock, eds, *Human Bioarchaeology at the Transition to Agriculture*, pp. 63–86. Chichester: Wiley-Blackwell.

Güldemann, T. 2008 A linguist's view: Khoe-Kwadi speakers as the earliest food-producers of southern Africa. *Southern African Humanities* 20:93–132.

Güleç, E., White, T. et al. 2009 The Lower Pleistocene lithic assemblage from Dursunlu (Konya), central Anatolia, Turkey. *Antiquity* 83:11–22.

Gunz, P., Bookstein, F. et al. 2009 Early modern human diversity suggests subdivided population structure and a complex out-of-Africa scenario. *Proceedings of the National Academy of Sciences (USA)* 106:6094–8.

Haak, W., Balanovsky, O. et al. 2010 Ancient DNA from European early Neolithic farmers reveals their Near eastern affinities. *Plos Biology* 8(11):e1000536.

Haak, W., Forster, P. et al. 2005 Ancient DNA from the first European farmers in 7500-year-old Neolithic sites. *Science* 310:1016–8.

Haberle, S. and David, B. 2002 Climates of change. *Quaternary International* 118–9:165–79.

Habgood, P. and Franklin, N. 2008 The revolution that didn't arrive: a review of Pleistocene Sahul. *Journal of Human Evolution* 55:187–222.

Habu, J. 2004 *Ancient Jomon of Japan*. Cambridge: Cambridge University Press.

Hamilton, M. and Buchanan, B. 2007 Spatial gradients in Clovis-age radiocarbon dates across North America suggest rapid colonization from the north. *Proceedings of the National Academy of Sciences (USA)* 104:15625–30.

Hammer, M., Karafet, T. et al. 2006 Dual origins of the Japanese: common ground for hunter–gatherer and farmer Y chromosomes. *Journal of Human Genetics* 51(1):47–58.

Hammer, M., Woerner, A. et al. 2011 Genetic evidence for archaic admixture in Africa. *Proceedings of the National Academy of Sciences (USA)* 108:15123–8.

Hammond, N. 2007 Recovering Maya civilization. *Proceedings of the British Academy* 151:1–25.

Handford, S. 1951 *De Bello Gallico* (Caesar's *Gallic Wars*). Harmondsworth: Penguin.

Hansen, J. 1992 Franchthi Cave and the beginnings of agriculture in Greece and the Aegean. In P. Anderson, ed., *Préhistoire de l'Agriculture*, pp. 231–48. Paris: CNRS.

Hard, R. and Roney, J. 2007 Cerros de trincheras in northwestern Chihuahua. In S. Fish, P.R. Fish et al., eds, *Trincheras Sites in Time, Space and Society*, pp. 11–52. Tucson: University of Arizona Press.

Harlow, G., Murphy, A. et al. 2006 Pre-Columbian jadeite axes from Antiqua, West Indies. *The Canadian Mineralogist* 44:305–21.

Harris, D., ed. 2010 *Origins of Agriculture in Western Central Asia*. Philadelphia: University of Pennsylvania Museum of Archaeology.

Harry, K. and Frink, L. 2009 The Arctic cooking pot: why was it adopted? *American Anthropologist* 111:330–43.

Hart, J., Brumback, H. et al. 2007 Extending the phytolith evidence for early maize and squash in central New York. *American Antiquity* 72:563–83.

Haslam, M., Clarkson, C. et al. 2010 The 74ka Toba super-eruption and southern Indian hominins. *Journal of Archaeological Science* 37:3370–84.

Hassan, F. 1988 The predynastic of Egypt. *Journal of World Prehistory* 2:135–86.

Hassan, F. 2002 Archaeology and linguistic diversity in North Africa. In P. Bellwood and C. Renfrew, eds, *Examining the Farming/Language Dispersal Hypothesis*, pp. 127–34. Cambridge: McDonald Institute.

Headland, T. 1997 Limitation of human rights – Agta Negritos. *Human Organisation* 56:79–90.

Headland, T. and Reid, L. 1989 Hunter–gatherers and their neighbors from prehistory to the present. *Current Anthropology* 30:43–66.

Heckenberger, M. 2002 Rethinking the Arawak diaspora: hierarchy, regionality and the Amazonian Formarive. In J. Hill and F. Santos-Granero, eds, *Comparative Arawakan Histories*, pp. 99–122. Urbana: University of Illinois Press.

Heckenberger, M. 2005 *The Ecology of Power*. New York: Routledge.

Heckenberger, M. 2013 Amazonia: archaeology. In I. Ness and P. Bellwood, eds, *Encyclopedia of Global Human Migration*. Volume 1, *Prehistory*, pp. 392–400. Malden, MA and Oxford: Wiley-Blackwell.

Heckenberger, M. and Neves, E. 2009 Amazonian archaeology. *Annual Review of Anthropology* 38:251–66.

Heggarty, P. 2013 Europe and Western Asia: Indo-European linguistic history. In I. Ness and P. Bellwood, eds, *Encyclopedia of Global Human Migration*. Volume 1, *Prehistory*, pp. 157–67. Malden, MA and Oxford: Wiley-Blackwell.

Heggarty, P. and Beresford-Jones, D. 2010 Agriculture and language dispersals: limitations, refinements, and an Andean exception? *Current Anthropology* 51:163–92.

Heggarty, P. and Beresford-Jones, D., eds, 2012 *Archaeology and Language in the Andes*. Proceedings of the British Academy 173. Oxford: Oxford University Press.

Heggarty, P. and Beresford-Jones, D. 2013 Andes: linguistic history. In I. Ness and P. Bellwood, eds, *Encyclopedia of Global Human Migration*. Volume 1, *Prehistory*, pp. 401–9. Malden, MA and Oxford: Wiley-Blackwell.

Hemphill, B. 2009 Harappa: the role of an urbanized Bronze Age populace in the population history of South Asia. Presented to 13th Harvard Round Table, Ethnogenesis of South and Central Asia, Research Institute for Humanity and Nature, Kyoto (unpublished conference proceedings, pp. 19–21).

Hemphill, B., Lukacs, J. et al. 1991 Biological adaptations and affinities of Bronze Age Harappans. In R.H. Meadow, ed., *Harappa Excavations 1986–1990*, pp. 137–82. Madison: Prehistory Press.

Henn, B., Gignoux, C. et al. 2008 Y-chromosomal evidence of a pastoralist migration through Tanzania to southern Africa. *Proceedings of the National Academy of Sciences (USA)* 105:10693–98.

Henn, B., Gignoux, C. et al. 2011 Hunter-gatherer genomic diversity suggests a southern African origin for modern humans. *Proceedings of the National Academy of Sciences (USA)* 108:5154–62.

Henn, B., Cavalli-Sforza, L. et al. 2012 The great human expansion. *Proceedings of the National Academy of Sciences (USA)* 109:17758–64.

Henshilwood, C. and Dubreuil, B. 2011 The Still Bay and Howieson's Poort, 77–59 ka. *Current Anthropology* 52:335–60.

Henshilwood, C., d'Errico, F. et al. 2011 A 100,000-year-old ochre processing workshop at Blombos Cave, South Africa. *Science* 334:219–22.

Hertler, C., Bruch, A. et al. 2013 The earliest stages of hominin dispersal in Africa and Eurasia. In I. Ness and P.Bellwood, eds, *Encyclopedia of Global Human Migration*. Volume 1, *Prehistory*, pp. 9–17. Malden, MA and Oxford: Wiley-Blackwell.

Heyer, E. and Rocha, J. 2013 Sub-Saharan Africa: human genetics. In I. Ness and P. Bellwood, eds, *Encyclopedia of Global Human Migration*. Volume 1, *Prehistory*, pp. 115–24. Malden, MA and Oxford: Wiley-Blackwell.

Hiebert, F. 1994 *Origins of the Bronze Age Oasis Civilization in Central Asia*. American School of Prehistoric Research Bulletin 42. Cambridge MA: Peabody Museum, Harvard University.

Hiebert, F. 2003 *A Central Asian Village at the Dawn of Civilization*. Philadelphia: University of Pennsylvania Museum.

Higham, C. 2001 *The Civilization of Angkor*. London: Weidenfeld and Nicholson.

Higham, C. 2002 *Early Cultures of Mainland Southeast Asia*. Bangkok: River Books.

Higham, C. 2013 Southeast Asian mainland: archaeology. In I. Ness and P. Bellwood, eds, *Encyclopedia of Global Human Migration*. Volume 1, *Prehistory*, pp. 269–75. Malden, MA and Oxford: Wiley-Blackwell.

Higham, C and Kijngam, A. 2010 *The Excavation of Ban Non Wat: The Neolithic Occupation*. Bangkok: Thai Fine Arts Department.

Higham, C. and Thosarat, R. 1994 *Khok Phanom Di*. Fort Worth: Harcourt Brace.

Higham, C. and Thosarat, R. 2004 Khok Phanom Di in wider perspective. In C. Higham and R. Thosarat, eds, *The Excavation of Khok Phanom Di*, Volume VII, Summary and Conclusions, pp. 127–58. London: Society of Antiquries.

Higham, T., Barton, H. et al. 2009 Radiocarbon dating of charcoal from tropical sequences: results from the Niah Great Cave. *Journal of Quaternary Science* 24:189–97.

Higham, T., Jacobi, R. et al. 2010 Chronology of the Grotte du Renne (France). *Proceedings of the National Academy of Sciences (USA)* 107(47):20147–8.

Higham, C., Xie, G. et al. 2011a The prehistory of a friction zone: first farmers and hunter-gatherers in Southeast Asia. *Antiquity* 85:529–43.

Higham, T., Compton, T. et al. 2011b The earliest evidence for anatomically modern humans in northwestern Europe. *Nature* 479:521–4.

Hildebrand, E. and Grillo, K. 2012 Early herders and monumental sites in eastern Africa. *Antiquity* 86:338–52.

Hill, J. 2001 Proto-Uto-Aztecan: a community of cultivators in central Mexico? *American Anthropologist* 103:913–34.

Hill, J. 2002 Proto-Uto-Aztecan cultivation and the Northern Devolution. In P. Bellwood and C. Renfrew, eds, *Examining the Farming/Language Dispersal Hypothesis*, pp. 331–40. Cambridge: McDonald Institute.

Hill, J. 2006 The historical linguistics of maize cultivation in Mesoamerica and North America. In J. Staller, Tykot, R. et al., eds, *Histories of Maize*, pp. 631–47. Amsterdam: Elsevier.

Hill, J. 2008 Northern Uto-Aztecan and Kiowa-Tanoan. *International Journal of American Linguistics* 74:155–88.

Hill, J. 2010 New evidence for a Mesoamerican homeland for Proto-Uto-Aztecan. *Proceedings of the National Academy of Sciences (USA)* 107:E33.

Hill, J. 2013 Mesoamerica and the Southwestern USA: linguistic history. In I. Ness and P. Bellwood, eds, *Encyclopedia of Global Human Migration*. Volume 1, *Prehistory*, pp. 362–8. Malden, MA and Oxford: Wiley-Blackwell.

Hill, C., Soares, P. et al. 2007a Phylogeography and ethnogenesis of Aboriginal Southeast Asians. *Molecular Biology and Evolution* 23:2480–91.

Hill, C., Soares, P. et al. 2007b A mitochondrial stratigraphy for Island Southeast Asia. *American Journal of Human Genetics* 80:29–43.

Hill, K., Walker, R. et al. 2011 Co-residence patterns in hunter-gatherer societies show unique human social structure. *Science* 331:1286–8.

Hillman, G. 1996 Late Pleistocene changes in wild plant-foods available to hunter–gatherers of the northern Fertile Crescent: possible preludes to cereal cultivation. In D. Harris, ed., *The Origins and Spread of Agriculture and Pastoralism in Eurasia*, pp.159–203. London: UCL Press.

Hillman, G., Hedges, R. et al. 2001 New evidence of late glacial cereal cultivation at Abu Hureyra on the Euphrates. *The Holocene* 11:383–93.

Hills, C. 2003 *Origins of the English*. London: Duckworth.

Hines, J. 1996 Britain after Rome. In P. Graves-Brown, S. Jones et al., eds, *Cultural Identity and Archaeology*, pp. 256–70. London: Routledge.

Hiscock, P. 2008 *Archaeology of Ancient Australia*. Abingdon: Routledge.

Hiscock, P. 2013a Early Old World migrations of *Homo sapiens*: archaeology. In I. Ness and P. Bellwood, eds, *Encyclopedia of Global Human Migration*. Volume 1, *Prehistory*, pp. 38–48. Malden, MA and Oxford: Wiley-Blackwell.

Hiscock, P. 2013b The human colonization of Australia. In I. Ness and P. Bellwood, eds, *Encyclopedia of Global Human Migration*. Volume 1, *Prehistory*, pp. 55–60. Malden, MA and Oxford: Wiley-Blackwell.

Hiscock, P. and Attenbrow, V. 1998 Early Holocene backed artefacts from Australia. *Archaeology in Oceania* 33:49–62.

Hodder, I. and Meskell, L. 2011 A "curious and sometimes a trifle macabre artistry". *Current Anthropology* 52:235–64.

Hoeffecker, J., Powers, W. et al. 1993 The colonization of Beringia and the peopling of the New World. *Science* 259:46–53.

Hofman, C., Bright, A. et al. 2007 Island rhythms: the web of social relationships and interaction networks in the lesser Antillean Archipelago between 400 BC, AD 1492. *American Antiquity* 18:243–68.

Holdaway, S. and Porch, N. 1995 Dates as data. In J. Allen, ed., *Report of the Southern Forests Archaeological Project*, pp. 251–77. Melbourne: School of Archaeology, La Trobe University.

Holden, C. 2002 Bantu language trees reflect the spread of farming across sub-Saharan Africa: a maximum parsimony analysis. *Proceedings of the Royal Society of London, Series B* 269:793–9.

Holman, E., Brown, C. et al. 2011 Automated dating of the world's language families based on lexical similarity. *Current Anthropology* 52:841–75.

Holtby, I., Scarre, C. et al. 2012 Disease, CCR5-Δ32 and the European spread of agriculture? *Antiquity* 86:207–10.

Hornborg, A. 2005 Ethnogenesis, regional interaction, and ecology in prehistoric Amazonia: toward a system perspective. *Current Anthropology* 46:589–620.

Hou Y.M. and Zhao, L.X. 2010 An archaeological view for the presence of early humans in China. *Quaternary International* 223–4:10–9.

Housley, R., Gamble, C. et al. 1997 Radiocarbon evidence for late glacial human recolonisation of northern Europe. *Proceedings of Prehistoric Society* 63:25–54.

Hovers, E. and Braun, D., eds, 2009 *Interdisciplinary Approaches to the Oldowan*. Dordrecht: Springer.

Howells, W.W. 1960 *Mankind in the Making*. London: Secker and Warburg.

Hsieh, J., Hsing, Y. et al. 2011 Studies on ancient rice. *Rice* 4:178–83.

Hu, Y., Ambrose, S. et al. 2006 Stable isotopic analysis of human bones from Jiahu site. *Journal of Archaeological Science* 33:1319–30.

Huang, X., Kurata, N. et al. 2012 A map of rice genome variation reveals the origin of cultivated rice. *Nature* 490:497–501.

Hubbe, M., Neves, W. et al. 2010 Testing evolutionary and dispersion scenarios for the settlement of the New World. *PloS One* 5(6):e11105.

Hublin, J-J. 2007 What can Neanderthals tell us about modern origins? In P. Mellars, O. Bar-Yosef et al., eds, *Rethinking the Human Revolution*, pp. 235–48. Cambridge: McDonald Institute.

Huckell, B., Huckell, L. et al. 2002 Maize agriculture and the rise of mixed farming-foraging economies in southeastern Arizona during the second millennium BC. In S. Schlanger, ed., *Traditions, Transitions and Technologies*, pp. 137–59. Boulder: University Press of Colorado.

Hudjashov, G., Kivisild, T. et al. 2007 Revealing the prehistoric settlement of Australia by Y chromosome and mtDNA analysis. *Proceedings of the National Academy of Sciences (USA)* 104:8726–30.

Hudson, M. 1999 *Ruins of Identity: Ethnogenesis in the Japanese Islands*. Honolulu: University of Hawaii Press.

Hudson, M. 2013 Japan: archaeology. In I. Ness and P. Bellwood, eds, *Encyclopedia of Global Human Migration*. Volume 1, *Prehistory*, pp. 224–9. Malden, MA and Oxford: Wiley-Blackwell.

Human Ecology 1991 *Special Issue: Human Foragers in Tropical Rain Forests.* Vol. 19, No. 2, June 1991.

Hung, H-c. 2005 Neolithic interaction between Taiwan and northern Luzon. *Journal of Austronesian Studies* 1(1):109–34.

Hung, H-c., Carson, M. et al. 2011 The first settlement of Remote Oceania: the Philippines to the Marianas. *Antiquity* 329:909–26.

Hung, H-c., Carson, M. et al. 2012 Earliest settlement in the Marianas. *Antiquity* 86:910–4.

Hunley, K., Dunn, M. et al. 2008 Genetic and linguistic coevolution in northern Island Melanesia. *PLoS Genetics* 4(10):e1000239.

Hunt, H., Vander Linden, M. et al. 2008 Millets across Eurasia. *Vegetation History and Archaeobotany* 17 (Supplement):S5–18.

Huysecom, E., Rasse, M. et al. 2009 The emergence of pottery in Africa during the tenth millennium cal BC. *Antiquity* 83:905–17.

Hyodo, M., Matsu'ura, S. et al. 2011 High-resolution record of the Matuyama-Brunhes transition constrains the age of Javanese *Homo erectus* in the Sangiran dome. *Proceedings of the National Academy of Sciences (USA)* 108:19563–8.

Ikawa-Smith, F. 2009 Living on the edge of the continent: the Japanese archipelago 30,000–8000 cal. BC. *North Pacific Prehistory* 3:49–69.

Indriati, E., ed. 2007 *Recent Advances on Southeast Asian Palaeoanthropology.* Indonesia: Gadjah Mada University, Yogyakarta.

Irwin, G. 1992 *The Prehistoric Exploration and Colonization of the Pacific.* New York: Cambridge University Press.

Irwin, G. 2010 Pacific voyaging and settlement. In J. Anderson, H. Barrett et al., eds, *The Global Origins and Development of Seafaring*, pp. 131–42. Cambridge: McDonald Institute Monograph.

Isaac, G. 1978 Food sharing and human evolution. *Journal of Anthropological Research* 34:311–25.

Izuho, M. 2011 Presentation at conference on Modern Human Behavior held in the National Museum of Nature and Science in Tokyo, December 2011.

Jarrige, C. 2007–8a The figurines of the first farmers at Mehrgarh and their offshoots. *Pragdahara* 18:155–66. Lucknow.

Jarrige, J-F. 2007–8b Mehrgarh Neolithic. *Pragdahara* 18:135–54. Lucknow.

Jenkins, D., Davis, L.et al. 2012 Clovis age western stemmed projectile points and human coprolites at the Paisley Caves. *Science* 337:223–28.

Jinam, T., Hong, L-H. et al. 2012 Evolutionary history of continental South East Asians. *Molecular Biology and Evolution* 29:3513–27.

Jochim, M. 2000 The origins of agriculture in south-central Europe. In D. Price, ed., *Europe's First Farmers*, pp. 183–96. New York: Cambridge University Press.

Jones, M. and Brown, T. 2008 Selection, cultivation and reproductive isolation. In T. Denham, ed., *Rethinking Agriculture*, pp. 36–49. Walnut Creek: Left Coast Press.

Jordeczka, M., Krolik, H. et al. 2011 Early Holocene pottery in the Western Desert of Egypt. *Antiquity* 85:99–115.

Jungers, W. and Baab, K. 2009 The geometry of hobbits: *Homo floresiensis* and human evolution. *Significance* 6(4):159–64.

Kaczanowska, M. and Kozlowski, J. 2003 Origins of the linear pottery complex and the Neolithic transition in central Europe. In A. Ammerman and P. Biagi, eds, *The Widening Harvest*, pp. 227–48. Boston: Archaeological Institute of America.

Kaifu, Y. and Fujita, M. 2012 Fossil record of early modern humans in East Asia. *Quaternary International* 248:2–11.

Kaifu, Y., Baba, H. et al. 2005 Taxonomic affinities and evolutionary history of the Early Pleistocene hominids of Java: dentognathic evidence. *American Journal of Physical Anthropology* 128:709–26.

Kaifu, Y., Aziz, F. et al. 2008 Cranial morphology of Javanese *Homo erectus*: new evidence for continuous evolution, specialization, and terminal extinction. *Journal of Human Evolution* 55:551–80.

Kaifu, Y., Baba, T. et al. 2011 Craniofacial morphology of *Homo floresiensis*: description, taxonomic affinities, and evolutionary implication. *Journal of Human Evolution* 61:644–82.

Karafet, T. and Hallmark, B. 2010 Major east-west division underlies Y-chrosome stratification across eastern Indonesia. *Molecular Biology and Evolution* 27:1833–44.

Karafet, T., Lansing, J.S. et al. 2005 A Balinese Y-chromosome perspective on the peopling of Indonesia. *Human Biology* 77:93–114.

Karafet, T., Zegura, S. et al. 2009 Y-chromosome Japanese roots. In P.N. Peregrine, I. Peiros et al., eds, *Ancient Human Migrations*, pp. 137–48. Salt Lake City: University of Utah Press.

Kari, J. 2010 The concept of geolinguistic conservatism in Ne-Dene prehistory. In J. Kari and B. Potter, eds, *The Dene-Yeniseian Connection*, pp. 194–222. Fairbanks: University of Alaska Fairbanks, Department of Anthropology.

Kari, J. and Potter, B. 2010 The Dene-Yeniseian connection: bridging Asia and North America. In J. Kari and B. Potter, eds, *The Dene-Yeniseian Connection*, pp. 1–24. Fairbanks: University of Alaska Fairbanks, Department of Anthropology.

Kayser, M., Brauer, S. et al. 2001 Independent histories of human Y chromosomes from Melanesia and Australia. *American Journal of Human Genetics* 68:173–90.

Kayser, M., Lao, O. et al. 2008 Genome-wide analysis indicates more Asian than Melanesian ancestry of Polynesians. *American Journal of Human Genetics* 82:194–8.

Keates, S. 2010 The chronology of Pleistocene modern humans in China, Korea, and Japan. *Radiocarbon* 52:428–65.

Keegan, W. 2013 Caribbean Islands: archaeology. In I. Ness and P. Bellwood, eds, *Encyclopedia of Global Human Migration*. Volume 1, *Prehistory*, pp. 376–83. Malden, MA and Oxford: Wiley-Blackwell.

Keeley, L. 1992 The introduction of agriculture to the western North European Plain. In A.B. Gebauer and T.D. Price, eds, *Transitions to Agriculture in Prehistory*, pp. 81–96. Madison: Prehistory Press.

Keinan, A. and Clarke, G. 2012 Recent explosive human population growth has resulted in an excess of rare genetic variants. *Science* 336:740–3.

Kelly, R. 1985 *The Nuer Conquest*. Ann Arbor: University of Michigan Press.

Kelly, R. and Todd, L. 1988 Coming in to the country: early Paleoindian hunting and mobility. *American Antiquity* 53:231–44.

Kemp, B., Malhi, R. et al. 2007 Genetic analysis of early Holocene skeletal remains from Alaska. *American Journal of Physical Anthropology* 132:605–21.

Kemp, B., Gonzalez-Oliver, A. et al. 2010 Evaluating the farming-language dispersal hypothesis with genetic variation exhibited by populations in the Southwest and Mesoamerica. *Proceedings of the National Academy of Sciences (USA)* 107:6759–64.

Kennett, D., Piperno, D. et al. 2010 Pre-pottery farmers on the Pacific coast of southern Mexico. *Journal of Archaeological Science* 37:3401–11.

Kenoyer, J.M. 2009 The origin, context and function of the Indus script: recent insights from Harappa. In Toshiki Osada, ed., *Linguistics, Archaeology and Human Past in South Asia*, pp. 13–32. New Delhi: Manohar.

Kidd, J., Friedlaender, F. et al. 2011 Single nucleotide polymorphisms and haplotypes in Native American populations. *American Journal of Physical Anthropology* 146:495–502.

King, R. 2007 *Origins: An Atlas of Human Migration*. Sydney: ABC Books.

King, G. and Bailey, G. 2006 Tectonics and human evolution. *Antiquity* 80:265–86.

King, R., Özcan, S. et al. 2008 Differential Y-chromosome Anatolian influences on the Greek and Cretan Neolithic. *Annals of Human Genetics* 72:205–14.

Kirch, P. 1994 *The Wet and the Dry*. Chicago: University of Chicago Press.

Kirch, P. 1997 *The Lapita Peoples*. Blackwell, Oxford.

Kirch, P. 2010 Peopling of the Pacific. *Annual Review of Anthropology* 39:131–48.

Kirch, P. and Green, R. 1987 History, phylogeny, and evolution in Polynesia. *Current Anthropology* 28:431–56.

Kirch, P. and Green, R. 2001 *Hawaiki: Ancestral Polynesia*. Cambridge: Cambridge University Press.

Kislev, M., Weiss, E. et al. 2004 Impetus for sowing and the beginning of agriculture: ground collecting of wild cereals. *Proceedings of the National Academy of Sciences (USA)* 101:2692–5.

Kitchen, A., Miyamoto, M. et al. 2008 A three-stage colonization model for the peopling of the Americas. *PloS ONE* 3(2):e1596.

Kitchen, A., Ehret, C. et al. 2009 Bayesian phylogenetic analysis of Semitic languages. *Proceedings of the Royal Society of London, Series B* 276:2703–10.

Kitson, P. 1996 British and European river names. *Transactions of the Philological Society* 94:73–118.

Klein, R. 2009a *The Human Career*. Third edition. University of Chicago Press.

Klein, R. 2009b Darwin and the recent African origin of modern humans. *Proceedings of the National Academy of Sciences (USA)* 106:16007–9.

Klieman, K. 2003 *The Pygmies were our Compass*. Portsmouth: Heinemann.

Knapp, M., Horsburgh, A. et al. 2013 Complete mitochondrial DNA genome sequences from the first New Zealanders. *Proceedings of the National Academy of Sciences (USA)* 109:18350–4.

Kohl, P. 2007 *The Making of Bronze Age Eurasia*. Cambridge: Cambridge University Press.

Kohl, P. 2009 Perils of carts before horses. *American Antiquity* 111:109–11.

Kohler-Rollefson, I. 1988 The aftermath of the Levantine Neolithic Revolution. *Paléorient* 14(1):87–94.

Krantz, G. 1976 On the nonmigration of hunting peoples. *Northwestern Anthropology Research Notes* 10:209–16.

Krantz, G. 1988 *Geographical Development of European Languages*. New York: Lang.

Krause, J., Orlando, L. et al. 2007 Neanderthals in central Asia and Siberia. *Nature* 449:902–4.

Krause, J., Fu, Q. et al. 2010 The complete mitochondrial DNA genome of an unknown hominin from southern Siberia. *Nature* 464:894–7.

Kröpelin S., Verschuren, D. et al. 2008 Climate-driven ecosystem succession in the Sahara: the past 6000 years. *Science* 320:765–8.

Kuijt, I. 2008 Demography and storage systems during the southern Levantine Neolithic demographic transition. In J-P. Bocquet-Appel and O. Bar-Yosef, eds, *The Neolithic Demographic Transition and its Consequences*, pp. 287–314. Dordrecht: Springer.

Kuijt, I. and Finlayson, B. 2009 Evidence for food storage and pre-domestication granaries 11,000 years ago in the Jordan Valley. *Proceedings of the National Academy of Sciences (USA)* 106:10966–70.

Kuijt, I. and Goring-Morris, N. 2002 Foraging, farming and social complexity in the Pre-Pottery Neolithic of the southern Levant. *Journal of World Prehistory* 16:361–440.

Kumar, V., Reddy, A. et al. 2007 Y-chromosome evidence suggests a common paternal heritage of Austro-Asiatic populations. *BMC Evolutionary Biology* 7:47.

Kuper, R. and Kröpelin S. 2006 Climate-controlled Holocene occupation in the Sahara. *Science* 313:803–7.

Kushnareva, O. 1997 *The Southern Caucasus in Prehistory*. Philadelphia: University of Pennsylvania.

Kuzmin, Y., Jull, A. et al. 1998 Early agriculture in Primorye, Russian Far East: new radiocarbon and pollen data from Late Neolithic sites. *Journal of Archaeological Science* 25:813–6.

Kuzmin, Y., Keates, S. et al. 2007 Introduction: microblades and beyond. In Y. Kuzmin, S.G. Keates et al., eds, *Origin and Spread of Microblade Technology in Northern Asia and North America*, pp. 1–6. Burnaby, British Columbia: Archaeology Press.

Kuzmina, E. 2007 *The Origin of the Indo-Aryans*. Leiden: Brill.

Kyparissi-Apostolica, N. 2006 The beginning of the Neolithic in Thessaly. In I. Gatsov and H. Schwartzenberg, eds, *Aegean-Marmara-Black Sea*, pp. 59–68. Langenweissbach: Beier and Beran.

Lacan, M., Kayser, C. et al. 2011 Ancient DNA reveals male diffusion through the Neolithic Mediterranean route. *Proceedings of the National Academy of Sciences (USA)* 108:9788–91.

Lahr, M. and Foley, R. 1998 Towards a theory of modern human origins. *Yearbook of Physical Anthropology* 41:137–76.

Lamberg-Karlovsky K. 2002 Archaeology and language: the Indo-Iranians. *Current Anthropology* 43:63–88.

Lane, G. 1970 *Tocharian: Indo-European and Non-Indo-European relationships*. In G. Cardona et al., eds, *Indo-European and Indo-Europeans*, pp. 73–88. Philadelphia: University of Pennsylvania Press.

Langbroek, M. 2004 *'Out of Africa': An Investigation into the Earliest Occupation of the Old World*. Oxford: Archaeopress.

Lansing, J., Cox, M. et al. 2011 An ongoing Austronesian expansion in Island Southeast Asia. *Journal of Anthropological Archaeology* 30:262–72.

LaPolla, R. 2001 The role of migration and language contact in the development of the Sino-Tibetan language family. In A. Aikhenvald and R. Dixon, eds, *Areal Diffusion and Genetic Inheritance*, pp. 225–54. Oxford: Oxford University Press.

Larsen, C. 2006 The agricultural revolution as environmental catastrophe. *Quaternary International* 150:12–20.

Larson, G., Albarella, U. et al. 2007 Ancient DNA, pig domestication, and the spread of the Neolithic into Europe. *Proceedings of the National Academy of Sciences (USA)* 104:15276–81.

Larson, G., Liu, R. et al. 2010 Patterns of East Asian pig domestication, migration, and turnover revealed by modern and ancient DNA. *Proceedings of the National Academy of Sciences (USA)* 107:7686–91.

Larson, G., Karlsson, E. et al. 2013 Rethinking dog domestication by integrating genetics, archaeology and biogeography. *Proceedings of the National Academy of Sciences (USA)* 109:8878–83.

Lawler, A. 2012 Rethinking the thundering hordes. *Archaeology* 65:42–7.

Leach, H. 2005 *Ufi kumara*, the sweet potato as yam. In C. Ballard, P. Brown et al., eds, *The Sweet Potato in Oceania: A Reappraisal*, pp. 63–70. Pittsburgh: Ethnology Monograph 19.

Leakey, M., Spoor, F. et al. 2012 New fossils from Koobi Fora in northern Kenya confirm taxonomic diversity in early *Homo*. *Nature* 488:201–4.

LeBlanc, S. 2003 *Constant Battles*. New York: St Martin's.

LeBlanc, S. 2008 The case for an early farmer migration into the American Southwest. In L. Webster and M. McBrinn, eds, *Archaeology Without Borders*, pp. 107–42. Boulder: University Press of Colorado.

LeBlanc, S. 2013 Mesoamerica and the Southwestern USA: archaeology. In I. Ness and P. Bellwood, eds, *Encyclopedia of Global Human Migration*. Volume 1, *Prehistory*, pp. 369–75. Malden, MA and Oxford: Wiley-Blackwell.

LeBlanc, S., Kreisman, L. et al. 2007 Quids and aprons: ancient DNA from artifacts from the American Southwest. *Journal of Field Archaeology* 32:161–75.

LeBlanc, S, Turner, C. et al. 2008 Genetic relationships based on discrete dental traits: Basketmaker II and Mimbres. *International Journal of Osteoarchaeology* 17:1–22.

Lee, G-A. 2011 The transition from foraging to farming in prehistoric Korea. *Current Anthropology* 52 (Supplement 4): S307–30.

Lee, S. and Hasegawa, T. 2011 Bayesian phylogenetic analysis supports an agricultural origin of Japonic languages. *Proceedings of the Royal Society of London, Series B* 278:3662–9.

Leonard, J., Wayne, R. et al. 2002 Ancient DNA evidence for Old World origins of New World dogs. *Science* 298:1613–6.

Lepre, C., Roche, H. et al. 2011 An earlier origin for the Acheulian. *Nature* 477:82–5.

Leroy, S., Arpe, K. et al. 2011 Vegetation context and climatic limits of the Early Pleistocene hominin dispersal in Europe. *Quaternary Science Reviews* 30:1448–63.

Lertrit, P., Poolsuwan, S. et al. 2008 Genetic history of Southeast Asian populations as revealed by ancient and modern human mitochondrial DNA analysis. *American Journal of Physical Anthropology* 137:425–40.

Lesure, R., Borejsza, A. et al. 2006 Chronology, subsistence, and the earliest Formative of Central Tlaxcala, Mexico. *Latin American Archaeology* 474–92.

Levine, M., Rassamakin, Y. et al. 1999 *Late Prehistoric Exploitation of the Eurasian Steppes.* Cambridge: McDonald Institute for Archaeological Research.

Lev-Yadun, S., Gopher, A. et al. 2000 The cradle of agriculture. *Science* 288:1602–3.

Li, J., Absher, D. et al. 2008 Worldwide human relationships inferred from genome-wide patterns of variations. *Science* 319:1100–4.

Li, X., Dodson, J. et al. 2009 Increases of population and expansion of rice agriculture in Asia, and anthropogenic methane emissions since 5000 BP. *Quaternary International* 202:41–50.

Li, C., Li, H. et al. 2010 Evidence that a West–East admixed population lived in the Tarim Basin as early as the early Bronze Age. *BMC Biology* 8:15.

Lichter, C., ed. 2005 *How did Farming Reach Europe?* Istanbul: Ege Yayinlari.

Linderholm, A. 2011 The genetics of the Neolithic transition. In R. Pinhasi and J. Stock, eds, *Human Bioarchaeology at the Transition to Agriculture*, pp. 385–402. Chichester: Wiley-Blackwell.

Lisiecki, L. and Raymo, M. 2005 A Plio-Pleistocene stack of 57 globally distributed benthic $\delta^{18}O$ records. *Paleoceanography* 20:PA1003.

Liu, L. 2004 *The Chinese Neolithic.* Cambridge: Cambridge University Press.

Liu, Y. 2007 The earliest Austronesians and their movements inside Taiwan. In S. Chiu and C. Sand, eds, *From Southeast Asia to the Pacific*, pp. 49–74. Taipei: Center for Archaeological Studies, Academia Sinica.

Liu, F. and Feng, Z. 2012 A dramatic climatic transition at ~4000 cal. yr BP and its cultural response in Chinese cultural domains. *The Holocene* 22:1181–97.

Liu, L., Lee, G. et al. 2007 Evidence for the early beginning (c.9000 cal. BP) of rice domestication in China: a response. *The Holocene* 17:1059–68.

Liu, W., Jin, C-Z. et al. 2010 Human remains from Zhirendong, south China, and modern human emergence in East Asia. *Proceedings of the National Academy of Sciences (USA)* 107:19201–6.

Loftus, R. and Cunningham, P. 2000 Molecular genetic analysis of African zeboid populations. In R. Blench and K. MacDonald, eds, *The Origins and Development of African Livestock*, pp. 251–8. London: UCL Press.

Lombard, M. and Phillipson, L. 2010 Indications of bow and stone-tipped arrow use 64 000 years ago in KwaZulu-Natal, South Africa. *Antiquity* 84:635–48.

Long, J. and Bortolini, M. 2011 New developments in the origins and evolution of Native American populations. *American Journal of Physical Anthropology* 146:491–4.

Lourandos, H. and David, B. 2002 Long-term archaeological and environmental trends. In P. Kershaw, B. David et al., eds, *Bridging Wallace's Line*, pp. 307–38. Reiskirchen: Catena Verlag GMBH.

Lu, T.L-D. 2010 Early pottery in South China. *Asian Perspectives* 49:1–42.

Lu, H., Zhang, J. et al. 2009 Earliest domestication of common millet (Panicum miliaceum) in East Asia extended to 10,000 years ago. *Proceedings of the National Academy of Sciences (USA)* 106:7367–72.

Lucas, L., Colledge, S. et al. 2011 Crop introduction and accelerated island evolution. *Vegetation History and Archaeobotany* 21:117–29.

Lucier, C. and VanStone, J. 1992 *Historic pottery of Kotzebue Sound Iñupiat*. Chicago: Field Museum of Natural History.

Luis, J., Rowold, D. et al. 2004 The Levant versus the Horn of Africa: evidence for bidirectional corridors of human migrations. *American Journal of Human Genetics* 74:532–44.

Lyras, G., Dermitzakis, M. et al. 2008 The origin of *Homo floresiensis* and its relation to evolutionary processes under isolation. *Anthropological Science* 117:33–43.

Mabry, J. 2002 The role of irrigation in the transition to agriculture and sedentism in the Southwest. In S. Schlanger, ed., *Traditions, Transitions and Technologies*, pp. 178–99. Boulder: University Press of Colorado.

Mabry, J. 2005 Changing knowledge and ideas about the first farmers in southern Arizona. In B. Vierra, ed., *The Late Archaic Across the Borderlands*, pp. 41–83. Austin: University of Texas Press.

Mabry, J. and Doolittle, W. 2008 Modeling the early agricultural frontier in the desert borderlands. In L. Webster and M. McBrinn, eds, *Archaeology Without Borders*, pp. 53–70. Boulder: University Press of Colorado.

Mabry, J., Carpenter, J. et al. 2008 Archaeological models of Uto-Aztecan prehistory in the Arizonas-Sonora borderlands. In L. Webster and M. McBrinn, eds, *Archaeology without Borders: Contact, Commerce, and Change in the U.S. Southwest and Northwestern Mexico*, pp. 155–84. Boulder: University Press of Colorado.

Macaulay, V., Hill. C. et al. 2005 Single, rapid coastal settlement of Asia revealed by analysis of complete mitochondrial genomes. *Science* 308:1034–6.

Mace, R. and Holden, C. 2005 A phylogenetic approach to human evolution. *Trends in Ecology and Evolution* 20(3):116–21.

Mace, R. and Pagel, M. 1994 The comparative method in anthropology. *Current Anthropology* 35:549–64.

Macknight, C. 1976 *The Voyage to Marege*. Melbourne: Melbourne University Press.

Macknight, C. 2008 Harvesting the memory: open beaches in Makassar and Arnhem Land. In P. Veth, P. Sutton et al., eds, *Strangers on the Shore*, pp. 33–47. Canberra: National Museum of Australia.

Magill, C., Ashley, G. et al. 2013 Water, plants, and early human habitats in eastern Africa. *Proceedings of the National Academy of Sciences (USA)* 110:1175–80.

Maier, U. 1996 Morphological studies of free-threshing wheat ears from a Neolithic site in southwest Germany, and the history of naked wheats. *Vegetation History and Archaeobotany* 5:39–55.

Majid, Z., ed. 2005 *The Perak Man and other Skeletons of Malaysia*. Penang: Penerbit Universiti sains Malaysia.

Majumder, P. 2010 The human genetic history of South Asia. *Current Biology* 20:R184–7.

Malhi, R., Mortensen, H. et al. 2003 Native American mtDNA prehistory in the American Southwest. *American Journal of Physical Anthropology* 120:108–24.

Malhi, R., Kemp, B. et al. 2007 Mitochondrial haplogroup M discovered in prehistoric North Americans. *Journal of Archaeological Science* 34:642–8.

Mallory, J. 1989 *In Search of the Indo-Europeans*. London: Thames and Hudson.

Mallory, J. 1997 The homelands of the Indo-Europeans. In R. Blench and M. Spriggs, eds, *Archaeology and Language I*, pp. 93–121. London: Routledge.

Mallory, J. and Mair, V. 2000 *The Tarim Mummies*. London: Thames and Hudson.

Malmstrom, H., Gilbert, M. et al. 2009 Ancient DNA reveals lack of continuity between Neolithic hunter–gatherers and contemporary Scandinavians. *Current Biology* 19:1758–62.

Mann, C. 2008 Ancient earthmovers of the Amazon. *Science* 321:1148–52.

Manning, P. 2005 *Migration in World History*. New York: Routledge.

Manning, S., McCartney, C. et al. 2010a The earlier Neolithic in Cyprus. *Antiquity* 84: 693–706.

Manning, K., Pelling, R. et al. 2010b 4500-year old domesticated pearl millet (*Pennisetum glaucum*) from the Tilemsi Valley, Mali. *Journal of Archaeological Science* 38:312–22.

Marean, C. 2007 Heading north: an Africanist perspective on the replacement of Neanderthals by modern humans. In P. Mellars, O. Bar-Yosef et al., eds, *Rethinking the Human Revolution*, pp. 367–82. Cambridge: McDonald Institute.

Marean, C. 2010 Pinnacle Point Cave 13B (Western Cape Province, South Africa) in context. *Journal of Human Evolution* 59:425–43.

Marean, C., Bar-Matthews, M. et al. 2007 Early human use of marine resources and pigment in South Africa during the Middle Pleistocene. *Nature* 449:905–8.

Marsella, A. and Ring, E. 2003 Human migration and immigration: an overview. In L. Adler and U. Gielen, eds, *Migration*, pp. 3–22. Westport: Praeger.

Marshall, F. and Weissbrod, L. 2011 Domestication processes and morphological change. *Current Anthropology* 52 (Supplement 4): S397–413.

Martin, S. 2008 Languages past and present: archaeological approaches to the appearance of Northern Iroquoian speakers in the Lower Great Lakes region of North America. *American Antiquity* 73:441–63.

Marwick, B. 2005 The interpersonal origins of language. *Linguistics and the Human Sciences* 1(2):197–224.

Masson, V.N. 1988 *Altyn-Depe*. Philadelphia: University of Pennsylvania Museum.

Matson, R.G. 2002 The spread of maize agriculture into the US Southwest. In P. Bellwood and C. Renfrew, eds, *Examining the Farming/Language Dispersal Hypothesis*, pp. 341–56. Cambridge: McDonald Institute.

Matson, R.G. 2007 The Archaic origins of the Zuni: preliminary observations. In D. Gregory and D. Wilcox, eds, *Zuni Origins*, pp. 97–117. Tucson: University of Arizona Press.

Matson, R.G. and Magne, M. 2007 *Athapaskan Migrations*. Tucson: University of Arizona Press.

Matson, R.G. and Magne, M. 2013 North America: Na Dene/Athapaskan archaeology and linguistics. In I. Ness and P. Bellwood, eds, *Encyclopedia of Global Human Migration*. Volume 1, *Prehistory*, pp. 333–9. Malden, MA and Oxford: Wiley-Blackwell.

Matsui, A. and Kanehara, M. 2006 The question of prehistoric plant husbandry during the Jomon period in Japan. *World Archaeology* 38:259–73.

Matsumura, H. and Hudson, M. 2005 Dental perspectives on the population history of Southeast Asia. *American Journal of Physical Anthropology* 127:182–209.

Matsumura, H. and Oxenham, M. 2013 Eastern Asia and Japan: human biology. In I. Ness and P. Bellwood, eds, *Encyclopedia of Global Human Migration*. Volume 1, *Prehistory*, pp. 217–23. Malden, MA and Oxford: Wiley-Blackwell.

Matsumura, H., Minoru, Y. et al. 2008a Terminal Pleistocene human skeleton from Hang Cho cave, northern Vietnam: Implications for the biological affinities of Hoabinhian people. *Anthropological Science* 116:135–48.

Matsumura, H., Oxenham, M. et al. 2008b Morphometric affinity of the late Neolithic human remains from Man Bac, Ninh Binh Province, Vietnam: *Anthropological Science* 116:135–48.

Matsumura, H., Oxenham, M. et al. 2011 Population history of MSEA: the two layer model in the context of northern Vietnam. In N. Enfield, ed., *Dynamics of Human Diversity*, pp. 153–78. Canberra: Pacific Linguistics.

Matthews, K. 1995 Archaeological data, sub-cultures and social dynamics. *Antiquity* 69:586–94.

McArthur, N., Saunders, I. et al. 1976 Small population isolates: a micro-simulation study. *Journal of the Polynesian Society* 85:307–26.

McBrearty, S. 2012 Sharpening the mind. *Nature* 491:531-2.

McBrearty, S. and Brooks, A. 2000 The revolution that wasn't: a new interpretation of the origin of modern human behaviour. *Journal of Human Evolution* 39:453–563.

McConvell, P. 1990 The linguistic prehistory of Australia. *Australian Archaeology* 31:3–27.

McConvell, P. 1996 Backtracking to Babel. *Archaeology in Oceania* 31:125–44.

McConvell, P. 2010 The archaeo-linguistics of migration. In J. Lucassen, L. Lucassen et al, eds, *Migration History in World History*, pp. 155–88. Leiden: Brill.

McConvell, P. 2013 Australia: linguistic history. In I. Ness and P. Bellwood, eds *Encyclopedia of Global Human Migration*. Volume 1, *Prehistory*, pp. 327–32. Malden, MA and Oxford: Wiley-Blackwell.

McConvell, P. and Bowern, C. 2011 The prehistory and internal relationships of Australian languages. *Language and Linguistics Compass* 5:19–32.

McDougall, I., Brown, F. et al. 2005 Stratigraphic placement and age of modern humans from Kibish, Ethiopia. *Nature* 433:733–6.

McGhee, R. 2005 *The Last Imaginary Place*. Chicago: University of Chicago Press.

McGovern, P., Zhang, J. et al. 2004 Fermented beverages of pre- and proto-historic China. *Proceedings of the National Academy of Sciences (USA)* 101:17593–8.

McGrail, S. 2010 The global origins of seagoing water transport. In J. Anderson, H. Barrett et al., eds, *The Global Origins and Development of Seafaring*, pp. 95–108. Cambridge: McDonald Institute for Archaeological Research.

McIntosh, I. 2008 Pre-Macassans at Dholtji? In P. Veth, P. Sutton et al., eds, *Strangers on the Shore*, pp. 165–80. Canberra: National Museum of Australia.

McKeown, A. 2004 Global migration, 1846–1940. *Journal of World History* 15:155–89.

McNiven, I, David, B. et al. 2011 New direction in human colonization of the Pacific. *Australian Archaeology* 72:1–6.

Meehan, B. 1990 Insights into the colonial process: Aborigines, Malays, and Europeans in Arnhem Land, Northern Australia. In J-P. Descoudres, ed., *Greek Colonists and Native Populations*, pp. 191–204. Oxford: Clarendon Press.

Meggers, B. 1987 The early history of man in Amazonia. In T.C. Whitmore and G.T. Prance, eds, *Biogeography and Quaternary History in Tropical America*, pp.151–74. Oxford: Clarendon Press.

Meggers, B. and Evans, C. 1983 Lowland South America and the Antilles. In J.D. Jennings, ed., *Ancient South Americans*, pp. 287–335. San Francisco: Freeman.

Meignen, L. 2011 Levantine perspectives on the Middle Paleolithic/Upper Paleolithic transition. In A. Derevianko and M. Shunkov, eds, *Characteristic Features of the Middle to Upper Paleolithic Transition in Eurasia*, pp. 164–73. Novosibirsk: Institute of Archaeology and Ethnography.

Mellars, P. 2011 The earliest modern humans in Europe. *Nature* 479:483–5.

Mellars, P. and French, J. 2011 Tenfold population increase in Western Europe at the Neanderthal-to-modern transition. *Science* 333:623–7.

Meltzer, D. 2009 *First Peoples in a New World*. Berkeley: University of California Press.

Meltzer, D. 2013 The human colonization of the Americas: archaeology. In I. Ness and P. Bellwood, eds, *Encyclopedia of Global Human Migration*. Volume 1, *Prehistory*, pp. 61–9. Malden, MA and Oxford: Wiley-Blackwell.

Mercader, J., Barton, H. et al. 2007 4,300-year-old chimpanzee sites and the origins of percussive stone technology. *Proceedings of the National Academy of Sciences (USA)* 104:3043–8.

Merrill, W., Hard, R. et al. 2009 The diffusion of maize to the southwestern United States and its impact. *Proceedings of the National Academy of Sciences (USA)* 106:21019–26.

Merriwether, A., Kemp, B. et al. 2000 Gene flow and genetic variation in the Yanomama as revealed by mirochondrial DNA. In C. Renfrew, ed., *America Past, America Present*, pp. 89–124. Cambridge: McDonald Institute for Archaeological Research.

Merriwether, D., Hodgson, J. et al. 2005 Ancient mitochondrial M haplogroups identified in the Southwest Pacific. *Proceedings of the National Academy of Science* 102:13034–9.

Metspalu, M., Romero, I. et al. 2011 Shared and unique components of human population structure and genome-wide signals of positive selection in South Asia. *American Journal of Human Genetics* 89:731–44.

Meyer, M., Kircher, M. et al. 2012 A high-coverage genome sequence from an archaic Denisovan individuial. *Science* 338:222–6.

Migliazza, E. 1982 Linguistic prehistory and the refuge model. In G. Prance, ed., *Biological Diversification in the Tropics*, pp. 497–522. New York: Columbia University Press.

Mijares, A., Detroit, F. et al. 2010 New evidence for a 67,000-year-old human presence at Callao Cave, Luzon, Philippines. *Journal of Human Evolution* 59:123–32.

Militarev, A. 2002 The prehistory of a dispersal: the Proto-Afrasian (Afroasiatic) farming lexicon. In P. Bellwood and C. Renfrew, eds, *Examining the Farming/Language Dispersal Hypothesis*, pp. 135-50. Cambridge: McDonald Institute.

Miller, J. 1958 *Early Victorian New Zealand*. London: Oxford University Press.

Mills, M., Armit, I. et al. 2004 Neolithic land-use and environmental degradation. *Antiquity* 78:886–95.

Mirabal, S., Herrera, K. et al. 2012 Increased Y-chromosome resulution of haplogroup O suggests genetic ties between the Ami aborigines of Taiwan and the Polynesian islands of Tonga and Samoa. *Gene* 493:339–48.

Mithun, M. 1984 Iroquoian origins: problems in reconstruction. In M. Foster, ed., *Extending the Rafters*, pp. 237–81. Albany: State University of New York Press.

Mithun, M. 1999 *The Native Languages of North America*. Cambridge: Cambridge University Press.

Molina, J., Sikora, M. et al. 2011 Molecular evidence for a single origin of rice. *Proceedings of the National Academy of Sciences (USA)* 108:8351–6.

Mona, S., Grunz, K. et al. 2009 Genetic admixture history of eastern Indonesia as revealed by Y-chromosome and mitochondrial DNA analysis. *Molecular Biology and Evolution* 26:1865–77.

Monah, F. 2007 The spread of cultivated plants in the region between the Carpathians and the Dniester, 6th–4th millennia cal BC. In S. Colledge and J. Conolly, eds, *The Origins and Spread of Domestic Plants in Southwest Asia and Europe*, pp. 111–24. Walnut Creek: West Coast Press.

Montgomery, J. 2010 Passports from the past. *Annals of Human Biology*, 37:325–46.

Moreau, C., Bherer, C. et al. 2011 Deep human genealogies reveal a selective advantage to be on an expanding wave front. *Science* 334:1148–50.

Morisaki, K. 2011 Presentation at conference on Modern Human Behavior held in the National Museum of Nature and Science in Tokyo, December 2011.

Morwood, M. and Aziz, F. 2009 Conclusions. In F. Aziz, M. Morwood et al., eds, *Pleistocene Geology, Palaeontology and Archaeology of the Soa Basin, Central Flores, Indonesia*, pp. 139–46. Bandung: Pusat Survei Geologi.

Morwood, M. and Jungers, W. 2009 Conclusions: implications of the Liang Bua excavations for hominin evolution and biogeography. *Journal of Human Evolution* 57:640–8.

Moseley, M. and Heckenberger, M. 2013 From village to empire in South America. In Scarre, ed., *The Human Past*, pp. 640–77. London: Thames and Hudson.

Mulvaney, D.J. 1985 Australian backed blade industries in perspective. In V.N. Misra and P. Bellwood, eds, *Recent Advances in Indo-Pacific Prehistory*, pp. 211–7. New Delhi: Oxford & IBH.

Mulvaney, D.J. 2008 French strangers on Tasmanian shores. In P. Veth, P. Sutton et al., eds, *Strangers on the Shore*, pp. 113–23. Canberra: National Museum of Australia.

Mulvaney, D.J. and Soejono, R.P. 1970 The Australian-Indonesian archaeological expedition to Sulawesi. *Asian Perspectives* 13:163–78.

Munson, P. 1973 Origins and antiquity of maize-beans-squash agriculture in eastern North America. In D. Lathrap, ed., *Variation in Anthropology*, pp. 107–36. Urbana: Inninois Archaeological Survey.

Myres, N., Rootsi, S. et al. 2011 A major Y-chromosome haplogroup R1b Holocene era founder effect in Central and Western Europe. *European Journal of Human Genetics* 19:96–101.

Nadel, D., Weiss, E. et al. 2004 Stone Age hut in Israel yield's world's oldest evidence of bedding. *Proceedings of the National Academy of Sciences (USA)* 101:6821–6.

Naderi, S., Rezaei, H. et al. 2008 The goat domestication process. *Proceedings of the National Academy of Sciences (USA)* 105:17659–64.

Nakamura, S-i. 2010 The origin of rice cultivation in the lower Yangtze region, China. *Archaeological and Anthropological Sciences* 2:107–14.

Neef, R. 2003 Overlooking the steppe-forest. *Neo-Lithics* 2(13):13–6.

Neff, H., Pearsall, D. et al. 2006 Early Maya adaptive patterns: mid-late Holocene paleoenvironmental evidence from Pacific Guatemala. *Latin American Archaeology* 17:287–315.

Ness, I. and Bellwood, P., eds, 2013 *Encyclopedia of Global Human Migration*. 5 volumes (Volume 1, *Prehistory*). Malden, MA and Oxford: Wiley-Blackwell.

Neumann, K. and Hildebrand, E. 2009 Early bananas in Africa: the state of the art. *Ethnobotanical Research and Applications* 7:335–62.

Neves, E. 2008 Ecology, ceramic chronology and distribution, long-term history, and political change in the Amazonian floodplain. In H. Silverman and W. Isbell, eds, *Handbook of South American Archaeology*, pp. 359–79. New York: Springer.

Neves, W. and Hubbe, M. 2005 Cranial morphology of early Americans from Lagoa Santa, Brazil: implications for the settlement of the New World. *Proceedings of the National Academy of Sciences (USA)* 102:18309–14.

Noelli, F. 1998 The Tupi: explaining origins and expansions in terms of archaeology and of historical linguistics. *Antiquity* 72:648–63.

O'Brien, M.J. and Wood, W.R. 1998 *The Prehistory of Missouri*. Columbia: University of Missouri Press.

O'Connell, J. and Allen, J. 2012 The restaurant at the end of the universe. *Australian Archaeology* 74:5–31.

O'Connell, J., Allen, J. et al. 2010 Pleistocene Sahul and the origins of seafaring. In J. Anderson, H. Barrett et al., eds, *The Global Origins and Development of Seafaring*, pp. 57–68. Cambridge: McDonald Institute for Archaeological Research.

O'Connor, S. 2010 Pleistocene migration and colonization in the Indo-Pacific region. In J. Anderson, H. Barrett et al., eds, *The Global Origins and Development of Seafaring*, pp. 41–56. Cambridge: McDonald Institute for Archaeological Research.

O'Connor, S. and Veth, P. 2005 Early Holocene shell fishhooks from Lene Hara Cave, East Timor. *Antiquity* 79:249–56.

O'Connor, S., Ono, R. et al. 2011a Pelagic fishing at 42,000 years before the present and the maritime skills of modern humans, *Science* 334:1117–20.

O'Connor, S., Barham, A. et al. 2011b The power of paradigms. *Journal of Pacific Archaeology* 2:1–25.

O'Fallon, B. and Fehren-Schmitz, L. 2011 Native Americans experienced a strong population bottleneck coincident with European contact. *Proceedings of the National Academy of Sciences (USA)* 108:20444–8.

O'Grady, G. and Fitzgerald, S. 1997 Cognate search in the Pama-Nyungan language family. In P. McConvell and N. Evans, eds, *Archaeology and Linguistics*, pp. 341–56. Oxford: Oxford University Press.

O'Regan, H., Turner, A. et al. 2011 Hominins without fellow travellers? *Quaternary Science Reviews* 30:1343–52.

O'Reilly, D. 2007 *Early Civilizations of Southeast Asia*. Lanham: Altamira.

O'Rourke, D. and Raff, J. 2010 The human genetic history of the Americas: the final frontier. *Current Biology* 20: R202–7.

Olivieri, A., Achilli, A. et al. 2006 The mtDNA legacy of the Levantine Early Upper Paleolithic in Africa. *Science* 314:1767–70.

Ono, R., Soegondho, S. et al. 2009 Changing marine exploitation during late Pleistocene in northern Wallacea. *Asian Perspectives* 48:318–41.

Oota, H., Kurosaki, K. et al. 2001 Genetic study of the Paleolithic and Neolithic Southeast Asians. *Human Biology* 73:225–31.

Oppenheimer, S. 1998 *Eden in the East*. London: Weidenfeld and Nicholson.

Oppenheimer, S. 2003 *Out of Eden*. London: Weidenfeld and Nicholson.

Oppenheimer, S. 2007 *The Origins of the British*. London: Robinson.

Oppenheimer, S. 2011 MtDNA variation and southward Holocene human dispersals within Mainland Southeast Asia. In N. Enfield, ed., *Dynamics of Human Diversity*, pp. 81–108. Canberra: Pacific Linguistics.

Oppenheimer, S. and Richards, M. 2002 Polynesians: devolved Taiwanese rice farmers or Wallacean maritime traders with fishing, foraging and horticultural skills? In P. Bellwood and C. Renfrew, eds, *Examining the Farming/Language Dispersal Hypothesis*, pp. 287–98. Cambridge: McDonald Institute.

Osborne, A., Vance, D. et al. 2008 A humid corridor across the Sahara for the migration of early modern humans out of Africa 120,000 years ago. *Proceedings of the National Academy of Sciences (USA)* 105:16444–7.

Oskarsson, M., Klutsch, C. et al. 2012 Mitochondrial DNA data indicate an introduction through Mainland Southeast Asia for Australian dingoes and Polynesian domestic dogs. *Proceedings of the Royal Society of London, Series B* 279:967–74.

Ostapirat, W. 2005 Kra-dai and Austronesians. In L. Sagart, R. Blench et al., eds, *The Peopling of East Asia: Putting Together Archaeology, Linguistics and Genetics*, pp. 107–31. London: RoutledgeCurzon.

Ostler, N. 2005 *Empires of the Word*. London: Harper Perennial.

Outram. A., Stear, N. et al. 2009 The earliest horse harnessing and milking. *Science* 323:1332–5.

Ovodov, N., Crockford, S. et al. 2011 A 33,000 year old incipient dog from the Altai Mountains of Siberia. *PLoS One* 6(7):e22821.

Owsley, D., Jodry, M. et al. 2010 *Arch Lake Woman*. College Station: Texas A & M University Press.

Oxenham, M. and Tayles, N., eds, 2006 *Bioarchaeology of Southeast Asia.* Cambridge: Cambridge University Press.

Oxenham, M., Matsumura, H. et al., eds, 2011 *Man Bac: The Excavation of a Neolithic Site in Northern Vietnam.* Canberra: Terra Australis vol. 33, ANU E Press.

Özdoğan, M. 2007 Amidst Mesopotamia-centric and Euro-centric approaches: the changing role of the Anatolian peninsula between the East and the West. *Anatolian Studies* 57:17–24.

Özdoğan, M. 2008 An alternative approach in tracing changes in demographic composition. In J-P. Bocquet-Appel and O. Bar-Yosef, eds, *The Neolithic Demographic Transition and its Consequences*, pp. 139–78. Dordrecht: Springer.

Özdoğan, M. 2011a Archaeological evidence on the westward expansion of farming communities from eastern Anatolia to the Aegean and the Balkans. *Current Anthropology* 52 (Supplement 4):S415–30.

Özdoğan, M. 2011b Eastern Thrace: the contact zone between Anatolia and the Balkans. In S. Steadman and G. McMahon, eds, *The Oxford Handbook of Ancient Anatolia*, pp. 657–82. Oxford: Oxford University Press.

Özdoğan, M. 2013 Anatolia and the Balkans: archaeology. In I. Ness and P. Bellwood, eds, *Encyclopedia of Global Human Migration.* Volume 1, Prehistory, pp. 139–45. Malden, MA and Oxford: Wiley-Blackwell.

Pachori, S. 1993 *Sir William Jones: a Reader.* Delhi: Oxford University Press.

Palsson, G. 2008 Genomic anthropology: coming in from the cold? *Current Anthropology* 49:545–68.

Pappu, S., Gunnell, Y. et al. 2011 Early Pleistocene presence of Acheulian hominins in South India. *Science* 331:1596–9.

Parpola, A. 1999 The formation of the Aryan branch of Indo-European. In R. Blench and M. Spriggs, eds, *Archaeology and Language III*, pp. 180–210. London: Routledge.

Parpola, A. 2008 Proto-Indo-European speakers of the late Tripolye culture as the inventors of wheeled vehicles: linguistic and archaeological considerations of the PIE homeland problem. In K. Jones-Bley, Annual UCLA Indo-European Conference et al., eds, *Proceedings of the Nineteenth Annual UCLA Indo-European Conference*, pp. 1–59. Journal of Indo-European Studies Monograph 54. Washington, DC: Institute for the Study of Man.

Pavlov, P., Svendsen, J. et al. 2001 Human presence in the European Arctic nearly 40,000 years ago. *Nature* 413:64–7.

Pawley, A. 2002 The Austronesian dispersal: languages, technologies and people. In P. Bellwood and C. Renfrew, eds, *Examining the Farming/Language Dispersal Hypothesis*, pp. 251–74. Cambridge: McDonald Institute.

Pawley, A. 2005 The chequered career of the Trans New Guinea hypothesis: recent research and its implications. In A. Pawley, R. Attenborough et al., eds, *Papuan Pasts*, pp. 67–108. Canberra: Pacific Linguistics.

Pawley, A. 2007 The origins of early Lapita culture: the testimony of historical linguistics. In S. Bedford, C. Sand et al., eds, *Oceanic Explorations*, pp. 17–49. Canberra: Terra Australis 26.

Pawley, A. and Pawley, M. 1994 Early Austronesian terms for canoe parts and seafaring. In A. Pawley and M. Ross, eds, *Austronesian Terminologies: Continuity and Change*, pp. 329–62. Canberra: Pacific Linguistics Series C-127.

Pearsall, D. 2003 Plant food resources of the Ecuadorian Formative. In J. Raymond and R. Burger, eds, *Archaeology of Formative Ecuador*, pp. 213–58. Washington, DC: Dumbarton Oaks Research Library.

Pearson, O. 2012 Interpretation of the genetic, anatomical and archaeological data for the African origins of modern humans. In S. Reynolds and A. Gallagher, eds, *African Genesis: Perspectives on Hominin Evolution*, pp. 423–8. Cambridge: Cambridge University Press.

Perego, U., Achilli, A. et al. 2009 Distinctive Paleo-Indian migration routes from Beringia marked by two rare mtDNA haplogroups. *Current Biology* 19:1–8.

Perlès, C. 1999 The distribution of *magoules* in eastern Thessaly. In P. Halstead, ed., *Neolithic Society in Greece*, pp. 42–56. Sheffield: Sheffield Academic Press.

Perlès, C. 2005 From the Near East to Greece: let's reverse the focus. In C. Lichter, ed., *How did Farming Reach Europe?* pp. 275–90. Istanbul: Ege Yayınlari.

Perry, G. and N. Dominy 2009 Evolution of the human pygmy phenotype. *Trends in Ecology and Evolution* 24:218–25.

Peterson, J. 1978 *The Ecology of Social Boundaries*. Urbana: University of Illinois Press.

Peterson, N., ed. 2003 *Donald Thomson in Arnhem Land*. Carlton, VIC: Miegunyah Press.

Petraglia, M. and Korisettar, R. 2012 The Toba super-eruption of 74,000 years ago: climate change, environments, and evolving humans. *Quaternary International* 258:119–34.

Petraglia, M., Korisettar, R. et al. 2007 Middle Paleolithic assemblages fom the Indian Subcontinent before and after the Toba super-eruption. *Science* 417:114–6.

Petraglia, M., Clarkson, C. et al. 2009 Population increase and environmental deterioration correspond with microlithic innovations in South Asia ca. 35,000 years ago. *Proceedings of the National Academy of Sciences (USA)* 106:11261–6.

Petraglia, M., Haslam, M. et al. 2010 Out of Africa: new evidence and hypotheses for the dispersal of *Homo sapiens* along the Indian Ocean rim. *Annals of Human Biology* 37(3):288–311.

Pettitt, P. 2013 The rise of modern humans. In Scarre, ed., *The Human Past*, pp. 124–73. London: Thames and Hudson.

Phillipson, D. 2005 *African Archaeology*. Third Edition. Cambridge: Cambridge University Press.

Pickering, R., Dirks, P. et al. 2011 *Australopithecus sediba* at 1.977 ma and implications for the origins of the genus *Homo*. *Science* 333:1421–3.

Pietrusewsky, M. 2006 A multivariate craniometric study of the prehistoric and modern inhabitants of Southeast Asia, East Asia and surrounding regions: a human keleidoscope? In M. Oxenham and N. Tayles, eds, *Bioarchaeology of Southeast Asia*, pp. 59–90. Cambridge: Cambridge University Press.

Pinhasi, R. 2013 Europe: Neolithic colonization. In I. Ness and P. Bellwood, eds, Volume 1, *Prehistory*, pp. 168–77. Malden, MA and Oxford: Wiley-Blackwell.

Pinhasi, R. and Cramon-Taubadel, N. 2009 Craniometric data supports demic diffusion model for the spread of agriculture into Europe. *Plos ONE* 4(8):e6747.

Pinhasi, R. and Heyer, E. 2013 Central Asia: genetics and archaeology. In I. Ness and P. Bellwood, eds, *Encyclopedia of Global Human Migration*. Volume 1, *Prehistory*, pp. 184–90. Malden, MA and Oxford: Wiley-Blackwell.

Pinhasi, R. and Stock, J., eds, 2011 *Human Bioarchaeology of the Transition to Agriculture*. Chichester: Wiley-Blackwell.

Pinhasi, R., Fort, J. et al. 2005 Tracing the origin and spread of agriculture in Europe. *PLoS Biology* 3:e410.

Pinhasi, R., Higham, T. et al. 2011 Revised age of late Neanderthal occupation and the end of the Middle Paleolithic in the northern Caucasus. *Proceedings of the National Academy of Sciences (USA)* 108:8611–6.

Pinhasi, R., Thomas, M. et al. 2012 The genetic hsitory of Europeans. *Trends in Genetics* 128:496–505.

Piper, P., Campos, F. et al. 2012 Early evidence for pig and dog husbandry from the site of An Son, Southern Vietnam. *International Journal of Osteoarchaeology* (advance online, DOI: 10.1002/oa.2226).

Piperno, D. 2011a Plant cultivation and domestication in the New World tropics. *Current Anthropology* 52 (Supplement 4):S453–70.

Piperno, D. 2011b Northern Peruvian Early and Middle Preceramic agriculture. In T. Dillehay, ed., *From Foraging to Farming in the Andes*, pp. 275–84. Cambridge: Cambridge University Press.

Piperno, D., Weiss, E. et al. 2004 Processing of wild cereal grains in the Upper Palaeolithic revealed by starch grain analysis. *Nature* 430:670-3.

Piperno, D., Ranere, A. et al. 2009 Starch grain and phytolith evidence for early ninth millennium B.P. maize from the central Balsas River Valley, Mexico. *Proceedings of the National Academy of Sciences (USA)* 106:5019–24.

Pitulko, V. 1993 An early Holocene site in the Siberian high Arctic. *Arctic Anthropology* 30:13–21.

Pitulko, V. 2003 The bear-hunters of Zhokhov Island, East Russian Arctic. *Senri Ethnological Studies* 63:141–152 (Osaka).

Pitulko, V., Nikolsky, P. et al. 2004 The Yana RHS site. *Science* 303:52–6.

Pitulko, V., Pavlova, E. et al. 2012 The oldest art of the Eurasian Arctic. *Antiquity* 86:642–59.

Pleurdeau, D., Imalwa, E. et al. 2012 Earliest direct evidence of caprine domestication in southern Africa. *PLoS ONE* 7(7):e40340.

Plomley, N. 1966 *Friendly Mission*. Kingsgrove, NSW: Halstead.

Potter, B. 2010 Archaeological patterning in northeast Asia and northwest North America. In J. Kari and B. Potter, eds, *The Dene-Yeniseian Connection*, pp. 138–67. Fairbanks: University of Alaska Fairbanks, Department of Anthropology.

Potts, R. 2012 Environmental and behavioral evidence pertaining to the evolution of early *Homo*. *Current Anthropology* 53 (Supplement 6):S299–317.

Prescott, G., Williams, D. et al. 2012 Quantitative global analysis of the role of climate and people in explaining Quaternary megafaunal extinctions. *Proceedings of the National Academy of Sciences (USA)* 109:4527–31.

Price, T., Bentley, A. et al. 2001 Prehistoric human migration in the *Linearbandkeramik* of central Europe. *Antiquity* 75:593–603.

Pucciarelli, H., Perez, S. et al. 2010 Early Holocene human remains from the Argentinian Pampas. *American Journal of Physical Anthropology* 143:298–305.

Pugach, I., Delfin, F. et al. 2013 Genome-wide data substantiate Holocene gene flow from India to Australia. *Proceedings of the National Academy of Sciences (USA)* 110:1803–8.

Quintana-Murci, L., Chaix, R. et al. 2004 Where west meets east: the complex mtDNA landscape of the Southwest and Central Asian corridor. *American Journal of Human Genetics* 74:827–45.

Radcliffe-Brown, A. 1922 *The Andaman Islanders*. Glencoe: Free Press.

Raff, J., Bolnick, D. et al. 2011 Ancient DNA perspective on American colonization and population history. *American Journal of Physical Anthropology* 146:503–14.

Ranere, A., Piperno, D. et al. 2009 The cultural and chronological context of early Holocene maize and squash domestication in the central Balsas River Valley, Mexico. *Proceedings of the National Academy of Sciences (USA)* 106:5014–8.

Rankama, T. and Kankaanpää, J. 2008 Eastern arrivals in post-glacial Lapland. *Antiquity* 82:884–99.

Rankin, R. 2006 Siouan tribal contacts and dispersions evidenced in the terminology for maize and other cultigens. In J. Staller, Tykot, R. et al., eds, *Histories of Maize*, pp.564–77. Amsterdam: Elsevier.

Rasmussen, M., Li, Y. et al. 2010 Ancient human genome sequence of an extinct Palaeo-Eskimo. *Nature* 463:757–62.

Rasmussen, M., Guo, X. et al. 2011 An Aboriginal Australian genome reveals separate human dispersals into Asia. *Science* 334:94–8.

Ratliff, M. 2010 *Hmong-Mien Language History*. Canberra: Pacific Linguistics.

Ray, N., Wegmann, D. et al. 2010 A statistical evaluation of models for the initial settlement of the American continent emphasizes the importance of gene flow with Asia. *Molecular Biology and Evolution* 27:337–45.

Reich, D. 2011 Evidence for at least four human dispersals between Africa and Eurasia. In A. Derevianko and M. Shunkov, eds, *Characteristic Features of the Middle to Upper Paleolithic Transition in Eurasia*, pp. 174–9. Novosibirsk: Institute of Archaeology and Ethnography.

Reich, D., Thangaraj, K. et al. 2009 Reconstructing Indian population history. *Nature* 461:489–94.

Reich, D., Green, R.et al. 2010 Genetic history of an archaic hominin from Denisova Cave in Siberia. *Nature* 468:1053–60.

Reich, D., Patterson, N. et al. 2011 Denisova admixture and the first modern human dispersals into Southeast Asia and Oceania. *American Journal of Human Genetics* 89:1–13.

Reich, D., Patterson, N. et al. 2012 Reconstructing Native American population history. *Nature* 488:370–4.

Reid, L. 1994 Unravelling the linguistic histories of Philippine Negritos. In T. Dutton and D. Tryon, eds, *Language Contact and Change in the Austroneaian World*, pp. 443–76. Berlin: Mouton de Gruyter.

Renfrew, C. 1987 *Archaeology and Language*. London: Jonathan Cape.

Renfrew, C. 1989 Models of change in language and archaeology. *Transactions of the Philological Society* 87:103–65.

Renfrew, C. 1991 Before Babel. *Cambridge Archaeological Journal* 1:3–23.

Renfrew, C. 1992a World languages and human dispersals: a minimalist view. In J. Hall and I. Jarvie, eds, *Transition to Modernity*, pp. 11–68. Cambridge: Cambridge University Press.

Renfrew, C. 1992b Archaeology, genetics and linguistic diversity. *Man* 27:445–78.

Renfrew, C. 1996 Language families and the spread of farming. In D. Harris, ed., *The Origins and Spread of Agriculture and Pastoralism in Asia*, pp. 70–92. London: UCL Press.

Renfrew, C. 1998 Word of Minos. *Cambridge Archaeological Journal* 8:239–64.

Renfrew, C. 1999 Time depth, convergence theory, and innovation in Proto-Indo-European. *Journal of Indo-European Studies* 27:257–93.

Renfrew, C. 2000 At the edge of knowability: towards a prehistory of languages. *Cambridge Archaeological Journal* 10:7–34.

Renfrew, C. 2001 The Anatolian origins of Proto-Indo-European and the autochthony of the Hittites. In R. Drews, ed., *Greater Anatolia and the Indo-Hittite Language Family*, pp. 36–63. Washington DC: Institute for the Study of Man.

Renfrew, C. 2002 'The emerging synthesis': the archaeogenetics of language / farming dispersals and other spread zones. In P. Bellwood and C. Renfrew, eds, *Examining the Farming/Language Dispersal Hypothesis*, pp. 3–16. Cambridge: McDonald Institute.

Rexova, K., Frynta, D. et al. 2003 Cladistic analysis of languages: Indo-European classification based on lexicostatistical data. *Cladistics* 19:120–7.

Richards, M. 2003 The Neolithic invasion of Europe. *Annual Review of Anthropology* 32:135–62.

Richards, M. and Trinkaus, E. 2009 Isotopic evidence for the diets of European Neanderthals and early modern humans. *Proceedings of the National Academy of Sciences (USA)* 106: 16034–9.

Richerson, P., Boyd, R. et al. 2001 Was agriculture impossible during the Pleistocene but mandatory during the Holocene? *American Antiquity* 66:387–411.

Rightmire, G. and Lordkipanidze, D. 2010 Fossil skulls from Dmanisi. In J. Fleagle, J.J. Shea et al., eds, *Out of Africa I*, pp. 225–44. Dordrecht: Springer.

Rimantiené, R. 1992 The Neolithic of the eastern Baltic. *Journal of World Prehistory* 6:97–143.

Ringe, D, Warnow, T. et al. 1998 Computational cladistics and the position of Tocharian. In V.H. Mair, ed., *The Bronze Age and Early Iron Age Peoples of Eastern Central Asia*, pp. 391–414. Philadelphia: Institute for the Study of Man.

Ringe, D., Warnow, T. et al. 2002 Indo-European and computational cladistics. *Transactions of the Philological Society* 100:59–129.

Rispoli, F. 2007 The incised and impressed pottery of Mainland Southeast Asia: following the paths of Neolithization. *East and West* 57:235–304.

Robertshaw, P. 2013 Sub-Saharan Africa: archaeology. In I. Ness and P. Bellwood, eds, *Encyclopedia of Global Human Migration*. Volume 1, *Prehistory*, pp. 107–14. Malden, MA and Oxford: Wiley-Blackwell.

Robertson, G., Attenbrow, V. et al. 2009 Multiple uses for Australian backed artefacts. *Antiquity* 83:296–308.

Robinson, D. 2007 Exploitation of plant resources in the Mesolithic and Neolithic of southern Scandinavia. In S. Colledge and J. Conolly, eds, *The Origins and Spread of Domestic Plants in Southwest Asia and Europe*, pp. 359–74. Walnut Creek: West Coast Press.

Robinson, B. 2008 Commentary: microblades and seasonality. *The Review of Archaeology* 29:21–40.

Rodriguez, J., Burjachs, F. et al. 2011 One million years of cultural evolution in a stable environment at Atapuerca (Burgos, Spain). *Quaternary Science Reviews* 30:1396–412.

Roebrooks, W. and Villa, P. 2011 On the earliest evidence for habitual use of fire in Europe. *Proceedings of the National Academy of Sciences (USA)* 108:5209–14.

Rohling, E.J., Grant, E. et al. 2008 High rates of sea-level rise during the last interglacial period. *Nature Geoscience* 1:38–42.

Rolett, B., Zheng, Z. et al. 2011 Holocene sea-level change and the emergence of Neolithic seafaring in the Fuzhou Basin. *Quaternary Science Reviews* 30:788–97.

Romney, A. 1957 The genetic model and Uto-Aztecan time perspective. *Davidson Journal of Anthropology* 3:35–41.

Roodenberg, J. and Alpaslan-Roodenberg, S. 2008 Ilıpınar and Menteşe. In D. Bailey, A. Whittle et al., eds, *Living Well Together?* pp. 8–16. Oxford: Oxbow.

Roostalu, U., Kutuev, J. et al. 2007 Origin and expansion of haplogroup H, the dominant human mitochondrial lineage in West Eurasia. *Molecular Biology and Evolution* 24(2):436–48.

Rose, J. 2010 New light on human prehistory in the Arabo-Persian Gulf oasis. *Current Anthropology* 51:849–83.

Rosenberg, M. 2003 The strength of numbers. In U. Esin, M. Ozdogan et al., eds, *Koyden Kente: From Villages to Cities*, Vol. 1, pp. 91–102. Istanbul: Arkeoloji ve Sanat Yayinlari.

Rosenswig, R. 2006 Sedentism and food production in early complex societies of Soconusco, Mexico. *World Archaeology* 38:330–55.

Roth, W.E. 1908 Australian canoes and rafts. *Man* 8(88):161–2.

Rotilio, G. and Marchese, E. 2010 Nutritional factors in human dispersals. *Annals of Human Biology* 37:312–24.

Rouse, I. 1986 *Migrations in Prehistory*. New Haven: Yale University Press.

Rowley-Conwy, P. 2004a Early domestic animals in Europe: imported or locally domesticated? In A. Ammerman and P. Biagi, eds, *The Widening Harvest*, pp. 99–120. Boston: Archaeological Institute of America.

Rowley-Conwy, P. 2004b How the West was lost. *Current Anthropology* 45 (Supplement):S83–113.

Rowley-Conwy, P. 2011 Westward Ho! The spread of agriculturalism from central Europe to the Atlantic. *Current Anthropology* 52 (Supplement 4):S431–52.

Rowley-Conwy, P. and Layton, R. 2013 Foraging and farming as niche construction. *Philosophical Transactions of the Royal Society of London, Series B* 366:849–62.

Ruddiman, W.F. 2003 The anthropogenic greenhouse era began thousands of years ago. *Climatic Change* 61:261–93.

Ruddiman, W.F. 2005 *Plows, Plagues and Petroleum*. Princeton: Princeton University Press.

Ruhlen, M. 1987 *A Guide to the World's Languages*. Volume 1. Stanford: Stanford University Press.

Ruhlen, M. 1994 *The Origin of Language*. New York: Wiley.

Ruhlen, M. 1998 The origin of the Na-Dene. *Proceedings of the National Academy of Sciences (USA)* 95:13994–6.

Rule, S., Brook, B. et al. 2012 The aftermath of megafaunal extinction: ecosystem transformation in prehistoric Australia. *Science* 335:1483–6.

Ruxton, G. and Wilkinson, D. 2011 Avoidance of overheating and selection for both hair loss and bipedality in humans. *Proceedings of the National Academy of Sciences (USA)* 108:20965–9.

Ryan, C. and Jetha, C. 2010 *Sex at Dawn*. Melbourne: Scribe.

Sagart, L. 2003 The vocabulary of cereal cultivation and the phylogeny of East Asian languages. *Bulletin of the Indo-Pacific Prehistory Association* 2:127–36.

Sagart, L. 2005a Sino-Tibetan-Austronesian: an updated and improved argument. In L. Sagart, R. Blench et al., eds, *The Peopling of East Asia*, pp. 161–76. London: RoutledgeCurzon.

Sagart, L. 2005b Tai-Kadai as a subgroup of Austronesian. In L. Sagart, R. Blench et al., eds, *The Peopling of East Asia*, pp. 177–81. London: RoutledgeCurzon.

Sagart, L. 2008 The expansion of *Setaria* farmers in East Asia. In A. Sanchez-Mazas, R. Blench et al., eds, *Past Human Migrations in East Asia*, pp. 133–57. London: RoutledgeCurzon.

Sagart, L. 2011 The Austroasiatics: east to west or west to east? In N. Enfield, ed., *Dynamics of Human Diversity*, pp. 345–60. Canberra: Pacific Linguistics.

Sahultime 2007 http://sahultime.monash.edu.au/explore.html.

Salque, M., Bogucki, P. et al. 2013 Earliest evidence for cheese making in the sixth millennium BC in northern Europe. *Nature* 493:522–5.

Sampietro, M., Lao, O. et al. 2007 Palaeogenetic evidence supports a dual model of Neolithic spreading into Europe. *Proceedings of the Royal Society of London, Series B* 274:2161–7.

Sarjeant, C. 2012a The Role of Potters at Neolithic An Son, Southern Vietnam. Unpublished PhD thesis, Australian National University.

Sarjeant, C. 2012b Defining the Neolithic of southern Vietnam: the ceramics of An Son. In D. Bonatz, A. Reinecke et al., eds, *Crossing Borders: Selected Papers from the 13th International Conference of the European Association of Southeast Asian Archaeologists, Volume 1*, pp. 143–63. Singapore: National University of Singapore.

Sato, H. and T. Tsutsumi 2007 The Japanese microblade industries: technology, raw material procurement, and adaptations. In Y. Kuzmin, S.G. Keates et al., eds, *Origin and Spread of Microblade Technology in Northern Asia and North America*, pp. 53–78. Burnaby, British Columbia: Archaeology Press.

Sato, Y-C., Yamanaka, S. et al. 2003 Evidence for Jomon plant cultivation based on DNA analysis of chestnut remains. *Senri Ethnological Studies* 63:187–97.

Savolainen, P., Leitner, T. et al. 2004 A detailed picture of the origin of the Australian dingo, obtained from the study of mitochondrial DNA. *Proceedings of the National Academy of Sciences (USA)* 101:12387–90.

Scally, A. and Durbin, R. 2012 Revising the human mutation rate: implications for understanding human evolution. *Nature Reviews, Genetics* 13(10):745–53.

Scarre, C., ed. 2013 *The Human Past*. Third edition. London: Thames and Hudson.

Scheidel, W. 2005 Human mobility in Roman Italy, 1: The free population. *Journal of Roman Studies* 95:1–26.

Scheu, A., Hartz, S. et al. 2008 Ancient DNA provides no evidence for independent domestication of cattle in Mesolithic Rosenhof, northern Germany. *Journal of Archaeological Science* 35:1257–64.

Schillaci, M. 2008 Human cranial diversity and evidence for an ancient lineage of modern humans. *Journal of Human Evolution* 54:814–26.

Schlebusch, C., Skoglund, P. et al. 2012 Genomic variation in seven Khoe-San groups reveals adaptation and complex African history. *Science* 338:374–9.

Schmidt, K. 2012 Göbekli Tepe. *A Stone Age Sanctuary in Southeast Anatolia*. Berlin: ex oriente.

Scholz, C., Johnson, T. et al. 2007 East African megadroughts between 135 and 75 thousand years ago and bearing on early-modern human origins. *Proceedings of the National Academy of Sciences (USA)* 104:16416–21.

Schooling, S. 1990 *Language Maintenance in Melanesia: Sociolinguistics and Social Networks in New Caledonia*. Dallas: Summer Institute of Linguistics.

Schoop, U-D. 2005 The late escape of the Neolithic from the central Anatolian Plain. In C. Lichter, ed., *How did Farming Reach Europe?* pp. 41–58. Istanbul: Ege Yayinlari.

Schulting, R. 2011 Mesolithic-Neolithic transitions: an isotopic tour through Europe, pp. 17–42. In R. Pinhasi and J. Stock, eds, *Human Bioarchaeology at the Transition to Agriculture*, pp. 17–42. Chichester: Wiley-Blackwell.

Schwartzenberg, H. 2005 Prismatic polypod vessels and their way to Europe. In C. Lichter, ed., *How did Farming Reach Europe?* pp. 255–74. Istanbul: Ege Yayinlari.

Schwartzenberg, H. 2006 A new item for the Neolithic package? In I. Gatsov and H. Schwartzenberg, eds, *Aegean-Marmara-Black Sea*, pp. 127–34. Langenweissbach: Beier and Beran.

Sellato, B. 1994 *Nomads of the Borneo Rainforest*. Honolulu: University of Hawaii Press.

Sémah, F. and Sémah, A. 2013 Pleistocene migrations in the Southeast Asian archipelagoes. In I. Ness and P. Bellwood, eds, *Encyclopedia of Global Human Migration. Volume 1, Prehistory*, pp. 49–54. Malden, MA and Oxford: Wiley-Blackwell.

Seong, C. 2008 Tanged points, microblades, and late Palaeolithic hunting in Korea. *Antiquity* 82:871–83.

Serva, M. and Petroni, F. 2008 Indo-European languages tree by Levenshtein distance. *EPL (Europhysics Letters)* 81(6).

Serva, M., Petroni, F. et al. 2011 Malagasy dialects and the peopling of Madagascar. *Journal of the Royal Society Interface* 9:54–67.

Shang, H., Tong, H. et al. 2007 An early modern human from Tianyuan Cave, Zhoukoudian, China. *Proceedings of the National Academy of Sciences (USA)* 104:6573–8.

Shea, J. 2010a Stone Age visiting cards revisited. In J. Fleagle, J.J. Shea et al., eds, *Out of Africa I*, pp. 47–64. Dordrecht: Springer.

Shea, J. 2010b Neanderthals and early *Homo sapiens* in the Levant. In E. Garcea, ed., *South-Eastern Mediterranean Peoples Between 130,000 and 10,000 Years Ago*, pp. 126–43. Oxford: Oxbow.

Shea, J. 2011 *Homo sapiens* is as *Homo sapiens* was. *Current Anthropology* 52:1–35.

Shea, J., Fleagle, J. et al. 2007 Context and chronology of early *Homo sapiens* fossils from the Omo Kibish Formation, Ethiopia. In P. Mellars, O. Bar-Yosef et al., eds, *Rethinking the Human Revolution*, pp. 219–34. Cambridge: McDonald Institute.

Shelach, G. 2012 On the invention of pottery. *Science* 336:1644–5.

Shen, G., Gao, X. et al. 2009 Age of Zhoukoudian *Homo erectus*. *Nature* 458:198–200.

Shennan, S. 2008 Population processes and their consequences in early Neolithic central Europe. In J-P. Bocquet-Appel and O. Bar-Yosef, eds, *The Neolithic Demographic Transition and its Consequences*, pp. 315–29. Dordrecht: Springer.

Shennan, S. 2009 Evolutionary demography and the population history of the European early Neolithic. *Human Biology* 81:339–55.

Shennan, S. and Edinburgh, K. 2007 Prehistoric population hsitory: from the late glacial to the late Neolithic in central and northern Europe. *Journal of Archaeological Science* 34:1339–45.

Sheppard, P. 2011 Lapita colonization across the near/remote Oceania bondary. *Current Anthropology* 52:799–840.

Sherratt, A. 2005 Settling the Neolithic: a *digestif*. In D. Bailey, A. Whittle et al., eds, *Unsettling the Neolithic*, pp. 140–6. Oxford: Oxbow.

Sherratt, A. 2007 Diverse origins: regional contributions ot the genesis of farming. In S. Colledge and J. Conolly, eds, *The Origins and Spread of Domestic Plants in Southwest Asia and Europe*, pp. 1–20. Walnut Creek: West Coast Press.

Shi, W., Q. Ayub et al. 2010 A worldwide survey of human male demographic history based on Y-SNP and Y-STR data from the HGDP–CEPH populations. *Molecular Biology and Evolution* 27(2):385–93.

Shinde, V, Osada, T. et al. 2008 Exploration in the Ghaggar Basin and excavations at Girawad, Farmana and Mitathal. In T. Osada and A. Uesugi, eds, *Linguistics, Archaeology and the Human Past*, pp. 77–158. Kyoto: Research Institute for Humanity and Nature.

Shipman, P. 2012 Do the eyes have it? *American Scientist* 100(3):198.

Shirai, N. 2005 Walking with herdsmen. *Neo-Lithics* 1(5):12–16. Berlin: ex oriente.

Sidwell, P. 2013 Southeast Asian mainland: linguistic hsitory. In I. Ness and P. Bellwood, eds, *Encyclopedia of Global Human Migration*. Volume 1, *Prehistory*, pp. 259–68. Malden, MA and Oxford: Wiley-Blackwell.

Sidwell, P. and Blench, R. 2011 The Austroasiatic Urheimat: the Southeastern Riverine Hypothesis. In N. Enfield, ed., *Dynamics of Human Diversity*, pp. 315–44. Canberra: Pacific Linguistics.

Sigurdsson, G. 2009a The north Atlantic expansion. In S. Brink, ed., *The Viking World*, pp. 562–70. London: Routledge.

Sigurdsson, J. 2009b Iceland. In S. Brink, ed., *The Viking World*, pp. 571–8. London: Routledge.

Simmons, A. 2004 Bitter hippos of Cyprus. In A. Peltenberg and A. Wasse, eds, *Neolithic Revolution*, pp. 1–14. Oxford: Oxbow.

Simmons, A. 2007 *The Neolithic Revolution in the Near East*. Tucson: University of Arizona Press.

Simmons, A. 2008 American researchers and the earliest Cypriots. *Near Eastern Archaeology* 71:21–9.

Sims-Williams, P. 2008 *Ancient Celtic Place-names in Europe and Asia Minor*. Oxford: Blackwell.

Skoglund, P., Malmstrom, H. et al. 2012 Origins and genetic legacy of Neolithic farmers and hunter–gatherers in Europe. *Science* 336:466–9.

Slimak, L., Svendsen, J. et al. 2011 Late Mousterian persistence near the Arctic Circle. *Science* 332:841–5.

Slimak, L., Svendsen, J. et al. 2012 Response to "Comment on Late Mousterian persistence near the Arctic Circle". *Science* 335:167c.

Sliva, R.J., ed. 2005 *Material Cultures and Lifeways of early Agricultural Communities in Southern Arizona*. Anthropological Papers 35. Tucson, Center for Desert Archaeology.

Smalley, J. and Blake, M. 2003 Sweet beginnings: stalk sugar and the domestication of maize. *Current Anthropology* 44:675–704.

Smith, K. 1995 *Landnam*: the settlement of Iceland in archaeologial and historical perspective. *World Archaeology* 26:319–47.

Smith, B. 2001 Low-level food production. *Journal of Archaeological Research* 9:1–43.

Smith, B. 2006 Eastern North America as an independent center of plant domestication. *Proceedings of the National Academy of Sciences (USA)* 1–3:12223–8.

Smith, A. 2008 Pastoral origins at the Cape, South Africa. *Southern African Humanities* 20:49–60.

Smith, B. 2011 The cultural context of plant domestication in eastern North America. *Current Anthropology* 52 (Supplement 4):S471–85.

Smith, D., Harrison, S. et al. 2011 The early Holocene sea level rise. *Quaternary Science Reviews* 30:1846–60.

Smith, F., Hutchinson, V. et al. 2012 Assimilation and modern human origins in the African peripheries. In S. Reynolds and A. Gallagher, eds, *African Genesis: Perspectives on Hominin Evolution*, pp. 365–93. Cambridge: Cambridge University Press.

Snow, D. 1994 *The Iroquois*. Oxford: Blackwell.

Snow, D. 1995 Migration in prehistory: the Northern Iroquoian case. *American Antiquity* 60:59–79.

Snow, D. 1996 The first Amerians and the differentiation of hunter-gatherer cultures. In B.G. Trigger and W.E. Washburn, eds, *The Cambridge History of the Native Peoples of the Americas*. Volume 1, *North America*, Part 1, pp. 125–99. Cambridge: Cambridge University Press.

Snow, D. 2013 Eastern North America: archaeology. In I. Ness and P. Bellwood, eds, *Encyclopedia of Global Human Migration*. Volume 1, *Prehistory*, pp. 354–61. Malden, MA and Oxford: Wiley-Blackwell.

Soares, P., Trejaut, J. et al. 2008 Climate change and human dispersals in Southeast Asia. *Molecular Biology and Evolution* 25:1209–18.

Soares, P., Achilli, A. et al. 2010 The archaeogenetics of Europe. *Current Biology* 20: R174–83.

Soares, P., Rito, T. et al. 2011 Ancient voyaging and Polynesian origins. *American Journal of Human Genetics* 88:1–9.

Soares, P., Alshamali, F. et al. 2012 The expansion of mtDNA haplogroup L3 within and out of Africa. *Molecular Biology and Evolution* 29:915–27.

Soffer, O. 2004 Recovering perishable technologies through use wear on stone tools. *Current Anthropology* 45:407–13.

Solberg, B. 1989 The Neolithic transition in southern Scandinavia. *Oxford Journal of Archaeology* 8:261–96.

Southerton, S. 2013 The human colonization of the Americas: genetics. In I. Ness and P. Bellwood, eds, *Encyclopedia of Global Human Migration*. Volume 1, *Prehistory*, pp. 70–6. Malden, MA and Oxford: Wiley-Blackwell.

Southworth, F. 2005 *Linguistic Archaeology of South Asia*. London and New York: RoutledgeCurzon.

Southworth, F. 2009 Proto-Dravidian Agriculture. In Toshiki Osada, ed., *Linguistics, Archaeology and Human Past in South Asia*, pp. 101–26. Delhi: Manohar.

Southworth, F. 2011 Rice in Dravidian. *Rice* 4:142–8.

Southworth, F. and McAlpin, D. 2013 South Asia: Dravidian linguistic history. In I. Ness and P. Bellwood, eds, *Encyclopedia of Global Human Migration*. Volume 1, *Prehistory*, pp. 235–44. Malden, MA and Oxford: Wiley-Blackwell.

Spencer, B. 1982 *The Aboriginal Photographs of Baldwin Spencer*. Melbourne: John Currey, O'Neil Pty Ltd.

Spriggs, M. 1997 *The Island Melanesians*. Oxford: Blackwell.

Spriggs, M. 2011 Archaeology and the Austronesian expansion: where are we now? *Antiquity* 85:510–29.

Spriggs, M. 2013 Oceania: Lapita migration. In I. Ness and P. Bellwood, eds, *Encyclopedia of Global Human Migration*. Volume 1, *Prehistory*, pp. 308–13. Malden, MA and Oxford: Wiley-Blackwell.

Staller, J., Tykot, R. et al., eds, 2006 *Histories of Maize*. Amsterdam: Elsevier.

Stark, M., Bowser, B. et al. 2008 Why breaking down boundaries matters for archaeological research on learning and cultural transmission. In M. Stark, B.J. Bowser et al., eds, *Cultural Transmission and Material Culture*, pp. 1–16. Tucson: University of Arizona Press.

Steele, J., Jordan, P. et al. 2010 Evolutionary approaches to cultural and linguistic diversity. *Philosophical Transactions of the Royal Society of London, Series B* 365:3781–5.

Stevens, C. 2007 Reconsidering the evidence. In S. Colledge and J. Conolly, eds, *The Origins and Spread of Domestic Plants in Southwest Asia and Europe*, pp. 375–90. Walnut Creek: West Coast Press.

Stevens, C. and Fuller, D. 2012 Did Neolithic farming fail? *Antiquity* 86:707–22.

Stewart, J. and Stringer, C. 2012 Human evolution out of Africa: the role of refugia and climate change. *Science* 335:1317–21.

Stoneking, M. and Delfin, F. 2010 The human genetic history of East Asia. *Current Biology* 20: R188–93.

Stoneking, M. and Harvati, K. 2013 Early Old World migrations of *Homo sapiens*: human biology. In I. Ness and P. Bellwood, eds, *Encyclopedia of Global Human Migration*. Volume 1, *Prehistory*, pp. 26–37. Malden, MA and Oxford: Wiley-Blackwell.

Storey, A., Athens, J. et al. 2012 Investigating the global dispersal of chickens in prehistory using ancient mitochondrial DNA signatures. *PLoS ONE* 7(7):e39171.

Storm, P. 2001 The evolution of humans in Australasia from an environmental perspective. *Palaeogeography, Palaeoclimatology, Palaeoecology* 171:363–83.

Strade, N. 1998 An interdisciplinary approach to the role of Uralic hunters and gatherers in the ethnohistory of the early Germanic area. In K. Julku and K. Wiik, eds, *The Roots of Peoples and Languages of North Eurasia*, pp. 168–79. Turku: Finno-Ugric Historical Society.

Stringer, C. 2007 The origin and dispersal of *Homo sapiens*. In P. Mellars, O. Bar-Yosef et al., eds, *Rethinking the Human Revolution*, pp. 15–20. Cambridge: McDonald Institute.

Summerhayes G. 2010 Lapita interaction – an update. In M. Gadu and Hsiu-man Lin, eds, *2009 International Symposium of Austronesian Studies*, pp. 11–40. Taitung, Taiwan: National Museum of Prehistory.

Summerhayes, G., Leavesley, M. et al. 2010 Human adaptation and plant use in Highland New Guinea 49,000 to 44,000 years ago. *Science* 330:78–81.

Sutlive V.H. 1978 *The Iban of Sarawak*. Arlington Heights: AHM Pub.

Szabo, K, Brumm, A. et al. 2007 Shell artefact production at 32,000 BP in Island Southeast Asia: thinking across media? *Current Anthropology* 48:701–24.

Taavitsainen, J.-P., Simola, H. et al. 1998 Cultivation history beyond the periphery. *Journal of World Prehistory* 12:199–253.

Tabbada, K.A., Trejaut, J. et al. 2010 Philippine mitochondrial DNA diversity: A populated viaduct between Taiwan and Indonesia? *Molecular Biology and Evolution* 27:21–31.

Tamm, E., Kivisild, T. et al. 2007 Beringian standstill and spread of Native American founders. *PloS One* 2(9): e829.

Tayles, N. 1999 *The Excavation of Khok Phanom Di*. Volume V, *The People*. London: Society of Antiquaries.

Telegin, D.J. 1987 Neolithic cultures of the Ukraine and adjacent areas and their chronology. *Journal of World Prehistory* 1:307–31.

Terrell, J. 1986 *Prehistory in the Pacific Islands*. Cambridge: Cambridge University Press.

Thangaraj, K., Chaubey, G. et al. 2005 Reconstructing the origin of the Andaman Islanders. *Science* 308:996.

Thiel, B. 1987 Early settlement of the Philippines, Eastern Indonesia, and Australia-New Guinea. *Current Anthropology* 28:236–41.

Thomas, M., Stumpf, M. et al. 2006 Evidence for an apartheid-like social structure in early Anglo-Saxon England. *Proceedings of the Royal Society of London, Series B* 273:2651–7.

Thomas, M., Kivisild, T. et al. 2013 Europe and Western Asia: genetics and population history. In I. Ness and P. Bellwood, eds, *Encyclopedia of Global Human Migration*. Volume 1, *Prehistory*, pp. 146–56. Malden, MA and Oxford: Wiley-Blackwell.

Thomas, N. et al., eds, 1996 *Observations Made During a Voyage Round the World*. Honolulu: University of Hawaii Press.

Timmreck, C., Graf, H. et al. 2012 Climate response to the Toba super-eruption: regional changes. *Quaternary International* 258:30–44.

Tipping, R., Bunting, M. et al. 2009 Modeling land use around an early Neolithic timber 'hall' in north east Scotland from high resolution pollen analyses. *Journal of Archaeological Science* 36:140–9.

Tishkoff, S., Reed, F. et al. 2009 The genetic structure and history of Africans and African Americans. *Science* 324:1035–44.

Tito, R., Belknap III, S. et al. 2011 DNA from early Holocene American dog. *American Journal of Physical Anthropology* 145:653–7.

Tomasello, M., Melis, A. et al. 2012 Two key steps in the evolution of human cooperation: the interdependence hypothesis. *Current Anthropology* 53:673–92.

Trinkaus, E. 2007 European early modern humans and the fate of the Neandertals. *Proceedings of the National Academy of Sciences (USA)* 104:7367–72.

Tsang C-h. 1992 *Archaeology of the P'eng-hu Islands*. Taipei: Institute of History and Philology, Academia Sinica.

Tsang, C-h. 2005 Recent discoveries at a Tapenkeng culture site in Taiwan: implications for the problem of Austronesian origins. In L. Sagart, R. Blench et al., eds, *The Peopling of East Asia*, pp. 63–73. London: RoutledgeCurzon.

Tsutsumi, T. 2012 MIS3 edge-ground axes and the arrival of the first *Homo sapiens* in the Japanese Archipelago. *Quaternary International* 248:70-8.

Tumonggor, M., Karafet, T. et al. 2013 The Indonesian archipelago: an ancient genetic highway linking Asia and the Pacific. *Journal of Human Genetics* advance online.

Tuniz, C., Gillespie, R. et al. 2009 *The Bone Readers*. Sydney: Allen and Unwin.

Turney, C. and Brown, H. 2007 Catastrophic early Holocene sea level rise, human migration and the Neolithic transition in Europe. *Quaternary Science Reviews* 26:2036–41.

Turney, C., Flannery, T. et al. 2008 Late surviving megafauna in Tasmania, Australia, implicate human involvement in their extinction. *Proceedings of the National Academy of Sciences (USA)* 105:12150–3.

Uerpmann, H., Potts, D. et al. 2009 Holocene (re-)occupation of eastern Arabia. In M. Petraglia and J. Rose, eds, *The Evolution of Human Populations in Arabia*, pp. 205–14. Springer Science + Business Media.

Valamoti, S. and Kotsakis, K. 2007 Transitions to agriculture in the Aegean: the archaeobotanical evidence. In S. Colledge and J. Conolly, eds, *The Origins and Spread of Domestic Plants in Southwest Asia and Europe*, pp. 75–92. Walnut Creek: West Coast Press.

Vamplew, W., ed. 1987 *Australians: Historical Statistics*. Sydney: Fairfax, Syme and Weldon.

Van Andel, T. and Runnels, C. 1995 The earliest farmers in Europe. *Antiquity* 69:481–500.

Van den Bergh, G., de Vos, J. et al. 2001 The Late Quaternary palaeogeography of mammal evolution in the Indonesian Archipelago. *Palaeogeography, Palaeoclimatology, Palaeoecology* 171:385–408.

Van der Geer, A., Lyras, G. et al. 2010 *Evolution of Island Mammals*. Oxford: Wiley-Blackwell.

Van der Made, J. 2011 Biogeography and climatic change as a context to human dispersal out of Africa and within Eurasia. *Quaternary Science Reviews* 30:1353–67.

Van Driem, G. 2011 Rice and the Austroasiatic and Hmong-Mien homelands. In N. Enfield, ed., *Dynamics of Human Diversity*, pp. 361–90. Canberra: Pacific Linguistics.

Van Heekeren, H. 1972 *The Stone Age of Indonesia*, second edition. The Hague: Nijhoff.

Van Heteren, A. and Sankhyan, A. 2009 Hobbits and pygmies: trends in evolution. In A.R. Sankhyan, ed., *Asian Perspectives on Human Evolution*, pp. 172–87. New Delhi: Serials Publications.

VanPool, T., Palmer, C. et al. 2008 Horned serpents, tradition, and the tapestry of culture. In M.J. O'Brien, ed., *Cultural Transmission and Archaeology*, pp. 77–90. Washington DC: Society for American Archaeology.

Vennemann, T. 1994 Linguistic reconstruction in the context of European prehistory. *Transactions of the Philological Society* 92:215–84.

Verhoeven, M. 2011 The birth of a concept and the origins of the Neolithic. *Paléorient* 37:75–87.

Vermeersch, P. 2010 Middle and Upper Palaeolithic in the Egyptian Nile valley. In E. Garcea, ed., *South-Eastern Mediterranean Peoples Between 130,000 and 10,000 Years Ago*, pp. 66–88. Oxford: Oxbow.

Vierra, B. and Ford, R. 2006 Early maize agriculture in the northern Rio Grande valley, New Mexico. In J. Staller, Tykot, R. et al., eds, *Histories of Maize*, pp. 497–510. Amsterdam: Elsevier.

Vigne, J-D. 2008 Zooarchaeological aspects of the Neolithic diet transition in the Near East and Europe. In J-P. Bocquet-Appel and O. Bar-Yosef, eds, *The Neolithic Demographic Transition and its Consequences*, pp. 179–206. Dordrecht: Springer.

Vigne, J-D., Carrère, I. et al. 2011 The early process of mammal domestication in the Near East. *Current Anthropology* 52 (Supplement 4):S255–73.

Volodko, N., Starikovskaya, E. et al. 2008 Mitochondrial genome diversity in Arctic Siberians. *American Journal of Human Genetics* 82:11084–100.

VonHoldt, B., Pollinger, J. et al. 2010 Genome-wide SNP and haplotype analyses reveal a rich history underlying dog domestication. *Nature* 464:898–903.

Vovin, A. 2000 Did the Xiong-nu speak a Yeniseian language? *Central Asian Journal* 44:87–104, 389–94.

Vovin, A. 2013 Northeastern and Central Asia: Altaic linguistic prehistory. In I. Ness and P. Bellwood, eds, *Encyclopedia of Global Human Migration*. Volume 1, *Prehistory*, pp. 197–203. Malden, MA and Oxford: Wiley-Blackwell.

Wainwright, F.T. 1962 *Archaeology and Place-names and History*. London: Routledge and Kegan Paul.

Walker, R. and Hamilton, M. 2011 Social complexity and linguistic diversity in the Austronesian and Bantu population expansions. *Proceedings of the Royal Society of London, Series B* 278:1399–404.

Walker, R. and Ribeiro, L. 2011 Bayesian phylogeography of the Arawak expansion in lowland South America. *Proceedings of the Royal Society of London, Series B* 278:2562–7.

Wallaert, H. 2008 The way of the potter's mother. In M. Stark, B.J. Bowser et al., eds, *Cultural Transmission and Material Culture*, pp. 178–98. Tucson: University of Arizona Press.

Walter, R., Buffler, R. et al. 2000 Early human occupation of the Red Sea coast of Eritrea during the last interglacial. *Nature* 405:65–9.

Walter, R., Jacomb, C. et al. 2010 Colonization, mobility and exchange in New Zealand prehistory. *Antiquity* 84:497–513.

Warmuth, V., Eriksson, A. et al. 2012 Reconstructing the origin and spread of horse domestication in the Eurasian steppe. *Proceedings of the National Academy of Sciences (USA)* 109:8202–6.

Warnow, T. 1997 Mathematical approaches to computational linguistics. *Proceedings of the National Academy of Sciences (USA)* 94:6585–90.

Waters, M. and Stafford, T. 2007 Redefining the age of Clovis: implications for the peopling of the Americas. *Science* 315:1122–6.

Waters, M., Forman, S. et al. 2011a The Buttermilk Creek Site and the origins of Clovis. *Science* 331:1599–603.

Waters, M., Stafford, T. et al. 2011b Pre-Clovis mastodon hunting 13,800 years ago at the Manis Site, Washington. *Science* 334:351–3.

Watkins, C. 1998 Proto-Indo-European: comparison and reconstruction. In A.G. Ramat and P. Ramat, eds, *The Indo-European Languages*, pp. 25–73. London: Routledge.

Watson, P. 2012 *The Great Divide*. London: Weidenfeld and Nicholson.

Weale, M., Weiss, D. et al. 2002 Y chromosome evidence for Anglo-Saxon mass migration. *Molecular Biology and Evolution* 19:1008–21.

Weaver, T. 2009 The meaning of Neanderthal skeletal morphology. *Proceedings of the National Academy of Sciences* 106:16028–33.

Weber, S., Lehman, H. et al. 2010 Rice or millets: early farming strategies in prehistoric central Thailand. *Archaeological and Anthropological Sciences* 2:79–88.

Webster, D. 2011 Backward bottlenecks: ancient teosinte / maize selection. *Current Anthropology* 52:77–104.

Weiss, E., Wetterstrom, W. et al. 2004 The broad spectrum revisited. *Proceedings of the National Academy of Sciences (USA)* 101:9551–5.

Weiss, E., Kislev, M. et al. 2006 Autonomous cultivation before domestication. *Science* 312:1608–10.

Wells, S. 2006 *Deep Ancestry*. Washington, DC: National Geographic.

Wen, B., Li, H. et al. 2004 Genetic evidence supports demic diffusion of Han culture. *Nature* 431:302–5.

Westaway, K., Morwood, M. et al. 2009 *Homo floresiensis* and the late Pleistocene environments of eastern Indonesia. *Quaternary Science Reviews* 28:2897–912.

Wetterstrom, W. 1998 The origins of agriculture in Africa. *Review of Archaeology* 19(2):30–46.

Wichmann, S., Müller, A. et al. 2010 Homelands of the world's language families: A quantitative approach. *Diachronica* 27:247–76.

Widianto, H. 2006 Austronesian prehistory from the perspective of skeletal anthropology. In T. Simanjuntak, ed., *Austronesian Diaspora and the Ethnogeneses of People in the Indonesian Archipelago*, pp. 174–85. Jakarta: LIPI Press.

Wiik, K. 2000 Some ancient and modern linguistic processes in northern Europe. In C. Renfrew, A. McMahon et al., eds, *Time Depth in Historical Linguistics*, pp. 463–80. Cambridge: McDonald Institute for Archaeological Research.

Willcox, G. 2012 Pre-domestication cultivation during the Late Pleistocene and Early Holocene in the northern Levant. In P. Gepts, T.R. Famula et al., eds, *Biodiversity in Agriculture*, pp. 92–109. Cambridge: Cambridge University Press.

Willcox, G. and Stordeur, D. 2012 Large-scale cereal processing before domestication during the tenth millennium cal BC in northern Syria. *Antiquity* 86:99–114.

Willcox, G., Fornite, S. et al. 2008 Early Holocene cultivation before domestication in northern Syria. *Vegetation History and Archaeobotany* 17:313–25.

Williams, M., Ambrose, S. et al. 2009 Environmental impact of the 73 ka Toba super-eruption in South Asia. *Palaeogeography, Palaeoclimatology, Palaeoecology* 284:295–314.

Wilmshurst, J., Hunt, T. et al. 2011 High-precision radiocarbon dating shows recent and rapid initial human colonization of East Polynesia. *Proceedings of the National Academy of Sciences (USA)* 108:1815–20.

Wilson, S. 2007 *The Archaeology of the Caribbean*. Cambridge: Cambridge University Press.

Winter, J. and Hogan, P. 1986 Plant husbandry in the Great Basin and adjacent North Colorado Plateau. In C. Londie and D. Fowler, eds, *Anthropology of the Desert West*, pp. 119–44. Salt Lake City: University of Utah Press.

Winter, O., Clark, G. et al. 2012 Austronesian sailing to the northern Marianas. *Antiquity* 86:898–909.

Wiriyaromp, W. 2010 The wider relationships of the Neolithic 1 ceramics. In C. Higham and A. Kijngam, eds, *The Excavation of Ban Non Wat: The Neolithic Occupation*, pp. 107–24. Bangkok: Thai Fine Arts Department.

Witzel, M. 2003 *Linguistic Evidence for Cultural Exchange in Prehistoric Western Central Asia*. Sino-Platonic Papers 129. Philadelphia: Department of East Asian Languages and Civilizations, University of Pennsylvania.

Witzel, M. 2005 Central Asian roots and acculturation in South Asia. In T. Osada, ed., *Linguistics, Archaeology and the Human Past*, pp. 87–211. Occasional Paper 1. Kyoto: Indus Project, Research Institute for Humanity and Nature.

Wolff, J. 2010 *Proto-Austronesian Phonology with Glossary*. 2 volumes. Ithaca: Cornell Southeast Asia Program Publications.

Wollstein, A., Lao, O. et al. 2010 Demographic history of Oceania inferred from genome-wide data. *Current Biology* 20:1983–92.

Wolpoff, M. and Lee, S-H. 2012 The African origin of recent humanity. In S. Reynolds and A. Gallagher, eds, *African Genesis: Perspectives on Hominin Evolution*, pp. 347–64. Cambridge: Cambridge University Press.

Wood, B. 2011 Did early *Homo* migrate "out of" or "in to" Africa? *Proceedings of the National Academy of Sciences* 108:10375–6.

Wood, B. 2012 Facing up to complexity. *Nature* 488:162–3.

Woodman, N. and Beavan, N. 2009 Post-Clovis survival of American mastodon in the southern Great Lakes region of North America. *Quaternary Research* 72:359–63.

Wrangham, R. 2009 *Catching Fire: How Cooking Made Us Human*. London: Profile.

Wu, X., Zhang, C. et al. 2012 Early pottery at 20,000 years ago in Xiarendong Cave, China. *Science* 336:1696–700.

Wurster, C.M., Bird, M. et al. 2010 Forest contraction in north equatorial Southeast Asia during the last glacial period. *Proceedings of the National Academy of Sciences (USA)* 107:15508–11.

Xu, S. 2012 Human population admixture in Asia. *Genomics and Informatics* 10(3):133–44.

Xu, S., Pugach, I. et al. 2012 Genetic dating indicates that the Asian-Papuan admixture through Eastern Indonesia corresponds to the Austronesian expansion. *Proceedings of the National Academy of Sciences (USA)* 109:4574–9.

Yamaoka, T. 2012 Use and maintenance of trapezoids in the initial Early Upper Paleolithic of the Japanese Islands. *Quaternary International* 248:32–42.

Yan, W. 2004 The cradle of eastern civilization. In Yang Xiaoneng, ed., *New Perspectives on China's Past*, pp. 48–75. New Haven and London: Yale University Press.

Yang Xiaoneng, ed. 2004 *New Perspectives on China's Past*. New Haven and London: Yale University Press.

Yesner, D. and Pearson, G. 2002 Microblades and migrations. In R. Elston and S. Kuhn, eds, *Thinking Small: Global Perspectives on Microlithization*, pp. 134–61. Archeological Papers of the American Anthropological Association 12. Arlington: American Anthropological Association.

Yokoyama, Y., Falgueres, C. et al. 2008 Gamma-ray spectrometcis dating of late *Homo erectus* skulls from Ngandong and Sambungmacan, Central Java. *Journal of Human Evolution* 55: 274–7.

Zaidner, Y., Yeshurun, R. et al. 2010 Early Pleristocene hominins outside of Africa: recent excavations at Bizat Ruhama, Israel. *PaleoAnthropology* 2010:162–95.

Zeder, M. 2006 Central questions in the domestication of plants and animals. *Evolutionary Anthropology* 15:105–17.

Zeder, M. 2008 Domestication and early agriculture in the Mediterranean Basin. *Proceedings of the National Academy of Sciences (USA)* 105:11597–604.

Zeder, M. 2011 The origins of agriculture in the Near East. *Current Anthropology* 52 (Supplement 4):S221–36.

Zegura, S., Karafet, T. et al. 2009 The peopling of the Americas as viewed from the Y chromosome. In P.N. Peregrine, I. Peiros et al., eds, *Ancient Human Migrations*, pp. 127–36. Salt Lake City: University of Utah Press.

Zerjal, T., Xue, Y. et al. 2003 The genetic legacy of the Mongols. *American Journal of Human Genetics* 72:717–21.

Zhang, C. and Hung, H-c. 2008 The Neolithic cultures of southern China: origin; development and dispersal. *Asian Perspectives* 47(2):299–330.

Zhang, C. and Hung, H-c. 2010 The emergence of agriculture in southern China. *Antiquity* 84:11–25.

Zhang, C. and Hung, H-c. 2012 Late hunter-gatherers in southern China, 18000–3000 BC. *Antiquity* 86:11–29.

Zhang, C. and Hung, H-c. 2013 Eastern Asia: archaeology. In I. Ness and P. Bellwood, eds, *Encyclopedia of Global Human Migration*. Volume 1, *Prehistory*, pp. 209–16. Malden, MA and Oxford: Wiley-Blackwell.

Zhang, P., Huang, W. et al. 2010 Acheulian handaxes from Fengshudao, Bose sites of South China. *Quaternary International* 223–4:440–3.

Zhang, D., Lee, H. et al. 2011 The causality analysis of climate change and large-scale human crisis. *Proceedings of the National Academy of Sciences (USA)* 108:17296–301.

Zhang, J., Lu, H. et al. 2012. Early mixed farming of millet and rice 7800 years ago in the middle Yellow River region, China. *PLoS ONE* 7(3):e52146.

Zhao, Z. 2010 New data and new issues for the study of origin of rice agriculture in China. *Archaeological and Anthropological Sciences* 2:99–106.

Zhao, Z. 2011 New archaeobotanic data for the study of the origins of agriculture in China. *Current Anthropology* Supplement 4: S295–306.

Zhao, M., Kong, Q. et al. 2009 Mitochondrial genome evidence reveals successful late Paleolithic settlement on the Tibetan Plateau. *Proceedings of the National Academy of Sciences (USA)* 106:21230–5.

Zilhão, J. 2000 From the Mesolithic to the Neolithic in the Iberian Peninsula. In D. Price, ed., *Europe's First Farmers*, pp. 144–82. Cambridge: Cambridge University Press.

Zilhão, J. 2001 Radiocarbon evidence for maritime pioneer colonization at the origins of farming in west Mediterranean Europe. *Proceedings of the National Academy of Sciences (USA)* 98:14180–5.

Zilhão, J. 2010 Aliens from outer time? In S. Condemi and G. Weniger, eds, *Continuity and Discontinuity in the Peopling of Europe*, pp. 331–66. Dordrecht: Springer.

Zilhão, J. 2011 Time is on my side. In A. Hadjikoumis, E. Robinson et al., eds, *The Dynamics of Neolithisation in Europe*, pp. 46–65. Oxford: Oxbow.

Zilhão, J. and d'Errico F. 1999 The chronology and taphonomy of the earliest Aurignacian. *Journal of World Prehistory* 13:1–68.

Zilhão, J. and Wong, K. 2010 Did Neanderthals think like us? *Scientific American* 302(6):72–5.

Zilhão, J., Cardoso, J. et al. 2011 Gruta Nova da Columbeira (Bombarral, Portugal). *Quartär* 58:930112.

Zimmermann, A., Hilpert, J. et al. 2009 Estimations of population density for selected periods between the Neolithic and AD 1800. *Human Biology* 81:357–80.

Zong, Y., Chen, Z. et al. 2007 Fire and flood management of coastal swamp enabled first rice paddy cultivation in east China. *Nature* 449:459–62.

Zorc, D. 1994 Austronesian culture history through reconstructed vocabulary. In A. Pawley and M. Ross, eds, *Austronesian Terminologies: Continuity and Change*, pp. 541–95. Canberra: Pacific Linguistics Series C-127.

Zwyns, N., Roebroeks, W. et al. 2012 Comment on "Late Mousterian persistence near the Arctic Circle". *Science* 335:167b.

Index